CHILDREN ACT 1989

CHILDREN ACT 1989

Annotated by

STUART BELL M.P.,
Barrister

SHAW & SONS LTD
Shaway House
21 Bourne Park
Bourne Road
Crayford
Kent DA1 4BZ

Published in October 1990 by Shaw & Sons Ltd
of Shaway House, 21 Bourne Park, Bourne Road,
Crayford, Kent DA1 4BZ.

ISBN 0-7219-1075-0

British Library Cataloguing in Publication Data
Great Britain
[240.4] The Children Act 1989 – (Shaw's annotated Acts series).
1. Great Britain. Children. Care. Law
I. [240.4] II. Title III. Bell, Stuart
344.104327

© Shaw & Sons Ltd 1990
Text typeset by Input Typesetting Ltd, London
Printed in Great Britain by Bell & Bain Ltd, Glasgow

CONTENTS

ACKNOWLEDGEMENTS

I am grateful to Her Majesty's Stationery Office for the use of Crown and Parliamentary copyright material in the preparation of these annotations. Their "Introduction to the Children Act 1989" is a useful introduction to the new framework for the care and upbringing of children, which is what the Act is all about. I am also grateful to my daughter Yvonne who did much of the background work and research which enabled me to make these annotations as comprehensive as possible.

INTRODUCTION

Background to the Act

The Children Act received the Royal Assent 16 November 1989.

The then Minister of State at the Department of Health, David Mellor QC, MP, described the Act as "the most comprehensive and far-reaching reform of child law to have come before Parliament in living memory". According to the Minister, prior to the Act legislation covering the welfare of children had been "confusing, piecemeal, outdated, often unfair and, in important respects, ineffective". Indeed, the Minister might have gone further, for large tracts of child care law which had been placed on the statute book had never been implemented; in fact, he did go further, for he promised that the whole of the Act, with the concomitant regulations and rules of court, would be implemented in October 1991. Some of the provisions of the Act, of course, became effective upon the Royal Assent, but the annotations herein treat the entirety of the Act as already in force.

With so much criticism of former child care law one wonders why it had taken Parliament so many years to put so many wrongs to right. There had been the report of the House of Commons Social Services Committee 1983–84 entitled "Children in Care". This had been followed by a government White Paper entitled "The Law on Child Care and the Family". There had been The Law Commission's "Family Law, Review of Child Law, Guardianship and Custody". There had been unfortunate events such as the death of Jasmine Beckford, who had died at the hands of her stepfather in a suburb of London. And there had been the publication of the report of Lord Justice Butler-Sloss following a judicial enquiry into events in Cleveland, where the local authority, acting under former legislation, had applied for and obtained 276 place of safety orders over a seven month period, with 174 of these having been obtained from justices of the peace signing the orders in their home rather than applications granted by the bench during the regular hours of the court.

The public outcry that ensued, followed by the publication of the Butler-Sloss report, provided the impetus for the government to integrate the public and private law relating to children, thus creating what they hoped would be a single rationalised system. The difficulties, however, remained. How should one define what was in the best interests of a child? How best could the child's welfare be promoted? And how did this relate to a family of which the child was a part? The massive majority of families have no need of the parental state, of outside interference in their affairs—they know what is in the best interests of their children. But for those parents, guardians and other interested parties, not least the child, who are involved with the parental state, how best should they interface? The parental state itself is a series of interlocking establishments—a local authority covering education and social services, voluntary child care and other agencies dealing with the family, a police authority, and the High Court acting within its inherent jurisdiction. How could a child in need wend his way through such a labyrinth of interests, yet find his interests paramount and his welfare promoted?

A view had been expressed in the seventies that "from birth till death it is now the privilege of the parental state to take major decisions—objective, unemotional. The state weighs up what is best for the child." The parental state had clearly not known what had been in the best interests of Jasmine Beckford, who had been removed from her family because of suspected physical abuse but who had been allowed to return home from the care of a local authority. How had the parental state protected children and families the subject of so many precipitate place of safety orders in Cleveland, where the local authority had, in the words of Lord Justice Butler-Sloss, operated a policy she described as "highly interventionist"? How could the parental state be so redefined, in the light of these experiences, whilst recognising that parents, too, had fundamental rights over their own children?

It would be for the Children Act to define the duties and obligations of the parental state towards children in need, balancing such duties and obligations with the need not to intrude upon the rights of parents in regard to their own children and, where intrusion is necessary in the interests of the child, not to deprive parents of their rights. This balance would be achieved through the development of two basic principles: that the welfare of the child is paramount and that the prime repsonsibility for the upbringing of children rests with their parents. As to the first principle, David Mellor would say: "We aim to provide a comprehensive and comprehensible framework of powers and responsibilities that we hope will secure our central goal, that children receive the care, upbringing and protection that they deserve". As to the second, there would be major reforms dealing with parental responsibility, guardianship and the powers of the court to make orders in respect of children in family proceedings.

But if parents are to be responsible for bringing up their children, the parental state should be ready to reduce the risk of family breakdown. Thus the intervention of a local authority should be by way of a voluntary partnership that should develop in such a way that family relationships are promoted. This means that any transfer of parental responsibility for caring for a child to a local authority will require a court order. There will be due process of law and the court will have to be satisfied that this is in the best interests of the child. In such proceedings, parents and children shall have full party status. Decisions can no longer be taken on family life without parents not only being fully informed but having the right of representation. There are also emergency powers to remove a child at serious immediate risk, though the period should be as short as possible and subject to court review if challenged by parents, guardians or other interested parties.

These emergency powers are to be found in the Emergency Protection Order and the Child Assessment Order which replace the Place of Safety Order. The Emergency Protection Order is limited to a maximum of eight days and can be extended by the court to up to fifteen days, but it may be challenged after seventy-two hours. The Order is designed for those very serious situations where there is a deep concern for the welfare of a child and where the child should be removed from the home for its own safety. The Child Assessment Order is for less serious situations where the child can be assessed within the family home, and where the Order may run for seven days. The intention is that the child be assessed in the family home, save for "an afternoon or two," in the words of David Mellor, "and only rarely overnight".

The Act also provides that where local authorities are caring for a child away from home, their powers and responsibilities, and those of the child's parents in such circumstances, should be clear-cut. The Act also rationalises local authorities' responsibilities towards children in need, including disabled children and their families. The Act also restricts the use of wardship as a means of giving local authorities compulsory powers over a child, and outlines arrangements for child care cases to be heard at the level of court appropriate to the complexity of the case.

The Solicitor General, Sir Nicholas Lyell QC MP, explained to the House of Commons that whilst there would be no such thing as a family court, in the sense of a courthouse consisting of bricks and mortar, there would be a unified specialist jurisdiction in child care matters that would include the magistrates' courts, the county courts and the family division of the High Court. Within each county court and magistrates' court there would be created a family division which, together with the family division of the High Court, would operate as a family court. The Lord Chancellor would, by rules of court, specify the procedures to be followed in order to identify the welfare of the child, to avoid unnecessary formality, to reduce delay and inconvenience to the public in resolving family disputes, to reduce the harm to children and families which might occur from the court process, and bring in methods of conciliation that would assist in the resolution of disputes.

Set out below are the main legislative provisions contained in the various parts of the Children Act.

Part I of the Act deals with the welfare of the child, parental responsibility for children, the meaning of parental responsibility, the acquisition of parental responsibility by a father, the appointment of guardians and welfare reports. It deals with the private law of the land, establishing the general welfare principle that the child's interest should be paramount and implements the recommendations of the Law Commission in its report on guardianship and custody. Part I also enunciates the general principles and matters which would govern the decisions of courts concerning a child's upbringing and the administration of his property. It also provides for the substance and incidence of parental status at law and how this can be acquired, by order or agreement. It concludes by providing for the availability of welfare reports in proceedings under the Act.

Part II introduces four new orders relating to children: the residence order, the contact order, the specific issues order and the prohibited steps order. These are the so-called section 8 orders and replace former orders for custody, legal custody, care and control and access that were previously on the statute book. The new orders seek to concentrate the minds of the parties and the courts on the concrete issues relating to the day-to-day care of the child and are designed to encourage parents to continue to participate fully in the child's upbringing, subject only to any particular matter provided for by a court order.

Part III sets out local authorities' responsibilities towards children and their families. "Children" includes children in need, disabled children, under fives and children being looked after by local authorities. Clauses in **Part III** replace, supplement or update various provisions in the Child Care Act 1980 and other enactments dealing with services for disabled children and their families. **Part III** also clarifies the responsibility of local authorities in relation to the children they are looking after, whether under voluntary arrangements, or as a result of compulsory care proceedings.

Also under **Part III** of the Act, the local authority will have an absolute duty to safeguard and promote the welfare of any child in its care, to review the child's needs at specified intervals, to promote contact between the child and his family and to consult the family on decisions. The local authority will also be required to establish procedures for the consideration of complaints, with bodies independent of the authority being involved in the procedure. A local authority will also have enhanced responsibilities for preparing children they are looking after for the day when they leave care; also for helping those children accommodated away from home who, when they reach sixteen, leave that accommodation.

In short, it will be the duty of a local authority to advise, assist and befriend such children in care and prepare them for the outside world.

Part IV deals with care orders, the effect of such orders, parental contact with children in care, supervision orders, including education supervision orders, and interim orders. It also deals with the powers of the court in certain family proceedings, the discharge and variation of care and supervision orders and the right of guardians ad litem to have access to local authority records. **Part IV** also makes clear that the effect of a care order is to give parental responsibility for the child to the local authority looking after him.

The courts may also now make an order as to contact which distinguishes the new law from the old where a court could only intervene to grant access when that had been stopped or prevented: "an arbitrary restriction", as described by David Mellor QC MP. A guardian ad litem will have to be appointed by the court to safeguard the child's interests in all care proceedings, including those arising in family proceedings, unless, in exceptional circumstances, the court considers such an appointment unnecessary. Previously, appointments were made only where there was a conflict of interest between the child and the parents.

Part V deals with the reform of the statutory framework for the protection of children through Child Assessment Orders and Emergency Protection Orders. It deals with the duration of Emergency Protection Orders and other supplemental provision and with removal and accommodation of children by police in cases of emergency. **Part V** defines the local authority's duty to investigate and those powers to assist in discovery of children who may be in need of emergency protection. Although this is a civil Act, **Part V** covers the criminal offence of abduction of a child in care, with a liability on summary conviction to imprisonment for a term not exceeding six months or to a fine not exceeding level 5 on the standard scale, or to both. Refuges for children at risk are also covered.

Parts VI to **X** to deal with community homes, voluntary homes and voluntary organisations.

Part VI contains provisions which replace Part IV of the Child Care Act 1980 and requires local authorities to secure that community homes are available for children who are looked after by them. Part VI and Schedule 4 provide for the management and conduct of community homes.

Part VII provides for the registration and regulation of voluntary homes and for the welfare of children who are accommodated by or on behalf of voluntary organisations. These clauses and Schedule 5 re-enact, with amendments, Part VI of the Child Care Act 1980.

Part VIII re-enacts, with certain amendments, the provisions of the Children's Homes Act 1982 and provides for the registration and regulation of children's homes and the welfare of children accommodated in them.

Part IX replaces the provisions of the Foster Children Act 1980 and deals with private arrangements for fostering children. It provides for the notification and regulation of private fostering arrangements and the welfare of privately fostered children.

Part X deals with the Secretary of State's supervisory functions and responsibilities and provides for inspection, by persons authorised by the Secretary of State, of children's homes and other establishments, for inquiries and financial support by the Secretary of State and for returns of information.

Part XI deals with the abolition of the power of the court to make a care order in criminal proceedings and provides that the court should have the additional powers in relation to supervision orders given by the amendments to section 12 of the Children and Young Persons Act 1969. These are set out in Schedule 8 of the Children Act and allow the court to include in a supervision order the requirement that the child or young person reside in accommodation provided by or on behalf of the local authority and to specify that he may not live with a named person.

The intention of Clause 69 within Part XI is to prevent local authorities from using the High Court's inherent jurisdiction, including wardship, as an alternative to a care or supervision order, or as a means of their otherwise obtaining compulsory powers over children. Clause 69 seeks to protect children and families from compulsory care or supervision except where the statutory grounds for care exist under the Act and in other cases to preclude intervention by local authorities unless significant harm to the child is likely.

General

There are unlikely to be any financial effects arising from the application of Parts I and II of the Act, since these are private law provisions, but increased court and legal aid costs will result from the changes in the arrangements for local authority care and supervision and emergency protection. These may be offset, partly by savings from limiting access to wardship, as set out in Clause 69, and partly from more effective management of cases. The government nevertheless expects a net increase in court costs in the range of £0.6 million to £4.9 million, including £1 million for judicial and staff training. The effect on legal aid expenditure is likely to range between a saving of £0.6 million and an increase of £1.7 million.

The costs of local authorities on court-related work are also expected to increase, in particular in relation to guardians ad litem, but there are expected to be savings from the transfer of most local authority wardship applications to care proceedings in lower courts. A net increase of £2.1 million is expected in a full year.

The additional welfare responsibilities for local authorities to be introduced mainly by **Part III** will cost about £1.7 million and there will be a net increase of about £0.2 million in other local authority costs, including registration and inspection costs as a result of changes in respect of registered children's homes as set out in **Part VIII**.

The full annual cost of the Act is expected to be between £4 million and £11 million, of which £4 million will fall to local authorities, and from no additional cost to a possible £7 million to court administration and legal aid. There may also be one-off training costs for local authority staff training.

Clause 67 of the Act is expected to increase the number of care cases that will require additional legal staff and guardians ad litem and those new responsibilities introduced by **Part III** will also require additional staff. In total, the increase in local authority staff is estimated at 150 for England and Wales. There is not expected to be any increase in central government manpower.

Conclusion

This annotated edition of the Children Act is designed to be of assistance to those practitioners involved in child care within the context of family proceedings. The proper interpretation of the Act, its rules and regulations, will be a matter for the courts who will make their own jurisprudence. A child is referred to in the masculine but of course equally covers the feminine gender: this is for the purpose of ease and simplicity. A child means a person who is not yet eighteen years old, but there are some divergencies from this rule within the framework of the financial provisions to be found in Schedule 1.

In the main, the Act only applies to England and Wales but there are some extensions: Part X dealing with child minding and day care for young children also applies in Scotland. There are also a number of other amendments that apply to the law in Scotland and Northern Ireland—see section 90.

Note

A series of amendments to the Children Act 1989 were incorporated as Schedule 14 to the Courts and Legal Services Act as this made its way through Parliament. The last of these amendments were moved at report stage in the Commons on 25 July 1990. These amendments have been referred to in the annotations to the 1989 Act. The amendments are sometimes technical, sometimes minor and sometimes consequential. They are opportune in that they have been placed on the statute book in time for the implementation of the Children Act 1989, so that the body of law in relation to children, families, local authorities and the courts is properly integrated. The Secretary of State for Health indicated that his Department would indeed be implementing the Children Act during 1991: Col 1005 Hansard 18 July 1990.

The Act is due to be fully implemented by October 1991.

CHILDREN ACT 1989

(Chapter 41)

PART I

INTRODUCTORY

Section 1. Welfare of the child

1.—(1) When a court determines any question with respect to—

    (a) the upbringing of a child; or

    (b) the administration of a child's property or the application of any income arising from it,

the child's welfare shall be the court's paramount consideration.

(2) In any proceedings in which any question with respect to the upbringing of a child arises, the court shall have regard to the general principle that any delay in determining the question is likely to prejudice the welfare of the child.

(3) In the circumstances mentioned in subsection (4), a court shall have regard in particular to—

    (a) the ascertainable wishes and feelings of the child concerned (considered in the light of his age and understanding);

    (b) his physical, emotional and educational needs;

    (c) the likely effect on him of any change in his circumstances;

    (d) his age, sex, background and any characteristics of his which the court considers relevant;

    (e) any harm which he has suffered or is at risk of suffering;

    (f) how capable each of his parents, and any other person in relation to whom the court considers the question to be relevant, is of meeting his needs;

    (g) the range of powers available to the court under this Act in the proceedings in question.

(4) The circumstances are that—

    (a) the court is considering whether to make, vary or discharge a section 8 order, and the making, variation or discharge of the order is opposed by any party to the proceedings; or

    (b) the court is considering whether to make, vary or discharge an order under Part IV.

(5) Where a court is considering whether or not to make one or more orders under this Act with respect to a child, it shall not make the order or any of the orders unless it considers that doing so would be better for the child than making no order at all.

Annotation

Section 1: determines that the child's interest is paramount with respect to his upbringing or the administration of his property or the application of any income arising from it. A court shall have particular regard to certain specific matters in all care and supervision order cases and in contested family proceedings as these relate to the child's upbringing. A court shall not make an order unless it would be better for the child than making no order at all.

Section 1(1): reproduces with minor drafting improvements section 1 of the Guardianship of Minors Act 1971. Section 1(1) also covers the inherent *parentis patriae* jurisdiction of the High Court in respect of a child. It does not, however, cover orders about maintenance: these are covered by the provisions in Schedule 1(10) of the Act.

Section 1(2): declares the general principle that the court is to regard any delay in proceedings concerning the welfare of a child as likely to prejudice that welfare. A court shall be expected to draw up a timetable to ensure delay is kept to a minimum.

Section 1(3): defines particular matters to which a court is to have regard when applying the paramountcy principle in contested section 8 order applications and in all applications relating to local authority care and supervision of a child. The list of particular matters is in the manner of a checklist recommended by the Law Commission as "a means of providing greater consistency and clarity in the law and . . . a major step towards a more systematic approach to decisions concerning children".

Section 1(4): limits section 1(3) to contested section 8 order cases or where the court is considering making, varying, or discharging a care or supervision order under Part IV. The decision of a court to order a child into local authority care or under its supervision, or the supervision of a probation officer, or to vary or discharge such orders, bears directly upon the integrity and independence of a family. This integrity and independence must be balanced against the need to protect a child from serious harm, so a full investigation in accordance with the checklist is justified in every case.

Section 1(5): determines that an order shall be in the best interests of the child in accordance with the paramountcy rule, but that any order or orders must be better for the child than making no order at all. As the Law Commission has pointed out: "A tendency seems to have developed to assume that some order about the children should always be made whenever divorce or separation cases come to court and that they may be seen by solicitors as 'part of the package' for their matrimonial clients and by the court as part of their task of approving the arrangements made in divorce proceedings".

Section 2. Parental responsibility for children

2. — (1) Where a child's father and mother were married to each other at the time of his birth, they shall each have parental responsibility for the child.

(2) Where a child's father and mother were not married to each other at the time of his birth —

(a) the mother shall have parental responsibility for the child;
(b) the father shall not have parental responsibility for the child, unless he acquires it in accordance with the provisions of this Act.

(3) References in this Act to a child whose father and mother were, or (as the case may be) were not, married to each other at the time of his birth must be read with section 1 of the Family Law Reform Act 1987 (which extends their meaning).

(4) The rule of law that a father is the natural guardian of his legitimate child is abolished.

(5) More than one person may have parental responsibility for the same child at the same time.

(6) A person who has parental responsibility for a child at any time shall not cease to have that responsibility solely because some other person subsequently acquires parental responsibility for the child.

(7) Where more than one person has parental responsibility for a child, each of them may act alone and without the other (or others) in meeting that responsibility; but nothing in this Part shall be taken to affect the operation of any enactment which requires the consent of more than one person in a matter affecting the child.

(8) The fact that a person has parental responsibility for a child shall not entitle him to act in any way which would be incompatible with any order made with respect to the child under this Act.

(9) A person who has parental responsibility for a child may not surrender or transfer any part of that responsibility to another but may arrange for some or all of it to be met by one or more persons acting on his behalf.

(10) The person with whom any such arrangement is made may himself be a person who already has parental responsibility for the child concerned.

(11) The making of any such arrangement shall not affect any liability of the person making it which may arise from any failure to meet any part of his parental responsibility for the child concerned.

Annotation

Section 2: provides that the legal status of parents in relation to the care and upbringing of their children, that is to say their rights, powers, duties and responsibilities, shall be referred to collectively as parental responsibility: thus parenthood becomes a primary concept. Section 2 confers parental responsibility on both parents if married to each other, and on the mother alone if not. It also provides for those who share parental responsibility to act independently of each other and allows delegation of that responsibility. Section 2 in addition prohibits the outright surrender or transfer of parental responsibility and the exercise of that responsibility in a way that is incompatible with any child care order.

Section 2(1): confers parental responsibility on both parents if married to each other. Also included is a child who is treated as legitimate by virtue of section 1 of the Legitimacy Act 1976, a legitimated person within the meaning of section 10 of that Act, an adopted child within the meaning of Part IV of the Adoption Act 1976, or a child who is otherwise treated as legitimate.

Section 2(3): determines that a father shall not have parental responsibility unless he acquires it in accordance with the provisions of this Act. This should be read in conjunction with section 4 of the Family Law Reform Act 1987, which came into force 1 April 1989, and which allowed a court to give full parental rights and duties to a father in relation to a child. Any order in force under this Act shall be deemed to be an order under section 4 of the Children Act giving the father parental responsibility for the child: see Schedule 14(4).

Section 2(4): abolishes the rule of common law that the father is the sole natural guardian of his children. The Law Commission found this "archaic and confusing".

Section 2(5): determines that more than one person may have parental responsibility for the same child at the same time. Parents or others with parental responsibility shall have equal status and each shall be able to act independently in carrying out that responsibility, subject to any statutory provisions requiring the consent of them all. Such an example would be where one parent proposed to free a child for adoption.

Section 2(6): establishes that a person who has parental responsibility for a child shall not lose such responsibility solely because another person also acquires it. Such a person may be an unmarried father, a guardian or a local authority. Thus a father will not lose parental responsibility on divorce and a stepfather may acquire it by the making of a residence order. Parental responsibility is not lost where a child is looked after by a local authority, but the appropriate care order also confers parental responsibility upon the authority.

Section 2(7): provides for those who share parental responsibility to act independently of each other. However, no such independence can be exercised when it comes to freeing a child for adoption. Section 2(7) aims to encourage both parents who have parental responsibility to involve themselves in the welfare of a child, with a power to act independently unless and until such time as a court orders otherwise.

Section 2(8): establishes the principle that whilst a parent's power to carry out his parental responsibility may be modified or curtailed by residence or care orders, or other aspects of upbringing, a parent should only be prevented from acting in ways which are incompatible with the court's order.

Section 2(9): maintains the rule that parental responsibility cannot be surrendered or transferred without a court order, but a person may delegate the exercise of some or all of his responsibility. This may be towards others who have parental responsibility or outside organisations such as schools, holiday camps, foster parents or local authorities. Such delegation does not imply that all such arrangements shall be legally binding upon the person or persons delegating parental responsibility.

Section 2(10): establishes that the person with whom any such arrangement is made may himself be a person who already has parental responsibility. Equally, the delegation of parental responsibility does not imply that the person to whom the delegation is made, even though a person with parental responsibility, can make arrangements all of which are legally binding upon the person who has made the delegation to him.

Section 2(11): provides that notwithstanding the delegation of parental responsibility in accordance with section 2(9) and (10), a person with parental responsibility who has made the delegation shall remain liable for any failure to meet any part of his parental responsibility for the child concerned. See the proviso under section 2(9) and (10) above.

Section 3. Meaning of "parental responsibility"

3.—(1) In this Act "parental responsibility" means all the rights, duties, powers, responsibilities and authority which by law a parent of a child has in relation to the child and his property.

(2) It also includes the rights, powers and duties which a guardian of the child's estate (appointed, before the commencement of section 5, to act generally) would have had in relation to the child and his property.

(3) The rights referred to in subsection (2) include, in particular, the right of the guardian to receive or recover in his own name, for the benefit of the child, property of whatever description and wherever situated which the child is entitled to receive or recover.

(4) The fact that a person has, or does not have, parental responsibility for a child shall not affect—

(a) any obligation which he may have in relation to the child (such as a statutory duty to maintain the child); or

(b) any rights which, in the event of the child's death, he (or any other person) may have in relation to the child's property.

(5) A person who—

(a) does not have parental responsibility for a particular child; but

(b) has care of the child,

may (subject to the provisions of this Act) do what is reasonable in all the circumstances of the case for the purpose of safeguarding or promoting the child's welfare.

Annotation

Section 3: defines parental responsibility to include all the legal incidents of parenthood which relate to the care and upbringing of a child under eighteen. This applies equally to a child's estate or property. Additional powers are conferred upon guardians. Parental responsibility does not include rights of succession to a child's property or the child's rights of succession. The test of reasonableness is applied to those who have the physical care of a child but not parental responsibility.

Section 3(1): defines parental responsibility. Parenthood is a matter of responsibility as well as of rights. The Children Act is designed to move the emphasis away from rights and towards responsibility. It will be for the courts to interpret parental responsibility in accordance with the needs and circumstances of each child: see *Gillick* v. *West Norfolk and Wisbech Area Health Authority* (1986) [A.C.112]. The court might also apply subjective tests, such as the age and maturity of the individual child before it.

Section 3(2): provides that parental responsibility includes the rights, duties and powers which a guardian has in relation to the estate, or property of a child where the guardian was appointed prior to the operation of section 5. It clarifies prior law, which was obscure, as to whether the powers of parents and guardians in relation to the administration of a child's property are co-extensive.

Section 3(3): provides that parental responsibility includes the right of a guardian to receive and recover in his own name for the benefit of the child property of whatever description. Section 3(3) ensures that parents and guardians have the same powers to receive a legacy on the child's behalf.

Section 3(4): provides that whether a person does or does not have parental responsibility for a child, this shall not affect any obligation which he may have, or any rights in relation to the child's property. Thus an unmarried father or stepfather who has treated a child as one of his family may be ordered to pay maintenance even if he does not have parental responsibility. Further, parental responsibility does not affect rights in relation to a child's property where the child dies.

Section 3(5): provides for a test of reasonableness where a person does not have parental responsibility but has care of a child. Thus a child who goes on holiday with another family falls within the responsibility of those in charge of that family, who must take what steps are reasonable to safeguard or promote the child's welfare: see also section 2(9)(10). The element of reasonableness will imply not doing anything to override the child's wishes where he is of sufficient age and understanding to be entitled to decide matters for himself: see *Gillick* v. *West Norfolk and Wisbech Area Health Authority* (1986) [A.C.112].

Section 4. Acquisition of parental responsibility by father

4. — (1) Where a child's father and mother were not married to each other at the time of his birth —

(a) the court may, on the application of the father, order that he shall have parental responsibility for the child; or

(b) the father and mother may by agreement ("a parental responsibility agreement") provide for the father to have parental responsibility for the child.

(2) No parental responsibility agreement shall have effect for the purposes of this Act unless —

(a) it is made in the form prescribed by regulations made by the Lord Chancellor; and

(b) where regulations are made by the Lord Chancellor prescribing the manner in which such agreements must be recorded, it is recorded in the prescribed manner.

(3) Subject to section 12(4), an order under subsection (1)(a), or a parental responsibility agreement, may only be brought to an end by an order of the court made on the application —

(a) of any person who has parental responsibility for the child; or

(b) with leave of the court, of the child himself.

(4) The court may only grant leave under subsection (3)(b) if it is satisfied that the child has sufficient understanding to make the proposed application.

Annotation

Section 4: builds upon the scheme for acquisition by unmarried fathers of parental rights and duties contained in section 4 of the Family Law Reform Act 1987. This came into force 1 April 1989.

Section 4(1): does not preclude the mother from parental responsibility; rather it accords with section 4 of the Family Law Reform Act 1987. Section 4(1)(b) seeks to avoid court appearances and any private agreement parents may enter into shall be as binding as any court order.

Section 4(2): provides for any parental responsibility agreement to be made in a prescribed form. Both parents must understand the nature of the decision they are taking. Section 4(2) provides a straightforward way for unmarried parents to acknowledge their shared responsibility to cover the support and upbringing of their child. A distinction should be made between the private appointment of a father through a parental responsibility agreement during the lifetime of the mother and the private appointment of a guardian to take the place of a parent after his death.

Section 4(3): is consistent with section 4(3) of the Family Law Reform Act 1987 which provides that "a parental rights and duties order" under that section may only be discharged by a subsequent order made on the application of the father or mother of the child. Should the mother be dead the order may be discharged on the application of a guardian of the child who may have been appointed under the Guardianship of Minors Act 1971. This should be read in conjunction with section 12(1)(4).

Section 4(4): provides that whereas a child as well as either parent shall be able to apply to bring an order to an end, in the case of the child this right may only be exercised with leave of the court.

Section 5. Appointment of guardians

5.—(1) Where an application with respect to a child is made to the court by any individual, the court may by order appoint that individual to be the child's guardian if—

(a) the child has no parent with parental responsibility for him; or

(b) a residence order has been made with respect to the child in favour of a parent or guardian of his who has died while the order was in force.

(2) The power conferred by subsection (1) may also be exercised in any family proceedings if the court considers that the order should be made even though no application has been made for it.

(3) A parent who has parental responsibility for his child may appoint another individual to be the child's guardian in the event of his death.

(4) A guardian of a child may appoint another individual to take his place as the child's guardian in the event of his death.

(5) An appointment under subsection (3) or (4) shall not have effect unless it is made in writing, is dated and is signed by the person making the appointment or—

(a) in the case of an appointment made by a will which is not signed by the testator, is signed at the direction of the testator in accordance with the requirements of section 9 of the Wills Act 1837; or

(b) in any other case, is signed at the direction of the person making the appointment, in his presence and in the presence of two witnesses who each attest the signature.

(6) A person appointed as a child's guardian under this section shall have parental responsibility for the child concerned.

(7) Where—

    (a) on the death of any person making an appointment under subsection (3) or (4), the child concerned has no parent with parental responsibility for him; or

    (b) immediately before the death of any person making such an appointment, a residence order in his favour was in force with respect to the child,

the appointment shall take effect on the death of that person.

(8) Where, on the death of any person making an appointment under subsection (3) or (4)—

    (a) the child concerned has a parent with parental responsibility for him; and

    (b) subsection (7)(b) does not apply,

the appointment shall take effect when the child no longer has a parent who has parental responsibility for him.

(9) Subsections (1) and (7) do not apply if the residence order referred to in paragraph (b) of those subsections was also made in favour of a surviving parent of the child.

(10) Nothing in this section shall be taken to prevent an appointment under subsection (3) or (4) being made by two or more persons acting jointly.

(11) Subject to any provision made by rules of court, no court shall exercise the High Court's inherent jurisdiction to appoint a guardian of the estate of any child.

(12) Where rules of court are made under subsection (11) they may prescribe the circumstances in which, and conditions subject to which, an appointment of such a guardian may be made.

(13) A guardian of a child may only be appointed in accordance with the provisions of this section.

Annotation

Section 5: simplifies the procedures for the appointment of guardians and their acquisition of parental responsibility. The general rule is that the appointment of a guardian shall only take effect after the death of any surviving parent with parental responsibility. Such appointments shall be valid if made in writing and signed, thus enlarging the rule that they must be made by deed or will. All guardians shall have the same parental responsibility as parents but shall not become "liable relatives" under the Social Security Act 1986 or potentially subject to orders for financial provision or property adjustment. A local authority cannot be appointed a guardian.

Section 5(1): replaces the court's powers to appoint a guardian under its jurisdiction: the statutory powers of all courts contained in sections 3(1), (2) and 5 of the Guardianship of Minors Act 1971, and the High Court's jurisdiction, under section 6 of the 1971 Act, when it has removed a guardian from office to appoint another in his place.

Section 5(2): enables a court to appoint a guardian in other family proceedings before it where a parent could have done so but did not, or when a guardian appointed by a parent has died or refused to act. This power was to be found in sections 3(1)(2) and 5 of the Guardianship of Minors Act 1971 and is retained in section 5(2).

Section 5(3): provides that each parent may appoint a guardian to replace them on death. Under section 4(1) and (2) of the Guardianship of Minors Act such provision was also made, except the appointment had to be by deed or will. Section 5(3), when read with section 5(5), provides that a parent with parental responsibility shall also have power by signed writing, in addition to a will or a deed, to appoint a guardian to act after that parent's death.

Section 5(4): provides that a guardian of a child may appoint another individual to take his place as the child's guardian in the event of his death. It follows that if under section 5(3) each parent with parental responsibility should be able, jointly if necessary, to appoint a guardian to act after his death, guardians should also be able to do so: if appointing a guardian is an aspect of responsible parenthood, it can be no less an aspect of responsible guardianship.

Section 5(5): clarifies section 5(3) in that whilst a parent who has parental responsibility for his child may appoint another to be the child's guardian in the event of his death, he must do so in writing. No oral appointment is possible.

Section 5(6): provides that a person appointed a child's guardian shall have parental responsibility for the child concerned. In short, complete responsibility for the care and upbringing of a child if the parents die. Whilst parental responsibility as defined in section 3(1) shall be interpreted by the courts, a guardian shall have the parent's duty to see that the child is provided with adequate food, clothing, medical aid and lodging, pursuant to section 1(2)(a) of the Children and Young Persons Act 1933 and to educate the child properly, whether or not he is actually caring for the child. See also Schedule 12(2).

Section 5(7): provides an exception to the general rule that guardianship appointments shall only take effect after the death of both parents. It was the view of the Law Commission that if there is a court order that the child should live with the deceased, and not with the surviving parent, the appointment should take immediate effect. The guardian and surviving parent would then share responsibility. Any disputes would be resolved in the same way as they are between parents.

Section 5(9): reinforces the principle that appointments of guardians should generally only take effect after the death of any surviving parent with parental responsibility. Thus where a parent or guardian with the benefit of a residence order in respect of a child dies, and there is a surviving parent who shares the benefit of that residence order, then the court does *not* have power to appoint a guardian under section 5(1)(b); neither does section 7(1) operate to give immediate effect to any appointment of a guardian by the deceased.

Section 5(10): confirms that an appointment of a guardian by a parent or guardian under section 5(3) and (4) above may be made by two or more persons acting jointly.

Section 5(11): reflects the view of the Law Commission that guardianship of an estate of the child should be abolished and that all guardians should be given the same parental responsibility as parents. This, however, will be subject to rules of court.

Section 5(12): provides that the rules of court referred to in section 5(11) may prescribe the circumstances in which an appointment of a guardian of the estate of any child may be made. In the past, guardians of the estate have occasionally been appointed to receive foreign legacies or awards under the criminal injuries compensation scheme. The Law Commission has felt that trusteeship would adequately and more appropriately fill any gap.

Section 5(13): provides that guardians may only be appointed, by individuals or by the court, in accordance with section 5. It will no longer be possible to appoint a guardian for one specific purpose, for example to give or withhold consent to marriage.

Section 6. Guardians: revocation and disclaimer

6.—(1) An appointment under section 5(3) or (4) revokes an earlier such appointment (including one made in an unrevoked will or codicil) made by the same person in respect of the same child, unless it is clear (whether as the result of an express provision in the later appointment or by any necessary implication) that the purpose of the later appointment is to appoint an additional guardian.

(2) An appointment under section 5(3) or (4) (including one made in an unrevoked will or codicil) is revoked if the person who made the appointment revokes it by a written and dated instrument which is signed—

(a) by him; or
(b) at his direction, in his presence and in the presence of two witnesses who each attest the signature.

(3) An appointment under section 5(3) or (4) (other than one made in a will or codicil) is revoked if, with the intention of revoking the appointment, the person who made it—

(a) destroys the instrument by which it was made; or
(b) has some other person destroy that instrument in his presence.

(4) For the avoidance of doubt, an appointment under section 5(3) or (4) made in a will or codicil is revoked if the will or codicil is revoked.

(5) A person who is appointed as a guardian under section 5(3) or (4) may disclaim his appointment by an instrument in writing signed by him and made within a reasonable time of his first knowing that the appointment has taken effect.

(6) Where regulations are made by the Lord Chancellor prescribing the manner in which such disclaimers must be recorded, no such disclaimer shall have effect unless it is recorded in the prescribed manner.

(7) Any appointment of a guardian under section 5 may be brought to an end at any time by order of the court—

(a) on the application of any person who has parental responsibility for the child;
(b) on the application of the child concerned, with leave of the court; or
(c) in any family proceedings, if the court considers that it should be brought to an end even though no application has been made.

Annotation

Section 6: provides that where a guardian has been appointed the appointment may be revoked or disclaimed. Section 6 introduces a simple form of revocation to match the simple form of appointment. A later appointment shall automatically revoke an earlier one unless it is clearly an additional appointment and an appointment by will shall be revoked, not only in writing or by additional appointment, but where the will itself is revoked, for example on marriage. The Lord Chancellor is entitled to make regulations to prescribe a form of disclaimer under new powers granted to him.

Section 6(1): provides that where there has been an appointment by a parent or guardian under section 5(3) or (4), whether by deed, will or the new signed writing, then a later appointment of guardian by that person shall revoke the earlier appointment, including one made in an unrevoked will or codicil, unless it is clearly intended to add to an individual already appointed guardian.

Section 6(2): introduces a simple form of revocation to match the simple form of appointment. The Law Commission had recommended revocation by written and dated instrument; revocation was broadened, during the Bill's passage through Parliament, to include a written and dated instrument signed and dated at the direction of the person revokng the appointment, in his presence and in the presence of two witnesses.

Section 6(3): provides that an appointment be revoked where the new signed writing is destroyed either by the person who made the appointment or where it is destroyed by another in his presence, and where the document is destroyed with the intention of revoking the appointment.

Section 6(4): provides that an appointment of guardian by a parent or guardian in a will or codicil is revoked if the will or codicil is effectively revoked, either deliberately or by operation of law.

Section 6(5): provides that a guardian shall be able to disclaim his appointment within a reasonable time of it taking effect. Such a disclaimer must be in writing and signed by the appointee. To be effective, it must also be recorded in accordance with any regulations laid down by the Lord Chancellor.

Section 6(6): confers upon the Lord Chancellor the power to make regulations governing the procedure relating to disclaimers referred to in section 6(5); and further that no such disclaimer shall have effect unless recorded in accordance with the requirements of those regulations.

Section 6(7): provides a general power for all courts to remove a guardian whether appointed by a parent, a guardian or by the court. Under prior law, this power was limited to the High Court: see section 6 of the Guardianship of Minors Act 1971.

Section 7. Welfare reports

7.—(1) A court considering any question with respect to a child under this Act may—

(a) ask a probation officer; or
(b) ask a local authority to arrange for—
      (i) an officer of the authority; or
      (ii) such other person (other than a probation officer) as the authority considers appropriate,

to report to the court on such matters relating to the welfare of that child as are required to be dealt with in the report.

(2) The Lord Chancellor may make regulations specifying matters which, unless the court orders otherwise, must be dealt with in any report under this section.

(3) The report may be made in writing, or orally, as the court requires.

(4) Regardless of any enactment or rule of law which would otherwise prevent it from doing so, the court may take account of—

(a) any statement contained in the report; and
(b) any evidence given in respect of the matters referred to in the report,

in so far as the statement or evidence is, in the opinion of the court, relevant to the question which it is considering.

(5) It shall be the duty of the authority or probation officer to comply with any request for a report under this section.

Annotation

Section 7: provides that in all cases where orders about a child's upbringing may be made, a court shall have power to call for a report on any matter relevant to the child's welfare. A court will not be expected to request a report in every case before it: no welfare officer, probation officer or other appropriate expert could cope if this were to be the norm. To call for a report adds to the time it takes to process child care proceedings and one of the purposes of the Act is to reduce delays that harm the welfare of a child. Section 7 also deals with the admissibility as evidence of such welfare reports.

Section 7(1): empowers a court to obtain welfare reports on any aspect of the child. The prior law permitted a court, when considering the welfare of the child, and in cases dealing with custody or access, to call for a welfare officer's report. However, a court had no power to call for a report in proceedings relating to the removal of a guardian, or on applications before it in regard to parental rights and duties under the Family Law Act 1987.

Section 7(2): empowers the Lord Chancellor to specify in regulations the particular matters to be covered in any report unless the court orders to the contrary. The Law Commission felt those should cover in particular applications by non-parents for residence orders. The purpose of the regulations is to ensure homogeneity and consistency for both reporting officers and the court.

Section 7(3): provides that any report may be made in writing or orally as the court requires. In practice a report will be made in writing and submitted to the court, but it may be added to at any hearing by the officer reporting in person.

Section 7(4): provides that a court may take into account hearsay evidence, or even opinion, notwithstanding the provisions of the Civil Evidence Acts, provided the court feels such hearsay evidence or opinion is relevant. Hearsay or opinion may be accepted under the Guardianship Act 1973, the Children Act 1975 and the Domestic Proceedings and Magistrates' Courts Act 1978.

Section 7(5): emphasises the *duty* of a local authority or probation officer or any other appropriate expert to comply with the court's request for a report under section 7.

PART II

ORDERS WITH RESPECT TO CHILDREN IN FAMILY PROCEEDINGS

General

Section 8. Residence, contact and other orders with respect to children

8. —(1) In this Act—

"a contact order" means an order requiring the person with whom a child lives, or is to live, to allow the child to visit or stay with the person named in the order, or for that person and the child otherwise to have contact with each other;

"a prohibited steps order" means an order that no step which could be taken by a parent in meeting his parental responsibility for a child, and which is of a kind specified in the order, shall be taken by any person without the consent of the court;

"a residence order" means an order settling the arrangements to be made as to the person with whom a child is to live; and

"a specific issue order" means an order giving directions for the purpose of determining a specific question which has arisen, or which may arise, in connection with any aspect of parental responsibility for a child.

(2) In this Act "a section 8 order" means any of the orders mentioned in subsection (1) and any order varying or discharging such an order.

(3) For the purposes of this Act "family proceedings" means any proceedings —

(a) under the inherent jurisdiction of the High Court in relation to children; and
(b) under the enactments mentioned in subsection (4),

but does not include proceedings on an application for leave under section 100(3).

(4) The enactments are —

(a) Parts I, II and IV of this Act;
(b) the Matrimonial Causes Act 1973;
(c) the Domestic Violence and Matrimonial Proceedings Act 1976;
(d) the Adoption Act 1976;
(e) the Domestic Proceedings and Magistrates' Courts Act 1978;
(f) sections 1 and 9 of the Matrimonial Homes Act 1983;
(g) Part III of the Matrimonial and Family Proceedings Act 1984.

Annotation

Section 8: defines four categories of orders which may be made concerning children in family proceedings. It was the view of the Law Commission that the former system of orders dealt with "rights" – the interference of one parent whilst the other had custody, rather than each parent exercising those rights in accordance with his responsibility. The new orders are designed to deal with more practical questions, for example, with whom is the child to live and whom should he see, in addition to other specific matters which might require resolution.

Section 8(1): defines residence, contact and other orders with respect to children. Residence and contact orders resemble and replace the former custody and access orders but avoid the confusion as to differing degrees of custody. Prohibited steps and specific issue orders are more general in scope and are modelled on wardship jurisdiction.

Section 8(2): defines, for the purposes of the Act, the four orders in section 8(1) as section 8 orders. It is by this title they are expected to be known.

Section 8(3): does not include proceedings on an application for leave under section 100(3). Section 100(3) provides that no application for any exercise of the court's inherent jurisdiction with respect to children may be made by a local authority unless the authority have obtained the leave of the court.

Section 8(4): sets out a list of those enactments where proceedings are included in the definition "family proceedings" and where the court under this Act is to have power to make section 8(4) deal with custody and access, though the word contact is now preferred, the education of children in divorce and nullity or judicial separation proceedings.

Section 9. Restrictions on making section 8 orders

9. — (1) No court shall make any section 8 order, other than a residence order, with respect to a child who is in the care of a local authority.

(2) No application may be made by a local authority for a residence order or contact order and no court shall make such an order in favour of a local authority.

(3) A person who is, or was at any time within the last six months, a local authority foster parent of a child may not apply for leave to apply for a section 8 order with respect to the child unless —

    (a) he has the consent of the authority;
    (b) he is a relative of the child; or
    (c) the child has lived with him for at least three years preceding the application.

(4) The period of three years mentioned in subsection (3)(c) need not be continuous but must have begun not more than five years before the making of the application.

(5) No court shall exercise its powers to make a specific issue order or prohibited steps order—

- (a) with a view to achieving a result which could be achieved by making a residence or contact order; or
- (b) in any way which is denied to the High Court (by section 100(2)) in the exercise of its inherent jurisdiction with respect to children.

(6) No court shall make any section 8 order which is to have effect for a period which will end after the child has reached the age of sixteen unless it is satisfied that the circumstances of the case are exceptional.

(7) No court shall make any section 8 order, other than one varying or discharging such an order, with respect to a child who has reached the age of sixteen unless it is satisfied that the circumstances of the case are exceptional.

Annotation

Section 9: imposes restrictions on the making of section 8 orders. The effect of a care order is to confer parental responsibility on a local authority: see section 33(3). Statutory duties fall upon a local authority to care for a child under sections 22 and 23. In those circumstances, it is not thought appropriate for a court to have power through specific issue or prohibited steps orders to interfere in the way they discharge their duties, or to direct a local authority how to manage a child's upbringing in accordance with their parental responsibility. Section 9 prohibits any section 8 order being made in respect of a child who has reached sixteen, unless there are exceptional circumstances. Under prior law, a court had power to make custody and access orders endure until a child reached eighteen.

Section 9(1): precludes a court from making any section 8 order other than a residence order. The effect of making a residence order when a child is subject to a care order would be to discharge the care order: see section 91(1). It would also fulfil the purpose of a residence order, in accordance with section 7(1), that is to say settling the arrangements as to the person(s) with whom a child should live.

Section 9(2): precludes a local authority from applying for a section 8 residence or contact order, or from having the benefit of such orders. Without the provision of section 9(2) a local authority would be able to circumvent the provisions of sections 31(2) which limit the circumstances under which they may obtain parental responsibility. The purpose of section 31(2) is to provide protec-

tion to children and their families from excessive intrusion into
their lives by any local authority or authorised person. Hence the
significance of section 9(2).

Section 9(3): lays down the circumstances whereby a foster parent
may apply for a section 8 order with respect to a child. In the
original Bill before Parliament, a local authority foster parent
required the consent of that local authority before seeking leave
to apply for a section 8 order, but as the Bill proceeded through
its committee stages the constraint was broadened to permit leave
to apply where the foster parent is a relative of the child, or the
child has lived with him for three years preceding the application.

Section 9(4): clarifies the three year rule in section 9(3)(c) to take
into account the fact that a child may be in and out of foster care
over a lengthy period.

Section 9(5): enacts a recommendation of the Law Commission,
who wished to encourage a court to use a residence or contact
order rather than a specific issue or prohibited steps order. Section
9(5)(b) should be read in conjunction with section 100(2) which
prohibits a court from using specific issue and prohibited steps
orders to put a child compulsorily in the care, or under the supervision, of a local authority.

Section 9(6): provides that no court shall make any section 8
order that is to expire after a child has reached sixteen, unless
the circumstances are exceptional. A child may leave school when
he is sixteen; he may seek employment; he may become entitled
to social security allowance and benefits. Why then should he be
subject to a section 8 order?: see section 91(10).

Section 10. Power of court to make section 8 orders

10.—(1) In any family proceedings in which a question arises
with respect to the welfare of any child the court may make a
section 8 order with respect to the child if—

> (a) an application for the order has been made by a person
> who—
>> (i) is entitled to apply for a section 8 order with
>> respect to the child; or
>> (ii) has obtained the leave of the court to make
>> the application; or

> (b) the court considers that the order should be made even
> though no such application has been made.

(2) The court may also make a section 8 order with respect to
any child on the application of a person who—

    (a) is entitled to apply for a section 8 order with respect to the child; or

    (b) has obtained the leave of the court to make the application.

(3) This section is subject to the restrictions imposed by section 9.

(4) The following persons are entitled to apply to the court for any section 8 order with respect to a child—

    (a) any parent or guardian of the child;

    (b) any person in whose favour a residence order is in force with respect to the child.

(5) The following persons are entitled to apply for a residence or contact order with respect to a child—

    (a) any party to a marriage (whether or not subsisting) in relation to whom the child is a child of the family;

    (b) any person with whom the child has lived for a period of at least three years;

    (c) any person who—

        (i) in any case where a residence order is in force with respect to the child, has the consent of each of the persons in whose favour the order was made;

        (ii) in any case where the child is in the care of a local authority, has the consent of that authority; or

        (iii) in any other case, has the consent of each of those (if any) who have parental responsibility for the child.

(6) A person who would not otherwise be entitled (under the previous provisions of this section) to apply for the variation or discharge of a section 8 order shall be entitled to do so if—

    (a) the order was made on his application; or

    (b) in the case of a contact order, he is named in the order.

(7) Any person who falls within a category of person prescribed by rules of court is entitled to apply for any such section 8 order as may be prescribed in relation to that category of person.

(8) Where the person applying for leave to make an application for a section 8 order is the child concerned, the court may only grant leave if it is satisfied that he has sufficient understanding to make the proposed application for the section 8 order.

(9) Where the person applying for leave to make an application for a section 8 order is not the child concerned, the court shall,

in deciding whether or not to grant leave, have particular regard to —

> (a) the nature of the proposed application for the section 8 order;
> (b) the applicant's connection with the child;
> (c) any risk there might be of that proposed application disrupting the child's life to such an extent that he would be harmed by it; and
> (d) where the child is being looked after by a local authority—
>> (i) the authority's plans for the child's future; and
>> (ii) the wishes and feelings of the child's parents.

(10) The period of three years mentioned in subsection (5)(b) need not be continuous but must not have begun more than five years before, or ended more than three months before, the making of the application.

Annotation

Section 10: confers upon the court the power to make section 8 orders. In prior law, there were three ways of bringing in play the mechanism for making such orders – proceedings for divorce, nullity or judicial separation; upon the court's own motion in proceedings under the Matrimonial Causes Act 1973 or for financial relief between spouses under the Domestic Proceedings and Magistrates' Courts Act 1978; and by way of free-standing applications relating to custody, access or particular aspects of upbringing. Grandparents might also apply for access. Section 10 continues to provide ways in which section 8 orders may be made; it specifies the persons who are entitled to apply and the criteria for deciding such applications for leave. It also has the helpful effect of ensuring that, so far as possible, all applications relating to the same child can be dealt with together.

Section 10(1): enacts a recommendation of the Law Commission that section 8 orders can be made on application in the course of family proceedings, on the court's own motion in the course of those proceedings, and in the absence of any other proceedings. Section 10(1)(a)(i) provides that anyone with a genuine interest in a child's welfare can make applications relating to his upbringing, as could have been done in the past by making a child a ward of court. The requirement of leave in section 10(1)(a)(ii) is intended to protect the child and his family from unwarranted intrusion, whilst ensuring that a child's interests are respected.

Section 10(2): further enacts a Law Commission recommendation that section 8 orders can be made on free-standing applications in the absence of any other proceedings. Under the prior law, a free-standing application was brought by parents, with full parental rights and duties, guardians, joint guardians, other than for custody or access, and unmarried fathers. The same persons can initiate free-standing applications as can make applications in the course of family proceedings.

Section 10(3): is subject to the restrictions imposed by section 9. That is to say, the balance the Act seeks to strike between the rights of a parent and child within the family and the rights of a local authority as defined in section 9, shall not be disturbed by the powers of the court to make section 8 orders in accordance with this section.

Section 10(4): enacts another Law Commission recommendation that three categories of people should always be able to apply for a section 8 order – parents, with or without parental responsibility, guardians and people in whose favour there is a residence order in force. If it is right that a guardian will take over complete responsibility for the care and upbringing of a child if the parents die, it is equally right that he should be able to apply for a section 8 order and not be limited, as in the past, to a free-standing application. Those with parental responsibility should have parental access to the court.

Section 10(5): provides that three categories of persons are entitled to apply for a residence or contact order without leave of the court. Section 10(5)(a) precludes step parents, for they do not automatically acquire parental responsibility, though they have a right to apply for access and custody in matrimonial proceedings, and they may also be ordered to make financial provision for the child. See section 105 for the definition of what constitutes a child of the family. Section 10(5)(b) should be read in conjunction with section 10(10). The prior qualifications for custodianship required that the period included the three months before the application, with elaborate provision to forestall removal by parents or others just before the application could be made. Section 10(5)(a) reflects the former qualifications to apply for custodianship and applies to any person who makes the application with the consent of any of those persons whose position will be affected by it.

Section 10(6): provides, in the words of the Attorney General when he moved section 10(6) at report stage, that "just as a person may be entitled to apply for any section 8 order or some section 8 orders, so may a person apply for a variation or discharge".

Section 10(7): provides for rules of court to be made to cover other categories of persons who may emerge and to whom leave may be granted.

Section 10(8): provides that a child may make an application about his own upbringing. Under the Act, a child is able to apply for a guardian to be appointed or removed; he is also entitled to apply for the discharge of parental responsibility orders or agreements. Under section 10(8) he can further protect himself, with leave of the court, by having the power to apply for a section 8 order.

Section 10(9): provides that in deciding whether to grant leave on application by someone other than a child, the court is to have regard to the nature of the proposed application, the applicant's connection with the child and any risk of harmful disruption to the child's life because of the application. Section 10(9)(d) deals essentially with the position of local authority foster parents, but covers all children being looked after either under a care order or as a service. The thinking behind section 10(9)(d) is that confidence should be maintained by parents in the voluntary care system. They should not feel more at risk of losing their children by accepting the services of a local authority than they would by making private arrangements. A balance has to be struck, however, so that local authorities should feel confidence in their responsibility to plan the best possible future for children who may be in voluntary or compulsory care.

Section 10(10): supplements section 10(5)(b) and specifies that although the three year period need not be continuous, it must not have ended more than three months before, or begun more than five years before, the making of the application: see annotation to section 10(5).

Section 11. General principles and supplementary provisions

11.—(1) In proceedings in which any question of making a section 8 order, or any other question with respect to such an order, arises, the court shall (in the light of any rules made by virtue of subsection (2))—

(a) draw up a timetable with a view to determining the question without delay; and

(b) give such directions as it considers appropriate for the purpose of ensuring, so far as is reasonably practicable, that that timetable is adhered to.

(2) Rules of court may—

(a) specify periods within which specified steps must be taken in relation to proceedings in which such questions arise; and

(b) make other provision with respect to such proceedings for the purpose of ensuring, so far as is reasonably practicable, that such questions are determined without delay.

(3) Where a court has power to make a section 8 order, it may do so at any time during the course of the proceedings in question even though it is not in a position to dispose finally of those proceedings.

(4) Where a residence order is made in favour of two or more persons who do not themselves all live together, the order may specify the periods during which the child is to live in the different households concerned.

(5) Where—

(a) a residence order has been made with respect to a child; and

(b) as a result of the order the child lives, or is to live, with one of two parents who each have parental responsibility for him,

the residence order shall cease to have effect if the parents live together for a continuous period of more than six months.

(6) A contact order which requires the parent with whom a child lives to allow the child to visit, or otherwise have contact with, his other parent shall cease to have effect if the parents live together for a continuous period of more than six months.

(7) A section 8 order may—

(a) contain directions about how it is to be carried into effect;

(b) impose conditions which must be complied with by any person—

(i) in whose favour the order is made;

(ii) who is a parent of the child concerned;

(iii) who is not a parent of his but who has parental responsibility for him; or

(iv) with whom the child is living,

and to whom the conditions are expressed to apply;

(c) be made to have effect for a specified period, or contain provisions which are to have effect for a specified period;

(d) make such incidental, supplemental or consequential provision as the court thinks fit.

Annotation

Section 11: introduces the general principle that delay is likely to prejudice the welfare of the child and provides supplementary provisions to enable a court to oversee the progress of a case. Section 11 also contains provisions supplemental to section 8 in relation to the terms and duration of residence and contact orders and the putting into effect of matters supplemental to all section 8 orders.

Section 11(1): reflects a view put forward by the Law Commission that all delay in proceedings affecting a child will be prejudicial to his welfare. Such delay hardly assists those with parental responsibility and the relationship between them. Delay also prejudices a parent who is not living with the child. However, delay is often in the interests of one or other of the parties. Section 11(1) enables the court to take into account the time required, for example, to prepare welfare reports, yet set a timetable which is both reasonable and practical.

Section 11(2): provides, together with section 11(3), the means for the court to take the necessary practical action to oversee the progress of the case and ensure that it proceeds speedily. The Law Commission in its Working Paper on Care, Supervision and Interim Orders in Custody Proceedings, provisionally proposed that where there is a dispute about the child's upbringing the court should always set a fixed return date. It was suggested that the dispute should be heard within a maximum of three months. Section 11(2) provides for the requisite rules of court to provide for this, or other, time limits.

Section 11(3): provides that the court may make a section 8 order at any time in the course of the proceedings, whether or not it is yet in a position to make a final determination on the application for the relief claimed in those proceedings. Section 11(3) is by way of clarification, since the freedom of a court to make a section 8 order at any time is implicit in its powers to make orders for a specific period: see section 11(7)(a).

Section 11(4): supplements those provisions of section 10 which enable the court to make residence orders. It was the view of the Law Commission that residence orders should be flexible enough to cater for a wider variety of arrangements than custody orders in the past, including cases where the child is to live with two or more people who do not themselves live together. Section 11(4) provides that an order may then specify the period during which the child should live in each household.

Section 11(5): provides that it would be unrealistic to maintain in being a residence order in favour of one parent where both parents were now living together. In the event they should separate again, where the circumstances may be different, it would be appropriate to apply to the court for another order. Section 11(4) deals with a couple each of whom has parental responsibility; it does not apply to an unmarried father who has not acquired parental responsibility in accordance with section 4(1), or to spouses who are not both parents of the child.

Section 11(6): provides that a contact order requiring one parent to allow the child to visit the other shall lapse automatically if the parents live together for more than six months. Similar provisions for custody orders to lapse where the parties have lived together for more than six months may be found under section 25(1) of the Domestic Proceedings and Magistrates' Courts Act 1978 and under section 5A(1) of the Guardianship Act 1973. There are no such provisions under the Matrimonial Causes Act.

Section 11(7): ensures the maximum flexibility with regard to section 8 orders. Thus section 11(7)(a) permits the court to smooth any transition in those cases in which it may order a change in existing arrangements. It may, for example, enable a delay before a change is ordered in the child's residence and what the terms of contact will be. Section 11(7)(b) confers a power to enable the court to resolve specific disputes before it, or to direct how such a dispute should be dealt with. If an objection is raised that one parent can or may cause difficulties for the other in the way he exercises his parental responsibilities, the court may deal with these matters by attaching conditions or specifying limitations upon the independent action of one or the other parent. Section 11(7)(a) retains the flexibility which presently exists under the Matrimonial Causes Act 1973 where there is no rigid distinction between interim and final custody and access orders. The court will have the power to make the best order it can on the information available to it at the time. Section 11(7)(d) will assist the court where it is required to consider additional provision not falling within any of the more specific provisions in section 11(7)(a)(b) and (c).

Section 12. Residence orders and parental responsibility

12. —(1) Where the court makes a residence order in favour of the father of a child it shall, if the father would not otherwise have parental responsibility for the child, also make an order under section 4 giving him that responsibility.

(2) Where the court makes a residence order in favour of any person who is not the parent or guardian of the child concerned

that person shall have parental responsibility for the child while the residence order remains in force.

(3) Where a person has parental responsibility for a child as a result of subsection (2), he shall not have the right—

(a) to consent, or refuse to consent, to the making of an application with respect to the child under section 18 of the Adoption Act 1976;

(b) to agree, or refuse to agree, to the making of an adoption order, or an order under section 55 of the Act of 1976, with respect to the child; or

(c) to appoint a guardian for the child.

(4) Where subsection (1) requires the court to make an order under section 4 in respect of the father of a child, the court shall not bring that order to an end at any time while the residence order concerned remains in force.

Annotation

Section 12: deals with residence orders and parental responsibility and links a residence order made in favour of an unmarried father with his acquisition of parental responsibility where he does not already have such responsibility. It is a principle of the Act that it is the person with whom the child lives who has the primary role for his care and upbringing, but where the court makes a residence order in favour of a person who is not a parent or guardian then the person in whose favour the order is made is given parental responsibility for the child. Section 12 limits this in certain respects.

Section 12(1): provides that where the court makes a residence order in favour of an unmarried father, the court may equally order that he acquire parental responsibility in accordance with section 4(1)(a) and (b). In the event of such an order being made, the full range of parental responsibility shall then be accorded to him, including the power to withhold agreement to adoption and the appointment of a guardian.

Section 12(2): follows upon those principles laid down in section 10, that section 8 orders be available to those who are not parents as they are available between parents, and that a residence order in favour of a non-parent shall carry with it all parental responsibility subject to section 12(3). Parental responsibility shall last only as long as the residence order lasts.

Section 12(3): reflects the view of the Law Commission that a residence order in favour of a non-resident should carry with it all the parental responsibilities, apart from those specifically limited to parents or guardians. Thus, in accordance with section 12(3), the specific limitation applies to the giving or withholding of agreement to adoption and to the appointment of a guardian.

Section 12(4): reflects the principle that where an unmarried father has undertaken full responsibility, thus forming a paternal relationship with the child, it cannot be in the child's interests for him to be treated differently from any other father. Changes in a child's residence should interfere as little as possible in his relationship with both his parents.

Section 13. Change of child's name or removal from jurisdiction

13.—(1) Where a residence order is in force with respect to a child, no person may—

(a) cause the child to be known by a new surname; or
(b) remove him from the United Kingdom;

without either the written consent of every person who has parental responsibility for the child or the leave of the court.

(2) Subsection (1)(b) does not prevent the removal of a child, for a period of less than one month, by the person in whose favour the residence order is made.

(3) In making a residence order with respect to a child the court may grant the leave required by subsection (1)(b), either generally or for specified purposes.

Annotation

Section 13: deals with the change of a child's name or his removal from the jurisdiction where a residence order is in force. The Law Commission recommended that the surname of a child should not be changed without either the written consent of every person who has parental responsibility for the child or leave of the court. Also, children subject to a residence order may find themselves unable to leave England and Wales without applying for leave to a court: visits to Scotland would require just such an application. Section 13 prevents the change of surname without the consent of every person who has parental responsibility or the leave of the court, but permits removal from the jurisdiction for up to one month without the consent or leave by a person in whose favour the residence order is made.

Section 13(1): prescribes the principle in section 13(1)(a) to be found in the Matrimonial Causes Rules 1977 (r.92(8)) that custody or care and control orders automatically include conditions to preserve the principle that a child's surname is an important symbol of his identity. Section 13(1)(a) makes it clear that whilst it may be in the best interests of the child to be known by a new surname, this will not be a matter solely for the parent with whom he lives pursuant to a residence order. Section 13(1)(b) reflects the former position, that a divorce court order for custody or care and control had to provide for the child not to be removed from England and Wales without leave of the court and other than on the terms specified by the court.

Section 13(2): provides that a child may be removed from the jurisdiction for a period of less than one month by the person in whose favour a residence order is made, notwithstanding the provision of section 13(1)(b). In the past, unless an exception was made at the outset, a child could not be taken abroad, or to Scotland, even if there were an agreement between parents, without leave of the court. This meant expensive and time wasting applications for leave.

Section 13(3): confers a power on the court when making a residence order to grant leave for a child to leave the jurisdiction, for general or specified purposes, but for up to one month only.

Section 14. Enforcement of residence orders

14. — (1) Where —

(a) a residence order is in force with respect to a child in favour of any person; and

(b) any other person (including one in whose favour the order is also in force) is in breach of the arrangements settled by that order,

the person mentioned in paragraph (a) may, as soon as the requirement in subsection (2) is complied with, enforce the order under section 63(3) of the Magistrates' Courts Act 1980 as if it were an order requiring the other person to produce the child to him.

(2) The requirement is that a copy of the residence order has been served on the other person.

(3) Subsection (1) is without prejudice to any other remedy open to the person in whose favour the residence order is in force.

Annotation

Section 14: provides that where a residence order is in force with respect to a child in favour of any person, an order under section 63(3) of the Magistrates' Courts Act 1980 may be enforced against a person in breach of the residence order, the only requirement being that such a person has had served upon him a copy of the residence order. Section 63(3) of the Magistrates' Courts Act 1980 provides that where any person disobeys an order of a magistrates' court to do anything other than the payment of money, or to abstain from doing anything, the court may order him to pay a sum not exceeding £50 for every day during which he is in default, or commit him to custody until he has remedied his default.

Section 14(1): provides that an order under section 63(3) of the Magistrates' Courts Act 1980 has to be treated as if it were an order to produce the child. Failure to produce the child upon receipt of a copy of the residence order pursuant to section 14(2) would make the person who is in breach of the residence order liable to fines and imprisonment. A person who does not produce the child falls into breach not only of the residence order but also of the magistrates' court order and might be ordered to pay a sum for every day during which he is in default or be committed to custody until he has remedied his default. He cannot, by virtue of section 63(3) of the Magistrates' Courts Act 1980, be ordered to pay more than £1,000 or be committed for more than two months.

Section 14(2): provides that knowledge of the contents of a residence order, by way of its delivery upon a person in breach of its conditions, will be sufficient to trigger section 14(1) and the provisions of section 63(3) of the Magistrates' Courts Act 1980.

Section 14(3): provides that the remedies available to a person in whose favour the residence order is in force shall not be restricted to section 14(1) and section 63(3) of the Magistrates' Courts Act 1980.

Financial relief

Section 15. Orders for financial relief with respect to children

15.—(1) Schedule 1 (which consists primarily of the re-enactment, with consequential amendments and minor modifications, of provisions [section 6 of the Family Law Reform Act 1969] of the Guardianship of Minors Acts 1971 and 1973, the Children Act 1975 and of sections 15 and 16 of the Family Law Reform Act 1987) makes provision in relation to financial relief for children.

(2) The powers of a magistrates' court under section 60 of the

Note: The words within square brackets were inserted by the Courts and Legal Services Act 1990.

Magistrates' Courts Act 1980 to revoke, revive or vary an order for the periodical payment of money shall not apply in relation to an order made under Schedule 1.

Annotation

Section 15: incorporates into the Act, by way of schedule 1, the necessary provisions enabling the court to make orders for financial relief with respect to children. The various private law provisions relating to the upbringing of children which the Act assimilates all have associated powers to make orders for financial relief and, in some cases, adjustment of property rights for the benefit of the children concerned.

Section 15(1): reflects the thinking of the Law Commission that it was only practicable to incorporate into this Act those powers formerly contained in the Guardianship of Minors Act 1971 and 1973 and the Children Act 1975. In addition, the powers of the courts contained in section 15 and 16 of the Family Law Reform Act 1987, dealing with the variation of maintenance agreements, are included.

Section 15(2): excludes the power of a magistrates' court under section 60 of the Magistrates' Courts Act 1980 to revoke, revive or vary an order for the periodical payment of money from applying to any order made under Schedule 1. Schedule 1 covers financial provision for children, including orders for financial relief and other matters.

Family assistance orders

Section 16. Family assistance orders

16. — (1) Where, in any family proceedings, the court has power to make an order under this Part with respect to any child, it may (whether or not it makes such an order) make an order requiring —

(a) a probation officer to be made available; or
(b) a local authority to make an officer of the authority available,

to advise, assist and (where appropriate) befriend any person named in the order.

(2) The persons who may be named in an order under this section ("a family assistance order") are —

(a) any parent or guardian of the child;

    (b) any person with whom the child is living or in whose favour a contact order is in force with respect to the child;

    (c) the child himself.

(3) No court may make a family assistance order unless—

    (a) it is satisfied that the circumstances of the case are exceptional; and

    (b) it has obtained the consent of every person to be named in the order other than the child.

(4) A family assistance order may direct—

    (a) the person named in the order; or

    (b) such of the persons named in the order as may be specified in the order,

to take such steps as may be so specified with a view to enabling the officer concerned to be kept informed of the address of any person named in the order and to be allowed to visit any such person.

(5) Unless it specifies a shorter period, a family assistance order shall have effect for a period of six months beginning with the day on which it is made.

(6) Where—

    (a) a family assistance order is in force with respect to a child; and

    (b) a section 8 order is also in force with respect to the child,

the officer concerned may refer to the court the question whether the section 8 order should be varied or discharged.

(7) A family assistance order shall not be made so as to require a local authority to make an officer of theirs available unless—

    (a) the authority agree; or

    (b) the child concerned lives or will live within their area.

(8) Where a family assistance order requires a probation officer to be made available, the officer shall be selected in accordance with arrangements made by the probation committee for the area in which the child lives or will live.

(9) If the selected probation officer is unable to carry out his duties, or dies, another probation officer shall be selected in the same manner.

Annotation

Section 16: provides for the making of a family assistance order and the formalisation of the involvement of a welfare officer for a short period. The purpose of a welfare officer would be to assist the family to overcome the problems of conflict associated with their separation or divorce. Section 16 is aimed at situations where conciliation could help the family resolve what might be a temporary crisis and avoid the need for further involvement of the court. Section 16 contains further provisions concerning the duration of such orders.

Section 16(1): is aimed at the family rather than the child and its intention is to replace family proceedings supervision orders. The Law Commission contemplated that the welfare officer would usually be the officer who had compiled a welfare report for the court, and thus a probation officer in most cases, but it did not exclude the possibility of a local authority acting as welfare officers for this purpose, particularly where they have provided the report for the court; hence section 16(1)(b).

Section 16(2): lists those likely to benefit in a conciliation process. Any order made for the benefit of any of those specified in section 16(2) would include requirements for those persons to keep in touch with the welfare officer. There would not, however, be the much wider range of requirements that might be included in a full supervision order. For example, if there is an order about the child's residence or upbringing, the welfare officer should be able to refer to the court the question of whether it should be varied or discharged: see section 16(4).

Section 16(3): provides that a family assistance order should only be made in exceptional circumstances and should require the consent of every person named in the order, other than the child. It follows that if any order can only be made in exceptional circumstances the aim of the order can only be short-term assistance; see section 16(5). Nor would it be the appropriate for the welfare officer to have power to seek committal for care under a family assistance order, because no ground for this will have been established at the outset. In considering the exceptional circumstances, a court might refer the case to the local authority for investigation if cause for concern arose.

Section 16(4): provides for a family assistance order to include requirements for the people, or any of them named in it, to keep in touch with the probation or local authority officer. The aim of section 16(4) is to make a more limited form of order available in cases where, in the past, the full effect of a supervision order had to be invoked, even where it had not been needed: see section 16(2).

PART III

LOCAL AUTHORITY SUPPORT FOR CHILDREN AND FAMILIES

Provision of services for children and their families

Section 17. Provision of services for children in need, their families and others

17.—(1) It shall be the general duty of every local authority (in addition to the other duties imposed on them by this Part)—

(a) to safeguard and promote the welfare of children within their area who are in need; and

(b) so far as is consistent with that duty, to promote the upbringing of such children by their families,

by providing a range and level of services appropriate to those children's needs.

(2) For the purpose principally of facilitating the discharge of their general duty under this section, every local authority shall have the specific duties and powers set out in Part 1 of Schedule 2.

(3) Any service provided by an authority in the exercise of functions conferred on them by this section may be provided for the family of a particular child in need or for any member of his family, if it is provided with a view to safeguarding or promoting the child's welfare.

(4) The Secretary of State may by order amend any provision of Part I of Schedule 2 or add any further duty or power to those for the time being mentioned there.

(5) Every local authority—

(a) shall facilitate the provision by others (including in particular voluntary organisations) of services which the authority have power to provide by virtue of this section, or section 18, 20, 23 or 24; and

(b) may make such arrangements as they see fit for any person to act on their behalf in the provision of any such service.

(6) The services provided by a local authority in the exercise of functions conferred on them by this section may include giving assistance in kind or, in exceptional circumstances, in cash.

(7) Assistance may be unconditional or subject to conditions as to the repayment of the assistance or of its value (in whole or in part).

(8) Before giving any assistance or imposing any conditions, a local authority shall have regard to the means of the child concerned and of each of his parents.

(9) No person shall be liable to make any repayment of assistance or of its value at any time when he is in receipt of income support or family credit under the Social Security Act 1986.

(10) For the purposes of this Part a child shall be taken to be in need if—

    (a) he is unlikely to achieve or maintain, or to have the opportunity of achieving or maintaining, a reasonable standard of health or development without the provision for him of services by a local authority under this Part;

    (b) his health or development is likely to be significantly impaired, or further impaired, without the provision for him of such services; or

    (c) he is disabled,

and "family", in relation to such a child, includes any person who has parental responsibility for the child and any other person with whom he has been living.

(11) For the purposes of this Part, a child is disabled if he is blind, deaf or dumb or suffers from mental disorder of any kind or is substantially and permanently handicapped by illness, injury or congenital deformity or such other disability as may be prescribed; and in this Part

    "development" means physical, intellectual, emotional, social or behavioural development; and

    "health" means physical or mental health.

Annotation

Section 17: deals with the provision of services for children in need, their families and others. Part III of the Act represents an amalgamation of former powers and duties to provide services that were to be found under section 1 of the Child Care Act 1980 and other various enactments dealing with health and welfare. Sections 21 and 29 of the National Assistance Act 1948 and schedule 8 to the National Health Service Act 1977 largely cease to apply to children under eighteen, and section 1 of the Child Care Act 1980 is repealed. Section 17 applies to all children, including those who are disabled or handicapped within the meaning of section 29 of the National Assistance Act 1948. Section 17 imposes a new general duty upon a local authority to safeguard and promote the welfare of children within their area who are in need and to promote the upbringing of such children by their families.

Section 17(1): defines the new duty upon a local authority which seeks to clarify and highlight the role of the authority in supporting the families of children in need. Section 17(1) provides that the duty will relate to children in need generally and not to individual children. In *Attorney General* (ex rel Tilley) v. *London Borough of Wandsworth* (1981) [1 All ER 1162] the Court of Appeal held that section 1 of the Child Care Act should be interpreted as creating a specific requirement in relation to particular children as opposed to children in general. Section 17(1) excludes the effect of this decision from section 17. The kind of assistance available to families of children in need includes assistance in the home by way of a family home help, day-care schemes, child minding facilities and the provision of accommodation in residential homes or substitute families.

Section 17(3): enables a local authority to provide a service not only to the family of a particular child in need but also a member of the family where it is to be provided with a view to safeguarding or promoting the welfare of the child. A local authority will be required, *inter alia*, to identify the extent to which there are children in need in their area, assess individual children who they find to be in need, and consider what services should be made available to the child or his family, or members of that family.

Section 17(4): enables the Secretary of State to amend or add to, by order, the various powers and duties specified in schedule 2.

Section 17(5): allows for services to families under section 17 to be provided by persons other than a local authority and in particular by voluntary organisations. Section 17(5) replaces section 1(2) of the Child Care Act 1980.

Section 17(6): provides that a local authority may, in exceptional circumstances, make a cash payment to a family in need in accordance with the general duty defined in section 17(1) and in accordance with assistance to be rendered to promote the welfare of a child as defined throughout Part III of the Act. Payments to a family in need, by way of income support or family credit, are made under the Social Security Act 1986, but receipt of such benefit does not exclude the right to a cash payment in exceptional circumstances, in accordance with section 17(6).

Section 17(8): provides for the means testing of any cash payment to take into account not only the means of the parents but of the child. Section 17(8) will require some urgency on the part of a local authority to act quickly to ascertain the means of the parents and the child in order to make the payment, if such payment is to be made, to promote the child's welfare.

Section 17(9): provides that where assistance is rendered, in cash or in kind, in accordance with section 17(6) a recipient will not be liable for repayment where the recipient receives income support or family credit under the Social Security Act 1986.

Section 17(10): provides a definition of a child in need for the purposes of Part III of the Act. There has been no prior legislative definition, except in relation to disabled children. The rehabilitation duty of section 1 of the Child Care Act 1980 is no longer retained in the same form, diminishing the need to receive children into care or keep them in care under this Act, or to bring children before a juvenile court. The objective is not to discourage the use of local authority services where needed, particularly as far as disabled children are concerned: see section 17(11). It is an objective of the Act to ensure that, where possible and consistent with a child's welfare, a local authority should endeavour to promote the upbringing of children with their families (section 17(1)). See also paragraph 9 of schedule 2 dealing with maintenance of the family home and the duty to consider the discharge of a child in compulsory care in accordance with the new, improved regulation-making powers for reviews in section 26.

Section 17(11): reflects the definition of a disabled child to be found in section 29(1) of the National Assistance Act 1948. Such a child will be provided for under Part III of the Act rather than, as previously under health and welfare legislation, from which they are now generally excluded.

Section 18. Day care for pre-school and other children

18.—(1) Every local authority shall provide such day care for children in need within their area who are—

(a) aged five or under; and
(b) not yet attending schools,

as is appropriate.

(2) A local authority may provide day care for children within their area who satisfy the conditions mentioned in subsection (1)(a) and (b) even though they are not in need.

(3) A local authority may provide facilities (including training, advice, guidance and counselling) for those—

(a) caring for children in day care; or
(b) who at any time accompany such children while they are in day care.

(4) In this section "day care" means any form of care or supervised activity provided for children during the day (whether or not it is provided on a regular basis).

(5) Every local authority shall provide for children in need within their area who are attending any school such care or supervised activities as is appropriate—

(a) outside school hours; or
(b) during school holidays.

(6) A local authority may provide such care or supervised activities for children within their area who are attending any school even though those children are not in need.

(7) In this section "supervised activity" means an activity supervised by a responsible person.

Annotation

Section 18: imposes a new duty on a local authority to provide day care for children in need who are five or under and not yet attending school. Section 18 also confers a power upon a local authority to provide care or supervised activities for children who are attending school. A local authority is also empowered to provide day care services for children who are not in need: see section 17(9) for the definition of children in need. Further, to provide facilities which may include advice, guidance and counselling for carers and those who accompany children while they are in day care. Section 18 replaces and extends the provision in schedule 8 of the National Health Service Act 1977. It also complements a local authority's regulation of private care and child minding facilities under the Nurseries and Child Minders Regulation Act 1948, which this Act replaces.

Section 18(1): requires a local authority to provide such day care as they consider appropriate. The duty of a local authority to provide day care services for children in need is one way of discharging their general duty to children in need pursuant to section 15.

Section 18(2): empowers a local authority to provide day care for children who are not in need. This may be of assistance where one child within a family is in need, as this is defined in section 17(10), but another is not, yet they might be kept together as a family by attendance at the same day care facility.

Section 18(3): enables a local authority to provide facilities, including advice, guidance and counselling, to those who provide day care or who accompany children in day care. A local authority is empowered both to provide the facilities and also the training.

Section 18(4): defines day care, which includes care in day nurseries or with child minders and any other kind of supervised activity during the day. Day care was provided under prior legislation by local authorities, voluntary bodies, private or commercial organisations and private individuals. Independently provided services were registered by local authorities under the Nurseries and Child Minders Regulation Act 1948.

Section 18(5): enables a local authority to provide for children who are attending school such care or supervised activities outside school hours and during school holidays as they consider appropriate.

Section 18(6): provides for the definition of a supervised activity. Section 18(6) originally included a definition of a child minder as any person falling within paragraph (b) of Section 1(1) of the Nurseries and Child Minders Regulation Act 1948 and day nursery as any premises falling within pargagraph (a) of that section, but as we have seen, the provisions of the Nurseries and Child Minders Regulation Act 1948 are replaced by the present Act.

Section 19. Review of provision for day care, child minding etc.

19. — (1) Every local authority in England and Wales shall review —

    (a) the provision which they make under section 18;

    (b) the extent to which the services of child minders are available within their area with respect to children under the age of eight; and

    (c) the provision for day care within their area made for children under the age of eight by persons other, than the authority, required to register under section 71(1)(b).

(2) A review under subsection (1) shall be conducted —

    (a) together with the appropriate local education authority; and

    (b) at least once in every review period.

(3) Every local authority in Scotland shall, at least once in every review period, review —

    (a) the provision for day care within their area made for children under the age of eight by the local authority and by persons required to register under section 71(1)(b); and

(b) the extent to which the services of child minders are available within their area with respect to children under the age of eight.

(4) In conducting any such review, the two authorities or, in Scotland, the authority shall have regard to the provision made with respect to children under the age of eight in relevant establishments within their area.

(5) In this section —

"relevant establishment" means any establishment which is mentioned in paragraphs 3 and 4 of Schedule 9 (hospitals, schools and other establishments exempt from the registration requirements which apply in relation to the provision of day care); and

"review period" means the period of one year beginning with the commencement of this section and each subsequent period of three years beginning with an anniversary of that commencement.

(6) Where a local authority have conducted a review under this section they shall publish the result of the review —

(a) as soon as is reasonably practicable;
(b) in such form as they consider appropriate; and
(c) together with any proposals they may have with respect to the matters reviewed.

(7) the authorities conducting any review under this section shall have regard to —

(a) any representations made to any one of them by any relevant health authority or health board; and
(b) any other representations which they consider to be relevant.

(8) In the application of this section to Scotland, "day care" has the same meaning as in section 79 and "health board" has the same meaning as in the National Health Service (Scotland) Act 1978.

Annotation

Section 19: imposes a duty on every local authority in England and Wales to review provision for day care within their area. The Act applies principally to England and Wales, but there are exceptions, notably in regard to child minding and day care for young children, which equally apply to Scotland. Section 19(3)(4) and (5) ensures that every local authority in Scotland will also have to review their day care provision. Section 19 provides for a review every three years that involves inter-agency cooperation with local education authorities, other statutory agencies such as health authorities or their Scottish equivalent, and voluntary organisations. Its purpose is to ensure that a local authority will talk to and work with other agencies, in order to identify need and enable a proper, strategic and long-term planning to emerge with regard to day care provision.

Section 19(1): provides for the review of day care provision for pre-school and other children, the extent to which child minders are available, and for the registration by persons who provide day care for children under the age of eight on premises other than domestic premises. A further purpose of the review is that there will be coherence, coordination, cooperation and, where possible, integration in the provision of services for the under-eights.

Section 19(2): reflects the need for the involvement of a local education authority. The Lord Chancellor, speaking in the Lords, said he was sympathetic to the view that a local authority, in consort with a local education authority, should keep day care service provision under review and the Solicitor General, speaking in the Commons, said that section 19(2) was "a good way to ensure that social service authorities, working with local or education authorities, pay attention to day care services for young children, and that such activities are effectively and efficiently coordinated".

Section 19(3): extends the provisions of section 19 to Scotland. Part X dealing with child minding and day care provision for young children equally applies to Scotland: see section 79. Section 71(b) referred to in section 19(3) imposes a duty on a local authority to maintain a register of persons who provide day care for children under the age of eight on premises other than domestic premises, within their area.

Section 19(4): provides that the review is intended not only to identify those areas where provision is needed but also to consider existing provision and whether this is sufficient. The review will be as wide as possible and require maximum cooperation between an education authority and a local authority where the two are different. Within the varied structures of local government, a local authority may include their own education and their own social services department, which in this case would be expected to act together and in harmony. An earlier legislative proposal was that the review be carried out by a local authority and education authority for day care provision up to the age of five, but this was extended in the committee and report stage proceedings of the Act up to the age of eight.

Section 19(5): defines "relevant establishment" and "review period". In the case of relevant establishment, section 19(5) extends the provisions of section 19 to a number of schools described in paragraph 3 of Schedule 9, and to a number of children's, voluntary and community homes described in paragraph 4 of Schedule 9. In the case of the review period, section 19(5) requires that the review begin within a year of the commencement of this section and each subsequent period of three years beginning with an anniversary of that commencement. Though the full Act is to be implemented not later than eighteen months after the Royal Assent (in November 1989) there is no reason why section 19(5) should not have been taken to commence immediately upon Royal Assent: there should be no delay in beginning the review proceedings.

Section 19(6): confers a duty upon a local authority not only to conduct a review with a local education authority but also to publish their findings and put forward proposals. Hence a local authority shall be held accountable for their own and other under-eight provision within their area, and for being positive about the review so that proposals may ensue as to how such provision can be improved.

Section 19(7): provides that in addition to there being cooperation between a local authority and an education authority, this may be extended to any relevant authority or Scottish health board. Thus it extends the principle of inter-agency cooperation for the benefit of children under eight. Section 19(7) also invites the participation of other agencies, such as the National Society for the Prevention of Cruelty to Children, who receive statutory recognition in the Act.

Section 19(8): defines day care in its application to Scotland as any form of care or of activity supervised by a responsible person provided for children during the day, whether or not it is provided on a regular basis.

Provision of accommodation for children

Section 20. Provision of accommodation for children: general

20. —(1) Every local authority shall provide accommodation for any child in need within their area who appears to them to require accommodation as a result of—

(a) there being no person who has parental responsibility for him;

(b) his being lost or having been abandoned; or

(c) the person who has been caring for him being prevented (whether or not permanently, and for whatever reason) from providing him with suitable accommodation or care.

(2) Where a local authority provide accommodation under subsection (1) for a child who is ordinarily resident in the area of another local authority, that other local authority may take over the provision of accommodation for the child within—

(a) three months of being notified in writing that the child is being provided with accommodation; or

(b) such other longer period as may be prescribed.

(3) Every local authority shall provide accommodation for any child in need within their area who has reached the age of sixteen and whose welfare the authority consider is likely to be seriously prejudiced if they do not provide him with accommodation.

(4) A local authority may provide accommodation for any child within their area (even though a person who has parental responsibility for him is able to provide him with accommodation) if they consider that to do so would safeguard or promote the child's welfare.

(5) A local authority may provide accommodation for any person who has reached the age of sixteen but is under twenty-one in any community home which takes children who have reached the age of sixteen if they consider that to do so would safeguard or promote his welfare.

(6) Before providing accommodation under this section, a local authority shall, so far as is reasonably practicable and consistent with the child's welfare—

(a) ascertain the child's wishes regarding the provision of accommodation; and

(b) give due consideration (having regard to his age and understanding) to such wishes of the child as they have been able to ascertain.

(7) A local authority may not provide accommodation under this section for any child if any person who—

(a) has parental responsibility for him; and

(b) is willing and able to—

(i) provide accommodation for him; or

          (ii) arrange for accommodation to be provided for
              him,
objects.

(8) Any person who has parental responsibility for a child may at any time remove the child from accommodation provided by or on behalf of the local authority under this section.

(9) Subsections (7) and (8) do not apply while any person—

    (a) in whose favour a residence order is in force with respect to the child; or

    (b) who has care of the child by virtue of an order made in the exercise of the High Court's inherent jurisdiction with respect to children,

agrees to the child being looked after in accommodation provided by or on behalf of the local authority.

(10) where there is more than one such person as is mentioned in subsection (9), all of them must agree.

(11) Subsections (7) and (8) do not apply where a child who has reached the age of sixteen agrees to being provided with accommodation under this section.

Annotation

Section 20: reflects the thinking in the White Paper entitled "The Law on Child Care and Family Services", that a local authority have a duty to receive a child into their care in specified circumstances, generally where there is a need for care for the child away from home because of the absence or incapacity of parents. The provision of a service by a local authority to enable a child who is not under a care order to be looked after away from home should be seen in a wider context and as part of the range of services a local authority can offer to parents and families in need of help with the care of their children: see section 17. It was the view expressed in the White Paper that such a service provided by a local authority should, in appropriate circumstances, be seen as a positive response to the needs of families and not as a mark of failure, either on the part of the family or those professionals and others working to support them.

Section 20(1): confers a duty on a local authority to provide accommodation for certain children is need. Section 21(b) covers abandonment. When a child appears to have been abandoned, the local authority will be under a duty to provide accommodation and maintenance, to search out the parents and investigate the possibility of returning the child to them if it is in his best interests.

However, if it is confirmed that the child has been abandoned it will not be possible for the local authority to apply for guardianship under the Guardianship of Minors Act 1971, since under the Children Act no local authority or voluntary organisation can be a guardian, since they are not individuals.

Section 20(2): provides for an authority to take over responsiblity for accommodating a child accommodated by another authority if the child is ordinarily resident in their area. The provision of accommodation by a local authority to enable a child in need who is not under a care order to be looked after away from home is one of a range of services which a local authority can provide to discharge their general duty under section 17.

Section 20(3): requires a local authority to provide accommodation, in addition to section 20(1), for children aged 16 whose welfare would otherwise be seriously prejudiced. This covers a situation where a local authority are seriously concerned about the care of a child. A local authority would no longer be able to acquire parental responsibility over the child, since parental responsibility can only be acquired through the court and not through administrative resolution of the authority.

Section 20(4): enables a local authority to accommodate any child if they consider it would promote or safeguard the child's welfare, even where he is in the hands of a person with parental responsibility over him. Service under section 21(4) covers respite care for handicapped children. The Review of Child Care Law distinguished between short-term respite care and longer term shared-care in considering voluntary arrangements between parents and a local authority to promote a child's welfare. But the White Paper, "The Law on Child Care and Family Services", considered that such a distinction in law would be unhelpful.

Section 20(5): enables a local authority to accommodate a person aged between 16 and 21 in a community home if they consider that to do so would safeguard or promote the young person's welfare. Section 20(5) replaces section 72 of the Child Care Act 1980 and recognises that those young people who are employed, seeking employment, still being educated or trained, or are disabled, may need help with accommodation even if not strictly "in need" as defined: for the provision of a community home see section 53(1). An additional proviso would be that such a community home takes children over 16.

Section 20(6): requires a local authority to ascertain and have regard to the child's wishes before providing him with accommodation. Section 20(6) reflects the duty in section 18 of the 1980

Act which is to be maintained in respect of all local authority actions concerning a child accommodated by them, or on their behalf. Regulations and guidance will stress the importance of written arrangements being made with the child, his parents or anyone else, such as a relative, who was looking after the child before the authority provided accommodation. Such regulations will set out, among other things, the purpose of the child's stay in local authority accommodation, the arrangements for contact with the child and any delegation of parental responsibility which may be necessary.

Section 20(7): prevents a local authority from accommodating a child under section 20 if a person with parental responsibility for him objects. Children accommodated under section 20 are "being looked after" by the local authority. Their accommodation is provided on a voluntary basis. A local authority also cannot acquire parental responsibility by taking a child in need of care away from his home in order to look after him: see section 20(3).

Section 20(8): enables a person with parental responsibility to remove a child from such accommodation at any time. In line with the concept of voluntary partnership, a local authority will no longer have power to set a period of notice 28 days or more before a parent wishing to take back a child from their care can do so where the child has been in care for more than six months. This was the prior law which is now abolished. There are, however, exceptions: see sections 20(9) and (10).

Section 20(9): disapplies section 20(7) and (8) where a person with a residence order, or an order made by virtue of the High Court's inherent jurisdiction in respect of the child, agrees to a local authority looking after the child, or where the child is over 16 and himself agrees to being provided with accommodation under section 20. Section 20(9) replaces, in part, section 8(2) of the Child Care Act 1980.

Section 20(10): provides that where there is more than one such person referred to in section 20(9), all of them must agree. If the person who has a residence order in his favour agrees to the provision of accommodation, the other parent cannot object to it being provided or remove the child. If he wished to take care of the child he would have to get the residence order discharged.

Section 21. Provision of accommodation for children in police protection or detention or on remand, etc.

21.—(1) Every local authority shall make provision for the reception and accommodation of children who are removed or kept away from home under Part V.

(2) Every local authority shall receive, and provide accommodation for, children—

(a) in police protection whom they are requested to receive under section 46(3)(f);

(b) whom they are requested to receive under section 38(6) of the Police and Criminal Evidence Act 1984;

(c) who are—

(i) on remand under section [16(3A) or] 23(1) of the Children and Young Persons Act 1969; or

(ii) the subject of a supervision order imposing a residence requirement under section 12AA of that Act,

and with respect to whom they are the designated authority.

(3) Where a child has been—

(a) removed under Part V; or

(b) detained under section 38 of the Police and Criminal Evidence Act 1984,

and he is not being provided with accommodation by a local authority or in a hospital vested in the Secretary of State, any reasonable expenses of accommodating him shall be recoverable from the local authority in whose area he is ordinarily resident.

Annotation

Section 21: interfaces a local authority with a police constabulary in the provision of accommodation for children in police protection. Section 38(6) of the Police and Criminal Evidence Act 1984 referred to in section 21(b) deals with a situation where a custody officer authorises an arrested juvenile to be kept in police detention. The custody officer shall, unless he certifies that it is impracticable to do so, make arrangements for the arrested juvenile to be taken into care of a local authority and detained by the authority and it shall be lawful to detain him in pursuance of the arrangement. Section 23(1) of the Children and Young Persons Act deals with a situation where a court remands or commits for trial a child charged with homicide, remands a child convicted of homicide, or remands a young person charged with or convicted of one or more offences or commits him for trial or sentence, without releasing him on bail. Then the court shall commit him to the care of

Note: The words within square brackets were inserted by the Courts and Legal Services Act 1990.

a local authority in whose area it appears he resides, or the offence or one of the offences was committed.

Section 21(1): provides for the accommodation of children who are in police protection, or detention, or are on remand. Such provision covers those children who are removed or kept away from home under Part V which covers the emergency protection of children at risk of significant harm. Part V also provides for police protection of children in cases of emergency.

Section 21(2): provides for the accommodation of a child in police protection in accordance with section 46(3)(f) of the present Act. Section 40 deals with the removal and accommodation of children by police in cases of emergency and section 46(3)(f) deals with a situation where a child is taken into police protection, specifying that he should be moved into accommodation provided by a local authority. Section 21(2) also deals with a child whom a local authority is requested to receive under section 38(6) of the Police and Criminal Evidence Act 1984, which deals with a person arrested for an offence otherwise than under a warrant endorsed for bail, and where a court remands under section 23(1) of the Children and Young Persons Act 1969, or commits a child charged with homicide.

Section 21(3): provides that where a child is removed under Part V or detained under section 38 of the Police and Criminal Evidence Act, the local authority may recover any reasonable expenses in accommodating him from the local authority where he is ordinarily resident.

Duties of local authorities in relation to children looked after by them

Section 22. General duty of local authority in relation to children looked after by them

22.—(1) In this Act, any reference to a child who is looked after by a local authority is a reference to a child who is—

    (a) in their care; or
    (b) provided with accommodation by the authority in the exercise of any functions (in particular those under this Act) which stand referred to their social services committee under the Local Authority Social Services Act 1970.

(2) In subsection (1) "accommodation" means accommodation which is provided for a continuous period of more than 24 hours.

(3) It shall be the duty of a local authority looking after any child—

(a) to safeguard and promote his welfare; and
(b) to make such use of services available for children cared for by their own parents as appears to the authority reasonable in his case.

(4) Before making any decision with respect to a child whom they are looking after, or proposing to look after, a local authority shall, so far as is reasonably practicable, ascertain the wishes and feelings of—

(a) the child;
(b) his parents;
(c) any person who is not a parent of his but who has parental responsibility for him; and
(d) any other person whose wishes and feelings the authority consider to be relevant,

regarding the matter to be decided.

(5) In making any such decision a local authority shall give due consideration—

(a) having regard to his age and understanding, to such wishes and feelings of the child as they have been able to ascertain;
(b) to such wishes and feelings of any person mentioned in subsection (4)(b) to (d) as they have been able to ascertain; and
(c) to the child's religious persuasion, racial origin and cultural and linguistic background.

(6) If it appears to a local authority that it is necessary, for the purpose of protecting members of the public from serious injury, to exercise their powers with respect to a child whom they are looking after in a manner which may not be consistent with their duties under this section, they may do so.

(7) If the Secretary of State considers it necessary, for the purpose of protecting members of the public from serious injury, to give directions to a local authority with respect to the exercise of their powers with respect to a child whom they are looking after, he may give such directions to the authority.

(8) Where any such directions are given to an authority they shall comply with them even though doing so is inconsistent with their duties under this section.

Annotation

Section 22: defines the general duty of a local authority to promote and safeguard the welfare of children whom they are looking after: this is often described as "a cornerstone duty". A local authority must have regard to the wishes and feelings of the child, any parent or other person with parental responsibility and any other person whose wishes and feelings they consider relevant, as well as to other factors. These responsibilities are subject to any directions the Secretary of State may give in order to protect members of the public from serious injury.

Section 22(1): describes a child to whom section 22 applies. A child is looked after by a local authority in the exercise of their social service functions.

Section 22(2): defines accommodation as meaning accommodation which is provided for more than twenty four hours. Social service functions are defined in Schedule 1 of the Local Authority Social Services Act 1970, as amended by Schedules 13 and 15 of the Children Act.

Section 22(3): confers a duty upon a local authority to safeguard and promote the welfare of each child whom they look after. This duty replaces the more vague duty to give "first consideration" to the need to safeguard and promote the child's welfare in section 18 of the Child Care Act 1980, which is replaced. As under prior law, the authority are required to make reasonable use, for the benefit of children who are looked after, of the services and facilities which are available for children cared for by their parents.

Section 22(4): emphasises the role of the child, his parents, and any person who has parental responsibility. This requires the involvement of parents and others in decision making. Section 22(4) reflects the need to involve those people who are important in the child's life. Thus, before a decision is taken with respect to a child whom a local authority are looking after, or proposing to look after, they must, so far as is reasonably practicable, ascertain the views of those people referred to in section 22(4).

Section 22(5): provides that when a local authority come to a decision on how best to promote the welfare of a child, they must give due consideration to the wishes and feelings, taking into account in the child's case his age and understanding, of those people referred to in section 22(4). Section 22(5)(a) provides that the child's religious persuasion, racial origin and cultural and linguistic background must be taken into account, even if there has been insufficient time to investigate the wishes and feelings of the child and others.

Section 22(6): enables a local authority to dispense with the duties defined in section 21 if it is necessary to protect members of the public from serious injury.

Section 22(7): provides that in the circumstances referred to in section 22(6), the Secretary of State may be able to give directions to the local authority about the care of the child.

Section 22(8): requires a local authority to act in accordance with any directions the Secretary of State might give. Such directions will deal with where the child should live. In each case the authority must maintain the child: see section 23(1)(b).

Section 23. Provision of accommodation and maintenance by local authority for children whom they are looking after

23. —(1) It shall be the duty of any local authority looking after a child—

> (a) when he is in their care, to provide accommodation for him; and
> (b) to maintain him in other respects apart from providing accommodation for him.

(2) A local authority shall provide accommodation and maintenance for any child whom they are looking after by—

> (a) placing him (subject to subsection (5) and any regulations made by the Secretary of State) with—
>
>> (i) a family;
>> (ii) a relative of his; or
>> (iii) any other suitable person,
>
> on such terms as to payment by the authority and otherwise as the authority may determine;
> (b) maintaining him in a community home;
> (c) maintaining him in a voluntary home;
> (d) maintaining him in a registered children's home;
> (e) maintaining him in a home provided [in accordance with arrangements made] by the Secretary of State under section 82(5) on such terms as the Secretary of State may from time to time determine; or
> (f) making such other arrangements as—

Note: The words within square brackets were inserted by the Courts and Legal Services Act 1990.

(i) seem appropriate to them; and
(ii) comply with any regulations made by the Secretary of State.

(3) Any person with whom a child has been placed under subsection (2)(a) is referred to in this Act as a local authority foster parent unless he falls within subsection (4).

(4) A person falls within this subsection if he is—

(a) a parent of the child;
(b) a person who is not a parent of the child but who has parental responsibility for him; or
(c) where the child is in care and there was a residence order in force with respect to him immediately before the care order was made, a person in whose favour the residence order was made.

(5) Where a child is in the care of a local authority, the authority may only allow him to live with a person who falls within subsection (4) in accordance with regulations made by the Secretary of State.

[(5A) For the purposes of subsection (5) a child shall be regarded as living with a person if he stays with that person for a continuous period of more than 24 hours.]

(6) Subject to any regulations made by the Secretary of State for the purposes of this subsection, any local authority looking after a child shall make arrangements to enable him to live with—

(a) a person falling within subsection (4); or
(b) a relative, friend or other person connected with him,

unless that would not be reasonably practicable or consistent with his welfare.

(7) Where a local authority provide accommodation for a child whom they are looking after, they shall, subject to the provisions of this Part and so far as is reasonably practicable and consistent with his welfare, secure that—

(a) the accommodation is near his home; and
(b) where the authority are also providing accommodation for a sibling of his, they are accommodated together.

(8) Where a local authority provide accommodation for a child whom they are looking after and who is disabled, they shall, so

Note: The words within square brackets were inserted by the Courts and Legal Services Act 1990.

far as is reasonably practicable, secure that the accommodation is not unsuitable to his particular needs.

(9) Part II of Schedule 2 shall have effect for the purposes of making further provision as to children looked after by local authorities and in particular as to the regulations that may be made under subsections (2)(a) and (f) and (5).

Annotation

Section 23: requires a local authority looking after a child to accommodate him in specified ways and provides for the making of regulations in respect of particular types of placement. Thus, section 23 provides for a child who is looked after by a local authority to be fostered or maintained in a community home or a voluntary home, or maintained by the making of such other arrangements as the local authority consider appropriate.

Section 23(1): provides for a local authority to maintain and accommodate any child whom they are looking after. In the making of their arrangements, a local authority will need to have regard to the different racial groups to which children within their area who are in need belong: see paragraph 11 of schedule 2.

Section 23(2): provides a range of options for a local authority. Section 23(2)(a) deals with a family placement – a relative or another suitable person. Under the prior law, these placements were referred to as boarding out and charge and control placements, depending on with whom the child was placed.

Section 23(3): provides that where a child is placed with a family, formerly known as boarded out, the child is to be described as having been placed with local authority foster parents. This establishes a terminology which distinguishes local authority fostering arrangements from private fostering arrangements.

Section 23(4): provides clarification of the terminology of a local authority foster parent in section 23(3) and excludes from such terminology a parent, any other person who has parental responsibility for the child, or in the case of a child in care, any person in whose favour a residence order was in force immediately before the care order was made. Such a person will have had parental responsibiliy for the child until the care order brought the residence order to an end.

Section 23(5): provides that if a child who is in care is placed with a person falling within those categories defined in section 23(4)(a)(b) and (c), the placement will be subject to regulations which derive from the Accommodation of Children (Charge and

Control) Regulations 1988. The regulation-making power of the Secretary of State replaces that which was introduced by section 1 of the Children and Young Persons (Amendment) Act 1986.

Section 23(6): refers to other regulations which can be made by the Secretary of State. Family placements will be subject to local fostering regulations which derive from the Boarding Out of Children (Foster Placement) Regulations 1988. Unlike the prior law, placement with relatives and friends of a child are classed as foster placements rather than the equivalent of home placements (charge and control) except where such a person has, or had in the case of a care order, parental responsibility for the child under a residence order.

Section 23(7): gives effect to Part II of Schedule 2 which deals with regulations as to the placement of children with local foster parents and is part of those provisions covered by the Boarding Out of Children (Foster Placement) Regulations 1988 and the Accommodation of Children (Care and Control) Regulations 1988 which cover children.

Advice and assistance for certain children

Section 24. Advice and assistance for certain children

24. — (1) Where a child is being looked after by a local authority, it shall be the duty of the authority to advise, assist and befriend him with a view to promoting his welfare when he ceases to be looked after by them.

(2) In this Part "a person qualifying for advice and assistance" means a person within the area of the authority who is under twenty-one and who was, at any time after reaching the age of sixteen but while still a child—

(a) looked after by a local authority;
(b) accommodated by or on behalf of a voluntary organisation;
(c) accommodated in a registered children's home;
(d) accommodated—
　　(i) by any health authority or local education authority; or
　　(ii) in any residential care home, nursing home or mental nursing home,

　　for a consecutive period of at least three months; or

(e) privately fostered,

but who is no longer so looked after, accommodated or fostered.

(3) Subsection (2)(d) applies even if the period of three months mentioned there began before the child reached the age of sixteen.

(4) Where—

(a) a local authority know that there is within their area a person qualifying for advice and assistance;

(b) the conditions in subsection (5) are satisfied; and

(c) that person has asked them for help of a kind which they can give under this section,

they shall (if he was being looked after by a local authority or was accommodated by or on behalf of a voluntary organisation) and may (in any other case) advise and befriend him.

(5) The conditions are that—

(a) it appears to the authority that the person concerned is in need of advice and being befriended;

(b) where that person was not being looked after by the authority, they are satisfied that the person by whom he was being looked after does not have the necessary facilities for advising or befriending him.

(6) Where as a result of this section a local authority are under a duty, or are empowered, to advise and befriend a person, they may also give him assistance.

(7) Assistance given under subsections (1) to (6) may be in kind or, in exceptional circumstances, in cash.

(8) A local authority may give assistance to any person who qualifies for advice and assistance by virtue of subsection (2)(a) by—

(a) contributing to expenses incurred by him in living near the place where he is, or will be—

(i) employed or seeking employment; or

(ii) receiving education or training; or

(b) making a grant to enable him to meet expenses connected with his education or training.

(9) where a local authority are assisting the person under subsection (8) by making a contribution or grant with respect to a course of education or training, they may—

(a) continue to do so even though he reaches the age of twenty-one before completing the course; and

(b) disregard any interruption in his attendance on the course
if he resumes it as soon as is reasonably practicable.

(10) Subsections (7) to (9) of section 17 shall apply in relation
to assistance given under this section (otherwise than under subsection (8)) as they apply in relation to assistance given under
that section.

(11) Where it appears to a local authority that a person whom
they have been advising and befriending under this section, as a
person qualifying for advice and assistance, proposes to live, or
is living, in the area of another local authority, they shall inform
that other local authority.

(12) Where a child who is accommodated —

(a) by a voluntary organisation or in a registered children's
home;
(b) by any health authority or local education authority; or
(c) in any residential care home, nursing home or mental
nursing home,

ceases to be so accommodated, after reaching the age of sixteen,
the organisation, authority or (as the case may be) person carrying
on the home shall inform the local authority within whose area
the child proposes to live.

(13) Subsection (12) only applies, by virtue of paragraph (b)
or (c), if the accommodation has been provided for a consecutive
period of at least three months.

[(14) Every local authority shall establish a procedure for considering any representations (including any complaint) made to
them by a person qualifying for advice and assistance about the
discharge of their functions under this part in relation to him.

(15) In carrying out any consideration of representations under
subsection (14), a local authority shall comply with any regulations
made by the Secretary of State for the purposes of this subsection.]

Annotation

Section 24: replaces sections 27, 28, 29 and 69 of the Child Care
Act 1980. It also extends those provisions which deal with a local
authority's powers and duties in respect of young persons aged
under twenty-one who were, but are no longer, accommodated
by or on behalf of a local authority. Accommodation might equally
be provided by a voluntary organisation or voluntary home or a

Note: The words within square brackets were inserted by the Courts and Legal
Services Act 1990.

registered children's home; or where a child has been privately fostered.

Section 24(1): imposes a duty upon a local authority to promote the welfare of a child after leaving care or other accommodation provided by them or on their behalf. The use of the words "advise, assist and befriend" provide a context and a language sufficiently clear for a local authority to comprehend the nature of their duties. The nature of assistance is further defined in subsection (7).

Section 24(2): defines a person qualifying for after care provision. Under sections 28 and 69 of the Child Care Act 1980 a duty lay upon a local authority to advise and befriend a person qualifying for after care provision up to the age of eighteen; now the age is extended to twenty-one. The duty that falls upon the authority is one of advising, assisting and befriending those persons defined in subsection 24(1) who, having been parted from their families for relatively long periods, may face problems on leaving the accommodation also defined in this subsection.

Section 24(3): extends the definition contained in section 24(2) to a person who may have spent three months in accommodation provided by any health or local authority, in any residential care home, nursing home or mental nursing home before that person reached the age of eighteen. Note that the definition is *not* extended under section 24(3) to a person who has been privately fostered.

Section 24(4): extends the powers of a local authority to advise and befriend. In the case of section 24(2)(a) and (b), a local authority have an obligation to advise and befriend a person who, living within their area, is qualified to receive such advice and assistance, but the local authority shall be empowered to provide such advice and assistance under this subsection where such a person asks the authority for help.

Section 24(5): lays down the conditions to which subsection (4) shall be subordinated.

Section 24(6): provides for a local authority not only to befriend and advise but also to assist, thus adding specificity to section 24(1): the purpose of this subsection, however, is to ensure that assistance may be material as well as moral.

Section 24(7): defines such assistance as being in cash or in kind, but the cash to be only in exceptional circumstances. The "exceptional circumstances" hurdle has to be cleared in relation to subsections 1–6 and does not apply to subsection 8.

Section 24(8) provides a discretionary power to a local authority either to contribute to the expenses of a person who qualifies for advice and assistance and who is employed or seeking employment – such contribution of expenses may be repayable in whole or in part – or to provide a grant to enable him to meet expenses connected with education or training.

Section 24(9): provides for the extension of any contribution or grant with respect to education or training, but no extension of any contribution towards employment or the search for employment as provided under subsection 8.

Section 24(10) provides that such financial assistance may be unconditional or subject to repayment, in whole or in part, with the local authority, when considering the provision of such financial assistance, to have regard to the means of the person and his family. There is no liability for repayment if the person is in receipt of income support or family credit.

Section 24(11): imposes a duty on a local authority to provide another local authority with information concerning a person to whom they have been providing advice and friendship, that such a person is, or proposes to live, within the area of that authority. The subsection imposes no such duty upon a local authority who have been providing assistance in accordance with subsections (6), (7), (8), or (9).

Section 24(12): concerns notification to be given to a local authority of a person who has been accommodated but who has now ceased to be accommodated and such notification shall be made either to the local authority where the person has lived or the local authority where the person proposes to live. No notification is required under this subsection where a private fostering arrangement comes to an end, notwithstanding that a person who has been privately fostered may be a person qualifying for advice and assistance under subsection 2.

Section 24(13) requires that such notification be given only if a person has been provided accommodation for a consecutive period of three months.

Secure accommodation

Section 25. Use of accommodation for restricting liberty

25.—(1) Subject to the following provisions of this section, a child who is being looked after by a local authority may not be placed, and, if placed, may not be kept, in accommodation provided for the purpose of restricting liberty ("secure accommodation") unless it appears—

    (a) that—

        (i) he has a history of absconding and is likely to abscond from any other description of accommodation; and

        (ii) if he absconds, he is likely to suffer significant harm; or

    (b) that if he is kept in any other description of accommodation he is likely to injure himself or other persons.

    (2) The Secretary of State may by regulations—

    (a) specify a maximum period—

        (i) beyond which a child may not be kept in secure accommodation without the authority of the court; and

        (ii) for which the court may authorise a child to be kept in secure accommodation;

    (b) empower the court from time to time to authorise a child to be kept in secure accommodation for such further period as the regulations may specify; and

    (c) provide that applications to the court under this section shall be made only by local authorities.

    (3) It shall be the duty of a court hearing an application under this section to determine whether any relevant criteria for keeping a child in secure accommodation are satisfied in his case.

    (4) If a court determines that any such criteria are satisfied, it shall make an order authorising the child to be kept in secure accommodation and specifying the maximum period for which he may be so kept.

    (5) On any adjournment of the hearing of an application under this section, a court may make an interim order permitting the child to be kept during the period of the adjournment in secure accommodation.

    (6) No court shall exercise the powers conferred by this section in respect of a child who is not legally represented in that court unless, having been informed of his right to apply for legal aid and having had the opportunity to do so, he refused or failed to apply.

    (7) The Secretary of State may by regulations provide that—

    (a) this section shall or shall not apply to any description of children specified in the regulations;

(b) this section shall have effect in relation to children of a description specified in the regulations subject to such modifications as may be so specified;

(c) such other provisions as may be so specified shall have effect for the purpose of determining whether a child of a description specified in the regulations may be placed or kept in secure accommodation.

(8) The giving of an authorisation under this section shall not prejudice any power of any court in England and Wales or Scotland to give directions relating to the child to whom the authorisation relates.

(9) this section is subject to section 20(8).

Annotation

Section 25: defines the powers of a local authority in the use of accommodation to restrict liberty. Section 25 replaces section 21A of the Child Care Act 1980. It is designed to be flexibile, giving discretion to a local authority, yet at the same time circumscribing restrictions on liberty within a tight framework of law. These restrictions are such that secure accommodation should be a last resort and subject to regulations that may be issued by the Secretary of State.

Section 25(1): defines the criteria by which a child, already in the care of a local authority, may be placed in secure accommodation.

Section 25(2): provides that only a local authority may apply to a court for an order to restrict the liberty of a child within the care of that authority. Not all restrictions on a child's liberty require a court order and it will be for the Secretary of State to specify a maximum period up to which a child may be kept in secure accommodation without the authority of the court.

Section 25(3): lays a duty upon a court to determine whether the criteria defined in section 25(1) are satisfied before making an order for keeping a child in secure accommodation.

Section 25(4): defines the duty upon the court not to go beyond the criteria defined in section 25(1) and once satisfied to make the order. The court may, however, take all the relevant facts of the case, including the criteria, into account when specifying the maximum period for which a child should be kept in secure accommodation.

Section 25(5) provides for an interim order to be made where a child is in secure accommodation and is likely to be kept in such accommodation beyond the maximum period to be established by the Secretary of State, but where the local authority are not ready to bring a full application to the court.

Section 25(6): provides that the court may not act where a child is not legally represented and does not have an opportunity to seek to rebut allegations to criteria laid down in section 25(1). A court may act on such criteria, however, where a child is not legally represented but where he was informed as to his rights to apply for legal aid and refused or failed to apply.

Section 25(7): enables the Secretary of State to make regulations regarding those children who may find their liberty restricted whilst in local authority care. Clearly, the widest category of children in care will be subject to the provisions of section 25 where, whilst in care, the criteria laid down in subsection (1) are fulfilled. Children who have been, but are no longer, in care would not be included for the purposes of this subsection.

Section 25(8): provides that any court making an order in accordance with section 25 shall not be constrained by limiting itself solely to such an order and may give other directions in relation to the child before it pursuant to other powers already conferred upon the court.

Section 25(9): subordinates section 25 to section 20(8) which confers a right upon any person who has parental responsibility for a child to remove a child from accommodation provided by or on behalf of a local authority. This right would be exercised directly with a local authority where a child had been placed in secure accommodation not subject to a court order, but where there had been a court order a person with parental responsibility would need to seek to exercise that right through the court. That right might equally be circumscribed by section 25(8).

Supplemental

Section 26. Review of cases and inquiries into representations

26. — (1) The Secretary of State may make regulations requiring the case of each child who is being looked after by a local authority to be reviewed in accordance with the provisions of the regulations.

(2) The regulations may, in particular, make provision —

(a) as to the manner in which each case is to be reviewed;
(b) as to the considerations to which the local authority are to have regard in reviewing each case;

(c) as to the time when each case is first to be reviewed and the frequency of subsequent reviews;

(d) requiring the authority, before conducting any review, to seek the views of—

(i) the child;

(ii) his parents;

(iii) any person who is not a parent of his but who has parental responsibility for him; and

(iv) any other person whose views the authority consider to be relevant,

including, in particular, the views of those persons in relation to any particular matter which is to be considered in the course of the review;

(e) requiring the authority to consider, in the case of a child who is in their care, whether an application should be made to discharge the care order;

(f) requiring the authority to consider, in the case of a child in accommodation provided by the authority, whether the accommodation accords with the requirements of this Part;

(g) requiring the authority to inform the child, so far as is reasonably practicable, of any steps he may take under this Act;

(h) requiring the authority to make arrangements, including arrangements with such other bodies providing services as it considers appropriate, to implement any decision which they propose to make in the course, or as a result, of the review;

(i) requiring the authority to notify details of the result of the review and of any decision taken by them in consequence of the review to—

(i) the child;

(ii) his parents;

(iii) any person who is not a parent of his but who has parental responsibility for him; and

(iv) any other person whom they consider ought to be notified;

(j) requiring the authority to monitor the arrangements which they have made with a view to ensuring that they comply with the regulations.

(3) Every local authority shall establish a procedure for considering any representations (including any complaint) made to them by—

(a) any child who is being looked after by them or who is not being looked after by them but is in need;

(b) a parent of his;

(c) any person who is not a parent of his but who has parental responsibility for him;

(d) any local authority foster parent;

(e) such other person as the authority consider has a sufficient interest in the child's welfare to warrant his representations being considered by them,

about the discharge by the authority of any of their functions under this Part in relation to the child.

(4) the procedure shall ensure that at least one person who is not a member or officer of the authority takes part in—

(a) the consideration; and

(b) any discussions which are held by the authority about the action (if any) to be taken in relation to the child in the light of the consideration.

(5) In carrying out any consideration of representations under this section a local authority shall comply with any regulations made by the Secretary of State for the purpose of regulating the procedure to be followed.

(6) The Secretary of State may make regulations requiring local authorities to monitor the arrangements that they have made with a view to ensuring that they comply with any regulations made for the purposes of subsection (5).

(7) Where any representation has been considered under the procedure established by a local authority under this section, the authority shall—

(a) have due regard to the findings of those considering the representation; and

(b) take such steps as are reasonably practicable to notify (in writing)—

(i) the person making the representation;

(ii) the child (if the authority consider that he has sufficient understanding); and

(iii) such other persons (if any) as appear to the authority to be likely to be affected,

of the authority's decision in the matter and their reasons for taking that decision and of any action which they have taken, or propose to take.

(8) Every local authority shall give such publicity to their pro-

cedure for considering representations under this section as they consider appropriate.

Annotation

Section 26: requires a local authority to review the case of every child who is looked after by them. They shall do so in accordance with regulations laid down by the Secretary of State insofar as the Secretary of State lays down any regulations at all. The section emphasises the need to seek the views of the child, so far as is practicable, and the views of parents or others with parental responsiblity, or those who have an interest, before any review is conducted.

Section 26(1): provides authority for the Secretary of State to make regulations requiring the review of the case of each child in the care of a local authority. There is no binding duty upon the Secretary of State to make regulations but these would include requirements for inquiries into representations made.

Section 26(2): replaces in part section 20 of the Child Care Act 1980. This was never implemented. Although section 26(2) describes the scope of any regulations the Secretary of State may make and may be considered broad enough to enable a local authority to begin its review procedures, nevertheless a constraint may be placed upon them by section 26(5) which calls for a local authority to act in accordance with any regulations the Secretary of State may make.

Section 26(3): also replaces in part section 20 of the Child Care Act 1980. Access to the review procedure shall be accorded to any child being looked after by the local authority as well as a parent, a person not a parent but having parental responsibility, any local authority foster parent and any outside person such as a Member of Parliament who has sufficient interest to warrant the local authority's considering representations. Representations include complaints.

Section 26(4): provides that at least one person not connected with the authority takes part in the proceedings. This provision is designed to ensure some impartiality in the proceedings, so that a local authority cannot be judge and jury in their own case.

Section 26(5): imposes a duty on a local authority to comply with any regulations issued by the Secretary of State where the Secretary of State makes such regulations. Where no such regulations are made, a local authority might be expected to set up procedures to comply with the criteria laid down in section 26(2).

Section 26(6): provides for an overview of any arrangements made by a local authority by the authority itself, thus instituting a further check and balance in accordance with any regulations the Secretary of State may make.

Section 26(7): imposes a duty on a local authority not only to note the findings of the body considering the representations but to act upon such findings; to notify those concerned not only of their decisions but the reasons for such decisions and consequent action.

Section 26(8): requires a local authority to publicise their procedures but not their findings; and even in relation to the procedures that they should be publicised as a local authority think appropriate.

Section 27. Co-operation between authorities

27. — (1) Where it appears to a local authority that any authority [*or other person*] mentioned in subsection (3) could, by taking any specified action, help in the exercise of any of their functions under this Part, they may request the help of that other authority [*or person*], specifying the action in question.

(2) an authority whose help is so requested shall comply with the request if it is compatible with their own statutory or other duties and obligations and does not unduly prejudice the discharge of any of their functions.

(3) The [*persons*] [authorities] are—

  (a) any local authority;
  (b) any local education authority;
  (c) any local housing authority;
  (d) any health authority [or National Health Service Trust]; and
  (e) any person authorised by the Secretary of State for the purposes of this section.

(4) Every local authority shall assist any local education authority with the provision of services for any child within the local authority's area who has special educational needs.

Annotation

Section 27: responds to the often expressed need for more multi-disciplinary cooperation between the statutory agencies and makes

Note: The words within square brackets were inserted by the Courts and Legal Services Act 1990.
Note: The words within square brackets were inserted by the Courts and Legal Services Act 1990.

provision for a local authority to call upon the specialist skills or facilities of another in order better to promote the welfare of a child who may be in local authority care.

Section 27(1): introduces the concept of multi-disciplinary proceedings and makes provision for a local authority to call upon another local authority, or another statutory body, specifying the action that may be necessary and requires to be taken.

Section 27(2): imposes a duty upon such statutory authority to respond favourably, provided that in doing so it does not breach its own statutory obligations or is hindered in the discharge of its own functions.

Section 27(3): lists the statutory bodies who may be of assistance in providing education, housing or health facilities, in addition to the assistance that may be given by any other local authority, and leaves the door open for any person who also may be able to help and who may be authorised by the Secretary of State.

Section 27(4): imposes a new duty on a local authority to assist a local education authority where a child, not necessarily in the care of a local authority, has special educational needs. The definition of special educational needs can be found in the Education Act 1981.

Section 28. Consultation with local education authorities

28. — (1) Where —

(a) a child is being looked after by a local authority; and
(b) the authority propose to provide accommodation for him in an establishment at which education is provided for children who are accommodated there,

they shall, so far as is reasonably practicable, consult the appropriate local education authority before doing so.

(2) Where any such proposal is carried out, the local authority shall, as soon as is reasonably practicable, inform the appropriate local education authority of the arrangements that have been made for the child's accommodation.

(3) Where the child ceases to be accommodated as mentioned in subsection (1)(b), the local authority shall inform the appropriate local education authority.

(4) In this section "the appropriate local education authority" means —

(a) the local education authority within whose area the local authority's area falls; or,

(b) where the child has special educational needs and a statement of his needs is maintained under the Education Act 1981, the local education authority who maintain the statement.

Annotation

Section 28: provides for consultation between a local authority and a local education authority where it is proposed to place a child in an establishment where education is provided for children who live there. The appropriate local education authority would be the authority within whose area the local education authority falls, or in the case of a child with special educational needs, as defined in the Education Act 1981, the local education authority who maintain a statement of his needs.

Section 28(1): provides for consultation with local education authorities, so far as this is reasonably practicable.

Section 28(2): imposes a duty upon a local authority who has placed a child pursuant to section 28(1) to so inform the local education authority as soon as is reasonably practicable.

Section 28(3): imposes a similar duty where a child ceases to be so accommodated pursuant to section 28(1).

Section 28(4): defines the appropriate local education authority as one covering the area of the local authority or where a child has special educational needs, and where the local educational authority maintaining the statement of educational need is situated elsewhere than in the area of the local authority.

Section 29. Recoupment of cost of providing services etc.

29. —(1) Where a local authority provide any service under section 17 or 18, other than advice, guidance or counselling, they may recover from a person specified in subsection (4) such charge for the service as they consider reasonable.

(2) Where the authority are satisfied that that person's means are insufficient for it to be reasonably practicable for him to pay the charge, they shall not require him to pay more than he can reasonably be expected to pay.

(3) No person shall be liable to pay any charge under subsection (1) at any time when he is in receipt of income support or family credit under the Social Security Act 1986.

(4) The persons are—

(a) where the service is provided for a child under sixteen, each of his parents;

(b) where it is provided for a child who has reached the age of sixteen, the child himself; and

(c) where it is provided for a member of the child's family, that member.

(5) any charge under subsection (1) may, without prejudice to any other method of recovery, be recovered summarily as a civil debt.

(6) Part III of Schedule 2 makes provision in connection with contributions towards the maintenance of children who are being looked after by local authorities and consists of the re-enactment with modifications of provisions in Part V of the Child Care Act 1980.

(7) Where a local authority provide any accommodation under section 20(1) for a child who was (immediately before they began to look after him) ordinarily resident within the area of another local authority, they may recover from that other authority any reasonable expenses incurred by them in providing the accommodation and maintaining him.

(8) Where a local authority provide accommodation under section 21(1) or (2)(a) or (b) for a child who is ordinarily resident within the area of another local authority and they are not maintaining him in—

(a) a community home provided by them;

(b) a controlled community home; or

(c) a hospital vested in the Secretary of State,

they may recover from that other authority any reasonable expenses incurred by them in providing the accommodation and maintaining him.

(9) Where a local authority comply with any request under section 27(2) in relation to a child or other person who is not ordinarily resident within their area, they may recover from the local authority in whose area the child or person is ordinarily resident any [*expenses reasonably*] [reasonable expenses] incurred by them in respect of that person.

Annotation

Section 29: provides for a local authority to charge for services provided under sections 17 and 18, except for advice, guidance

Note: The words *in italics* within square brackets were deleted by the Courts and Legal Services Act 1990.
Note: The words within square brackets were inserted by the Courts and Legal Services Act 1990.

or counselling and defines who may be liable to be charged. It also limits a charge to what may be considered reasonable and imposes restrictions on who may be charged at all. Section 29 mirrors section 17 of the Health and Social Services and Social Security Adjudications Act 1983 which provides for the recovery of charges for local authority services rendered, for example, on behalf of a disabled child.

Section 29(1): empowers a local authority to recover the cost of providing a service, limits the exercise of that discretion to a person specified in subsection (4) and provides that where the right is exercised a local authority shall only charge what they consider reasonable.

Section 29(2): establishes that where the authority are satisfied that the means of a person to be charged are insufficient, any charge shall not be more than he can reasonably be expected to pay. Thus the test of reasonableness in section 29(1) is objective to the local authority; in section 29(2) it becomes subjective to the means of the person.

Section 29(3): declares that no person shall be liable to pay any charge under section 29(1) when he is in receipt of income support or family credit. The test of reasonableness shall not apply. Section 29(3) leaves open, however, whether a person shall be liable under section 29(1) and (2) where he ceases to be a recipient of income support or family credit for any services rendered whilst he was in receipt of such benefit.

Section 29(4): defines those who may be liable to be charged and limits any liability to each of his parents where the service is provided for a child under sixteen rather than to those who may have, or who may acquire, parental responsibility pursuant to sections 2, 3, 4 and 5 of the Act. A child who reaches the age of sixteen may himself become liable, and so too may a member of a family who has been the beneficiary of collateral services.

Section 29(5): renders any charges levied in accordance with section 29(1) as liable to recovery as a civil debt.

Section 29(6): introduces Part III of Schedule 2 which describes contributions towards the maintenance of children looked after by local authorities. It replaces provisions, with modifications, of Part V of the Child Care Act 1980.

Section 29(7): provides for the recovery of any charges incurred by a local authority who have provided any accommodation for a child who was ordinarily resident within the area of another local authority immediately before the first local authority began to look after him. Again, the recovery of any charges is discretionary.

Section 29(8): provides for the recovery of charges by one local authority from another where one local authority are maintaining a child who is in police protection or whom they are requested to receive under section 38(6) of the Police and Criminal Evidence Act 1984 where that child is ordinarily resident in the area of another. No such charge for reasonable expenses may be made if a child is being maintained in a community home, a controlled community home or a hospital vested in the Secretary of State.

Section 29(9): provides for a local authority to claim from another any reasonable expenses incurred where they have complied with the request of that authority to assist a child or other person not ordinarily resident in their area. Note again the test of reasonableness shall be applied.

Section 30. Miscellaneous

30. —(1) Nothing in this Part shall affect any duty imposed on a local authority by or under any other enactment.

(2) Any question arising under section 20(2), 21(3) or 29(7) to (9) as to the ordinary residence of a child shall be determined by agreement between the local authorities concerned or, in default of agreement, by the Secretary of State.

(3) Where the functions conferred on a local authority by this Part and the functions of a local education authority are concurrent, the Secretary of State may by regulations provide by which authority the functions are to be exercised.

(4) The Secretary of State may make regulations for determining, as respects any local education authority functions specified in the regulations, whether a child who is being looked after by a local authority is to be treated, for purposes so specified, as a child of parents of sufficient resources or as a child of parents without resources.

Annotation

Section 30: is the final section in Part III of the Act dealing with local authority support for children and the provision of services for children and their families. It includes a provision that local authority duties provided for in other Acts shall not be affected by the provisions or application of Part III. It also provides for the intervention of the Secretary of State to determine residence where the definition is in dispute and for regulations on the status of a child and his family as being with or without sufficient resources.

Section 30(1): is a miscellaneous provision to ensure that any duty imposed on a local authority by or under any other enactment shall not be affected by the provisions of Part III. Note that this refers to duties as opposed to powers.

Section 30(2): provides for the intervention of the Secretary of State where there is a conflict between two local authorities on the definition of residence. Section 105 interprets "ordinary residence" and in its determination disregards any period in which a child lives in any place which is a school or other institution, in accordance with the requirements of a supervision order, or while he is being provided with accommodation by or on behalf of a local authority.

Section 30(3): provides the Secretary of State with a discretion to decide whether functions, that is powers and duties, conferred on a local authority which may be concurrent with those of a local education authority shall be exercised either by one authority or another.

Section 30(4): provides the Secretary of State with a further discretion, in relation to any local education authority functions, whether a child being looked after by a local authority is to be treated as a child of parents of sufficient resources or as a child of parents without resources. Part of this subsection may be found in section 30 of the Child Care Act 1980.

PART IV

CARE AND SUPERVISION

General

Section 31. Care and supervision orders

31. — (1) On the application of any local authority or authorised person, the court may make an order —

   (a) placing the child with respect to whom the application is made in the care of a designated local authority; or
   (b) putting him under the supervision of a designated local authority or of a probation officer.

(2) A court may only make a care order or supervision order if it is satisfied —

(a) that the child concerned is suffering, or is likely to suffer, significant harm; and

(b) that the harm, or likelihood of harm, is attributable to—

(i) the care given to the child, or likely to be given to him if the order were not made, not being what it would be reasonable to expect a parent to give to him; or

(ii) the child's being beyond parental control.

(3) No care order or supervision order may be made with respect to a child who has reached the age of seventeen (or sixteen, in the case of a child who is married).

(4) An application under this section may be made on its own or in any other family proceedings.

(5) The court may—

(a) on an application for a care order, make a supervision order;

(b) on an application for a supervision order, make a care order.

(6) Where an authorised person proposes to make an application under this section he shall—

(a) if it is reasonably practicable to do so; and

(b) before making the application,

consult the local authority appearing to him to be the authority in whose area the child concerned is ordinarily resident.

(7) An application made by an authorised person shall not be entertained by the court if, at the time when it is made, the child concerned is—

(a) the subject of an earlier application for a care order, or supervision order, which has not been disposed of; or

(b) subject to—

(i) a care order or supervision order;

(ii) an order under section 7(7)(b) of the Children and Young Persons Act 1969; or

(iii) a supervision requirement within the meaning of the Social Work (Scotland) Act 1968.

(8) The local authority designated in a care order must be—

(a) the authority within whose area the child is ordinarily resident; or

(b) where the child does not reside in the area of a local

authority, the authority within whose area any circumstances arose in consequence of which the order is being made.

(9) In this section—

"authorised person" means

(a) the National Society for the Prevention of Cruelty to Children and any of its officers; and

(b) any person authorised by order of the Secretary of State to bring proceedings under this section and any officer of a body which is so authorised;

"harm" means ill-treatment or the impairment of health or development;

"development" means physical, intellectual, emotional, social or behavioural development;

"health" means physical or mental health; and

"ill-treatment" includes sexual abuse and forms of ill-treatment which are not physical.

(10) Where the question of whether harm suffered by a child is significant turns on the child's health or development, his health or development shall be compared with that which could reasonably be expected of a similar child.

(11) In this Act—

"a care order" means (subject to section 105(1)) an order under subsection (1)(a) and (except where express provision to the contrary is made) includes an interim care order made under section 38; and

"a supervision order" means an order under subsection (1)(b) and (except where express provision to the contrary is made) includes an interim supervision order made under section 38.

Annotation

Section 31: provides that a court may make a care or supervision order on the application of any local authority or authorised person defined in section 31(9). The section sets out the grounds on which a court must be satisfied prior to making an order and equally provides that a care order may be made on its own or in relation to other family proceedings. Consequent upon section 31, police and local education authorities may no longer apply for care and supervision orders; new grounds are made for the making of these orders and a local authority may no longer acquire compulsory powers over children by different routes. However, see section 36 for the creation of a new order – the education supervision order.

Section 31(1): empowers a court, on the application of any local authority or authorised person to make either a care or supervision order. The court need not place a child under the supervision of a local authority but may, if it so wishes, place a child under the supervision of a probation officer.

Section 31(2): sets out the criteria on which the granting of care and supervision orders shall be based. An override to these criteria may, however, be found in section 1(1) and 1(5), that the interests of a child are paramount and that the court shall not make any order at all unless it considers that doing so would be better for the child than making no order at all.

Section 31(3): limits the powers of a court to grant care or supervision orders to a child who is less than seventeen years old, less than sixteen in the case of a child who is married. Section 31(3) should be read in conjunction with section 91(12) and (13) which provides that care other than an interim care or supervision order ceases to have effect after a child subject to such an order reaches the age of eighteen.

Section 31(4): provides that an application for a care or supervision order may be made either in care or family proceedings, that is to say those proceedings brought under the inherent jurisdiction of the High Court in relation to children and as these proceedings are defined by section 8(3) of this Act.

Section 31(5): defines the duties of the court in relation to care and supervision orders and enables the court, on the facts before it, to issue one order or the other, notwithstanding the terms of the application.

Section 31(6): circumscribes the powers of an authorised person to make an application and restrains him to making the application only after he has consulted, if it is reasonably practical to do so, with the appropriate local authority. An authorised person would be expected to work in close cooperation with a local authority rather than independently.

Section 31(7): further circumscribes the powers of an authorised person to make an application and provides that a court shall not entertain such application where a child is already subject to a care or supervision order or other orders designated in subsection b(ii) and (iii).

Section 31(8): defines a designated local authority either as one where a child named in an order is ordinarily resident, or, failing residence within an area, the area where circumstances arose and incidents occurred which gave rise to an application being made. Sometimes it may not be possible for a local authority to ascertain where a child lives, but it can identify the circumstances or incident which gave rise to an application and, therefore, the criteria for determining a designated local authority become unequivocal.

Section 31(9): defines "authorised person" as the National Society for the Prevention of Cruelty to Children and any of its officers and any person, that is to say agency as well as individual, or any officer of a body which the Secretary of State may authorise. The National Society for the Prevention of Cruelty to Children already had the right to initiate proceedings on the authority of the Secretary of State by order made pursuant to section 1 of the Children and Young Persons Act 1969. Section 31(9) also describes sexual abuse as a form of ill-treatment within the civil law.

Section 31(10): establishes a test of comparability in relation to harm affecting a child's health or development as these have been defined in section 31(9), the comparison to be made with the health or development of a similar child. There is no comparability test in relation to ill treatment.

Section 31(11): defines care and supervision orders and links the definition to section 105(1) which also provides that a reference to a child who is in the care of a local authority is a reference to a child who is in their care by virtue of a care order.

Section 32. Period within which application for order under this Part must be disposed of

32.—(1) A court hearing an application for an order under this Part shall (in the light of any rules made by virtue of subsection (2))—

    (a) draw up a timetable with a view to disposing of the application without delay; and

    (b) give such directions as it considers appropriate for the purpose of ensuring, so far as is reasonably practicable, that that timetable is adhered to.

(2) Rules of court may—

    (a) specify periods within which specified steps must be taken in relation to such proceedings; and

    (b) make other provision with respect to such proceedings for the purpose of ensuring, so far as is reasonably practicable, that they are disposed of without delay.

Annotation

Section 32: introduces a timetabling process for a court to apply when hearing an application for a care or supervision order: justice delayed may be justice denied, a process which applies no less to children, except that in their case the delay can be more harmful. Section 32 mirrors the provision made in section 11(1) and (2) dealing with section 8 orders and section 38(5) imposes time limits for interim care orders.

Section 32(1): repeats word for word section 11(1) dealing with general principles and supplementary provisions as these relate to section 8 orders. The care and supervision orders provided for under Part IV, section 31 are part of the same family of orders as those in section 8: the disadvantages of delay in respect of those orders apply no less to those provided for under section 31.

Section 32(2): repeats word for word section 11(2) dealing with rules of court in relation to speeding up proceedings on section 8 orders. The purpose of rules of court as provided for under section 11(1) and (2) is to apply a general principle that delay in disposing of an application for a care or supervision order is likely to prejudice the welfare of the child and his early return to the family.

Care orders

Section 33. Effect of care order

33.—(1) Where a care order is made with respect to a child it shall be the duty of the local authority designated by the order to receive the child into their care and to keep him in their care while the order remains in force.

(2) Where—

(a) a care order has been made with respect to a child on the application of an authorised person; but
(b) the local authority designated by the order was not informed that that person proposed to make the application,

the child may be kept in the care of that person until received into the care of the authority.

(3) While a care order is in force with respect to a child, the local authority designated by the order shall—

(a) have parental responsibility for the child; and
(b) have the power (subject to the following provisions of this section) to determine the extent to which a parent

or guardian of the child may meet his parental responsibility for him.

(4) The authority may not exercise the power in subsection (3)(b) unless they are satisfied that it is necessary to do so in order to safeguard or promote the child's welfare.

(5) Nothing in subsection (3)(b) shall prevent a parent or guardian of the child who has care of him from doing what is reasonable in all the circumstances of the case for the purpose of safeguarding or promoting his welfare.

(6) While a care order is in force with respect to a child, the local authority designated by the order shall not—

    (a) cause the child to be brought up in any religious persuasion other than that in which he would have been brought up if the order had not been made; or

    (b) have the right—

        (i) to consent or refuse to consent to the making of an application with respect to the child under section 18 of the Adoption Act 1976;

        (ii) to agree or refuse to agree to the making of an adoption order, or an order under section 55 of the Act of 1976, with respect to the child; or

        (iii) to appoint a guardian for the child.

(7) While a care order is in force with respect to a child, no person may—

    (a) cause the child to be known by a new surname; or

    (b) remove him from the United Kingdom,

without either the written consent of every person who has parental responsibility for the child or the leave of the court.

(8) Subsection (7)(b) does not—

    (a) prevent the removal of such a child, for a period of less than one month, by the authority in whose care he is; or

    (b) apply to arrangements for such a child to live outside England and Wales (which are governed by paragraph 19 of Schedule 2).

(9) The power in subsection (3)(b) is subject (in addition to being subject to the provisions of this section) to any right, duty, power, responsibility or authority which a parent or guardian of the child has in relation to the child and his property by virtue of any other enactment.

Annotation

Section 33: provides for a local authority to take a child into care and keep him in care until expiry of the court order. A local authority shall thus acquire parental responsibility for the child. Section 33 also provides that an authority may determine the extent to which a parent or guardian may meet his parental responsibility by a local authority.

Section 33(1): imposes an absolute duty on a local authority designated in a care order to receive the child into their care and keep him in care while the order remains in force.

Section 33(2): provides for a child to be maintained in the care of an authorised person where the local authority had already been designated by a court to receive into care that child. Section 33(2) seeks to anticipate confusion that may arise between an authorised person and a local authority, notwithstanding the provisions of section 31(6) and (7). Care of the child by an authorised person can only be until such time as the child shall be received into care by the designated local authority but no time limit has been set on such time.

Section 33(3): provides that a local authority designated by a care order shall have parental responsibility for the child and equally shall have power to determine the extent of the parental responsibility of a parent or guardian, subject to the restrictions imposed upon a designated local authority by section 33(5) and (6).

Section 33(4): provides that a designated local authority may not exercise the power in section 33(3)(b) unless they are satisfied that they need to do so in order to safeguard or promote the child's welfare: thus section 33(4) buttresses section 17(1), but also means that decisions of a local authority in relation to a child in its care shall be made, in respect to the exercise of parental responsibility, with the promotion of the child's welfare in mind.

Section 33(5): provides that the duties of a parent or guardian are not vitiated by the fact that a child is in the care of a designated authority and the duty rests upon such parent or guardian to do what is reasonable in the circumstances to safeguard or promote his welfare. The converse is that a designated authority shall not stand in the way of a parent or guardian in his endeavour to improve the child's welfare in accordance with all the circumstances of the case that can be considered reasonable.

Section 33(6): limits the parental responsibility of a designated authority in respect to a child in their care.

Section 33(7): relates to section 13(1) and provides that whilst a designated local authority cannot cause the child to be known by a new surname or remove him from the United Kingdom without either the written consent of those who may have parental responsibility, nevertheless a designated local authority have also acquired parental responsibility. Their consent would also be required in relation to the change of a child's name or removal from the jurisdiction pursuant to section 13(1) and section 33(7).

Section 33(8): provides a local authority with the right to send a child in their care abroad for a period of less than one month without application to the court and thus mirrors section 13(2) in relation to residence orders. A designated local authority may only arrange for, or assist in arranging for, any child in their care to live outside England and Wales with the approval of the court: see paragraph 19 of Schedule 2.

Section 33(9): limits the power of a local authority in relation to a parent or guardian defined in section 33(3)(b). Section 33 as a whole provides a local authority with a power to acquire parental responsibility as well as determining the extent to which a parent or guardian of the child may meet his parental responsibility. This power is subordinated to other provisions in section 33 but is further subordinated to any right, duty, responsibility or power which a parent or guardian may have vested in him by virtue of any other enactment.

Section 34. Parental contact etc. with children in care

34. — (1) Where a child is in the care of a local authority, the authority shall (subject to the provisions of this section) allow the child reasonable contact with —

    (a) his parents;
    (b) any guardian of his;
    (c) where there was a residence order in force with respect to the child immediately before the care order was made, the person in whose favour the order was made; and
    (d) where, immediately before the care order was made, a person had care of the child by virtue of an order made in the exercise of the High Court's inherent jurisdiction with respect to children, that person.

(2) On an application made by the authority or the child, the court may make such order as it considers appropriate with respect to the contact which is to be allowed between the child and any named person.

(3) On an application made by —

(a) any person mentioned in paragraphs (a) to (d) of subsection (1); or

(b) any person who has obtained the leave of the court to make the application,

the court may make such order as it considers appropriate with respect to the contact which is to be allowed between the child and that person.

(4) On an application made by the authority or the child, the court may make an order authorising the authority to refuse to allow contact between the child and any person who is mentioned in paragraphs (a) to (d) of subsection (1) and named in the order.

(5) When making a care order with respect to a child, or in any family proceedings in connection with a child who is in the care of a local authority, the court may make an order under this section, even though no application for such an order has been made with respect to the child, if it considers that the order should be made.

(6) an authority may refuse to allow the contact that would otherwise be required by virtue of subsection (1) or an order under this section if—

(a) they are satisfied that it is necessary to do so in order to safeguard or promote the child's welfare; and

(b) the refusal—

(i) is decided upon as a matter of urgency; and
(ii) does not last for more than seven days.

(7) An order under this section may impose such conditions as the court considers appropriate.

(8) The Secretary of State may by regulations make provision as to—

(a) the steps to be taken by a local authority who have exercised their powers under subsection (6);

(b) the circumstances in which, and conditions subject to which, the terms of any order under this section may be departed from by agreement between the local authority and the person in relation to whom the order is made;

(c) notification by a local authority of any variation or suspension of arrangements made (otherwise than under an order under this section) with a view to affording any person contact with a child to whom this section applies.

(9) The court may vary or discharge any order made under this

section on the application of the authority, the child concerned or the person named in the order.

(10) An order under this section may be made either at the same time as the care order itself or later.

(11) Before making a care order with respect to any child the court shall—

   (a) consider the arrangements which the authority have made, or propose to make, for affording any person contact with a child to whom this section applies; and
   (b) invite the parties to the proceedings to comment on those arrangements.

Annotation

Section 34: enables a court to consider contact between a child in care and his parents or other persons. In the past, a local authority had power to control and deny access to and by a child in compulsory care; now there is a presumption of reasonable contact between a child in care and his parents and certain others. A designated local authority shall be expected to agree on contact with parents and others at an early stage and in any case where agreement cannot be reached this can be dealt with by the court at the time the application for a care order is made. Subsequently, such a person shall be entitled to apply for a contact order. Contact orders may be subject to restrictions pursuant to section 34(7).

Section 34(1): imposes a duty on a designated local authority to allow the child reasonable contact with his parents, any guardian, or where there was a residence order immediately before the care order was made, with the person in whose favour the residence order was granted. A court would be expected to ensure that reasonable contact proposals were before it when considering a local authority or authorised person application and that parents or other parties to the proceedings would be entitled to comment on them before any order was made.

Section 34(2): provides that a court may make an order as to contact on an application made by the authority or the child.

Section 34(3): provides that a court may make an order as to contact on an application by parents of a child, his guardian or where a person had in his favour a residence order, that person. In the past, prior to the Children Act, contact could only be challenged by parents or other interested parties when contact was terminated or refused. Such parents or other interested parties could not challenge a decision by a local authority severely to restrict contact, and access could only be dealt with in separate proceedings, not on an application that the child should be taken into care.

Section 34(4): provides that where an application has been made by the authority or the child to refuse contact by parents of a child, his guardian, or where a person had in his favour a residence order that person, the court may make such an order even where such a person has been named as entitled to contact. Such an order would be made where the court felt that such an order would promote the welfare of the child.

Section 34(5): provides that a court may make an order as to contact without an application having been made and in any family proceedings in connection with a child who is in the care of a local authority, and where the court feels such an order should be made.

Section 34(6): provides a local authority with a power to deny contact in order to safeguard or promote the child's welfare, and where the refusal is decided upon as a matter of urgency and does not last for more than seven days. After this time a local authority would be required to apply for a court order pursuant to section 34(4) and the parents or other interested parties who had been denied contact would be entitled to make submissions.

Section 34(7): provides for the court to impose conditions as it feels appropriate, given all the circumstances of the case.

Section 34(8): provides that the Secretary of State may make regulations in order to define the circumstances under which a local authority may exercise its power to refuse contact. It is intended to limit and circumscribe the power of a local authority to refuse contact and this the Secretary of State would do by regulation. The regulations would also cover variation or suspension of arrangements made.

Section 34(9): provides the court with the power, if it so wishes, to vary or discharge any order made on the application of the authority, the child concerned or the person named in the order. The intention is that since contact is such a sensitive, emotional issue, the road to the court should always be open to all of the parties involved.

Section 34(10): provides that an order may be made either at the same time as the care order itself or later. A departure from earlier proceedings when contact – known as access – could only be dealt with in separate proceedings and not at the initial care hearing.

Section 34(11): provides for the court to examine the proposals for contact as to their logistical detail, not simply dates and times, and provides equally for parties to the proceedings to comment on those details.

Supervision orders

Section 35. Supervision orders

35. — (1) While a supervision order is in force it shall be the duty of the supervisor —

    (a) to advise, assist and befriend the supervised child;

    (b) to take such steps as are reasonably necessary to give effect to the order; and

    (c) where —

        (i) the order is not wholly complied with; or

        (ii) the supervisor considers that the order may no longer be necessary,

    to consider whether or not to apply to the court for its variation or discharge.

(2) Parts I and II of Schedule 3 make further provision with respect to supervision orders.

Annotation

Section 35: deals with the duties imposed on a supervisor, who may be a local authority or a probation officer, though a more ample definition of who shall be appointed as a supervisor and the conditions under which a probation officer shall be appointed, may be found in Parts I and II of Schedule 3.

Section 35(1): defines the broad duties of a supervisor to advise, assist and befriend the supervised child. The power of a supervisor to give directions to a supervised child is further defined in Schedule 3, Part I, paragraph 2(1).

Section 35(2): refers to the further provision to be found in Parts I and II of Schedule 3, which deal with the meaning of "the responsible person" in relation to a supervised child, the imposition of obligations on a responsible person, and psychiatric and medical examinations among other things.

Section 36. Education supervision orders

36. — (1) On the application of any local education authority, the court may make an order putting the child with respect to whom the application is made under the supervision of a designated local education authority.

(2) In this Act "an education supervision order" means an order under subsection (1).

(3) A court may only make an education supervision order if it is satisfied that the child concerned is of compulsory school age and is not being properly educated.

(4) For the purposes of this section, a child is being properly educated only if he is receiving efficient full-time education suitable to his age, ability and aptitude and any special educational needs he may have.

(5) Where a child is —

(a) the subject of a school attendance order which is in force under section 37 of the Education Act 1944 and which has not been complied with; or
(b) a registered pupil at a school which he is not attending regularly within the meaning of section 39 of that Act,

then, unless it is proved that he is being properly educated, it shall be assumed that he is not.

(6) An education supervision order may not be made with respect to a child who is in the care of a local authority.

(7) The local education authority designated in an education supervision order must be —

(a) the authority within whose area the child concerned is living or will live; or
(b) where —

(i) the child is a registered pupil at a school; and
(ii) the authority mentioned in paragraph (a) and the authority within whose area the school is situated agree,

the latter authority.

(8) Where a local education authority propose to make an application for an education supervision order they shall, before making the application, consult the social services committee (within the meaning of the Local Authority Social Services Act 1970) of the appropriate local authority.

(9) The appropriate local authority is —

(a) in the case of a child who is being provided with accommodation by, or on behalf of, a local authority, that authority; and

(b) in any other case, the local authority within whose area the child concerned lives, or will live.

(10) Part III of Schedule 3 makes further provision with respect to education supervision orders.

Annotation

Section 36: introduces an education supervision order which, upon a successful application to the court, would place a child not being properly educated under the supervision of a local education authority. Only an education authority may make an application under section 36. Formerly a care order might be made in respect of a child of compulsory school age under section 1(2)(e) of the Children and Young Persons Act 1969. The grounds were that the child was not receiving efficient, full time education and was in need of care and control. The duties of a supervisor under an education supervision order and other provisions relating to the order, shall be found in Part III of Schedule 3.

Section 36(1): provides that the court may hear an application by a local education authority to make a supervision order to a designated local education authority. In the past, it has long been considered inappropriate that a child be placed in care on educational grounds only, but whilst the number of care orders on education grounds had been declining, the number of supervision orders on these grounds had increased.

Section 36(2): declares that an education supervision order is one made under section 36(1).

Section 36(3): provides that the court might make an education supervision order if it is satisfied the child is of compulsory school age and is not being properly educated. Since an education authority is excluded from seeking a care order other than an education supervision order, the facts before the court must deal only with the education of the child, not whether a care or supervision order can be made under section 31.

Section 36(4): defines what is meant by a proper education. Under section 1(2)(e) of the Children and Young Persons Act 1969 the grounds were that the child was not receiving efficient full time education; for the purposes of section 36(4) the failure to receive such efficient full time education will be relevant evidence where an application is made for an education supervision order.

Section 36(5): provides that where a child is subject to a school attendance order not being complied with, or is not attending school regularly, there shall be a presumption that the child is not being properly educated. The presumption may, however, be rebutted. The failure properly to educate a child may be evidence that the child is suffering significant harm, since such failure may impair his development: see the definition of harm under section 31(9).

Section 36(6): provides that an education supervision order may not be made with respect to a child who is in the care of a local authority. In short, a care order and an education supervision order are mutually exclusive.

Section 36(7): defines the catchment area of a local authority in respect of a child in whose name it is seeking an education supervision order. Where the child is not within this catchment area it may nevertheless apply to the court with the agreement of another local authority within whose area the child attends school.

Section 36(8): provides for consultation with the social services committee of a local authority rather than the in-house bureaucracy of social services. The committee is defined within the meaning of the Local Authority Social Services Act 1970. Consultation with the committee might mean discussions with a chairman and vice chairman, or might require a decision of a full committee. In either case, the promotion of the child's welfare would be paramount in the consultation process.

Section 36(9): defines the appropriate local authority with whom consultations must take place.

Section 36(10): declares that Part III of Schedule 3 makes further provision with respect to education supervision orders. Part III deals with the effect of the orders, their duration and discharge, information to be provided to a supervisor, persistent failure of a child to comply with directions and other provisions.

Powers of court

Section 37. Powers of court in certain family proceedings

37.—(1) Where, in any family proceedings in which a question arises with respect to the welfare of any child, it appears to the court that it may be appropriate for a care or supervision order to be made with respect to him, the court may direct the appropriate authority to undertake an investigation of the child's circumstances.

(2) Where the court gives a direction under this section the

local authority concerned shall, when undertaking the investigation, consider whether they should—

(a) apply for a care order or for a supervision order with respect to the child;

(b) provide services or assistance for the child or his family; or

(c) take any other action with respect to the child.

(3) where a local authority undertake an investigation under this section, and decide not to apply for a care order or supervision order with respect to the child concerned, they shall inform the court of—

(a) their reasons for so deciding;

(b) any service or assistance which they have provided, or intend to provide, for the child and his family; and

(c) any other action which they have taken, or propose to take, with respect to the child.

(4) The information shall be given to the court before the end of the period of eight weeks beginning with the date of the direction, unless the court otherwise directs.

(5) The local authority named in a direction under subsection (1) must be—

(a) the authority in whose area the child is ordinarily resident; or

(b) where the child [*does not reside*] [is not ordinarily resident] in the area of a local authority, the authority within whose area any circumstances arose in consequence of which the direction is being given.

(6) If, on the conclusion of any investigation or review under this section, the authority decide not to apply for a care order or supervision order with respect to the child—

(a) they shall consider whether it would be appropriateto review the case at a later date; and

(b) if they decide that it would be, they shall determine the date on which that review is to begin.

Annotation

Section 37: empowers a court in family proceedings where any question arises dealing with the welfare of a child to direct a local

Note: The words *in italics* within square brackets were deleted by the Courts and Legal Services Act 1990.
Note: The words within square brackets were inserted by the Courts and Legal Services Act 1990.

authority to enquire into the child's circumstances, with a view to that local authority's applying for a care or supervision order. Formerly, a court considering the facts of any case in family proceedings could upon its own motion make a care order where the court was minded to decide a child should not live with a parent or another person. Section 37 means that it shall no longer be open to a court to act upon its own motion to make out a care or supervision order, other than an interim order pursuant to section 38; rather that it should direct a local authority to make its own enquiries and to act upon those enquiries, should it think fit, by an appropriate application to the court. The purpose of the section is to ensure that no care order is made without a full and detailed examination of the child's circumstances by the local authority who would be responsible, in any event, upon a successful application being made, for the care of the child.

Section 37(1): provides the court with a power to intervene in family proceedings as these are defined in section 8(3) and (4) with a view to a care order being applied for and granted, should this promote the welfare of the child.

Section 37(2): imposes a duty upon a local authority to consider a variety of applications it may make, either for a care or supervision order, but also to make no application at all, rather to provide services or assistance for the child or his family, or take any other action on behalf of the child. The taking of a child into care should not be the stock response of any local authority in receipt of a direction from a court to undertake an investigation into a child's circumstances.

Section 37(4): provides not a timetable but a deadline for a local authority to comply with a direction from the court, that is eight weeks. We have already seen that the principle of delay is one which harms a child; section 37(4) provides that these delays should be kept to a minimum. Note that the eight weeks is a maximum limit and the maximum should not be turned into a minimum. The court can issue alternative directions.

Section 37(5): defines the appropriate authority which should be directed by the court to undertake an investigation of a child's circumstances and is consistent with other sections of the Act which place a duty upon a local authority to act where a child is ordinarily resident within its area, or where a circumstance arose within the area of a local authority: see section 31(8).

Section 37(6): imposes a duty upon a local authority where, upon completion of its investigation, it decides not to apply for a care order or supervision order, to determine whether it would be appropriate to review the case at a later date. Should they so determine, a date shall be fixed for the review to begin. The findings under section 37(6) shall be imparted to the court pursuant to section 37(3).

Section 38. Interim orders

38. —(1) Where —

(a) in any proceedings on an application for a care order or supervision order, the proceedings are adjourned; or
(b) the court gives a direction under section 37(1),

the court may make an interim care order or an interim supervision order with respect to the child concerned.

(2) A court shall not make an interim care order or interim supervision order under this section unless it is satisfied that there are reasonable grounds for believing that the circumstances with respect to the child are as mentioned in section 31(2).

(3) Where, in any proceedings on an application for a care order or supervision order, a court makes a residence order with respect to the child concerned, it shall also make an interim supervision order with respect to him unless satisfied that his welfare will be satisfactorily safeguarded without an interim order being made.

(4) An interim order made under or by virtue of this section shall have effect for such period as may be specified in the order, but shall in any event cease to have effect on whichever of the following events first occurs —

(a) the expiry of the period of eight weeks beginning with the date on which the order is made;
(b) if the order is the second or subsequent such order made with respect to the same child in the same proceedings, the expiry of the relevant period;
(c) in a case which falls within subsection (1)(a), the disposal of the application;
(d) in a case which falls within subsection (1)(b), the disposal of an application for a care order or supervision order made by the authority with respect to the child;
(e) in a case which falls within subsection (1)(b) and in which —

> (i) the court has given a direction under section 37(4), but
> (ii) no application for a care order or supervision order has been made with respect to the child,

the expiry of the period fixed by that direction.

(5) In subsection (4)(b) "the relevant period" means—

- (a) the period of four weeks beginning with the date on which the order in question is made; or
- (b) the period of eight weeks beginning with the date on which the first order was made if that period ends later than the period mentioned in paragraph (a).

(6) Where the court makes an interim care order, or interim supervision order, it may give such directions (if any) as it considers appropriate with regard to the medical or psychiatric examination or other assessment of the child; but if the child is of sufficient understanding to make an informed decision he may refuse to submit to the examination of other assessment.

(7) A direction under subsection (6) may be to the effect that there is to be—

- (a) no such examination or assessment; or
- (b) no such examination or assessment unless the court directs otherwise.

(8) A direction under subsection (6) may be—

- (a) given when the interim order is made or at any time while it is in force; and
- (b) varied at any time on the application of any person falling within any class of person prescribed by rules of court for the purposes of this subsection.

(9) Paragraphs 4 and 5 of Schedule 3 shall not apply in relation to an interim supervision order.

(10) Where a court makes an order under or by virtue of this section it shall, in determining the period for which the order is to be in force, consider whether any party who was, or might have been, opposed to the making of the order was in a position to argue his case against the order in full.

Annotation

Section 38: provides that interim care or supervision orders stand alongside section 8 orders as a means of promoting a child's welfare. In considering the child's welfare as paramount, a court may decide that it is better to make an interim order rather than making no order at all, and to have regard to the general principle that that delay in determining a question with respect to the upbringing of a child is likely to prejudice his welfare. Thus, section 38 sets out the grounds which have to be satisfied and provides time limits for interim orders. A court must be satisfied that the first limbs on the way to a full care order exist – harm or likely harm to a child attributable to the absence of a reasonable standard of parental care or adequate control – and that the power to remove or detain the child is necessary in order to safeguard his welfare during the interim period.

Section 38(1): provides a court with the power to make an interim care or supervision order only after care proceedings have been initiated, and whilst an interim order is similar in effect to a full order, the difference lies in that with interim orders the court may make certain directions. Under the Children and Young Persons Act 1969, a court could only make an interim care order where an application had been made for a care or supervision order, but the court was not in a position to decide which order, if any, to make. In these circumstances, the court would make an interim care order but not an interim supervision order. The grounds on which such orders are to be made are now clearly established.

Section 38(2): relates the granting of an interim care or supervision order to section 31(2) which sets out the criteria for the granting of a full care or supervision order. The interim orders cannot be made simply because they are thought to be desirable; the court must be satisfied that there are reasonable grounds for believing that the conditions in section 31(2) are fulfilled. If the conditions are not fulfilled, it remains open to the court to decide to make a section 8 order or no order at all.

Section 38(3): acknowledges the rule that where a local authority is seeking a care or supervision order and the court chooses to make a residence order at the interim stage, the court shall have to consider carefully whether the child will be sufficiently protected without an interim supervision order.

Section 39. Discharge and variation etc. of care orders and supervision orders

39. —(1) A care order may be discharged by the court on the application of —

    (a) any person who has parental responsibility for the child;
    (b) the child himself; or
    (c) the local authority designated by the order.

(2) A supervision order may be varied or discharged by the court on the application of —

    (a) any person who has parental responsibility for the child;
    (b) the child himself; or

(c) the supervisor.

(3) On the application of a person who is not entitled to apply for the order to be discharged, but who is a person with whom the child is living, a supervision order may be varied by the court in so far as it imposes a requirement which affects that person.

(4) Where a care order is in force with respect to a child the court may, on the application of any person entitled to apply for the order to be discharged, substitute a supervision order for the care order.

(5) When a court is considering whether to substitute one order for another under subsection (4) any provision of this Act which would otherwise require section 31(2) to be satisfied at the time when the proposed order is substituted or made shall be disregarded.

Annotation

Section 39: provides for the discharge and variation of care and supervision orders. The court may substitute a care for a supervision order. A care order and a supervision order are mutually exclusive: see section 91(3) and Paragraph 10 of Schedule 3. The Children and Young Persons Act 1969 provided that a care order might be varied or discharged, but the power to vary a care order has now been removed. Similarly, in considering an application to substitute a care order for a supervision order it is not necessary to re-prove the grounds for the original order. In addition, when considering whether to substitute a care order for a supervision order the court would need to make a decision by having regard to the check list in section 1(3). Equally, the court would be required not to make an order unless it considers that making the order is better than making no order at all: see section 1(5).

Section 39(1): provides that a care order may be discharged on the application of a local authority, the child concerned or any person who has parental responsibility for him. Under prior law, only the child or the local authority could apply for the discharge of an order made in care proceedings; the child's parents might be able to apply on the child's behalf, but could not do so on their own account. Section 39(1)(a) extends the right to parents, or those with parental responsibility, and thus strengthens the rights of parents with regard to their own children.

Section 39(2): provides that a supervision order may be varied by the imposition or modification of requirements, or the extension of its duration, or discharged on the application of the supervisor, the supervised child, or a person who has parental responsibility for him. Note that a care order cannot be varied by the court, only a supervision order.

Section 39(3): provides for the variation of a supervision order if a person who is not entitled to apply for the order to be discharged but with whom the child is living, does in fact apply, but only insofar as the original order imposes a requirement on that person. Thus, a foster parent or a relative with whom the child is living, and where such a person is subject to requirements, may apply to have the supervision order varied.

Section 39(4): provides that where a care order is in force and a person who is entitled to do so applies for its discharge, the court may substitute a supervision order for the care order. A court must be satisfied that the discharge of the care order would be in the best interests of the child and that in reaching its decision the court is satisfied that if control is needed it will be provided under the supervision order.

Section 39(5): provides that where the court is considering whether it should substitute a care order for a supervision order it does not require to be established again the original conditions on the basis of which the care order was granted. The former ground for the discharge of a care order – that in the court's view it was appropriate – did not focus sufficiently on the child's interests and was not retained in the present Act. Section 39(5) reflects the criterion that a child's welfare is paramount and should be invoked in line with the general principles to be found in section 1.

Section 40. Orders pending appeals in cases about care or supervision orders

40. —(1) Where—

(a) a court dismisses an application for a care order; and
(b) at the time when the court dismisses the application, the child concerned is the subject of an interim care order,

the court may make a care order with respect to the child to have effect subject to such directions (if any) as the court may see fit to include in the order.

(2) Where—

(a) a court dismisses an application for a care order, or an application for a supervision order; and
(b) at the time when the court dismisses the application, the child concerned is the subject of an interim supervision order,

the court may make a supervision order with respect to the child to have effect subject to such directions (if any) as the court may see fit to include in the order.

(3) Where a court grants an application to discharge a care order or supervision order, it may order that—

(a) its decision is not to have effect; or
(b) the care order, or supervision order, is to continue to have effect but subject to such directions as the court sees fit to include in the order.

(4) An order made under this section shall only have effect for such period, not exceeding the appeal period, as may be specified in the order.

(5) Where—

(a) an appeal is made against any decision of a court under this section; or
(b) any application is made to the appellate court in connection with a proposed appeal against that decision,

the appellate court may extend the period for which the order in question is to have effect, but not so as to extend it beyond the end of the appeal period.

(6) In this section "the appeal period" means—

(a) where an appeal is made against the decision in question, the period between the making of that decision and the determination of the appeal; and
(b) otherwise, the period during which an appeal may be made against the decision.

Annotation

Section 40: deals with orders pending appeal and provides a court with power to order that a child remain in care or to place him under supervision pending an appeal when dismissing an application for a care order. Similarly, a court will be able to order that a child remain under supervision pending appeal when a supervision order is refused. Such powers are available only when the child is subject to an interim order. A court is also empowered to order that the child remain in care pending appeal when the court is discharging a care or supervision order.

Section 40(1): provides that a care order may be made where the court dismisses an application for a care order and at the time of dismissal the child is the subject of an interim care order. Section 40(1) provides a power to the court to stay its decision pending an appeal. Usually, pending any appeal in care and related proceedings, the child's position would conform with the decision which is being appealed. The power of the court to stay its decision will only be exercised where it is in the child's best interests.

Section 40(2): provides that a supervision order may be made if the court dismisses an application for a care or supervision order and at the time of dismissal the child is the subject of an interim supervision order. The same principle applies as under section 40(1) – that where a court dismisses an application a child should be free of any compulsory local authority powers or care pending an appeal. However, since an interim order is already extant, and in order to further the child's best interests, the court has power to make a supervision order until such time as the appeal is heard.

Section 40(3): provides that where a court grants an application to discharge a care or supervision order it may order that the discharge should not have effect, or that the care or supervision order should continue in force subject to directions. The fact that the court refuses to make a care order would not prevent a local authority from seeking an emergency protection order if it thought the child were at risk. Where the court orders that the care or supervision order should continue in accordance with section 40(3), this mitigates the need for such a course of action.

Section 40(4): provides that an order made under this section shall only have effect for such period, not exceeding the appeal period, as may be specified in the order. Thus, the effects of an order under section 40(1)(2) and (3) are intended to maintain protection for the child which would otherwise cease until such time as an appeal has been heard. Rules of court will define who may appeal against decisions made by courts under the Act. Unlike the situation under prior law, the local authority, the child and his parents are able to appeal against decisions concerning care and supervision orders.

Section 40(5): provides that appeals may be made against the decision of a court in respect of an order pending appeal. The appellate court may extend the duration of the care or supervision order which is in question if such an appeal is made, or if an application is made to it in connection with the proposed appeal.

Section 40(6): defines the meaning of appeal period within the framework of section 40. Appeals from care and related proceedings should be held in the same court. This would be a family court were one to be introduced. Meanwhile, it means that those appeals not heard in the High Court should now be referred to that Court and not to the Crown Court.

Guardians ad litem

Section 41. Representation of child and of his interests in certain proceedings

41.—(1) For the purpose of any specified proceedings, the court shall appoint a guardian ad litem for the child concerned unless satisfied that it is not necessary to do so in order to safeguard his interests.

(2) The guardian ad litem shall—

    (a) be appointed in accordance with rules of court; and

    (b) be under a duty to safeguard the interests of the child in the manner prescribed by such rules.

(3) Where—

    (a) the child concerned is not represented by a solicitor; and

    (b) any of the conditions mentioned in subsection (4) is satisfied,

the court may appoint a solicitor to represent him.

(4) The conditions are that—

    (a) no guardian ad litem has been appointed for the child;

    (b) the child has sufficient understanding to instruct a solicitor and wishes to do so;

    (c) it appears to the court that it would be in the child's best interests for him to be represented by a solicitor.

(5) Any solicitor appointed under or by virtue of this section shall be appointed, and shall represent the child, in accordance with rules of court.

(6) In this section "specified proceedings" means any proceedings—

    (a) on an application for a care order or supervision order;

    (b) in which the court has given a direction under section 37(1) and has made, or is considering whether to make, an interim care order;

    (c) on an application for the discharge of a care order or the variation or discharge of a supervision order;

    (d) on an application under section 39(4);

    (e) in which the court is considering whether to make a residence order with respect to a child who is the subject of a care order;

    (f) with respect to contact between a child who is the subject of a care order and any other person;

(g) under Part V;

(h) on an appeal against—

> (i) the making of, or refusal to make, a care order, supervision order or any order under section 34;
>
> (ii) the making of, or refusal to make, a residence order with respect to a child who is the subject of a care order; or
>
> (iii) the variation or discharge, or refusal of an application to vary or discharge, an order of a kind mentioned in sub-paragraph (i) or (ii);
>
> (iv) the refusal of an application under section 39(4); or
>
> (v) the making of, or refusal to make, an order under Part V; or

(i) which are specified for the time being, for the purposes of this section, by rules of court.

(7) The Secretary of State may by regulations provide for the establishment of panels of persons from whom guardians ad litem appointed under this section must be selected.

(8) Subsection (7) shall not be taken to prejudice the power of the Lord Chancellor to confer or impose duties on the Official Solicitor under section 90(3) of the Supreme Court Act 1981.

(9) The regulations may, in particular, make provision—

(a) as to the constitution, administration and procedures of panels;

(b) requiring two or more specified local authorities to make arrangements for the joint management of a panel;

(c) for the defrayment by local authorities of expenses incurred by members of panels;

(d) for the payment by local authorities of fees and allowances for members of panels;

(e) as to the qualifications for membership of a panel;

(f) as to the training to be given to members of panels;

(g) as to the co-operation required of specified local authorities in the provision of panels in specified areas; and

(h) for monitoring the work of guardians ad litem.

(10) Rules of court may make provision as to—

(a) the assistance which any guardian ad litem may be required by the court to give to it;

(b) the consideration to be given by any guardian ad litem, where an order of a specified kind has been made in the proceedings in question, as to whether to apply for the variation or discharge of the order;

(c) the participation of guardians ad litem in reviews, of a kind specified in the rules, which are conducted by the court.

(11) Regardless of any enactment or rule of law which would otherwise prevent it from doing so, the court may take account of—

(a) any statement contained in a report made by a guardian ad litem who is appointed under this section for the purpose of the proceedings in question; and

(b) any evidence given in respect of the matters referred to in the report,

in so far as the statement or evidence is, in the opinion of the court, relevant to the question which the court is considering.

[(12) The Secretary of State may, with the consent of the Treasury, make such grants with respect to expenditure of any local authority—

(a) in connection with the establishment and administration of guardian ad litem panels in accordance with this section;

(b) in paying expenses, fees, allowances and in the provision of training for members of such panels,

as he considers appropriate.]

Annotation

Section 41: provides that in certain proceedings a court shall appoint a guardian ad litem for the child unless satisfied that it is not necessary to do so in the interests of the child. Section 41 also provides for legal representation of the child and sets out the circumstances in which the court may appoint a solicitor to represent him where there is no guardian ad litem. It is expected, however, that rules of court will provide that a guardian ad litem should usually appoint a solicitor pursuant to section 41(2). Section 41 also provides for new panels from which individual guardians ad litem will be drawn and this means that they will be distanced from a particular local authority in a way which has been difficult to achieve in the past.

Section 41(1): requires a court in proceedings specified in section 41(6) to appoint a guardian ad litem unless satisfied that it is not

Note: The words within square brackets were inserted by the Courts and Legal Services Act 1990.

necessary to do so to safeguard the child's interests. Formerly, under section 32B of the Children and Young Persons Act 1969, the appointment of a guardian ad litem was limited to cases where there was, or was likely to be, conflict between the parents and child, and the court did not consider an appointment unnecessary for safeguarding the interest of the child.

Section 41(2): provides for a guardian ad litem to be appointed and to be responsible for safeguarding the child's interests as prescribed by court rules. In order to represent the child a guardian ad litem may instruct a solicitor for the child and act as an independent expert in matters relating to the child's welfare or any other matters, making a report to the court and carrying out any other duties which it directs. Section 41(2) does not prevent a child, when old enough, as a party to the proceedings, appointing a solicitor if the guardian ad litem or court have not done so.

Section 41(3): enables a court to appoint a solicitor for a child where he is not already represented and in accordance with conditions determined in section 41(4). A court would only appoint a solicitor where it is in the child's best interests that such an appointment be made. Formerly, the question of whether a child should be legally represented was decided by the court or by the guardian ad litem after obtaining the court's views. This was in accordance with rules of court: The Magistrates' Courts (Children and Young Persons) Rules 1988.

Section 41(4): defines those conditions which require to be satisfied in order that the court might appoint a solicitor. As under prior law, in most family proceedings a child will not be legally represented, but rules of court to be made pursuant to the Act will provide that parents and others with parental responsibility will be parties as a matter of course, and as such entitled to legal representation. See also section 10(8) where a child may himself apply for leave for a section 8 order affecting him where he has sufficient understanding to make the application.

Section 41(5): provides for any solicitor appointed under section 41 to represent the child in accordance with rules of court. These rules of court may require a solicitor appointed by a guardian ad litem to be instructed by the solicitor. The rules will provide that a guardian ad litem should usually appoint a solicitor for the child under section 41(2).

Section 41(6): defines specified proceedings for the purposes of section 41(1) in relation to the appointment of a guardian. Thus, section 41(6) extends the duty of the court to appoint a guardian ad litem, except where it is satisfied that it is not necessary to do so in order to safeguard the child's interests. Section 41(6) embraces care and supervision orders, but not education supervision orders, and also Part V orders, principally emergency protection and child assessment orders. These are important reforms in regard to the alignment of practice in these proceedings and will lead to an increase in the use of guardians ad litem, for which financial provision has been made.

Section 41(7): enables the Secretary of State to make regulations providing for the establishment of panels of guardians ad litem for the purpose of section 41. The section replaces, with amendments, most of the regulation-making power in respect of the establishment of panels of guardians ad litem in section 103 of the Children Act 1975. The regulation-making power is extended to cover cooperative arrangements between local authorities for administering panels: see section 41(9).

Section 41(8): provides that the regulation-making power in section 41(7) shall not prejudice the Lord Chancellor's powers in relation to the duties of the Official Solicitor. Appropriately trained members of the Official Solicitor's staff are to be encouraged to join local panels of guardians ad litem. Where a member of his staff is appointed guardian ad litem, that member will be bound by the same rules as apply to other panel guardians, including the rules which require the appointment of a solicitor for the child.

Section 41(9): follows upon section 41(7). The regulation-making powers under section 41(9) specify particular aspects of panel administration which may be provided; these include a power to require two or more authorities to make joint arrangements and to make provision as regards qualifications, training and monitoring of guardians ad litem. There had been some concern in the past that guardians ad litem were often unable to provide a properly independent service to the courts as panels were administered by the same local authorities as were involved in the proceedings. Section 41(9) enables the Secretary of State to require that where panels are administered on an area basis and there are no appropriate arrangements for joint operations between authorities, then there should be improved management, training and monitoring facilities available to panels.

Section 41(10): provides for rules of court to deal with particular responsibilities of a guardian ad litem and is intended to enable a guardian to play a role throughout the proceedings. For example, he may advise a court about the making of interim orders, or concerning questions relating to contact with the child, also in relation to directions about the examination or assessment of the child and directions which may be made to ensure that a timetable is adhered to in order to avoid unnecessary delay so harmful to the child's welfare. Section 41(10)(c) also provides for the guardian to play an active role by applying for directions to be made or for interim orders to be discharged if they are no longer needed.

Section 41(11): provides for the use of hearsay evidence as under the Civil Evidence Acts 1968 and 1972. One of the aims of the Children Act has been to move away from the quasi-criminal model towards a civil model with more advance disclosure so that respondents, that is to say the child or the child and his parents, know the elements of the case for an order. Section 41(11) enabling the use of hearsay evidence is helpful to this end.

Section 42. Right of guardian ad litem to have access to local authority records

42. —(1) Where a person has been appointed as a guardian ad litem under this Act he shall have the right at all reasonable times to examine and take copies of—

(a) any records of, or held by, a local authority [or an authorised person] which were compiled in connection with the making, or proposed making, by any person of any application under this Act with respect to the child concerned; [*or*]

(b) any [*other*] records of, or held by, a local authority which were compiled in connection with any functions which stand referred to their social services committee under the Local Authority Social Services Act 1970, so far as those records relate to that child [; or]

[(c) any records of, or held by, an authorised person which were compiled in connection with the activities of that person, so far as those records related to that child.]

(2) Where a guardian ad litem takes a copy of any record which he is entitled to examine under this section, that copy or any part of it shall be admissible as evidence of any matter referred to in any—

(a) report which he makes to the court in the proceedings in question; or

(b) evidence which he gives in those proceedings.

(3) Subsection (2) has effect regardless of any enactment or

Note: The words within square brackets were inserted by the Courts and Legal Services Act 1990.
Note: The words *in italics* within square brackets were deleted by the Courts and Legal Services Act 1990.

rule of law which would otherwise prevent the record in question being admissible in evidence.

[(4) In this section "authorised person" has the same meaning as in section 31.]

Annotation

Section 42: provides that a guardian ad litem should have a statutory right to local authority records. The White Paper, "The Law on Child Care and Family Services", reflected the concern that had been expressed that an applicant – normally a local authority – would be required to disclose their case automatically but the respondent only on the direction of the court. It was proposed that a respondent should be required as a minimum to give an outline of their reasons for contesting the application when practicable. The Review of Child Care Law canvassed the idea of discovery of documents – a process by which parties can have access to other parties' records, even though they may not be produced in court. It was felt this was not practical, but that it was important that the guardian ad litem of a child had access as a statutory right: hence section 42.

Section 42(1): provides a guardian ad litem with the statutory right to have access to local authority records compiled in connection with the bringing of proceedings and those which relate to the child concerned and compiled under the functions of the social services department: see Schedule 1 of the Local Authority Social Services Act 1970. During the report stage of the Bill, an enquiry was made whether a guardian ad litem could make use of information in the records of such bodies as the National Society for the Prevention of Cruelty to Children, which might be compiled in relation to a child subject to an application for a care order. The Solicitor General replied that the NSPCC, as an authorised person within the meaning of section 31(a), may be required to provide access to such documents as a guardian ad litem may need.

Section 42(2): provides that copies of records taken will be admissible as evidence of any matter referred to in either the guardian's report or in evidence which the guardian gives in the proceedings. Section 42(2) enables a guardian ad litem representing a child subject to an application by a local authority freely to make use of all records relevant to the child before making a decision as to his welfare and to rely on these records before a court.

Note: The words within square brackets were inserted by the Courts and Legal Services Act 1990.

Section 42(3): provides that such records are admissible in evidence, even if there is otherwise a rule of law which excludes it.

PART V

PROTECTION OF CHILDREN

Section 43. Child assessment orders

43.—(1) On the application of a local authority or authorised person for an order to be made under this section with respect to a child, the court may make the order if, but only if, it is satisfied that—

    (a) the applicant has reasonable cause to suspect that the child is suffering, or is likely to suffer, significant harm;

    (b) an assessment of the state of the child's health or development, or of the way in which he has been treated, is required to enable the applicant to determine whether or not the child is suffering, or is likely to suffer, significant harm; and

    (c) it is unlikely that such an assessment will be made, or be satisfactory, in the absence of an order under this section.

(2) In this Act "a child assessment order" means an order under this section.

(3) A court may treat an application under this section as an application for an emergency protection order.

(4) No court shall make a child assessment order if it is satisfied—

    (a) that there are grounds for making an emergency protection order with respect to the child; and

    (b) that it ought to make such an order rather than a child assessment order.

(5) A child assessment order shall—

    (a) specify the date by which the assessment is to begin; and

    (b) have effect for such period, not exceeding 7 days beginning with that date, as may be specified in the order.

(6) Where a child assessment order is in force with respect to a child it shall be the duty of any person who is in a position to produce the child—

    (a) to produce him to such person as may be named in the order; and

    (b) to comply with such directions relating to the assessment of the child as the court thinks fit to specify in the order.

(7) A child assessment order authorises any person carrying out the assessment, or any part of the assessment, to do so in accordance with the terms of the order.

(8) Regardless of subsection (7), if the child is of sufficient understanding to make an informed decision he may refuse to submit to a medical or psychiatric examination or other assessment.

(9) The child may only be kept away from home—

    (a) in accordance with directions specified in the order;
    (b) if it is necessary for the purposes of the assessment; and
    (c) for such period or periods as may be specified in the order.

(10) Where the child is to be kept away from home, the order shall contain such directions as the court thinks fit with regard to the contact that he must be allowed to have with other persons while away from home.

(11) Any person making an application for a child assessment order shall take such steps as are reasonably practicable to ensure that notice of the application is given to—

    (a) the child's parents;
    (b) any person who is not a parent of his but who has parental responsibility for him;
    (c) any other person caring for the child;
    (d) any person in whose favour a contact order is in force with respect to the child;
    (e) any person who is allowed to have contact with the child by virtue of an order under section 34; and
    (f) the child,

before the hearing of the application.

(12) Rules of court may make provision as to the circumstances in which—

    (a) any of the persons mentioned in subsection (11); or
    (b) such other person as may be specified in the rules,

may apply to the court for a child assessment order to be varied or discharged.

(13) In this section "authorised person" means a person who is an authorised person for the purposes of section 31.

E

Annotation

Section 43: provides for a court to make a child assessment order. The order is entirely new and is designed to run parallel to an emergency protection order. Section 43 provides for an application to be made to a court by a local authority or authorised person where there is serious concern about the welfare of a child. In the case of a local authority, it may be carrying out its investigative duty with regard to a child; in the case of an authorised person, he may be enquiring into the circumstances of the child. Neither investigation nor enquiry may justify an application for an emergency protection order, but if there has been a failure to produce the child, clearly no assessment can take place. Section 43 enables a court to make an order permitting a sensible assessment of a child with appropriate safeguards and directions to be given by the court.

Section 43(1): provides that an application may be made for a child assessment order by a local authority or authorised person. Section 43(1) reflects section 31(2)(a) dealing with the making of a care or supervision order and is similar to section 44(1)(a) dealing with the granting of an emergency protection order. Section 43(1)(b) and (c) indicates that the purpose of the child assessment order is quite different from that of the emergency protection order. A court would also have to take into account, before making the assessment order, what is the paramount interest of the child and whether an assessment order should be made rather than no order at all: see section 1(1) and (5).

Section 43(2): provides that under the Act "a child assessment order" means an order under section 43. The order was preferred in committee and at report stage of the Bill to a child production notice which would have allowed a local authority to serve notice on those with parental responsibility requiring them to produce the child before a doctor or a health visitor where it was feared the child was suffering, or likely to suffer, significant harm. In the event of non-compliance with a child production notice, a local authority would then have applied for an emergency protection order. However, it was decided that a child production order gave too much power to a local authority.

Section 43(3): provides that a court may treat an application under section 43 as an application for an emergency protection order. Once a court has satisfied itself of the welfare principle under section 1(1) and the desirability of making an order, rather than no order at all under section 1(5), it must address its mind to the making of a child assessment order or an emergency protection order. A court would then require to fall back upon scrutiny of section 43(1) and section 44(1) which make it clear that the purpose of a child assessment order is entirely different from an emergency protection order. The first is to *assess* the child; the second is to *protect* it.

Section 43(4): provides that in some circumstances, a court may take the view that those making the application have under-estimated the gravity of the case. Section 43(4) provides that it is then open to the court to make an emergency protection order instead of a child assessment order. Emergencies and non-emergencies are not self-defining categories. Section 43(4) provides that where a court hears the evidence and it believes that an emergency protection order is needed, it can so order.

Section 43(5): provides for the departure date for an assessment order to be specified by the court, together with its duration. An assessment order may only last for up to seven days and does not involve the child being kept away from home unless the court so directs. The duration of the assessment order is entirely a matter for the court and not a matter for the applicant. Section 43(5) provides for a maximum duration of a child assessment order – a lesser period may be prescribed by the court and the number of days so prescribed need not be consecutive.

Section 43(6): provides the court with a power not only to ensure that the child is produced but to comply with any directions the court may issue. Section 43(6)(b) provides the court with a power to direct the nature of the assessment that is to take place, its purpose, who is to carry out the assessment, where it shall take place, and whether conditions shall be attached. Also to direct what experts should be involved, whether there should be more than one expert working in tandem and whether such experts might be appointed by those with parental responsibility for the child as well as by the applicant.

Section 43(7): provides that whilst there is no restriction on the type of assessment which may be carried out, nevertheless each order shall authorise the person carrying out the assessment to do so in accordance with its terms.

Section 43(8): reflects provisions made in section 38(6) in respect of an interim care order and section 44(7) in respect of an emergency protection order. A court may appoint a guardian ad litem to protect the interests of a child in proceedings relating to child assessment orders: see section 41(6)(g).

Section 43(9): provides that a court may give directions to enable a child to be assessed away from home. At report stage the Minister of Health declared "For the most part the assessment will take place without the requirement to take the child away, save for the period of an afternoon or two afternoons for an assessment to be made. However, there may be rare occasions when an overnight stay is required."

Section 43(10): provides that a court and not an applicant will make provision for contact a child may have with other persons while away from home. A child assessment order deals only with assessment – no parental responsibility passes as it does with an emergency protection order.

Section 43(11): provides for notice to be given by any person making an application for a child assessment order to those parties defined in the section. Prior notice is also to be given to a person in whose favour an order relating to contact is in force with respect to the child, whether the contact order is made under section 8 or under section 34. Applications for a child assessment order will be made *inter partes*, not *ex partes*, as for most emergency protection orders.

Section 43(12): provides for rules of court to be made in relation to the variation or discharge of a child assessment order. A further application for a child assessment order may not be made, without the leave of the court, within six months of the disposal of the previous one or the disposal of an application for the discharge of a care order or supervision order: see section 95(15).

Section 43(13): provides that the National Society for the Prevention of Cruelty to Children and any of its officers, and any person authorised by the Secretary of State, may make an application for a child assessment order under section 43.

Section 44. Orders for emergency protection of children

44.—(1) Where any person ("the applicant") applies to the court for an order to be made under this section with respect to a child, the court may make the order if, but only if, it is satisfied that—

    (a) there is reasonable cause to believe that the child is likely to suffer significant harm if—

        (i) he is not removed to accommodation provided by or on behalf of the applicant; or
        (ii) he does not remain in the place in which he is then being accommodated;

    (b) in the case of an application made by a local authority—

        (i) enquiries are being made with respect to the child under section 47(1)(b); and

(ii) those enquiries are being frustrated by access to the child being unreasonably refused to a person authorised to seek access and that the applicant has reasonable cause to believe that access to the child is required as a matter of urgency; or

(c) in the case of an application made by an authorised person—

(i) the applicant has reasonable cause to suspect that a child is suffering, or is likely to suffer, significant harm;

(ii) the applicant is making enquiries with respect to the child's welfare; and

(iii) those enquiries are being frustrated by access to the child being unreasonably refused to a person authorised to seek access and the applicant has reasonable cause to believe that access to the child is required as a matter of urgency.

(2) In this section—

(a) "authorised person" means a person who is an authorised person for the purposes of section 31; and

(b) "a person authorised to seek access" means—

(i) in the case of an application by a local authority, an officer of the local authority or a person authorised by the authority to act on their behalf in connection with the enquiries; or

(ii) in the case of an application by an authorised person, that person.

(3) Any person—

(a) seeking access to a child in connection with enquiries of a kind mentioned in subsection (1); and

(b) purporting to be a person authorised to do so,

shall, on being asked to do so, produce some duly authenticated document as evidence that he is such a person.

(4) While an order under this section ("an emergency protection order") is in force it—

(a) operates as a direction to any person who is in a position to do so to comply with any request to produce the child to the applicant;

(b) authorises—

(i) the removal of the child at any time to accommodation provided by or on behalf of the applicant and his being kept there; or

    (ii) the prevention of the child's removal from any hospital, or other place, in which he was being accommodated immediately before the making of the order; and

  (c) gives the applicant parental responsibility for the child.

(5) Where an emergency protection order is in force with respect to a child, the applicant—

  (a) shall only exercise the power given by virtue of subsection (4)(b) in order to safeguard the welfare of the child;

  (b) shall take, and shall only take, such action in meeting his parental responsibility for the child as is reasonably required to safeguard or promote the welfare of the child (having regard in particular to the duration of the order); and

  (c) shall comply with the requirements of any regulations made by the Secretary of State for the purposes of this subsection.

(6) Where the court makes an emergency protection order, it may give such directions (if any) as it considers appropriate with respect to—

  (a) the contact which is, or is not, to be allowed between the child and any named person;

  (b) the medical or psychiatric examination or other assessment of the child.

(7) Where any direction is given under subsection (6)(b), the child may, if he is of sufficient understanding to make an informed decision, refuse to submit to the examination or other assessment.

(8) A direction under subsection (6)(a) may impose conditions and one under subsection (6)(b) may be to the effect that there is to be—

  (a) no such examination or assessment; or

  (b) no such examination or assessment unless the court directs otherwise.

(9) A direction under subsection (6) may be—

  (a) given when the emergency protection order is made or at any time while it is in force; and

  (b) varied at any time on the application of any person falling within any class of person prescribed by rules of court for the purposes of this subsection.

(10) Where an emergency protection order is in force with respect to a child and— .

(a) the applicant has exercised the power given by subsection (4)(b)(i) but it appears to him that it is safe for the child to be returned; or

(b) the applicant has exercised the power given by subsection (4)(b)(ii) but it appears to him that it is safe for the child to be allowed to be removed from the place in question,

he shall return the child or (as the case may be) allow him to be removed.

(11) Where he is required by subsection (10) to return the child the applicant shall—

(a) return him to the care of the person from whose care he was removed; or

(b) if that is not reasonably practicable, return him to the care of—

(i) a parent of his;

(ii) any person who is not a parent of his but who has parental responsibility for him; or

(iii) such other person as the applicant (with the agreement of the court) considers appropriate.

(12) Where the applicant has been required by subsection (10) to return the child, or to allow him to be removed, he may again exercise his powers with respect to the child (at any time while the emergency protection order remains in force) if it appears to him that a change in the circumstances of the case makes it necessary for him to do so.

(13) Where an emergency protection order has been made with respect to a child, the applicant shall, subject to any direction given under subsection (6), allow the child reasonable contact with—

(a) his parents;

(b) any person who is not a parent of his but who has parental responsibility for him;

(c) any person with whom he was living immediately before the making of the order;

(d) any person in whose favour a contact order is in force with respect to him;

(e) any person who is allowed to have contact with the child by virtue of an order under section 34; and

(f) any person acting on behalf of any of those persons.

(14) Wherever it is reasonably practicable to do so, an emer-

gency protection order shall name the child; and where it does not name him it shall describe him as clearly as possible.

(15) A person shall be guilty of an offence if he intentionally obstructs any person exercising the power under subsection (4)(b) to remove, or prevent the removal of, a child.

(16) A person guilty of an offence under subsection (15) shall be liable on summary conviction to a fine not exceeding level 3 on the standard scale.

Annotation

Section 44: introduces an emergency protection order which replaces the place of safety order which could be obtained under section 28(1) of the Children and Young Persons Act 1969. There were several weaknesses which became apparent with the former place of safety order. It simply required a court to be satisfied that the applicant had reasonable cause to believe that the grounds for a care order were met and did not address the emergency nature nor the need to remove the child. A place of safety order became an instrument for commencing care proceedings and open to abuse. In Cleveland, between 1 January and 31 July 1987, 276 place of safety orders were applied for by the local authority. Of those, 174 were heard by a single magistrate at home during the hours of court sittings, despite a clear understanding between the clerk to the justices and the social services department that social workers would make these applications in the first instance to the full court: see Lord Justice Butler-Sloss, Report of the Inquiry into Child Abuse in Cleveland 1987, paragraph 10.9. HMSO Cm. 412.

Section 44(1): enables a court to make an emergency protection order. An application may be made to the court by any person; this distinguishes the order from a child assessment order which might only be applied for by a local authority or an authorised person. Section 44(1)(a) requires that the court rather than the applicant alone must be satisfied that there is reasonable cause to believe the child is likely to suffer significant harm. Section 44(1)(a)(ii) would cover a child who is already in hospital and who is likely to suffer if he is allowed to return home. In the case of section 44(1)(b) the court's decision will be based upon the evidence provided by a local authority alone, since it will not have been appropriate and practicable to serve notice of the application on the person caring for the child. Section 44(1)(c) is similar to section 44(1)(b), except that it may only be used by the authorised person who is carrying out inquiries into the child's welfare.

Section 44(2): defines "authorised person" pursuant to section 31, that is to say the National Society for the Prevention of Cruelty to Children and a person so authorised by the Secretary of State, or those persons who have been delegated the authority to seek access. Section 44(2)(a) recognises that although they are not under a statutory duty to investigate children at risk, the NSPCC play an important role alongside a local authority. They are therefore given the same powers as those authorities to protect children in need.

Section 44(3): provides that where a person is seeking access to a child he must produce evidence of his authority should he be asked to do so. Failure to produce such evidence may make refusal of access reasonable. A court will not automatically make an emergency protection order even where the conditions of section 44(1) are satisfied. The welfare principle under section 1(1) must be met and the "no order" presumption under 1(5) rebutted, although the section 1(2) checklist does not require to be applied.

Section 44(4): provides that parental responsibility for the child during the period of the emergency protection order, which was not defined in the former place of safety order, will be with the applicant. Section 44(4)(c) distinguishes an emergency protection order from a child assessment order where parental responsibility does not pass: see section 43.

Section 44(5): provides that whilst parental responsibility passes to the applicant he must exercise that responsibility as required to promote the child's welfare pursuant to section 1(1). The rights, duties, powers and responsibilities embracing parental responsibility under section 3(1) are constrained only by the duration of the order; an applicant acquiring parental responsibility would not be expected to arrange for the child to move to a new school, but he might, if appropriate, make temporary arrangements for the child's education whilst the order lasts. An applicant acquiring parental responsibility would be expected to comply with such regulations; for example, on boarding out, as are appropriate in the circumstances: section 44(5)(c).

Section 44(6): provides that where a court makes an emergency protection order it may also give directions in relation to the order. Thus, a court may decide that a person who is suspected of alleged abuse should lose his right to reasonable contact to the child, or that a named person's contact might be restricted by certain conditions. There is, however, a presumption of reasonable access by those who had parental responsibility, unless the court directs otherwise.

Section 44(7): reflects provisions made in section 38(6) in respect of an interim care order and section 43(8) in respect of a child assessment order.

Section 44(8): empowers a court, when giving directions to impose conditions, that there be no examinations or assessments, unless the court directs otherwise. These powers are the same as those which arise when a child is in interim care or under an interim supervision order: see section 38(7). The reasoning behind the power is that the court may direct no assessment or examination where it believes this will be harmful to the child.

Section 44(9): provides that a direction under section 44(6) may be given at the time that the emergency protection order is made and varied at any time on the application of any class of person specified by rules of court. Thus, for example, a person with parental responsibility who is denied access on a direction given at the time the emergency protection order is made may apply to the court for a variation of the original direction to provide access where that person belongs to a class of person specified by rules of court.

Section 44(10): provides for a child to be returned within the period of the emergency protection order where the applicant is satisfied it is safe for him to do so, or to be allowed to return from any safe place if it is equally safe for him to do so. The paramount interest of the child would not be served in keeping him away from those capable of looking after him as defined in section 44(11)(b). An applicant does not need to return to the court to obtain such a decision to return the child. It is nevertheless a requirement upon him to return the child where he is satisfied that it is safe to do so: see section 44(12).

Section 44(11): provides that the applicant should be looking to see if it is at all possible for the child to be returned to the person from whose care the child was removed in the first place, provided it is safe to do so, and to other classes of persons if this is reasonably practicable. The applicant should be seeking to promote the child's welfare by returning him to his own environment as quickly as possible even within the duration of the emergency protection order.

Section 44(12): confers a power upon an applicant, within the duration of the emergency protection order, to remove the child again, in the exercise of his parental responsibility, should the circumstances have changed. Thus, where an alleged perpetrator of child abuse has been removed from the family home, making it ostensibly safe for the child to return, should the alleged perpetrator move back in section 44(12) empowers the applicant to remove the child again, but only within the duration of the emergency protection order. An emergency protection order may only be extended once: see section 45(6).

Section 44(13): requires the applicant to allow the child reasonable contact with those persons specified, subject to any direction given the court under section 44(4). Section 44(13)(f) covers, for example, a doctor or an independent social worker, but subject to the court's directions, it is for the applicant to decide what constitutes reasonable contact; it may only be reasonable to allow a person suspected of alleged abuse to have contact under supervision.

Section 44(14): provides that wherever possible an emergency protection order should name or identify a child to whom it relates. Rules which prevent the publication of details of children's cases which are heard in private in the High Court and county courts continue to have effect: see section 12 of the Administration of Justice Act 1960, as amended by Schedule 13 paragraph 14. The Act enables rules of court to permit a magistrates' court to sit in private in proceedings in which powers under it may be exercised with respect to a child: see section 97(1)

Section 44(15): provides for it to be a criminal offence for anyone intentionally to obstruct any person exercising the power under section 44(4)(b) to remove or prevent the removal of a child where an emergency protection order has been made in his name. A warrant may be issued to a constable to assist using reasonable force if necessary, where such person has been or is likely to be prevented from exercising powers under an emergency protection order by being refused entry to the premises concerned or access to the child concerned: see section 48(9).

Section 44(16): provides that a person guilty of an offence under section 44(15) shall be liable on summary conviction to a fine. The Act is essentially a civil act, drawing together and simplifying former child care legislation. Nevertheless, sometimes the civil law gives rise to ramifications falling within the criminal law. Sections 44(15) and (16) are among them.

Section 45. Duration of emergency protection orders and other supplemental provisions

45.—(1) an emergency protection order shall have effect for such period, not exceeding eight days, as may be specified in the order.

(2) Where—

(a) the court making an emergency protection order would,

but for this subsection, specify a period of eight days as the period for which the order is to have effect; but

(b) the last of those eight days is a public holiday (that is to say, Christmas Day, Good Friday, a bank holiday or a Sunday),

the court may specify a period which ends at noon on the first later day which is not such a holiday.

(3) Where an emergency protection order is made on an application under section 46(7), the period of eight days mentioned in subsection (1) shall begin with the first day on which the child was taken into police protection under section 46.

(4) Any person who—

(a) has parental responsibility for a child as the result of an emergency protection order; and

(b) is entitled to apply for a care order with respect to the child,

may apply to the court for the period during which the emergency protection order is to have effect to be extended.

(5) On an application under subsection (4) the court may extend the period during which the order is to have effect by such period, not exceeding seven days, as it thinks fit, but may do so only if it has reasonable cause to believe that the child concerned is likely to suffer significant harm if the order is not extended.

(6) An emergency protection order may only be extended once.

(7) Regardless of any enactment or rule of law which would otherwise prevent it from doing so, a court hearing an application for, or with respect to, an emergency protection order may take account of—

(a) any statement contained in any report made to the court in the course of, or in connection with, the hearing; or

(b) any evidence given during the hearing,

which is, in the opinion of the court, relevant to the application.

(8) Any of the following may apply to the court for an emergency protection order to be discharged—

(a) the child;

(b) a parent of his;

(c) any person who is not a parent of his but who has parental responsibility for him; or

(d) any person with whom he was living immediately before the making of the order.

(9) No application for the discharge of an emergency protection order shall be heard by the court before the expiry of the period of 72 hours beginning with the making of the order.

[*(10) No appeal may be made against the making of, or refusal to make, an emergency protection order or against any direction given by the court in connection with such an order.*]

[(10) No appeal may be made against—

(a) the making of, or refusal to make, an emergency protection order;
(b) the extension of, or refusal to extend, the period during which such an order is to have effect;
(c) the discharge of, or refusal to discharge, such an order; or
(d) the giving of, or refusal to give, any direction in connection with such an order.]

(11) Subsection (8) does not apply—

(a) where the person who would otherwise be entitled to apply for the emergency protection order to be discharged—

   (i) was given notice (in accordance with rules of court) of the hearing at which the order was made; and
   (ii) was present at that hearing; or

(b) to any emergency protection order the effective period of which has been extended under subsection (5).

(12) A court making an emergency protection order may direct that the applicant may, in exercising any powers which he has by virtue of the order, be accompanied by a registered medical practitioner, registered nurse or registered health visitor, if he so chooses.

Annotation

Section 45: provides for the duration of the emergency protection order and other supplemental provisions. The eight-day duration of the emergency protection order draws its inspiration from a proposal by a House of Commons social services select committee. It was recognised that there was a need to keep to a practical minimum the period for which the child is detained during which

Note: The words *in italics* within square brackets were deleted by the Courts and Legal Services Act 1990.
Note: The words within square brackets were inserted by the Courts and Legal Services Act 1990.

time there is no period of challenge by the child or those with parental responsibility for him. The eight-day period is designed to provide time for a local authority to investigate the case, decide whether or not to initiate care proceedings and obtain sufficient evidence to enable the court to decide whether to make a care order. An application to discharge the emergency protection order may be made after seventy two hours.

Section 45(1): provides that an emergency protection order has effect for the period specified in the order, which may not exceed eight days. Thus the order may be made for less. Unlike a child assessment order, which need not run on consecutive days, the emergency protection order will so run.

Section 45(2): excludes public holidays from the calculation of the eight day duration when such holidays fall on the eighth day, allowing an extra half day on the period of the eight days.

Section 45(3): provides that where an emergency protection order is obtained by the police, the period of the order will take account of the period the child was in police protection. The police are excluded from seeking child care orders under the Act but anyone may apply for an emergency protection order to protect a child's welfare. Where an emergency protection order is sought by the police they may apply on behalf of a local authority; see section 46(7).

Section 45(4): enables a person who, in the first instance, has parental responsibility acquired under an emergency protection order and, in the second, is entitled to apply for a care order under the provisions of section 31(1) to apply to the court for any emergency protection order to be extended. Thus, the police could not apply for an extension of an emergency protection order since they cannot apply for a care order under the provisions of section 31(1). The White Paper, "The Law on Child Care and Family Services", made it clear that only in exceptional circumstances would a person be permitted to apply for an extension of an emergency protection order for a further period of up to seven days to provide continued protection of the child.

Section 45(5): enables a court to extend any emergency protection order for a period of up to seven days. The purpose of the extension is to further protect the child; it is not to provide further time to prepare a care or supervision order unless the person making the application has reasonable grounds for not being ready.

Section 45(6): provides that an emergency protection order may only be extended once. A court must be satisfied that it has reasonable cause to believe that the child concerned is likely to suffer significant harm unless there is an extension. Extension hearings will be on notice.

Section 45(7): provides that the court may take into account any statement made in any report made to the court, or in any evidence given, which it considers relevant to the application. Applications to a court for the making of an emergency protection order pursuant to section 44(1) are made without offsetting statements either by the child or any person with parental responsibility. It might put the child whose welfare is being considered at greater risk if prior notice of any application under section 44(1) had to be given. Section 45(7) nevertheless, regardless of any enactment, allows the court to take into account any statement or evidence, and this may be favourable to the child or persons with parental responsibility.

Section 45(8): provides for the child, parent, any person with parental responsibilities, or any other person with whom the child was living immediately before the order was made, to apply for any emergency order to be discharged. It was a recommendation of the White Paper that there should be an opportunity for the parents or child to challenge the making of the emergency protection order and apply for its discharge on the grounds that there is no risk to the child.

Section 45(9): provides that any application for a discharge cannot be heard until seventy-two hours after the order was made. The right of a person who formerly had parental responsibility to seek the discharge of the order contrasts sharply with the former place of safety order which had a maximum duration of twenty-eight days with no right of appeal. Section 45(9) is one of those subsections which strikes a new balance between family autonomy and the protection of children.

Section 45(10): provides no right of appeal by an applicant against the decision of a court to refuse to make an emergency protection order. The welfare of a child would not be assisted by an appeals procedure once a court had made its decision. An applicant could always make a fresh application under section 31(1) for a care or supervision order where a court was satisfied that there was no reasonable cause to believe that a child was likely to suffer significant harm in accordance with section 44(1). Alternatively, an applicant could seek a child assessment order under the provisions of section 43. Similarly, no rights of appeal lie where a court has refused to discharge an emergency protection order, or where the order has been extended.

Section 45(11): provides that in the case of a person having been given notice of the original application for the emergency order and having been present at the hearing at which the order was made, such person will not be entitled to apply for a discharge of the order. It is anticipated to be rare indeed that such a notice would be served upon a person having parental responsibility for the child, since this is unlikely to be in the child's best interests.

Section 45(12): enables the court to direct that the applicant may be accompanied by a medical practitioner, nurse or health visitor when exercising powers under the order. The decision, however, lies with the applicant.

Section 46. Removal and accommodation of children by police in cases of emergency

46.—(1) Where a constable has reasonable cause to believe that a child would otherwise be likely to suffer significant harm, he may—

(a) remove the child to suitable accommodation and keep him there; or

(b) take such steps as are reasonable to ensure that the child's removal from any hospital, or other place, in which he is then being accommodated is prevented.

(2) For the purposes of this Act, a child with respect to whom a constable has exercised his powers under this section is referred to as having been taken into police protection.

(3) As soon as is reasonably practicable after taking a child into police protection, the constable concerned shall—

(a) inform the local authority within whose area the child was found of the steps that have been, and are proposed to be, taken with respect to the child under this section and the reasons for taking them;

(b) give details to the authority within whose area the child is ordinarily resident ("the appropriate authority") of the place at which the child is being accommodated;

(c) inform the child (if he appears capable of under-standing)—

(i) of the steps that have been taken with respect to him under this section and of the reasons for taking them; and

(ii) of the further steps that may be taken with respect to him under this section;

(d) take such steps as are reasonably practicable to discover the wishes and feelings of the child;

(e) secure that the case is inquired into by an officer designated for the purposes of this section by the chief officer of the police area concerned; and

(f) where the child was taken into police protection by being removed to accommodation which is not provided—

(i) by or on behalf of a local authority; or
(ii) as a refuge, in compliance with the requirements of section 51,

secure that he is moved to accommodation which is so provided.

(4) As soon as is reasonably practicable after taking a child into police protection, the constable concerned shall take such steps as are reasonably practicable to inform—

(a) the child's parents;
(b) every person who is not a parent of his but who has parental responsibility for him; and
(c) any other person with whom the child was living immediately before being taken into police protection,

of the steps that he has taken under this section with respect to the child, the reasons for taking them and the further steps that may be taken with respect to him under this section.

(5) On completing any inquiry under subsection (3)(e), the officer conducting it shall release the child from police protection unless he considers that there is still reasonable cause for believing that the child would be likely to suffer significant harm if released.

(6) No child may be kept in police protection for more than 72 hours.

(7) While a child is being kept in police protection, the designated officer may apply on behalf of the appropriate authority for an emergency protection order to be made under section 44 with respect to the child.

(8) An application may be made under subsection (7) whether or not the authority know of it or agree to its being made.

(9) While a child is being kept in police protection—

(a) neither the constable concerned nor the designated officer shall have parental responsibility for him; but
(b) the designated officer shall do what is reasonable in all the circumstances of the case for the purpose of safeguarding or promoting the child's welfare (having regard in particular to the length of the period during which the child will be so protected).

(10) Where a child has been taken into police protection, the designated officer shall allow—

(a) the child's parents;
(b) any person who is not a parent of the child but who has parental responsibility for him;
(c) any person with whom the child was living immediately before he was taken into police protection;
(d) any person in whose favour a contact order is in force with respect to the child;
(e) any person who is allowed to have contact with the child by virtue of an order under section 34; and
(f) any person acting on behalf of any of those persons,

to have such contact (if any) with the child as, in the opinion of the designated officer, is both reasonable and in the child's best interests.

(11) Where a child who has been taken into police protection is in accommodation provided by, or on behalf of, the appropriate authority, subsection (10) shall have effect as if it referred to the authority rather than to the designated officer.

Annotation

Section 46: provides for a child to be taken into police protection for up to seventy-two hours where a constable believes that the child might otherwise suffer significant harm. Section 41 replaces with significant amendments the non-criminal provisions of section 28(2) to (5) of the Children and Young Persons Act 1969. Section 46 sets out the responsibilities and powers of the police, which include power to apply for an emergency protection order on behalf of the local authority.

Section 46(1): provides a police constable with the power to protect a child from significant harm. The White Paper, "The Law on Child Care and Family Services", recommended that the police retain a power to detain a child without recourse to a magistrate in a place of protection. Note in relation to section 46(1)(b) that under the Police and Criminal Evidence Act 1984, the police may enter and search premises "to save life and limb": section 17(i)(e).

Section 46(2): provides that where a police constable acts to protect a child from significant harm the child is taken into police protection rather than police custody. The grounds for the exercise of a police constable's powers match those for an emergency protection order and should be used only in emergencies.

Section 46(3): clarifies police responsibilities while the child is in police protection and links these provisions with those for emergency protection elsewhere in this part of the Act. The child should be moved to accommodation provided by or on behalf of the local authority as soon as possible. As soon as is reasonably practicable after taking a child into police protection, the constable must secure that the case is inquired into by an officer who has been designated for this purpose. Designation is by the chief officer of the police area concerned.

Section 46(4): requires the police constable to inform the child's parents, any person having parental responsibility and any other person with whom the child was living before being taken into police protection. No parental responsibility passes to the police constable but rests with those in whom parental responsibility is vested at the time the child is taken into police protection and until such time as an emergency protection order is made, should one be applied for: see section 46(7).

Section 46(5): requires the designated officer, having enquired into the case pursuant to section 46(3)(e), to release the child unless he considers the child would be likely to suffer significant harm if he did. Such an enquiry would require to be completed within seventy-two hours: see section 46(6).

Section 46(6): limits the period for which a child may be in police protection to seventy-two hours. Under the prior law this was eight days. Within the seventy-two hours all of the requirements imposed upon the police constable and designated officer pursuant to section 46 should be completed and the designated officer should be in a situation either to release child pursuant to section 46(5) or to be able to apply for an emergency protection order on behalf of the local authority pursuant to section 46(7).

Section 46(7): provides that the designated officer may apply on behalf of the local authority for an emergency protection order in accordance with the provisions of section 44(1). The designated officer, in such event, falls within the scope of "any person" provided for in section 44(1) and permits the court not only to make an emergency protection order but also to make directions. In the event the court makes an emergency protection order, parental responsibility shall pass to the local authority on whose behalf the application was made by the designated officer.

Section 46(8): provides that a designated officer may apply for an emergency protection order whether or not a local authority knows of it or agrees to it being made. A designated officer will only apply for an emergency protection order where he feels significant harm is likely. During this time a child is in police protection, but where parental responsibility cannot be exercised over him. The Act makes it clear that delay in court proceedings is generally harmful to the child and should be avoided. Section 46(8), therefore, does not require that a local authority be advised beforehand that an emergency protection order is being applied for in its name.

Section 46(9): provides that neither a police constable nor a designated officer acquires parental responsibility for the child. This does not obviate from the designated officer the duty to take such steps as are necessary to safeguard or promote the welfare of the child, having regard in particular to the period the child will be under police protection. Such reasonable steps will fall far short of those required under the definition of parental responsibility to be found in section 3.

Section 46(10): requires the designated officer to allow the child's parents and other specified persons such contact as, in his opinion, is reasonable and in the child's interests. An order under section 46(10)(e) relating to contact may be a section 8 order or an order made under section 34.

Section 46(11): provides for the requirement of section 46(10) to apply to the local authority where the child has been moved to accommodation provided by them or on their behalf. The provisions of section 46(10) will last either until the child is returned pursuant to section 46(5) or until there is made an emergency protection order pursuant to an application made under section 46(7), at which time the provisions of section 46(11) shall be subject to any directions the court may make.

Section 47. Local authority's duty to investigate

47.—(1) Where a local authority—

(a) are informed that a child who lives, or is found, in their area—

(i) is the subject of an emergency protection order; or

(ii) is in police protection; or

(b) have reasonable cause to suspect that a child who lives, or is found, in their area is suffering, or is likely to suffer, significant harm,

the authority shall make, or cause to be made, such enquiries as they consider necessary to enable them to decide whether they should take any action to safeguard or promote the child's welfare.

(2) Where a local authority have obtained an emergency protection order with respect to a child, they shall make, or cause to be made, such enquiries as they consider necessary to enable them to decide what action they should take to safeguard or promote the child's welfare.

(3) The enquiries shall, in particular, be directed towards establishing—

(a) whether the authority should make any application to the court, or exercise any of their other powers under this Act, with respect to the child;

(b) whether, in the case of a child—

(i) with respect to whom an emergency protection order has been made; and

(ii) who is not in accommodation provided by or on behalf of the authority,

it would be in the child's best interests (while an emergency protection order remains in force) for him to be in such accommodation; and

(c) whether, in the case of a child who has been taken into police protection, it would be in the child's best interests for the authority to ask for an application to be made under section 46(7).

(4) Where enquiries are being made under subsection (1) with respect to a child, the local authority concerned shall (with a view to enabling them to determine what action, if any, to take with respect to him) take such steps as are reasonably practicable—

(a) to obtain access to him; or

(b) to ensure that access to him is obtained, on their behalf, by a person authorised by them for the purpose,

unless they are satisfied that they already have sufficient information with respect to him.

(5) Where, as a result of any such enquiries, it appears to the authority that there are matters connected with the child's education which should be investigated, they shall consult the relevant local education authority.

(6) Where, in the course of enquiries made under this section—

(a) any officer of the local authority concerned; or

(b) any person authorised by the authority to act on their behalf in connection with those enquiries—

(i) is refused access to the child concerned; or

(ii) is denied information as to his whereabouts,

the authority shall apply for an emergency protection order, a child assessment order, a care order or a supervision order with respect to the child unless they are satisfied that his welfare can be satisfactorily safeguarded without their doing so.

(7) If, on the conclusion of any enquiries or review made under this section, the authority decide not to apply for an emergency protection order, a child assessment order, a care order or a supervision order they shall—

(a) consider whether it would be appropriate to review the case at a later date; and
(b) if they decide that it would be, determine the date on which that review is to begin.

(8) Where, as a result of complying with this section, a local authority conclude that they should take action to safeguard or promote the child's welfare they shall take that action (so far as it is both within their power and reasonably practicable for them to do so).

(9) Where a local authority are conducting enquiries under this section, it shall be the duty of any person mentioned in subsection (11) to assist them with those enquiries (in particular by providing relevant information and advice) if called upon by the authority to do so.

(10) Subsection (9) does not oblige any person to assist a local authority where doing so would be unreasonable in all the circumstances of the case.

(11) The persons are—

(a) any local authority;
(b) any local education authority;
(c) any local housing authority;
(d) any health authority [or National Health Service trust]; and
(e) any person authorised by the Secretary of State for the purposes of this section.

(12) Where a local authority are making enquiries under this section with respect to a child who appears to them to be ordinarily resident within the area of another authority, they shall consult that other authority, who may undertake the necessary enquiries in their place.

Note: The words within square brackets were inserted by the Courts and Legal Services Act 1990.

Annotation

Section 47: imposes an investigative duty on a local authority in three specific circumstances: where they have reasonable cause to suspect that a child who lives or is found in their area is suffering or is likely to suffer significant harm; where they have obtained an emergency protection order in respect of a child; and where they are informed that a child who lives or is found in their area is subject to an emergency protection order or is in police protection. In all three circumstances the investigative duty is the same, namely to make or cause to be made, for example by another agency such as the NSPCC, such enquiries as they consider necessary to safeguard or promote the child's welfare. It also provides for other persons, mainly other authorities, to assist them in their enquiries.

Section 47(1): replaces the enquiry duty to be found in section 2(1) of the Children and Young Persons Act 1969 with more positive requirements. Formerly a local authority had to enquire into a case if they received information suggesting that there were grounds for bringing care proceedings in respect of a child in their area. The Review of Child Care Law proposed that there should be a more active duty to investigate any case where it is suspected that the child is suffering harm, or is likely to do so. See also the Jasmine Beckford Report, "A Child in Trust: The Report of the Panel of Inquiry into the circumstances surrounding the death of Jasmine Beckford" 1985 ISBN 0–95110680–5.

Section 47(2): imposes a duty upon a local authority to have enquiries made in order to decide whether they should take action to safeguard or promote the child's welfare where they have obtained an emergency protection order. An emergency protection order cannot be extended simply because a local authority have not made enquiries unless there is a sensible reason why they have not done so: see section 45(5). Even where the authority carry out enquiries through another agency, it is a matter for the authority to decide whether to take further action with respect to the child.

Section 47(3): provides for a series of enquiries to be made by a local authority to establish whether the authority need to exercise any of their powers under the Act with respect to the child. They may decide that an application be made to a court for a care or supervision order, or they may decide to offer services to the child or his family under Part III of the Act. The Review of Child Care Law suggested that the enquiries made should be such as are necessary to enable a local authority to decide what action, if any, they should take.

Section 47(4): provides for a local authority when carrying out their investigative duty to try to see the child so that they can properly decide whether they should take any action for his benefit. Unless they are satisfied that they already have sufficient information about the child – they may be already familiar with his present circumstances – they are required to take steps which are reasonably practicable either to obtain access to the child themselves or to ensure that access to him is obtained on their behalf by someone who is authorised by them for this purpose. This may be an officer of the NSPCC or a doctor.

Section 47(5): requires a local authority to consult with the relevant local education authority where there are matters concerning the child's education. The Children Act removes the power of a local education authority to initiate its own care proceedings but in cases of school non-attendance where care proceedings are not appropriate the local education authority can apply for a supervision order relating to educational need: see section 36.

Section 47(6): provides that where a local authority officer or a person authorised to act on behalf of a local authority is refused access to the child concerned or denied information about his whereabouts, the authority must apply for an order to protect the child unless they are satisfied that his welfare can be satisfactorily safeguarded by other means. The most common orders sought will be an emergency protection order, a child assessment order or a care or supervision order.

Section 47(7): provides that where a local authority decide not to apply for an emergency protection order, child assessment, care or supervision order, they must consider whether they should review the child's case later. If they decide to hold a review they must fix the date on which it is to begin. Certainty is in the best interests of the child.

Section 47(8): requires the local authority to take such action as they decide needs to be taken to safeguard or promote the welfare of the child if it is in their power and reasonably practicable for them to do so. For example, where a child may be at risk of ill-treatment at the hands of another person who is living on the same premises, the authority may decide to take steps other than the removal of the chiild. Cash may be provided to the person whom it is feared may ill-treat the child, so that he may find alternative accommodation: see Schedule 2, paragraph 5. Alternatively, the authority may advise and assist that person's spouse or cohabitee to apply for an order excluding him from their home. If the authority conclude that action, which they have power to take, should be taken in the child's interests, they are required to take this action pursuant to section 47(8).

Section 47(9): requires that those persons referred to in section 47(11) asked by a local authority to assist them with their enquiries shall do so provided that this is not unreasonble. As the Minister of State said during committee stage, "we have to make a sustained effort to improve the inter-agency cooperation that broke down in Cleveland, to restore inter-agency cooperation not only in Cleveland, but also to improve it throughout the country." See also Report of the Inquiry into Child Abuse in Cleveland 1987 HMSO Cm 412.

Section 47(10): provides that a person is not obliged to assist a local authority in accordance with section 47(9) if this would be unreasonable in all the circumstances. It may be unreasonable to request a local education authority to produce confidential school reports, or a local housing authority to produce confidential housing records, or a health authority to produce private medical records. Here, the age-old test of reasonableness applies, but the reasonableness has to be balanced with the commitment of the Act that the child's interest is paramout.

Section 47(11): provides a list of those persons who may be called upon to assist a local authority. The Jasmine Beckford Report declared that there were powerful reasons why the duty on local authorities or health authorities to cooperate under section 22 of the National Health Service Act 1977 should be made more specific, to include the duty to consult and the duty to assist by advice and the supply of information so as to help in the management of child care cases. Such a duty, it was argued, would operate as a positive and practical step to promote multi-disciplinary proceedings. Section 47(11) converts these declarations into law and extends the provision to any local authority, education as well as health. Probation services and police constabularies are not included but may be added, as with others, under section 47(11)(e).

Section 47(12): provides that where a local authority are investigating the circumstances of a child who usually lives in the area of another local authority, they must consult that other authority who may undertake the necessary enquiries in their area. Responsibility for any consequent course of action rests, however, with the enquiring authority.

Section 48. Powers to assist in discovery of children who may be in need of emergency protection

48.—(1) Where it appears to a court making an emergency protection order that adequate information as to the child's whereabouts—

(a) is not available to the applicant for the order; but
(b) is available to another person,

it may include in the order a provision requiring that other person to disclose, if asked to do so by the applicant, any information that he may have as to the child's whereabouts.

(2) No person shall be excused from complying with such a requirement on the ground that complying might incriminate him or his spouse of an offence; but a statement or admission made in complying shall not be admissible in evidence against either of them in proceedings for any offence other than perjury.

(3) an emergency protection order may authorise the applicant to enter premises specified by the order and search for the child with respect to whom the order is made.

(4) Where the court is satisfied that there is reasonable cause to believe that there may be another child on those premises with respect to whom an emergency protection order ought to be made, it may make an order authorising the applicant to search for that other child on those premises.

(5) Where—

(a) an order has been made under subsection (4);
(b) the child concerned has been found on the premises; and
(c) the applicant is satisfied that the grounds for making an emergency protection order exist with respect to him,

the order shall have effect as if it were an emergency protection order.

(6) Where an order has been made under subsection (4), the applicant shall notify the court of its effect.

(7) A person shall be guilty of an offence if he intentionally obstructs any person exercising the power of entry and search under subsection (3) or (4).

(8) A person guilty of an offence under subsection (7) shall be liable on summary conviction to a fine not exceeding level 3 on the standard scale.

(9) Where, on an application made by any person for a warrant under this section, it appears to the court—

(a) that a person attempting to exercise powers under an emergency protection order has been prevented from doing so by being refused entry to the premises concerned or access to the child concerned; or

(b) that any such person is likely to be so prevented from exercising any such powers,

it may issue a warrant authorising any constable to assist the person mentioned in paragraph (a) or (b) in the exercise of those powers, using reasonable force if necessary.

(10) Every warrant issued under this section shall be addressed to, and executed by, a constable who shall be accompanied by the person applying for the warrant if—

(a) that person so desires; and

(b) the court by whom the warrant is issued does not direct otherwise.

(11) A court granting an application for a warrant under this section may direct that the constable concerned may, in executing the warrant, be accompanied by a registered medical practitioner, registered nurse or registered health visitor if he so chooses.

(12) An application for a warrant under this section shall be made in the manner and form prescribed by rules of court.

(13) Wherever it is reasonably practicable to do so, an order under subsection (4), an application for a warrant under this section and any such warrant shall name the child; and where it does not name him it shall describe him as clearly as possible.

Annotation

Section 48: provides for powers to be available to the court in support of emergency protection orders. These include the power to issue a warrant authorising a police constable to enforce the applicant's rights. The warrant provision re-enacts a great deal of section 40 of the Children and Young Persons Act 1933. Section 48 also enables the court to direct that information about the child's whereabouts should be disclosed to the applicant. The section provides that the order may authorise the applicant to enter specified premises and search for the child; it also makes provision for cases where there may be another child on the premises.

Section 48(1): adopts from the Family Law Act 1986 a power for an applicant to apply to the court to compel disclosure by a person where there is reason to believe that he may have relevant information concerning the child's welfare. The former law relating to children who abscond or who are unlawfully taken away or detained was complicated and applied only to certain children in care: see also section 49.

Section 48(2): provides that no person who has been required to disclose information may refuse on the grounds that to do so might incriminate him or his spouse. Any statement made in complying with such a requirement would not, however, be admissible in evidence against them for any offence except perjury. Previously, a witness in equivalent proceedings under the Children and Young Persons Act 1969 might refuse to give evidence which would enable the court to decide what steps should be taken to protect the child concerned. In order to encourage witnesses to give evidence and to help avoid delay in children's cases (whilst awaiting the outcome of a criminal prosecution, for example) a person will no longer be able to refuse to give evidence or answer a question put to him while he gives evidence simply on the grounds of incrimination: see also section 98.

Section 48(3): gives effect to a recommendation of The White Paper, "The Law on Child Care and Family Services", that an emergency protection order may authorise the applicant to enter specified premises and search for the child the subject of the order. A constable coming to the aid of such a person will be able to use such force as may be necessary to give effect to the purpose of the order: see section 48(9).

Section 48(4): enables the court, if satisfied that there is reasonable cause to believe that there is another child on the premises in respect of whom an emergency protection order should be made, to make an order authorising the applicant to search for that child. Obstruction of this power may also be an offence; see section 48(7). The power is intended to secure that where an emergency protection order has been obtained in respect of one child, a search may be authorised for other children who may also need to be protected.

Section 48(5): provides that where the other child is found on the premises, and the applicant is satisfied that the grounds exist for making an emergency protection order in relation to that child, then the order made under section 48(4) has effect as if it were an emergency protection order. The child may also then be removed and the applicant acquires full parental responsibility for the child.

Section 48(6): requires the applicant, where an order is made under section 48(4), to notify the court of its effect. This also covers section 48(5)(c) where the applicant has exercised his judgement that the grounds for making an emergency protection order exist with respect to the other child. Otherwise an applicant may remove a child and acquire parental responsibility by the use of a discretionary power.

Section 48(7): provides that any intentional obstruction of the powers to assist in discovery of children who may be in need of emergency protection shall be an offence. Section 48(7) mirrors section 44(15) which provides for it to be a criminal offence for any person intentionally to obstruct any person exercising the power to remove or prevent the removal of a child where an emergency protection order has been made in his name.

Section 48(8): provides the penalty for any person found guilty of an offence under section 48(7). It mirrors the provision in section 44(16) which provides that a person found guilty of the offence of intentional obstruction in relation to an emergency protection order shall be liable on summary conviction to a fine. The scale of the fine is identical to that in section 44(16).

Section 48(9): enables the court, on application by any person, to issue a warrant authorising a constable to assist a person who has been prevented, or is likely to be prevented, from exercising powers under an emergency protection order. It is felt that with the addition of the warrant powers, an applicant should have sufficient legal powers to do what is necessary to protect a child in need of emergency protection.

Section 48(10): provides that the constable be accompanied by the person applying for the warrant unless the court directs otherwise. Thus an applicant will be acting in concert with the police, but responsibility for the child rests with the applicant in whom parental responsibility is vested.

Section 48(11): provides that a court may direct that the constable may be accompanied by a registered medical practitioner, registered nurse or registered health visitor if he so chooses. It mirrors section 45(12), dealing with an emergency protection order. As with section 45(12), the decision rests with the constable; the power of direction rests with the court.

Section 48(12): provides for an application for a warrant to be made in the manner and form prescribed by rules of court. Section 52, without prejudice to section 93 or any other power to make such rules, empowers that rules of court may be made with respect to the procedure to be followed in connection with proceedings under this Part of the Act.

Section 48(13): requires an order or warrant issued to name or identify the child where possible. It mirrors section 44(14) which provides that wherever possible an emergency protection order should name or identify a child to whom it relates. Rules which prevent the publication of details of children's cases which are heard in private in the High Court and county courts continue to have effect: see section 12 of the Administration of Justice Act 1960, as amended by Schedule 13 paragraph 14.

Section 49. Abduction of children in care etc.

49.—(1) A person shall be guilty of an offence if, knowingly and without lawful authority or reasonable excuse, he—

    (a) takes a child to whom this section applies away from the responsible person;

    (b) keeps such a child away from the responsible person; or

    (c) induces, assists or incites such a child to run away or stay away from the responsible person.

(2) This section applies in relation to a child who is—

    (a) in care;

    (b) the subject of an emergency protection order; or

    (c) in police protection,

and in this section "the responsible person" means any person who for the time being has care of him by virtue of the care order, the emergency protection order, or section 46, as the case may be.

(3) A person guilty of an offence under this section shall be liable on summary conviction to imprisonment for a term not exceeding six months, or to a fine not exceeding level 5 on the standard scale, or to both.

Annotation

Section 49: deals with the abduction of children in care and makes this an offence liable on summary conviction to imprisonment not exceeding six months or to a fine, or to both. The offence is that of abducting a child in care, under an emergency protection order, or in police protection, where this is done knowingly and without reasonable excuse. It replaces similar offences under the Child Care Act 1980; indeed, section 49 is a consolidation of former offences under the Child Care Act 1980 and the Children and Young Persons Act 1969.

Section 49(1): replaces similar offences defined in Part II of the Child Care Act 1980 and improves the prior law where the requirement "without reasonable excuse" did not always apply. The

White Paper, "The Law on Child Care and Family Services", proposed that there should be a single offence consisting of knowingly and, without reasonable excuse or lawful authority, taking the child or detaining or harbouring him or assisting, inducing or inciting him to run away.

Section 49(2): defines a child subject to this section as being in care, under an emergency protection order, or in police protection. However, the definition of a responsible person ensures that care is meant to cover a child the subject of a care order, not a child in care pursuant to voluntary arrangements.

Section 49(3): provides that a person guilty of an offence under this section shall be laible on summary conviction to imprisonment. Note the stiffer penalty in relation to the abduction of a child in care when compared with the standard fine for intentional obstruction as laid down in section 44(16) and section 48(8) when dealing with an emergency protection order.

Section 50. Recovery of abducted children etc.

50. — (1) Where it appears to the court that there is reason to believe that a child to whom this section applies —

(a) has been unlawfully taken away or is being unlawfully kept away from the responsible person;

(b) has run away or is staying away from the responsible person; or

(c) is missing,

the court may make an order under this section ("a recovery order").

(2) This section applies to the same children to whom section 49 applies and in this section "the responsible person" has the same meaning as in section 49.

(3) A recovery order —

(a) operates as a direction to any person who is in a position to do so to produce the child on request to any authorised person;

(b) authorises the removal of the child by any authorised person;

(c) requires any person who has information as to the child's whereabouts to disclose that information, if asked to do so, to a constable or an officer of the court;

(d) authorises a constable to enter any premises specified in the order and search for the child, using reasonable force if necessary.

(4) The court may make a recovery order only on the application of—

    (a) any person who has parental responsibility for the child by virtue of a care order or emergency protection order; or

    (b) where the child is in police protection, the designated officer.

(5) A recovery order shall name the child and—

    (a) any person who has parental responsibility for the child by virtue of a care order or emergency protection order; or

    (b) where the child is in police protection, the designated officer.

(6) Premises may only be specified under subsection (3)(d) if it appears to the court that there are reasonable grounds for believing the child to be on them.

(7) In this section—

"an authorised person" means—

(a) any person specified by the court;
(b) any constable;
(c) any person who is authorised—

    (i) after the recovery order is made; and
    (ii) by a person who has parental responsibility for the child by virtue of a care order or an emergency protection order,

to exercise any power under a recovery order; and

"the designated officer" means the officer designated for the purposes of section 46.

(8) where a person is authorised as mentioned in subsection (7)(c)—

    (a) the authorisation shall identify the recovery order; and
    (b) any person claiming to be so authorised shall, if asked to do so, produce some duly authenticated document showing that he is so authorised.

(9) A person shall be guilty of an offence if he intentionally obstructs an authorised person exercising the power under subsection (3)(b) to remove a child.

(10) a person guilty of an offence under this section shall be

liable on summary conviction to a fine not exceeding level 3 on the standard scale.

(11) No person shall be excused from complying with any request made under subsection (3)(c) on the ground that complying with it might incriminate him or his spouse of an offence; but a statement or admission made in complying shall not be admissible in evidence against either of them in proceedings for an offence other than perjury.

(12) Where a child is made the subject of a recovery order whilst being looked after by a local authority, any reasonable expenses incurred by an authorised person in giving effect to the order shall be recoverable from the authority.

(13) A recovery order shall have effect in Scotland as if it had been made by the Court of Session and as if that court had had jurisdiction to make it.

(14) In this section "the court", in relation to Northern Ireland, means a magistrates' court within the meaning of the Magistrates' Courts (Northern Ireland) Order 1981.

Annotation

Section 50: provides for the recovery of a child who has been abducted or has absconded from care or who is missing. Section 50 modifies the prior law in three ways: the power to arrest a child without warrant is repealed; a power is conferred upon a court to order that a person who has information regarding a child's whereabouts should disclose this to a constable or an officer of the court; and the legal effect of a recovery order is spelt out in a way that, in the words of the Minister of State, is more "comprehensible" than formerly.

Section 50(1): confers upon the court the power to make a recovery order. Under the prior law, where a child who was under a care or place of safety order was abducted or ran away from the person responsible for him, if he could not be found, a summons to produce the child or a search warrant might have been issued: see section 16 of the Child Care Act 1980 and section 32 of the Children and Young Persons Act 1969.

Section 50(2): applies to the same children as section 49. The responsible person defined in section 49(2) means, in practical terms, the person who is caring for him, for example a local authority foster parent or a person running a children's home where the child may have been living.

Section 50(3): defines the *modus operandi* of a recovery order

F

and reflects the view of both the White Paper, "The Law on Child Care and Family Services" and the "Review of Child Care Law", that the former power to arrest such a child without a warrant should be discontinued.

Section 50(4): provides that a recovery order may be applied for by the person who has parental responsibility for the child. It reflects the view of the White Paper, "The Law on Child Care and Family Services", that "a local authority should be able to seek an order authorising a constable, an officer of the court or a person specified by the authority to take charge of a child subject to a care order, who has absconded or been abducted": see also section 34(1) of the Family Law Act 1986 for children subject to custody orders.

Section 50(5): provides that a recovery order shall name the child and any person who has parental responsibility for him or a designated officer where the child is in police protection. It mirrors section 50(4) in that, in addition to the child, only those who have applied for the order may be named in it. Parental responsibility is not acquired by the police officer acting in furtherance of his duty in accordance with the powers conferred upon him by a recovery order.

Section 50(6): provides that premises may only be specified in a court order issued pursuant to section 50(1) where the court is satisfied that there are reasonable grounds for believing the child to be on them. A constable authorised under section 50(3)(d) may use reasonable force if necessary and this provision mirrors section 48(3) where a constable is empowered to use such force as may be necessary to give effect to the purpose of the emergency protection order.

Section 50(7): defines an authorised person for the purposes of section 50. A responsible person is generally one who carries parental responsibility in accordance with section 49(2) and section 50(4)(a). But parental responsibility is not acquired by the authority conferred upon other such persons specified in section 50(7)(a)(b) and (c)(i). A person specified by the court under section 50(7)(a) may be the court's tipstaff.

Section 50(8): provides that where a person is authorised under section 50(7)(c) such person must be able to produce a duly authenticated document providing that he is so authorised; that is where he is asked to do so. Such authorisation shall identify the recovery order and therefore is specific to that order; the same identification cannot be used for another recovery order.

Section 50(9): provides that it shall be an offence intentionally to obstruct a person authorised to remove a child: see also section 44(15) which provides for it to be a criminal offence for any person intentionally to obstruct any person exercising the power under section 44(4)(b) to remove or prevent the removal of a child where an emergency protection order has been made in his name: see also section 48(7) which provides that any intentional obstruction of the powers to assist in discovery of children who may be in need of emergency protection shall be an offence.

Section 50(10): provides for the scale of fine for the offence of intentional obstruction under section 50(9). Note the stiffer penalty in relation to the abduction of a child in care under section 49(3) when compared with the standard fine for intentional obstruction as laid down in section 44(16) and section 48(8) when dealing with an emergency protection order.

Section 50(11): provides that a person may not refuse to comply with a request to disclose information on the grounds of incrimination: see also section 50(3)(c). It mirrors section 48(2) that no person who has been required to disclose information may refuse on the grounds that to do so might incriminate him or his spouse: see also section 98.

Section 50(12): provides that where a child who is being looked after by a local authority is placed under a recovery order, the reasonable expenses of his recovery under the order may be charged to that local authority.

Section 50(13): provides that recovery orders may be enforced in Scotland as if they had been made by a court of session there. This in accordance with a recommendation of the White Paper, "The Law on Child Care and Family Services", that consideration would be given to permitting court orders for the recovery of a child to be served and enforced throughout the United Kingdom. It is also the hope that they be served and enforced in the Isle of Man and the Channel Islands: see regulations under section 101.

Section 50(14): provides that recovery orders may be made by a court in England, Wales or Northern Ireland. They may only be served and enforced in Scotland. Generally, the Children Act applies only to England and Wales. There are important exceptions in Part X dealing with child minding and day care for young children, which applies to Scotland. There are also a number of consequential amendments made to the law in Scotland and Northern Ireland: see section 90.

Section 51. Refuges for children at risk

51. — (1) Where it is proposed to use a voluntary home or registered children's home to provide a refuge for children who appear to be at risk of harm, the Secretary of State may issue a certificate under this section with respect to that home.

(2) Where a local authority or voluntary organisation arrange for a foster parent to provide such a refuge, the Secretary of State may issue a certificate under this section with respect to that foster parent.

(3) In subsection (2) "foster parent" means a person who is, or who from time to time is, a local authority foster parent or a foster parent with whom children are placed by a voluntary organisation.

(4) The Secretary of State may by regulations—

(a) make provision as to the manner in which certificates may be issued;
(b) impose requirements which must be complied with while any certificate is in force; and
(c) provide for the withdrawal of certificates in prescribed circumstances.

(5) Where a certificate is in force with respect to a home, none of the provisions mentioned in subsection (7) shall apply in relation to any person providing a refuge for any child in that home.

(6) Where a certificate is in force with respect to a foster parent, none of those provisions shall apply in relation to the provision by him of a refuge for any child in accordance with arrangements made by the local authority or voluntary organisation.

(7) The provisions are—

(a) section 49;
(b) section 71 of the Social Work (Scotland) Act 1968 (harbouring children who have absconded from residential establishments etc.), so far as it applies in relation to anything done in England and Wales;
(c) section 32(3) of the Children and Young Persons Act 1969 (compelling, persuading, inciting or assisting any person to be absent from detention, etc.), so far as it applies in relation to anything done in England and Wales;
(d) section 2 of the Child Abduction Act 1984.

Annotation

Section 51: provides that where it is proposed to use a voluntary home or registered children's home to provide a refuge for children who appear to be at risk of harm, such home may be issued with a certificate by the Secretary of State. Where such a certificate is in force those running the home, whether as a home or as foster parents, cannot be prosecuted for offences involving, for example, harbouring. Regulations which the Secretary of State may impose under section 51(4) are designed to impose rigorous requirements on those homes, and those acting for the Secretary of State are to examine the credentials of those seeking certificates with great care: Minister of State for Health, Hansard Col 609 23 October 1989.

Section 51(1): provides for the issue of a certificate. There is no statutory duty imposed upon the Secretary of State to issue such a certificate, only a discretion; this leaves it to the voluntary home or registered children's home to ensure that it seeks the appropriate certificate so that it falls within the provisions, and is granted the relief, of section 51. Assistance may be rendered in this regard by a local authority or voluntary organisation connected with the home and who have responsibility for the placement of children at risk within its confines.

Section 51(2): provides for the issue of a certificate to a foster parent. Again, since there is no statutory duty upon the Secretary of State to issue such a certificate, only a discretion, this leaves it to the foster parent to ensure the appropriate certificate is obtained so that the foster parent falls within the provisions of section 51.

Section 51(3): defines foster parent for the purpose of section 51(2). A foster parent defined by section 51(3) is likely to be a voluntary organisation foster parent rather than a foster parent on the books of a local authority.

Section 51(4): provides for regulations, the purpose of which is to permit homes – for example, those run by the Children's Society – which are places of refuge for children at risk to be free from potential prosecution, provided they act in accordance with the regulations issued by the Secretary of State. A requirement imposed by the Secretary of State will be that the person running the home must notify the police of the reception of a child.

Section 51(5): provides that immunity is given to those who provide refuge in a voluntary or registered children's home, such as those run by the Children's Society, or as a local authority, where a certificate is issued by the Secretary of State pursuant to section 51(5) and (6).

Section 51(6): provides that immunity is given to those who provide refuge, that is to say a foster parent, who is likely to be a voluntary organisation foster parent, not a foster parent on the books of a local authority, where a certificate is issued by the Secretary of State pursuant to section 51(5) and (6).

Section 51(7): ensures that where a person provides a refuge to a child who is at risk of harm, that is to say a child who is in care, the subject of an emergency protection order or in police protection, or who commits other child care offences defined in section 51(7), such a person shall not be criminally liable.

Section 52. Rules and regulations

52.—(1) Without prejudice to section 93 or any other power to make such rules, rules of court may be made with respect to the procedure to be followed in connection with proceedings under this Part.

(2) The rules may, in particular make provision—

    (a) as to the form in which any application is to be made or direction is to be given;

    (b) prescribing the persons who are to be notified of—

        (i) the making, or extension, of an emergency protection order; or

        (ii) the making of an application under section 45(4) or (8) or 46(7); and

    (c) as to the content of any such notification and the manner in which, and person by whom, it is to be given.

(3) The Secretary of State may by regulations provide that, where—

    (a) an emergency protection order has been made with respect to a child;

    (b) the applicant for the order was not the local authority within whose area the child is ordinarily resident; and

    (c) that local authority are of the opinion that it would be in the child's best interests for the applicant's responsibilities under the order to be transferred to them,

that authority shall (subject to their having complied with any requirements imposed by the regulations) be treated, for the purposes of this Act, as though they and not the original applicant had applied for, and been granted, the order.

(4) Regulations made under subsection (3) may, in particular, make provision as to—

    (a) the considerations to which the local authority shall have regard in forming an opinion as mentioned in subsection (3)(c); and

(b) the time at which responsibility under any emergency protection order is to be treated as having been transferred to a local authority.

Annotation

Section 52: provides for the making of rules of court in relation to the emergency protection of children and enables the Secretary of State to make regulations providing for the transfer of the benefit of an emergency protection order to a local authority where the local authority was not the applicant. Section 52 also links with section 47(2) which requires the local authority, where a child in their area is subject to an emergency protection order, to consider whether they should take any action to safeguard or promote the child's welfare.

Section 52(1): provides for the making of rules of court in relation to Part V of the Act dealing with the protection of children. This does not prejudice the terms of section 93 which deal with the power to make rules of court and regulations dealing with the entire Act.

Section 52(2): provides that rules of court may be made to cover the making or extension of an emergency protection order, the making of an application by any person who has parental responsibility for a child as a result of an emergency protection order, or a person who may seek to apply for the discharge of an emergency protection order, or where an application is made by a designated police officer.

Section 52(3): provides for the making of regulations to enable the local authority in whose area a child usually lives to take over the responsibility for a child who is subject to an emergency protection order. The local authority will then have parental responsibilty for the child and will take the decisions about where the child will be accommodated and whether an application should be made for the order to be extended.

Section 52(4): provides for further regulations to define the considerations to which a local authority shall have regard. Before transfer of parental responsibility may take place the authority will have to observe the requirements of the regulations, such as consultation with the original applicant, and where that person is the NSPCC, obtaining their consent to the transfer.

PART VI

COMMUNITY HOMES

Section 53. Provision of community homes by local authorities

53.—(1) Every local authority shall make such arrangements as they consider appropriate for securing that homes ("community homes") are available—

(a) for the care and accommodation of children looked after by them; and

(b) for purposes connected with the welfare of children (whether or not looked after by them),

and may do so jointly with one or more other local authorities.

(2) In making such arrangements, a local authority shall have regard to the need for ensuring the availability of accommodation—

(a) of different descriptions; and

(b) which is suitable for different purposes and the requirements of different descriptions of children.

(3) A community home may be a home—

(a) provided, managed, equipped and maintained by a local authority; or

(b) provided by a voluntary organisation but in respect of which a local authority and the organisation—

(i) propose that, in accordance with an instrument of management, the management, equipment and maintenance of the home shall be the responsibility of the local authority; or

(ii) so propose that the management, equipment and maintenance of the home shall be the responsibility of the voluntary organisation.

(4) Where a local authority are to be responsible for the management of a community home provided by a voluntary organisation, the authority shall designate the home as a controlled community home.

(5) Where a voluntary organisation are to be responsible for the management of a community home provided by the organisation, the local authority shall designate the home as an assisted community home.

(6) Schedule 4 shall have effect for the purpose of supplementing the provisions of this Part.

Annotation

Section 53: deals with the provision of community homes by a local authority and introduces Part VI of the Act which, together with Schedule 4, replaces with certain amendments Part IV of the Child Care Act 1980. Section 53 replaces section 31 of the Child Care Act 1980, which required a local authority to make arrangements for the provision of community homes to accommodate children looked after by them, and for purposes connected with their welfare.

Section 53(1): replaces section 31(1) of the Child Care Act 1980. It also replaces the terminology that a child is "in the care" of a local authority with the phrase that a child is "looked after" by them in accordance with other provisions of the Act: see also section 22(1). A child is looked after by a local authority if he is in their care or provided with accommodation by the authority in the exercise of their social service functions.

Section 53(2): re-enacts section 31(2) of the Child Care Act 1980 and requires a local authority to have regard to the need to provide accommodation of different descriptions suitable for different children and purposes. Note that so far as is reasonably practicable and consistent with the child's welfare, accommodation should be provided which is near to the child's home; also where accommodation is provided for siblings they should be accommodated together and, where a child is disabled, so far as is reasonably practicable, accommodation should not be unsuitable to his needs: see section 23(7)(a)(b) and section 23(8).

Section 53(3): re-enacts section 31(3) of the Child Care Act 1980 and provides that such homes may be provided by the local authority. Where they are so provided they are designated community homes. For the management and conduct of such community homes see Schedule 4 Part I.

Section 53(4): provides that where the home is managed by a local authority but provided by a voluntary organisation, the home shall be designed as a controlled community home. For the management and conduct of controlled community homes see Schedule 4 Part II.

Section 53(5): provides that where a home is managed, equipped and maintained by the voluntary organisation it is designated an assisted community home. For the management and conduct of such assisted community homes see Schedule 4 Part II.

Section 53(6): gives effect to the whole of Schedule 4, including Parts I, II and III, which concern the making of instruments of management for and management of such homes and regulations with respect to their conduct. The revised regulations will govern placement and the welfare of children living in them.

Section 54. Directions that premises be no longer used for community home

54.—(1) Where it appears to the Secretary of State that—

(a) any premises used for the purposes of a community home are unsuitable for those purposes; or
(b) the conduct of a community home—

    (i) is not in accordance with regulations made by him under paragraph 4 of Schedule 4; or
    (ii) is otherwise unsatisfactory,

he may, by notice in writing served on the responsible body, direct that as from such date as may be specified in the notice the premises shall not be used for the purposes of a community home.

(2) Where—

(a) the Secretary of State has given a direction under subsection (1); and
(b) the direction has not been revoked,

he may at any time by order revoke the instrument of management for the home concerned.

(3) For the purposes of subsection (1), the responsible body—

(a) in relation to a community home provided by a local authority, is that local authority;
(b) in relation to a controlled community home, is the local authority specified in the home's instrument of management; and
(c) in relation to an assisted community home, is the voluntary organisation by which the home is provided.

Annotation

Section 54: re-enacts section 40 of the Child Care Act 1980 and enables the Secretary of State to direct that specified premises shall no longer be used for the purpose of a community home, or a controlled or assisted community home. Section 54 provides that he gives such directions by notice in writing and that he then revokes the instrument of management for the home concerned.

Section 54(1): replaces section 40(1) of the Child Care Act 1980 and provides that the Secretary of State may, by giving notice in writing to the responsible body as defined in section 54(3), direct that specified premises be no longer used for the purposes of a community home. He may do so where it appears to him that the premises are unsuitable for that purpose, or where the conduct of the home is not in accordance with the regulations or is otherwise unsatisfactory.

Section 54(2): enables the Secretary of State to revoke the instrument of management for the home after giving a direction under section 54(1), provided he has not revoked that direction.

Section 54(3): defines "responsible body" as referred to in section 54(1) and links such responsible body to the definitions of maintained community home, controlled community home and assisted community home to be found in section 53(3)(4) and (5).

Section 55. Determination of disputes relating to controlled and assisted community homes

55. — (1) Where any dispute relating to a controlled community home arises between the local authority specified in the home's instrument of management and —

(a) the voluntary organisation by which the home is provided; or

(b) any other local authority who have placed, or desire or are required to place, in the home a child who is looked after by them,

the dispute may be referred by either party to the Secretary of State for his determination.

(2) Where any dispute relating to an assisted community home arises between the voluntary organisation by which the home is provided and any local authority who have placed, or desire to place, in the home a child who is looked after by them, the dispute may be referred by either party to the Secretary of State for his determination.

(3) Where a dispute is referred to the Secretary of State under this section he may, in order to give effect to his determination of the dispute, give such directions as he thinks fit to the local authority or voluntary organisation concerned.

(4) This section applies even though the matter in dispute may be one which, under or by virtue of Part II of Schedule 4, is reserved for the decision, or is the responsibility, of —

(a) the local authority specified in the home's instrument of management; or

(b) (as the case may be) the voluntary organisation by which the home is provided.

(5) Where any trust deed relating to a controlled or assisted community home contains provision whereby a bishop or any other ecclesiastical or denominational authority has power to decide questions relating to religious instruction given in the home, no dispute which is capable of being dealt with in accordance with that provision shall be referred to the Secretary of State under this section.

(6) In this Part "trust deed", in relation to a voluntary home, means any instrument (other than an instrument of management) regulating—

(a) the maintenance, management or conduct of the home; or

(b) the constitution of a body of managers or trustees of the home.

Annotation

Section 55: deals with the determination of disputes relating to controlled and assisted community homes and replaces section 42 of the Child Care Act 1980. It enables the Secretary of State, upon referral by either party, to determine any dispute between a local authority and a voluntary organisation relating to a controlled or assisted community home, or, in the case of a controlled community home, a dispute between local authorities. This applies even though the decision is, by virtue of Schedule 4, the responsibility of a local authority or voluntary organisation. It does not, however, apply where the question relates to religious instruction in the home and where a trust deed provides for an ecclesiastical authority to decide such a question.

Section 55(1): replaces section 42(1) of the Child Care Act 1980 and provides that where, in respect of a controlled community home, a dispute between the local authority named in the instrument of management and either the voluntary organisation providing the home, or with another local authority who have placed, or desire to place, a child in the home, arises, then any party may refer the matter to the Secretary of State for determination.

Section 55(2): re-enacts section 42(2) of the Child Care Act 1980. Section 55(2) makes a similar provision concerning assisted community homes where there is a dispute between the voluntary organisation and a local authority who have placed, or who wish to place, a child in the home.

Section 55(3): replaces section 42(3) of the Child Care Act 1980 and enables the Secretary of State to give the local authority or voluntary organisation directions as he thinks fit to determine the dispute.

Section 55(4): replaces section 42(4) of the Child Care Act 1980 and provides that section 55 applies even though the matter concerned may be the responsibility of the local authority or a voluntary organisation under Schedule 4 Part II dealing with the management of community homes.

Section 55(5): re-enacts section 42(5) of the Child Care Act 1980 and prevents the Secretary of State from determining disputes concerning religious instruction in the home in cases where power to determine such disputes is given to an ecclesiastical or denominational authority under a trust deed relating to the home.

Section 55(6): defines "trust deed" for the purposes of this part of the Act.

Section 56. Discontinuance by voluntary organisation of controlled or assisted community home

56.—(1) The voluntary organisation by which a controlled or assisted community home is provided shall not cease to provide the home except after giving to the Secretary of State and the local authority specified in the home's instrument of management not less than two years' notice in writing of their intention to do so.

(2) A notice under subsection (1) shall specify the date from which the voluntary organisation intend to cease to provide the home as a community home.

(3) Where such a notice is given and is not withdrawn before the date specified in it, the home's instrument of management shall cease to have effect on that date and the home shall then cease to be a controlled or assisted community home.

(4) Where a notice is given under subsection (1) and the home's managers give notice in writing to the Secretary of State that they are unable or unwilling to continue as its managers until the date specified in the subsection (1) notice, the Secretary of State may by order—

(a) revoke the home's instrument of management; and
(b) require the local authority who were specified in that instrument to conduct the home until—

(i) the date specified in the subsection (1) notice; or
(ii) such earlier date (if any) as may be specified for the purposes of this paragraph in the order,

as if it were a community home provided by the local authority.

(5) Where the Secretary of State imposes a requirement under subsection (4)(b) —

(a) nothing in the trust deed for the home shall affect the conduct of the home by the local authority;

(b) the Secretary of State may by order direct that for the purposes of any provision specified in the direction and made by or under any enactment relating to community homes (other than this section) the home shall, until the date or earlier date specified as mentioned in subsection (4)(b), be treated as a controlled or assisted community home;

(c) except in so far as the Secretary of State so directs, the home shall until that date be treated for the purposes of any such enactment as a community home provided by the local authority; and

(d) on the date or earlier date specified as mentioned in subsection (4)(b) the home shall cease to be a community home.

Annotation

Section 56: provides for the discontinuance by a voluntary organisation of a controlled or assisted community home and re-enacts section 43 of the Child Care Act 1980. Section 56 provides for the cessation of the provision of a controlled or assisted community home by a voluntary organisation, with two years notice required to be given to the Secretary of State. Where the home's managers are unable or unwilling to continue the home for the requisite two years, the Secretary of State may require a local authority to conduct the home until the expiry of the two-year period, or until an earlier date which he may specify, as if it were a community home provided by them.

Section 56(1): replaces section 43(1) of the Child Care Act 1980 and provides that a voluntary organisation shall not cease to conduct a controlled or assisted community home which it provides unless it gives in writing to the Secretary of State and the local authority two years notice of its intention to do so.

Section 56(2): replaces section 43(2) of the Child Care Act 1980 and provides that notice given under section 56(1) shall give the date on which the home shall cease to be provided.

Section 56(3): replaces section 43(2) of the Child Care Act 1980 and provides that the instrument of management for the home shall cease to have effect on the date given in the notice unless the notice is withdrawn before that date.

Section 56(4): replaces section 43(4) of the Child Care Act 1980 and enables the Secretary of State to require a local authority to conduct a controlled or assisted community home as if it were a community home provided by them, whenever the managers of the home are unable or unwilling to continue the home until the date specified in the notice. A local authority should continue to conduct the home until that date, or until such earlier date as the Secretary of State may specify.

Section 56(5): replaces section 43(5) of the Child Care Act 1980.

Section 57. Closure by local authority of controlled or assisted community home

57.—(1) The local authority specified in the instrument of management for a controlled or assisted community home may give —

(a) the Secretary of State; and
(b) the voluntary organisation by which the home is provided,

not less than two years' notice in writing of their intention to withdraw their designation of the home as a controlled or assisted community home.

(2) A notice under subsection (1) shall specify the date ("the specified date") on which the designation is to be withdrawn.

(3) Where —

(a) a notice is given under subsection (1) in respect of a controlled or assisted community home;
(b) the home's managers give notice in writing to the Secretary of State that they are unable or unwilling to continue as managers until the specified date; and
(c) the managers' notice is not withdrawn,

the Secretary of State may by order revoke the home's instrument of management from such date earlier than the specified date as may be specified in the order.

(4) Before making an order under subsection (3), the Secretary of State shall consult the local authority and the voluntary organisation.

(5) Where a notice has been given under subsection (1) and is not withdrawn, the home's instrument of management shall cease to have effect on—

(a) the specified date; or

(b) where an earlier date has been specified under subsection (3), that earlier date,

and the home shall then cease to be a community home.

Annotation

Section 57: provides for the closure by a local authority of a controlled or assisted community home. It re-enacts section 43A of the Child Care Act 1980 and enables a local authority named in the instrument of management of a controlled or assisted community home to give at least two years' notice to the Secretary of State and the voluntary organisation providing the home of its intention to withdraw the designation. If the home's managers are unable to unwilling to continue the home for such a period, the Secretary of State, after consulting the local authority and the voluntary organisation, may revoke the home's instrument of management at an earlier date.

Section 57(1): replaces section 43A(1) of the Child Care Act 1980 and enables a local authority to give notice of its intention to withdraw the designation of the home.

Section 57(2): requires the notice given under section 57(1) to specify the date on which the designation of the home will be withdrawn.

Section 57(3): provides that the Secretary of State may revoke the home's instrument of management on an earlier date if, notice having been given under section 57(1), the home's managers give notice that they are unable or unwilling to continue to conduct the home until the specified date and that notice is not withdrawn.

Section 57(4): provides for consultation wih the local authority and the voluntary organisation.

Section 57(5): replaces section 43A(5) and (6) of the Child Care Act 1980 and provides that the home shall cease to be a community home on the date given in the notice, or on an earlier date specified by the Secretary of State under section 57(3), provided the notice of intention to close the home has not been withdrawn.

Section 58. Financial provisions applicable on cessation of controlled or assisted community home or disposal etc. of premises

58.—(1) Where—

(a) the instrument of management for a controlled or assisted community home is revoked or otherwise ceases to have effect under section 54(2), 56(3) or (4)(a) or 57(3) or (5); or

(b) any premises used for the purposes of such a home are (at any time after 13th January 1987) disposed of, or put to use otherwise than for those purposes,

the proprietor shall become liable to pay compensation ("the appropriate compensation") in accordance with this section.

(2) Where the instrument of management in force at the relevant time relates —

(a) to a controlled community home; or
(b) to an assisted community home which, at any time before the instrument came into force, was a controlled community home,

the appropriate compensation is a sum equal to that part of the value of any premises which is attributable to expenditure incurred in relation to the premises, while the home was a controlled community home, by the authority who were then the responsible authority.

(3) Where the instrument of management in force at the relevant time relates —

(a) to an assisted community home; or
(b) to a controlled community home which, at any time before the instrument came into force, was an assisted community home,

the appropriate compensation is a sum equal to that part of the value of the premises which is attributable to the expenditure of money provided by way of grant under section 82, section 65 of the Children and Young Persons Act 1969 or section 82 of the Child Care Act 1980.

(4) Where the home is, at the relevant time, conducted in premises which formerly were used as an approved school or were an approved probation hostel or home, the appropriate compensation is a sum equal to that part of the value of the premises which is attributable to the expenditure —

(a) of sums paid towards the expenses of the managers of an approved school under section 104 of the Children and Young Persons Act 1933; or
(b) of sums paid under section 51(3)(c) of the Powers of Criminal Courts Act 1973 in relation to expenditure on approved probation hostels or homes.

(5) The appropriate compensation shall be paid—

    (a) in the case of compensation payable under subsection (2), to the authority who were the responsible authority at the relevant time; and

    (b) in any other case, to the Secretary of State.

(6) In this section—

"disposal" includes the grant of a tenancy and any other conveyance, assignment, transfer, grant, variation or extinguishment of an interest in or right over land, whether made by instrument or otherwise;

"premises" means any premises or part of premises (including land) used for the purposes of the home and belonging to the proprietor;

"the proprietor" means—

    (a) the voluntary organisation by which the home is, at the relevant time, provided; or

    (b) if the premises are not, at the relevant time, vested in that organisation, the persons in whom they are vested;

"the relevant time" means the time immediately before the liability to pay arises under subsection (1); and

"the responsible authority" means the local authority specified in the instrument of management in question.

(7) For the purposes of this section an event of a kind mentioned in subsection (1)(b) shall be taken to have occurred—

    (a) in the case of a disposal, on the date on which the disposal was completed or, in the case of a disposal which is effected by a series of transactions, the date on which the last of those transactions was completed;

    (b) in the case of premises which are put to different use, on the date on which they first begin to be put to their new use.

(8) The amount of any sum payable under this section shall be determined in accordance with such arrangements—

    (a) as may be agreed between the voluntary organisation by which the home is, at the relevant time, provided and the responsible authority or (as the case may be) the Secretary of State; or

    (b) in default of agreement, as may be determined by the Secretary of State.

(9) With the agreement of the responsible authority or (as the case may be) the Secretary of State, the liability to pay any sum under this section may be discharged, in whole or in part, by the transfer of any premises.

(10) This section has effect regardless of—

(a) anything in any trust deed for a controlled or assisted community home;

(b) the provisions of any enactment or instrument governing the disposition of the property of a voluntary organisation.

Annotation

Section 58: replaces with amendments section 44 of the Child Care Act 1980. The amendments arise out of an unreported case entitled *Dept of Health and Social Security* v. *Norton and Others*. The judge held in that case that when a home ceased to be a community home in the circumstances defined in section 44 of the Child Care Act 1980, the home had to be valued as existing at the date of closure and the parts of the home disposed of prior to closure could not be taken into account. Paragraph 83 of the White Paper, "The Law on Child Care and Family Services" called for a change in the law to provide that, when premises or parts of premises used for the purposes of a controlled or assisted community home are disposed of or put to alternative use before the home's designation as a community home has been withdrawn, that proportion of the value of the premises or parts disposed of, or put to alternative use, which is attributable to the expenditure of public money, will fall to be repaid by the voluntary organisation providing the home. Where the home is vested in trustees repayment will fall upon them.

Section 58(1): provides that the proprietor of a controlled or assisted community home shall repay any increase in the value of premises which is attributable to the expenditure of public money on these premises whenever they are disposed of or put to alternative use, or where the instrument of management is revoked. The date of 13 January 1987 is the date of the White Paper entitled "The Law on Child Care and Family Services" and is an example of retrospective legislation.

Section 58(2): provides that where the home is a controlled community home or is an assisted community home which was a controlled community home, then the repayment of the appropriate compensation shall be made to the authority specified in the instrument of management.

Section 58(3): provides that where the home is an assisted community home, or is a controlled community home which has been an assisted community home, the repayment should be to the Secretary of State. Reference is made to the expenditure of money provided by a grant under section 82 of the Child Care Act 1980, which is repealed in its entirety by the Children Act.

Section 58(4): re-enacts section 44(5) of the Child Care Act 1980 and makes similar provision in respect of premises which formerly were used as an approved school or an approved probation hostel or home.

Section 58(5): provides for the destination of the compensation.

Section 58(6): provides appropriate definitions for the purposes of section 58.

Section 58(7): makes new provisions regarding the date on which an event – disposal or the putting to alternative use of premises under section 58(1)(b) should be taken to have occurred. In the case of disposal, it is the date the disposal was completed or, if a series of transactions was undertaken, the date of the last transaction. For alternative use, it is the day the premises are first used for the new purpose.

Section 58(8): provides that where the amount to be repaid cannot be decided by agreement between the voluntary organisation and the local authority or Secretary of State, then the amount will be determined by the Secretary of State.

Section 58(9): replaces section 44(6) of the Child Care Act 1980 and permits any liability arising under this section to be discharged in whole or in part by the transfer of any premises, with the agreement of the local authority or Secretary of State, as appropriate.

Section 58(10): replaces section 44(7) of the Child Care Act 1980, providing that section 58 has effect regardless of anything in any trust deed of the relevant community home, or in any enactment or instrument relating to the disposal of the property of a voluntary organisation.

PART VII

VOLUNTARY HOMES AND VOLUNTARY ORGANISATIONS

Section 59. Provision of accommodation by voluntary organisations

59.—(1) Where a voluntary organisation provide accommodation for a child, they shall do so by—

(a) placing him (subject to subsection (2)) with—

(i) a family;
(ii) a relative of his; or
(iii) any other suitable person,

on such terms as to payment by the organisation and otherwise as the organisation may determine;

(b) maintaining him in a voluntary home;
(c) maintaining him in a community home;
(d) maintaining him in a registered children's home;
(e) maintaining him in a home provided by the Secretary of State under section 82(5) on such terms as the Secretary of State may from time to time determine; or
(f) making such other arrangements (subject to subsection (3)) as seem appropriate to them.

(2) The Secretary of State may make regulations as to the placing of children with foster parents by voluntary organisations and the regulations may, in particular, make provision which (with any necessary modifications) is similar to the provision that may be made under section 23(2)(a).

(3) The Secretary of State may make regulations as to the arrangements which may be made under subsection (1)(f) and the regulations may in particular make provision which (with any necessary modifications) is similar to the provision that may be made under section 23(2)(f).

(4) The Secretary of State may make regulations requiring any voluntary organisation who are providing accommodation for a child—

(a) to review his case; and
(b) to consider any representations (including any complaint) made to them by any person falling within a prescribed class of person,

in accordance with the provisions of the regulations.

(5) Regulations under subsection (4) may in particular make

provision which (with any necessary modifications) is similar to the provision that may be made under section 26.

(6) Regulations under subsections (2) to (4) may provide that any person who, without reasonable excuse, contravenes or fails to comply with a regulation shall be guilty of an offence and liable on summary conviction to a fine not exceeding level 4 on the standard scale.

Annotation

Section 59: provides for the accommodation of a child by a voluntary organisation and the making of regulations by the Secretary of State. A voluntary organisation is a body, other than a public or local authority, whose activities are not carried on for profit: see section 105(1). When it accommodates children, it does so chiefly in voluntary homes and community homes as these are referred to in section 59(1)(b) and (c), or by placing them with foster parents. The Children Act updates those provisions of the Child Care Act 1980 which applied to those placements. Under that Act, children were said to be "in the care of a voluntary organisation". To avoid confusion, the word care is not used by the Children Act in this context; rather children are referred to as provided with accommodation by the organisation.

Section 59(1): provides for the placement of a child by a voluntary organisation. Note that the return of a child to a parent or another person with parental responsiblity for him is not considered to be a placement: hence where section 59(1) refers to placement within a family, or with a relative or other suitable person, no reference is made to those persons who may have parental responsibility. Wherever the child is placed, the general duties of the voluntary organisation are the same: see section 61.

Section 59(2): provides that where a voluntary organisation places a child with foster parents, the placement will be governed by regulation-making powers which are equivalent to those which apply to local authorities when they use foster parents. If a voluntary organisation places a child on behalf of a local authority, the child is treated as placed with local authority foster parents: see section 23(2)(a).

Section 59(3): provides that the Secretary of State may make regulations similar to those under section 23(2)(f). Section 23(2) sets out a range of options for a local authority. The purpose of regulations under section 59(3) is to ensure that the duties and functions of a voluntary organisation towards children accommodated by them are the same as those which apply to a local authority.

Section 59(4): provides for the Secretary of State to make regulations for review of a case or to consider representations. Section 59(4)(a) seeks to bring a voluntary organisation into line with a local authority to review the case of every child who is looked after by them.

Section 59(5): provides that regulations under section 59(4) should mirror those under section 26. Section 26 emphasises the need to seek the views of the child, so far as is practicable, and also the views of parents or others with parental responsiblity, or those who have an interest, before any review is conducted.

Section 59(6): provides that it be an offence not to comply with regulations and sets the fine, on summary conviction, in accordance with the standard scale. Note that the failure to comply with regulations under section 59(6) makes the offender liable to a level 4 fine, whereas to carry on a voluntary home in contravention of section 60 incurs a liability to a level 5 fine: see Schedule 5 paragraph (5) and (6).

Section 60. Registration and regulation of voluntary homes

60. — (1) No voluntary home shall be carried on unless it is registered in a register to be kept for the purposes of this section by the Secretary of State.

(2) The register may be kept by means of a computer.

(3) In this Act "voluntary home" means any home or other institution providing care and accommodation for children which is carried on by a voluntary organisation but does not include —

(a) a nursing home, mental nursing home or residential care home;
(b) a school;
(c) any health service hospital;
(d) any community home;
(e) any home or other institution provided, equipped and maintained by the Secretary of State; or
(f) any home which is exempted by regulations made for the purposes of this section by the Secretary of State.

(4) Schedule 5 shall have effect for the purpose of supplementing the provisions of this Part.

Annotation

Section 60: provides for the registration and regulation of voluntary homes and re-enacts section 57(1) of the Child Care Act 1980. Note that a voluntary organisation cannot acquire parental responsibility without the authority of a court. Where appropriate a local authority may apply for a care order under section 31, or a voluntary organisation may apply for a section 8 order with or without leave, to prevent the removal of a child whom they are accommodating. But even without a court order it will always be possible for the voluntary organisation caring for a child to do what is necessary to safeguard and promote his welfare.

Section 60(1): re-enacts section 57(1) of the Child Care Act 1980 and provides that, unlike a children's home, a voluntary home shall be registered with the Secretary of State. Schedule 5 paragraph 7 deals with regulations which govern the placement of children in voluntary homes, the conduct of the homes and the welfare of children living there.

Section 60(2): introduces a new provision, that the Secretary of State shall be able to maintain the register of voluntary homes by means of a computer.

Section 60(3): provides that a voluntary home does not include a hospital, a school, a residential care home, a nursing home or certain other homes. Note that regulations will provide that certain persons are disqualified from involvement in voluntary homes without consent: see Schedule 5 paragraph 8.

Section 60(4): provides that Schedule 5 shall have effect for the purposes of supplementing the provisions of sections 59, 60, 61 and 62. These sections, with Schedule 5, replace with certain amendments the former provisions of Part VI of the Child Care Act 1980. Sections 64, 65, 66 and 67 of the Child Care Act 1980 dealing with a local authority's power to vest parental rights of a child in a voluntary organisation by means of administrative resolution are not replaced. Powers under section 64 have been used rarely and existing resolutions will be brought to an end six months after the Act comes into force: see Schedule 14, paragraph 31. Section 63 of the Child Care Act 1980 also empowered voluntary organisations to arrange for children to emigrate, but in future they will be subject to the general law regarding removal of children: see Schedule 12, paragraph 37 and Schedule 15.

Section 61. Duties of voluntary organisations

61.—(1) Where a child is accommodated by or on behalf of a voluntary organisation, it shall be the duty of the organisation—

    (a) to safeguard and promote his welfare;

    (b) to make such use of the services and facilities available for children cared for by their own parents as appears to the organisation reasonable in his case; and

(c) to advise, assist and befriend him with a view to promoting his welfare when he ceases to be so accommodated.

(2) Before making any decision with respect to any such child the organisation shall, so far as is reasonably practicable, ascertain the wishes and feelings of—

(a) the child;
(b) his parents;
(c) any person who is not a parent of his but who has parental responsibility for him; and
(d) any other person whose wishes and feelings the organisation consider to be relevant,

regarding the matter to be decided.

(3) In making any such decision the organisation shall give due consideration—

(a) having regard to the child's age and understanding, to such wishes and feelings of his as they have been able to ascertain;
(b) to such other wishes and feelings mentioned in subsection (2) as they have been able to ascertain; and
(c) to the child's religious persuasion, racial origin and cultural and linguistic background.

Annotation

Section 61: builds upon section 64A of the Child Care Act 1980 and imposes *inter alia* the general duty to safeguard and promote a child's welfare where he is accommodated by or on behalf of a voluntary organisation. The former duty on a voluntary organisation to ascertain the wishes and feelings of the child before making decisions about him is extended to include ascertaining the wishes and feelings of his parents, any persons not being parents but who have parental responsibility, and any other persons whose wishes and feelings the voluntary organisation considers relevant.

Section 61(1): makes it a duty for a voluntary organisation to safeguard and promote the welfare of any child who is accommodated by them or on their behalf. The welfare duty imposed on a voluntary organisation by section 61(1) applies equally to any persons carrying on the running of voluntary homes where these are not run by voluntary organisations. Section 61(1)(c) imposes a new duty on a voluntary organisation to prepare each child for the time when he ceases to be accommodated by them or on their behalf. The duty of a local authority to provide after care for children formerly looked after by a voluntary organisation under section 69 of the Child Care Act 1980 is now provided for in section 24.

Section 61(2): requires the voluntary organisation to ascertain, so far as is practicable, the wishes and feelings of the child, his parents, any other person not being a parent but who has parental responsibility, and any other person whose wishes and feelings they consider to be relevant before making any decision in respect of him. It mirrors section 22(4). Section 61(2) imposes positive and comprehensive duties upon a voluntary organisation to secure the welfare of a child and aligns these duties with the responsibilities of a local authority towards children whom they are looking after.

Section 61(3): provides that in making their decision the voluntary organisation should give due consideration to the child's age and understanding, wishes and feelings, and to the child's religious persuasion, racial origin and cultural background. It mirrors section 22(5)(c). These factors must be taken into account even if there has been insufficient time to investigate the wishes and feelings of the child and others.

Section 62. Duties of local authorities

62.—(1) Every local authority shall satisfy themselves that any voluntary organisation providing accommodation—

(a) within the authority's area for any child; or
(b) outside that area for any child on behalf of the authority,

are satisfactorily safeguarding and promoting the welfare of the children so provided with accommodation.

(2) Every local authority shall arrange for children who are accommodated within their area by or on behalf of voluntary organisations to be visited, from time to time, in the interests of their welfare.

(3) The Secretary of State may make regulations—

(a) requiring every child who is accommodated within a local authority's area, by or on behalf of a voluntary organisation, to be visited by an officer of the authority—

(i) in prescribed circumstances; and
(ii) on specified occasions or within specified periods; and

(b) imposing requirements which must be met by any local

authority, or officer of a local authority, carrying out functions under this section.

(4) Subsection (2) does not apply in relation to community homes.

(5) Where a local authority are not satisfied that the welfare of any child who is accommodated by or on behalf of a voluntary organisation is being satisfactorily safeguarded or promoted they shall—

(a) unless they consider that it would not be in the best interests of the child, take such steps as are reasonably practicable to secure that the care and accommodation of the child is undertaken by—

(i) a parent of his;
(ii) any person who is not a parent of his but who has parental responsibility for him; or
(iii) a relative of his; and

(b) consider the extent to which (if at all) they should exercise any of their functions with respect to the child.

(6) Any person authorised by a local authority may, for the purpose of enabling the authority to discharge their duties under this section—

(a) enter, at any reasonable time, and inspect any premises in which children are being accommodated as mentioned in subsection (1) or (2);

(b) inspect any children there;

(c) require any person to furnish him with such records of a kind required to be kept by regulations made under paragraph 7 of Schedule 5 (in whatever form they are held), or allow him to inspect such records, as he may at any time direct.

(7) Any person exercising the power conferred by subsection (6) shall, if asked to do so, produce some duly authenticated document showing his authority to do so.

(8) any person authorised to exercise the power to inspect records conferred by subsection (6)—

(a) shall be entitled at any reasonable time to have access to, and inspect and check the operation of, any computer and any associated apparatus or material which is or has been in use in connection with the records in question; and

(b) may require—

(i) the person by whom or on whose behalf the computer is or has been so used; or

(ii) any person having charge of, or otherwise concerned with the operation of, the computer, apparatus or material,

to afford him such assistance as he may reasonably require.

(9) Any person who intentionally obstructs another in the exercise of any power conferred by subsection (6) or (8) shall be guilty of an offence and liable on summary conviction to a fine not exceeding level 3 on the standard scale.

Annotation

Section 62: imposes duties upon a local authority in relation to those voluntary organisations within its area or outside its area where they are acting on behalf of the authority. Section 62 replaces section 68 of the Child Care Act 1980 and clarifies a duty formerly provided for in section 68(1) by imposing a new duty where a local authority are not satisfied as to the welfare of any child. The powers of a local authority to enter and inspect premises for the purposes of section 68 of the Child Care Act are re-enacted with amendments to ensure that they have full access to premises, to children and to any records that are kept.

Section 62(1): requires a local authority to satisfy themselves that any voluntary organisation providing accommodation for children is satisfactorily safeguarding and promoting the welfare of the child. Section 68(3) of the Child Care Act 1980 prevented a local authority from inspecting certain premises which were subject to inspection by another government department. This was applicable mainly to independent schools. This provision has not been replaced and thus ensures that the authority will be able to inspect such establishments insofar as they provide for the care and accommodation of children for whom the authority have responsibility, including those subject to care orders.

Section 62(2): imposes a duty on a local authority to arrange for any child who is accommodated by or on behalf of a voluntary organisation to be visited from time to time. This does not apply in relation to community homes: see section 62(4).

Section 62(3): provides that regulations may be made in relation to the duties of a local authority as they oversee the accommodation provided within their area, or outside their area on their behalf. Schedule 5 provides for regulations dealing with the registration of voluntary homes and their conduct. Section 62(3) provides for regulations as to the duties of a local authority in relation to these homes and their conduct. It also imposes standards upon a local authority in relation to these duties.

Section 62(4): relates to section 62(2).

Section 62(5): provides for the duties of a local authority in the event that they are not satisfied that a child's welfare is being satisfactorily safeguarded or promoted. A local authority should consider whether steps should be taken for the child to be accomodated by a parent, a relative or a person with parental responsiblity and consider whether to exercise any of their functions with respect to the child. These would include those defined under Part III, to provide, *inter alia*, advice and assistance, accommodation, or even secure accommodation.

Section 62(6): empowers an authorised person to enter premises in order to discharge his duties under section 62. The regulations under Schedule 5 Paragraph 7 referred to in section 62(6) deal with the placement of children in voluntary homes, the conduct of such homes and the welfare of children in such homes.

Section 62(7): requires the authorised person to produce evidence of his authority, if asked to do so, and mirrors section 50(8) providing for the recovery of a child who has been abducted or absconded from care, or who is missing. Such authorised person for the purposes of section 50 is also required to produce identification.

Section 62(8): gives the authorised person power to require access to any computer or associated material which is used in connection with the keeping of records, the provisions of the Data Protection Act notwithstanding. He may also require of the appropriate person such assistance as he may reasonably require in inspecting computer equipment or material.

Section 62(9): provides that it be an offence intentionally to obstruct a person in the exercise of powers under section 62. Upon summary conviction the liability is a fine not exceeding level 3 on the standard scale. Note the different levels of liability on summary conviction in relation to voluntary organisations. Note that the failure to comply with regulations under section 59(6) makes the offender liable to a level 4 fine, whereas to carry on a voluntary home in contravention of section 60 carries a liability to a level 5 fine.

PART VIII

REGISTERED CHILDREN'S HOMES

Section 63. Children not to be cared for and accommodated in unregistered children's homes

63.—(1) No child shall be cared for and provided with accommodation in a children's home unless the home is registered under this Part.

(2) The register may be kept by means of a computer.

(3) For the purposes of this Part, "a children's home"—

    (a) means a home which provides (or usually provides or is intended to provide) care and accommodation wholly or mainly for more than three children at any one time; but

    (b) does not include a home which is exempted by or under any of the following provisions of this section or by regulations made for the purposes of this subsection by the Secretary of State.

(4) A child is not cared for and accommodated in a children's home when he is cared for and accommodated by—

    (a) a parent of his;

    (b) a person who is not a parent of his but who has parental responsibility for him; or

    (c) any relative of his.

(5) A home is not a children's home for the purposes of this Part if it is—

    (a) a community home;

    (b) a voluntary home;

    (c) a residential care home, nursing home or mental nursing home;

    (d) a health service hospital;

    (e) a home provided, equipped and maintained by the Secretary of State; or

    (f) a school (but subject to subsection (6)).

(6) An independent school is a children's home if—

    (a) it provides accommodation for not more than fifty children; and

    (b) it is not approved by the Secretary of State under section 11(3)(a) of the Education Act 1981.

(7) A child shall not be treated as cared for and accommodated in a children's home when—

(a) any person mentioned in subsection (4)(a) or (b) is living at the home; or

(b) the person caring for him is doing so in his personal capacity and not in the course of carrying out his duties in relation to the home.

(8) In this Act "a registered children's home" means a children's home registered under this Part.

(9) In this section "home" includes any institution.

(10) Where any child is at any time cared for and accommodated in a children's home which is not a registered children's home, the person carrying on the home shall be—

(a) guilty of an offence; and

(b) liable to a fine not exceeding level 5 on the standard scale,

unless he has a reasonable excuse.

(11) Schedule 6 shall have effect with respect to children's homes.

(12) Schedule 7 shall have effect for the purpose of setting out the circumstances in which a person may foster more than three children without being treated as carrying on a children's home.

Annotation

Section 63: provides a definition as to what constitutes a registered children's home. Section 63, together with sections 64 and 65, replaces with various amendments the Children's Homes Act 1982. The 1982 Act, which was not implemented, made provision regarding the registration, inspection and conduct of private children's homes in which one or more children who were in the care of a local authority were accommodated. The effect of the amendments in sections 63, 64 and 65, when considered with other provisions in the Children Act concerning other children living away from home—for example, private foster children—is to ensure that all such children receive appropriate and sufficient attention from those who are looking after them.

Section 63(1): provides that a child may not be cared for and accommodated in a children's home unless it is registered. Section 63 replaces and amends sections 1 and 2 of the Children's Homes Act 1982. The 1982 Act applied only in respect of homes in which a child in the care of a local authority was accommodated. Protection is extended, except in respect of educational establishments referred to in section 63(5)(f), to any home whether or not a child who is looked after by a local authority is accommodated there, provided of course that such a home falls within the definitions set out in section 63.

Section 63(2): provides that registration may be made by computer. It is by Schedule 6 paragraph 1(1) that responsiblity for the maintenance of a register falls upon the local authority for the area in which the home is, or is to be, situated.

Section 63(3): provides for the definition of a children's home. Such a home is generally private sector and run for a profit. The duty to register a home with more than three children is in line with the provisions of the Registered Homes Act 1984. The regulation-making power contained in section 63(3)(c) enables certain accommodation, for example half-way houses for sixteen to seventeen year olds who are looked after by a local authority, to be exempted in appropriate circumstances.

Section 63(4): tightens the definition of a children's home in such a way that it excludes domestic arrangements. Thus a child does not constitute a child in a children's home where he is cared for and accommodated by a parent, a person not a parent who has parental responsibliity, or a relative. In the case of section 63(4)(c), this may constitute fostering.

Section 63(5): replaces section 1(2) of the Children's Homes Act 1982 and lists certain types of homes or installations which are not children's homes. Note the exclusion of educational establishments under section 63(5)(f) with the proviso in section 63(6).

Section 63(6): extends the definition of a children's home to include all independent schools which provide accommodation for not more than fifty pupils and which are not approved for special education. All such independent schools, in addition to being registered with the Department of Education and Science, will now have to register with the local authority within whose boundaries they lie. The Secretary of State may exempt other homes from the provisions of section 63, 64 and 65: see section 63(3).

Section 63(7): excludes from the definition of a child cared for and accommodated in a registered children's home the child who is accompanied by a parent of his or a person who is not a parent but who has parental responsibility, or by a person at the home caring for him in a personal capacity. It is not the purpose of section 63 to interfere in domestic arrangements, as any arrangement as defined in section 63(7) would be so considered.

Section 63(8): provides that the definition of a registered children's home is to run throughout the Act: thus where a local authority has options available to it for the placement of a child, a registered children's home in accordance with section 23(2)(d) is a home as defined in section 63.

Section 63(9): provides that any institution may be a children's home which provides care and accommodation wholly or mainly for more than three children. An institution which is a home does not cease to be a home simply because the numbers of children may drop: it remains a children's home if it usually provides or is intended to provide care and accommodation for more than three children: see section 63(3).

Section 63(10): provides that it be an offence to carry on an unregistered children's home without reasonable excuse. It replaces section 2(2) of the Children's Home Act 1982. Note the penalty on conviction of a fine not exceeding level 5, which mirrors the liability on summary conviction of carrying on a voluntary home in contravention of section 60.

Section 63(11): introduces Schedule 6 which makes provisions supplemental to sections 63, 64 and 65 concerning the registration and regulation of children's homes. Under Schedule 6, the Secretary of State may make regulations, *inter alia*, as to the placing of children in registered children's homes, the conduct of such homes, and the securing of the welfare of the children in such homes.

Section 63(12): provides that in accordance with Schedule 7 a home is not a children's home under section 63 if the children in the home are siblings: a private family household should not be required to register as a children's home. See also section 63(7).

Section 64. Welfare of children in children's homes

64.—(1) Where a child is accommodated in a children's home, it shall be the duty of the person carrying on the home to—

(a) safeguard and promote the child's welfare;
(b) make such use of the services and facilities available for children cared for by their own parents as appears to that person reasonable in the case of the child; and
(c) advise, assist and befriend him with a view to promoting his welfare when he ceases to be so accommodated.

(2) Before making any decision with respect to any such child the person carrying on the home shall, so far as is reasonably practicable, ascertain the wishes and feelings of—

(a) the child;
(b) his parents;

G

(c) any other person who is not a parent of his, but who has parental responsibility for him; and

(d) any person whose wishes and feelings the person carrying on the home considers to be relevant,

regarding the matter to be decided.

(3) In making any such decision the person concerned shall give due consideration —

(a) having regard to the child's age and understanding, to such wishes and feelings of his as he has been able to ascertain;

(b) to such other wishes and feelings mentioned in subsection (2) as he has been able to ascertain; and

(c) to the child's religious persuasion, racial origin and cultural and linguistic background.

(4) Section 62, except subsection (4), shall apply in relation to any person who is carrying on a children's home as it applies in relation to any voluntary organisation.

Annotation

Section 64: places similar duties upon the person carrying on a registered children's home in respect of the welfare of the children accommodated in the home as are placed upon voluntary organisations in section 61. These are nevertheless new provisions regarding the responsibilities of those persons in charge of children's homes towards the welfare of children accommodated. They also impose on a local authority the duty to satisfy themselves as to the welfare of such children.

Section 64(1): makes provision to have children in a registered children's home afforded the same protection as children in voluntary homes: see section 61(1). Under the unimplemented Children's Home Act 1982, the proprietor of a children's home had no specific responsibility towards the children in the home and a local authority had no responsibility beyond registration and inspection duties. But one of the aims of the Children Act is to ensure that the welfare of all the children away from home is secured.

Section 64(2): mirrors section 61(2). Note that section 64(2) imposes positive and comprehensive duties upon the person carrying on the registered children's home to secure the welfare of a child and aligns these duties with the responsibilities of a local authority towards children whom they are looking after: see section 22(4).

Section 64(3): mirrors section 61(3). The purpose of section 64(3)(c) is to encourage a registered children's home, along with a voluntary home under section 61(3)(c) or a local authority under section 22(5)(a) to take account of the ethnic composition of their areas and to have regard for the different racial groups of children in need: Minister of State, Hansard Col. 485, 23 April 1989.

Section 64(4): imposes a duty on a local authority to satisfy themselves as to the welfare of children accommodated in children's homes. This applies to a registered children's home as it applies to any voluntary organisation. The effect is to impose a duty to visit such children from time to time, to take certain action whenever they are not satisfied as to the welfare of the child and to give power to enter and inspect premises and to inspect children and records.

Section 65. Persons disqualified from carrying on, or being employed in, children's homes

65. —(1) A person who is disqualified (under section 68) from fostering a child privately shall not carry on, or be otherwise concerned in the management of, or have any financial interest in, a children's home unless he has—

(a) disclosed to the responsible authority the fact that he is so disqualified; and
(b) obtained their written consent.

(2) No person shall employ a person who is so disqualified in a children's home unless he has—

(a) disclosed to the responsible authority the fact that that person is so disqualified; and
(b) obtained their written consent.

(3) Where an authority refuse to give their consent under this section, they shall inform the applicant by a written notice which states—

(a) the reason for the refusal;
(b) the applicant's right to appeal against the refusal to a Registered Homes Tribunal under paragraph 8 of Schedule 6; and
(c) the time within which he may do so.

(4) Any person who contravenes subsection (1) or (2) shall be guilty of an offence and liable on summary conviction to imprisonment for a term not exceeding six months or to a fine not exceeding level 5 on the standard scale or to both.

(5) Where a person contravenes subsection (2) he shall not be guilty of an offence if he proves that he did not know, and had no reasonable grounds for believing, that the person whom he was employing was disqualified under section 68.

Annotation

Section 65: provides for the disqualification of persons from carrying on, or being employed in, a children's home. Contravention is to be an offence subject to imprisonment for a term not exceeding six months or a fine not exceeding level 4 on the standard scale. Section 65 replaces section 10 of the unimplemented Children's Home Act 1982.

Section 65(1): replaces sections 10(1) and (2) of the unimplemented Children's Home Act 1982, but instead of detailing the particular offences, disqualifies a person from being concerned in a children's home, unless he has disclosed his disqualification to a local authority and obtained the written consent of the authority. It subsequently applies by reference the provisions of section 68 which enable the Secretary of State to make regulations specifying persons to be disqualified from fostering a child privately. The regulation-making power will enable the Secretary of State to keep such a list up to date at all times in respect of both private fostering and registered children's homes.

Section 65(2): prevents any person from employing a person who is so disqualified unless he has first notified the local authority and obtained their consent. Failure to give consent may trigger an appeal to a Registered Homes Tribunal under section 65(3)(b). The appeal would be by the person who made the application, not the person who is disqualified.

Section 65(3): requires a local authority to give written notice to the applicant of any refusal to give consent under section 65(1) or 65(2)(b). An appeal against refusal of consent may be made to a Registered Homes Tribunal: see Schedule 6 paragraph 10, which links up with Schedule 6 paragraph 4, requiring a local authority to be satisfied that the proposed children's home will meet the requirements prescribed.

Section 65(4): provides that any contravention of section (1) or (2) shall be an offence subject to a penalty of imprisonment for up to six months or a fine not exceeding level 5, or both. Note that the penalty in relation to voluntary organisations under section 59(6) is liability on summary conviction to a fine not exceeding level 4 on the standard scale and under section 62(9) to a fine not exceeding level 3.

Section 65(5): provides for it not to be an offence to contravene section 65(2) if the applicant did not know, and had no reasonable cause to believe, that a person whom he employed was disqualified under section 68. Section 68 defines a person who is fostering a child privately and other terms. Notwithstanding lack of guilty intent in relation to section 65(2), an applicant would nevertheless have to meet the requirements provided for in Schedule 6.

PART IX

PRIVATE ARRANGEMENTS FOR FOSTERING CHILDREN

Section 66. Privately fostered children

66. — (1) In this Part —

(a) "a privately fostered child" means a child who is under the age of sixteen and who is cared for, and provided with accommodation by, someone other than —

(i) a parent of his;
(ii) a person who is not a parent of his but who has parental responsibility for him; or
(iii) a relative of his; and

(b) "to foster a child privately" means to look after the child in circumstances in which he is a privately fostered child as defined by this section.

(2) A child is not a privately fostered child if the person caring for and accommodating him —

(a) has done so for a period of less than 28 days; and
(b) does not intend to do so for any longer period.

(3) Subsection (1) is subject to —

(a) the provisions of section 63; and
(b) the exceptions made by paragraphs 1 to 5 of Schedule 8.

(4) In the case of a child who is disabled, subsection (1)(a) shall have effect as if for "sixteen" there were substituted "eighteen".

(5) Schedule 8 shall have effect for the purposes of supplementing the provision made by this Part.

Annotation

Section 66: introduces Part IX of the Act which replaces and amends the Foster Children Act 1980. Part IX, which comprises sections 66 to 70, provides for the notification and regulation of private fostering arrangements and the welfare of privately fostered children. Part IX should be read with Schedule 8. The general intention of these provisions, to provide safeguards for children cared for away from home, will be mostly unchanged but specific aspects are amended. Terminology is updated to distinguish between public and private fostering and the Nurseries and Child Minders Regulation Act 1948 is clarified.

Section 66(1): defines a privately fostered child. Note that "relative" referred to in section 66(1)(a)(iii) includes a step-parent and others as defined by section 105. A privately fostered child is one who is placed privately in what is clearly a family placement as opposed to an institutional home. The provisions in the Foster Children Act 1980 extended to children who were resident in institutions as well as domestic premises.

Section 66(2): provides that a child is privately fostered where his parents have placed him for twenty eight days by private arrangement with a family which is not related to the child or who have no parental responsiiblity for him. Payment may be made by the parents but this is not necessary. Unlike under the Foster Children Act 1980 placements for less than twenty eight days will not be classed as private fostering even if the person caring for the child is a regular foster parent.

Section 66(3): provides for the definition of a privately fostered child to be qualified by the provisions of section 63 and the exceptions made by paragraphs 1–5 of Schedule 8. The effect of section 63 is that a home providing care and accommodation for three or more children is to be treated as a registered children's home unless the local authority are satisfied that the children accommodated there should be treated as private foster children.

Section 66(4): applies Part IX of the Act to disabled children up to eighteen years of age. Thus, whereas provisions on private fostering continue as in the past to apply in respect of children below the upper limit of compulsory school age in accordance with section 66(1), the provisions of the Foster Children Act 1980 no longer apply to children over the age of sixteen, except for disabled children to whom they will apply up to the age of eighteen. Section 18 of the Foster Children Act 1980 extended the controls on private fostering to sixteen and seventeen year olds, but this is repealed.

Section 66(5): introduces Schedule 8 for the purposes of supplementing Part IX. Note that Schedule 8 makes certain exclusions from the definition of "privately fostered children" provided in section 66(1), and in accordance with section 66(3)(b).

Section 67. Welfare of privately fostered children

67. — (1) It shall be the duty of every local authority to satisfy themselves that the welfare of children who are privately fostered within their area is being satisfactorily safeguarded and promoted and to secure that such advice is given to those caring for them as appears to the authority to be needed.

(2) The Secretary of State may make regulations —

(a) requiring every child who is privately fostered within a local authority's area to be visited by an officer of the authority —

(i) in prescribed circumstances; and
(ii) on specified occasions or within specified periods; and

(b) imposing requirements which are to be met by any local authority, or officer of a local authority, in carrying out functions under this section.

(3) Where any person who is authorised by a local authority to visit privately fostered children has reasonable cause to believe that —

(a) any privately fostered child is being accommodated in premises within the authority's area; or
(b) it is proposed to accommodate any such child in any such premises,

he may at any reasonable time inspect those premises and any children there.

(4) Any person exercising the power under subsection (3) shall, if so required, produce some duly authenticated document showing his authority to do so.

(5) Where a local authority are not satisfied that the welfare of any child who is privately fostered within their area is being satisfactorily safeguarded or promoted they shall —

(a) unless they consider that it would not be in the best interests of the child, take such steps as are reasonably practicable to secure that the care and accommodation of the child is undertaken by —

(i) a parent of his;
(ii) any person who is not a parent of his but who has parental responsibility for him; or
(iii) a relative of his; and

(b) consider the extent to which (if at all) they should exercise any of their functions under this Act with respect to the child.

Annotation

Section 67: places a duty on a local authority to satisfy themselves as to the welfare of privately fostered children in their area and sets out the action they must take when not satisfied in particular cases. Section 67 empowers the Secretary of State to make regulations requiring privately fostered children to be visited. It also replaces a local authority's duties in respect of private foster children under section 3 of the Foster Children Act 1980.

Section 67(1): defines a local authority's welfare responsibiliy and requires them to give such advice to those caring for private foster children as is needed. The welfare duty which is owed by a local authority to privately fostered children is now the same as that owed to children living in children's homes and voluntary homes. The duty of a local authority is principally to be satisfied that each child is receiving an adequate standard of care and that their welfare is being promoted and safeguarded.

Section 67(2): enables the Secretary of State to make regulations requiring the authority to visit every private foster child in their area and specifying the visiting requirements. These may cover a local authority's visiting duty and any other requirements placed on a local authority under section 67.

Section 67(3): provides a local authority with the power to enter and inspect premises where they believe a private foster child is being, or will be, kept. Section 67(3) extends section 8 of the Foster Children Act 1980 to give power to inspect the children found on those premises.

Section 67(4): requires an officer to produce identification before seeking to inspect premises, if he is so required. It mirrors section 50(8)(b).

Section 67(5): defines a local authority's responsibilities where they are not satisfied as to the welfare of a private foster child. If they need to remove the child they may consider applying for an emergency protection order or a care order. A local authority can no longer remove a private foster child into their own care without such an order.

Section 68. Persons disqualified from being private foster parents

68.—(1) Unless he has disclosed the fact to the appropriate local authority and obtained their written consent, a person shall not foster a child privately if he is disqualified from doing so by regulations made by the Secretary of State for the purposes of this section.

(2) The regulations may, in particular, provide for a person to be so disqualified where—

(a) an order of a kind specified in the regulations has been made at any time with respect to him;

(b) an order of a kind so specified has been made at any time with respect to any child who has been in his care;

(c) a requirement of a kind so specified has been imposed at any time with respect to any such child, under or by virtue of any enactment;

(d) he has been convicted of any offence of a kind so specified, or has been placed on probation or discharged absolutely or conditionally for any such offence;

(e) a prohibition has been imposed on him at any time under section 69 or under any other specified enactment;

(f) his rights and powers with respect to a child have at any time been vested in a specified authority under a specified enactment.

(3) Unless he has disclosed the fact to the appropriate local authority and obtained their written consent, a person shall not foster a child privately if—

(a) he lives in the same household as a person who is himself prevented from fostering a child by subsection (1); or

(b) he lives in a household at which any such person is employed.

(4) Where an authority refuse to give their consent under this section, they shall inform the applicant by a written notice which states—

(a) the reason for the refusal;

(b) the applicant's right under paragraph 8 of Schedule 8 to appeal against the refusal; and

(c) the time within which he may do so.

(5) In this section—

"the appropriate authority" means the local authority within whose area it is proposed to foster the child in question; and

"enactment" means any enactment having effect, at any time, in any part of the United Kingdom.

Annotation

Section 68: prohibits a person from fostering children privately if he is disqualified by regulations made by the Secretary of State or lives in a household in which a disqualified person lives or is employed, unless he obtains the consent of the local authority. Section 68 replaces section 7 of the Foster Children Act 1980.

Section 68(1): provides for the making of regulations by the Secretary of State. Section 7 of the Foster Children Act 1980 listed a number of provisions which disqualified a person from keeping a private foster child unless he had disclosed the fact to the local authority and received their written consent, including a number of orders which, if made in respect of that person, would disqualify him. It is desirable that this list of orders and offences should be kept up to date at all times. Thus, in order to achieve this, disqualifications in respect of private fostering care are to be provided for in regulations to be made by the Secretary of State through section 68(1).

Section 68(2): provides for the regulations to specify various types of order, requirement or offence that would serve to disqualify a person. These will include care and supervision orders under the Act and the provisions of section 7 of the Foster Children Act 1980, with additions to be prescribed. Note that the making of an emergency protection order will not in itself disqualify a person as there would not have been a full court hearing into the child's circumstances. The fact that an emergency protection order has been made in the past while in the care of a putative foster parent will be one of the matters which should, however, be disclosed to a local authority on notification of their proposal to foster a child. This could be achieved by requiring notification under those regulations made under paragraph 7(1)(b) of Schedule 7.

Section 68(3): applies the same disqualifications and requirements as section 68(2) to persons who live in the same household as a person who would be disqualified or lives in a household which employs such a person. The note on section 68(2) applies equally to section 68(3).

Section 68(4): imposes a new duty on a local authority who refuse to give written consent under Section 68 to notify the applicant in writing for the reason for refusal and of his right of appeal under Schedule 8.

Section 68(5): provides for definitions of appropriate authority and enactment in accordance with this section. Note that generally the Children Act only applies to England and Wales. The most important exception is that Part X dealing with child minding and day care for young children applies also in Scotland. A number of consequential amendments are also made to the law in Scotland and Northern Ireland. Section 90 lists the provisions which apply to those countries.

Section 69. Power to prohibit private fostering

69.—(1) This section applies where a person—

(a) proposes to foster a child privately; or
(b) is fostering a child privately.

(2) Where the local authority for the area within which the child is proposed to be, or is being, fostered are of the opinion that—

(a) he is not a suitable person to foster a child;
(b) the premises in which the child will be, or is being, accommodated are not suitable; or
(c) it would be prejudicial to the welfare of the child for him to be, or continue to be, accommodated by that person in those premises,

the authority may impose a prohibition on him under subsection (3).

(3) A prohibition imposed on any person under this subsection may prohibit him from fostering privately—

(a) any child in any premises within the area of the local authority; or
(b) any child in premises specified in the prohibition;
(c) a child identified in the prohibition, in premises specified in the prohibition.

(4) A local authority who have imposed a prohibition on any person under subsection (3) may, if they think fit, cancel the prohibition—

(a) of their own motion; or
(b) on an application made by that person,

if they are satisfied that the prohibition is no longer justified.

(5) Where a local authority impose a requirement on any person under paragraph 6 of Schedule 8, they may also impose a prohibition on him under subsection (3).

(6) Any prohibition imposed by virtue of subsection (5) shall not have effect unless—

(a) the time specified for compliance with the requirement has expired; and

(b) the requirement has not been complied with.

(7) A prohibition imposed under this section shall be imposed by notice in writing addressed to the person on whom it is imposed and informing him of—

(a) the reason for imposing the prohibition;
(b) his right under paragraph 8 of Schedule 8 to appeal against the prohibition; and
(c) the time within which he may do so.

Annotation

Section 69: makes provisions enabling a local authority to prohibit persons from fostering a child privately. Section 69 replaces section 10 of the Foster Children Act 1980 which was a provision of equivalent effect. Section 69 also enables a local authority to prohibit persons from privately fostering a child where they consider the premises are not suitable, or that it would be prejudicial to the welfare of the child to continue to be so accommodated.

Section 69(1): provides when section 69 is to apply. Unlike section 10 of the Foster Children Act it applies where a person fosters a child privately without having given the required notice of his proposal so to do. Section 10 of the Foster Children Act 1980 enabled its safeguards to be evaded by a person who failed to give notice.

Section 69(2): sets out the grounds for a prohibition. For example, the person is an unsuitable person to foster a child, the premises are unsuitable, or it would be prejudicial to the welfare of the child to be fostered by that person in those premises. The welfare of the child remains paramount.

Section 69(3): specifies the nature of the prohibition. For example, it may be in respect of any child in specified premises, any child in any premises in their area, or a specified child in specified premises.

Section 69(4): enables a local authority to cancel the prohibition if they are satisfied that it is no longer justified. This can be done of the authority's own motion, or following an application from the person.

Section 69(5): enables a local authority to impose a prohibition on a person at the same time as a requirement is imposed under paragraph 6 of Schedule 8. Paragraph 6 allows the local authority to stipulate certain requirements which must be complied with by a person keeping or proposing to keep a private foster child.

Section 69(6): prevents a prohibition under section 69(5) from taking effect unless the person has failed to comply with the requirement within the time specified for compliance.

Section 69(7): requires the local authority to give written notice to a person who is prohibited under this section giving the reason for the prohibition and informing him of his rights of appeal under paragraph 8 of Schedule 8. The duty to give reasons is a new requirement.

Section 70. Offences

70. —(1) A person shall be guilty of an offence if—

(a) being required, under any provision made by or under this Part, to give any notice or information—

    (i) he fails without reasonable excuse to give the notice within the time specified in that provision; or
    (ii) he fails without reasonable excuse to give the information within a reasonable time; or
    (iii) he makes, or causes or procures another person to make, any statement in the notice or information which he knows to be false or misleading in a material particular;

(b) he refuses to allow a privately fostered child to be visited by a duly authorised officer of a local authority;

(c) he intentionally obstructs another in the exercise of the power conferred by section 67(3);

(d) he contravenes section 68;

(e) he fails without reasonable excuse to comply with any requirement imposed by a local authority under this Part;

(f) he accommodates a privately fostered child in any premises in contravention of a prohibition imposed by a local authority under this Part;

(g) he knowingly causes to be published, or publishes, an advertisement which he knows contravenes paragraph 10 of Schedule 8.

(2) Where a person contravenes section 68(3), he shall not be guilty of an offence under this section if he proves that he did not know, and had no reasonable ground for believing, that any person to whom section 68(1) applied was living or employed in the premises in question.

(3) A person guilty of an offence under subsection (1)(a) shall be liable on summary conviction to a fine not exceeding level 5 on the standard scale.

(4) A person guilty of an offence under subsection (1)(b), (c) or (g) shall be liable on summary conviction to a fine not exceeding level 3 on the standard scale.

(5) a person guilty of an offence under subsection (1)(d) or (f) shall be liable on summary conviction to imprisonment for a term not exceeding six months, or to a fine not exceeding level 5 on the standard scale, or to both.

(6) A person guilty of an offence under subsection (1)(e) shall be liable on summary conviction to a fine not exceeding level 4 on the standard scale.

(7) If any person who is required, under any provision of this Part, to give a notice fails to give the notice within the time specified in that provision, proceedings for the offence may be brought at any time within six months from the date when evidence of the offence came to the knowledge of the local authority.

(8) Subsection (7) is not affected by anything in section 127(1) of the Magistrates' Courts Act 1980 (time limit for proceedings).

Annotation

Section 70: provides for various offences which may lead on summary conviction to imprisonment for a term not exceeding six months or a fine not exceeding level 5 on the standard scale or both. Section 70 replaces section 16 of the Foster Children Act 1980 with provisions of equivalent effect, with more modern terminology and the addition of requirements that certain acts be "without reasonable excuse". Section 16(1)(f) of the 1980 Act is omitted from section 70 as it concerns the wilful obstruction of a person entitled to enter premises by virtue of a warrant. The issue of warrants is now covered in section 102.

Section 70(1): lists those offences of which a person shall be guilty if he contravenes one of a number of provisions under this Part of the Act or Schedule 8, including failure to give notice, refusal to allow a child to be visited, keeping a foster child in contravention of a prohibition, failure to comply with a requirement and placing an advertisement in contravention of Schedule 8. The offences in contravention of section 70(1) do not have equal weight under the law.

Section 70(2): replaces with an equivalent provision section 16(2) of the Foster Children Act 1980, namely that a person shall not be guilty of an offence of contravention of section 68(3) if he did not and could not be expected to know of the existence of the information. It also raises the defence of no guilty intent.

Section 70(3): provides that a person guilty of an offence under section 70(1)(a) shall be liable on summary conviction to a fine not exceeding level 5 on the standard scale. Note the defence of reasonable excuse. Originally, it was proposed that a standard fine or a term of imprisonment of up to six months should be the sentence on summary conviction of a breach of any of the requirements of section 70(1), but this was modified to take into account the different levels of seriousness of the various breaches.

Section 70(4): provides that a person guilty of an offence under section 70(1)(b)(c)(g) shall be liable on summary conviction to a fine not exceeding level 3 on the standard scale. Refusal to allow a privately fostered child to be visited by a duly authorised officer of a local authority in line with his duties is not the same as refusal to allow a visit to a child who may be considered at risk—hence the lighter sentence.

Section 70(5): provides that a person guilty of an offence under section 70(1)(d)(f) shall be liable on summary conviction to a term of imprisonment not exceeding six months or to a fine not exceeding level 5 on the standard scale, or to both. This applies to a person disqualified from being a private foster parent or who breaches a prohibition imposed by a local authority.

Section 70(6): provides that a perosn guilty of an offence under section 70(1)(c) shall be liable on summary conviction to a fine not exceeding level 4 on the standard scale. This covers a situation where a person fails without reasonable excuse to comply with any requirement imposed by a local authority and would cover breaches on the basis of negligence rather than of criminal intent.

Section 70(7): replaces the provisions of section 16(4) of the Foster Children Act 1980 with equivalent effect.

Section 70(8): replaces the provisions of section 16(4) of the Foster Children Act 1980 with equivalent effect as these relate to the bringing of proceedings for offences.

PART X

CHILD MINDING AND DAY CARE FOR YOUNG CHILDREN

Section 71. Registration

71.—(1) Every local authority shall keep a register of—

    (a) persons who act as child minders on domestic premises within the authority's area; and

    (b) persons who provide day care for children under the

age of eight on premises (other than domestic premises) within that area.

(2) For the purposes of this Part—

    (a) a person acts as a child minder if—

> (i) he looks after one or more children under the age of eight, for reward; and
> (ii) the period, or the total of the periods, which he spends so looking after children in any day exceeds two hours; and

    (b) a person does not provide day care for children unless the period, or the total of the periods, during which children are looked after exceeds two hours in any day.

(3) Where a person provides day care for children under the age of eight on different premises situated within the area of the same local authority, that person shall be separately registered with respect to each of those premises.

(4) A person who—

    (a) is the parent, or a relative, of a child;
    (b) has parental responsibility for a child; or
    (c) is a foster parent of a child,

does not act as a child minder for the purposes of this Part when looking after that child.

(5) Where a person is employed as a nanny for a child, she does not act as a child minder when looking after that child wholly or mainly in the home of the person so employing her.

(6) Where a person is so employed by two different employers, she does not act as a child minder when looking after any of the children concerned wholly or mainly in the home of either of her employers.

(7) a local authority may refuse to register an applicant for registration under subsection (1)(a) if they are satisfied that—

    (a) the applicant; or
    (b) any person looking after, or likely to be looking after, any children on any premises on which the applicant is, or is likely to be, child minding,

is not fit to look after children under the age of eight.

(8) A local authority may refuse to register an applicant for registration under subsection (1)(a) if they are satisfied that—

(a) any person living, or likely to be living, at any premises on which the applicant is, or is likely to be, child minding; or

(b) any person employed, or likely to be employed, on those premises,

is not fit to be in the proximity of children under the age of eight.

(9) A local authority may refuse to register an applicant for registration under subsection (1)(b) if they are satisfied that any person looking after, or likely to be looking after, any children on the premises to which the application relates is not fit to look after children under the age of eight.

(10) A local authority may refuse to register an applicant for registration under subsection (1)(b) if they are satisfied that—

(a) any person living, or likely to be living, at the premises to which the application relates; or

(b) any person employed, or likely to be employed, on those premises,

is not fit to be in the proximity of children under the age of eight.

(11) A local authority may refuse to register an applicant for registration under this section if they are satisfied—

(a) in the case of an application under subsection (1)(a), that any premises on which the applicant is, or is likely to be, child minding; or

(b) in the case of an application under subsection (1)(b), that the premises to which the application relates,

are not fit to be used for looking after children under the age of eight, whether because of their condition or the condition of any equipment used on the premises or for any reason connected with their situation, construction or size.

(12) In this section—

"domestic premises" means any premises which are wholly or mainly used as a private dwelling;

"premises" includes any vehicle.

(13) For the purposes of this Part a person acts as a nanny for a child if she is employed to look after the child by—

(a) a parent of the child;

(b) a person who is not a parent of the child but who has parental responsibility for him; or

(c) a person who is a relative of the child and who has assumed responsibility for his care.

(14) For the purposes of this section, a person fosters a child if—

(a) he is a local authority foster parent in relation to the child;

(b) he is a foster parent with whom the child has been placed by a voluntary organisation; or

(c) he fosters the child privately.

(15) Any register kept under this section—

(a) shall be open to inspection by members of the public at all reasonable times; and

(b) may be kept by means of a computer.

(16) Schedule 9 shall have effect for the purpose of making further provision with respect to registration under this section including, in particular, further provision for exemption from the requirement to be registered and provision for disqualification.

Annotation

Section 71: introduces Part X of the Act dealing with child minding and day care provision for young children. Part X, running from section 71 to section 79, builds upon the provisions of the Nurseries and Child Minders Regulation Act 1948 dealing with the registration of day care and short term residential facilities. This has been repealed. Section 71 places a duty on a local authority to maintain a register of child minders on domestic premises and those who provide day care for children under the age of eight on non-domestic premises. Section 71 also enables a local authority to refuse the registration of an applicant if they believe the person or the premises are unfit.

Section 71(1): imposes a duty upon a local authority to maintain a single register of those persons who act as child minders on domestic premises and those who provide day care on non-domestic premises in their area. The system of registration under the Nurseries and Child Minders Regulation Act 1948 provided for two registers to be maintained by a local authority, one for those persons providing care on domestic premises for reward—child minders—and one for non-domestic premises where care is provided—day nurseries and play groups. Section 71(1) replaces this system with a single register of those persons responsible for care provision on specified premises.

Section 71(2): qualifies section 71(1). The Nurseries and Child Minders Regulation Act 1948 applied to arrangements lasting for continuous periods of two hours up to six days. When an arrangement lasted for a longer period, the registration requirements of the 1948 Act gave way to the provisions of the Foster Children Acts. Under these Acts, private placements of foster children were notified to a local authority who were required to satisfy themselves of the child's wellbeing by visiting him from time to time.

Section 71(3): requires separate registration for each of the premises in which a person provides day care within the area of a local authority. Note that persons need not be registered in respect of day care where children are looked after in certain homes and hospitals and it is provided as part of the establishment's activities by the person who carries on the home or hospital or an authorised employee: see Schedule 9 paragraph 4.

Section 71(4): excludes certain persons who look after a child from the definition of child minder. Note that persons do not need to be registered in respect of child minding if the children concerned are being looked after in a school as part of the school's activities, except in respect of an independent nursery school which operates as a day nursery: see Schedule 9 paragraph 3.

Section 71(5): excludes a child's nanny from the definition of a child minder. A nanny is a person who is employed to look after the child by a parent, any other person who has parental responsibility for the child, or a relative who has assumed responsibility for his care: see section 71(13). Note that no further definition of nanny appears elsewhere in the Act.

Section 71(6): exempts a nanny who is employed by two different employers from registration as a child minder where she is looking after any of the children wholly or mainly in the home of her employers. See also section 71(5) and (13) dealing with the definition of a nanny,

Section 71(7): provides that a child minder must meet the test of "fitness" in order to be registered. In the words of the Minister of State: "Some people have urged that the legislation should be more specific about what constitutes a fit person, but we do not consider that that is necessary. We believe that it is a well-known legal concept; to be more specific could be too rigid for those who have to implement the legislation": see Hansard Col 389 Standing Committee B, 6 June 1989.

Section 71(8): provides additional grounds for a local authority's refusal to register an applicant under section 71(1)(a). Whilst the concept of "fitness" is well-known in legal terms, nevertheless new guidance in the form of specific regulations were promised by the Minister of State as part of the implementation exercise to cover the point: see Hansard Col 389 Standing Committee B, 6 June 1989.

Section 71(9): enables a local authority to refuse to register an applicant under section 71(1)(b). It is incumbent upon a local authority, when examining any application, to check whether an applicant is disqualified from being registered. Disqualification can arise if one of the circumstances prescribed in regulations applies to him, for example if he has committed certain offences or previously had a registration cancelled: see Schedule 9 paragraph 2.

Section 71(10): repeats the provisions of section 71(8) and applies them to applications for registration under section 71(1)(b).

Section 71(11): provides that a local authority may refuse to register an applicant either as a child minder or as a day care provider if they are satisfied that the premises are unfit for looking after children under the age of eight. This provision is similar to one to be found in the Nurseries and Child Minders Regulation Act 1948.

Section 71(15): provides that the maintenance of any register under section 71 may be on a computer and shall be available to the public.

Section 71(16): gives effect to Schedule 9. Exemptions defined in Schedule 9 are similar to those under the Nurseries and Child Minders Regulation Act 1948.

Section 72. Requirements to be complied with by child minders

72.—(1) Where a local authority register a person under section 71(1)(a), they shall impose such reasonable requirements on him as they consider appropriate in his case.

(2) In imposing requirements on him, the authority shall—

(a) specify the maximum number of children, or the maximum number of children within specified age groups, whom he may look after when acting as a child minder;

(b) require him to secure that any premises on which he so looks after any child, and the equipment used in those premises, are adequately maintained and kept safe;

(c) require him to keep a record of the name and address of—

(i) any child so looked after by him on any premises within the authority's area;

(ii) any person who assists in looking after any such child; and

(iii) any person living, or likely at any time to be living, at those premises;

(d) require him to notify the authority in writing of any change in the persons mentioned in paragraph (c)(ii) and (iii).

(3) The Secretary of State may by regulations make provision as to—

(a) requirements which must be imposed by local authorities under this section in prescribed circumstances;

(b) requirements of such descriptions as may be prescribed which must not be imposed by local authorities under this section.

(4) In determining the maximum number of children to be specified under subsection (2)(a), the authority shall take account of the number of other children who may at any time be on any premises on which the person concerned acts, or is likely to act, as a child minder.

(5) Where, in addition to the requirements mentioned in subsection (2), a local authority impose other requirements, those other requirements must not be incompatible with any of the subsection (2) requirements.

(6) A local authority may at any time vary any requirement imposed under this section, impose any additional requirement or remove any requirement.

Annotation

Section 72: imposes a duty on a local authority to attach conditions to the registration of child minders. Section 72 lists requirements to be specified by each local authority so that they may answer the specific needs and abilities of each individual case. These requirements include the number of children that may be looked after by a child minder, the obligation to maintain premises and equipment and to ensure that both of these are safe, the obligation to keep records and the requirement to notify any changes. A local authority are also given powers to change or remove any of the requirements set down and they may add to these. This differs from the Nurseries and Child Minders Regulation Act 1948 wherein local authorities were not under any duty to impose such requirements but could do so if they wished.

Section 72(1): places a duty on a local authority to impose requirements on registered child minders such as they consider reasonable and appropriate. The duty upon a local authority will be to tailor requirements to an individual case: see section 72(2). Note that if registration is granted a certificate must be issued. This certificate should specify any requirements which have been imposed on the applicant: see Schedule 9 paragraph 6.

Section 72(2): lists the requirements which a local authority shall impose and specify. The important difference in section 72 compared with the prior law is that a local authority will now have to impose certain requirements with which a registered person will have to comply, but they will also have the flexibility to add other conditions.

Section 72(3): enables the Secretary of State to make regulations providing that certain requirements must, or must not be, imposed by a local authority with regard to child minders. It was the view of the White Paper, "The Law on Child Care and Family Services", that there should be parallel arrangements for the supervision of private and voluntary accommodation by a local authority; hence there should be included a duty on a local authority to impose appropriate requirements in connection with registration.

Section 72(4): specifies that where requirements are imposed by a local authority regarding the maximum number of children to be looked after by any child minder, account should be taken of other children who may be on the premises at the time of child minding. These requirements should find their way into a certificate of registration to be issued in accordance with Schedule 9 paragraph 6.

Section 72(5): specifies that there should not be any incompatibility between the requirements imposed by virtue of section 72(2) and any other additional requirements imposed by a local authority.

Section 73. Requirements to be complied with by persons providing day care for young children

73.—(1) Where a local authority register a person under section 71(1)(b) they shall impose such reasonable requirements on him as they consider appropriate in his case.

(2) Where a person is registered under section 71(1)(b) with respect to different premises within the area of the same authority, this section applies separately in relation to each registration.

(3) In imposing requirements on him, the authority shall—

(a) specify the maximum number of children, or the

maximum number of children within specified age groups, who may be looked after on the premises;

(b) require him to secure that the premises, and the equipment used in them, are adequately maintained and kept safe;

(c) require him to notify the authority of any change in the facilities which he provides or in the period during which he provides them;

(d) specify the number of persons required to assist in looking after children on the premises;

(e) require him to keep a record of the name and address of—

   (i) any child looked after on the registered premises;
   (ii) any person who assists in looking after any such child; and
   (iii) any person who lives, or is likely at any time to be living, at those premises;

(f) require him to notify the authority of any change in the persons mentioned in paragraph (e)(ii) and (iii).

(4) The Secretary of State may by regulations make provision as to—

(a) requirements which must be imposed by local authorities under this section in prescribed circumstances;

(b) requirements of such descriptions as may be prescribed which must not be imposed by local authorities under this section.

(5) In subsection (3), references to children looked after are to children looked after in accordance with the provision of day care made by the registered person.

(6) In determining the maximum number of children to be specified under subsection (3)(a), the authority shall take account of the number of other children who may at any time be on the premises.

(7) Where, in addition to the requirements mentioned in subsection (3), a local authority impose other requirements, those other requirements must not be incompatible with any of the subsection (3) requirements.

(8) A local authority may at any time vary any requirement imposed under this section, impose any additional requirement or remove any requirement.

Annotation

Section 73: imposes duties upon a local authority in relation to the requirements to be complied with by those persons providing day care for young children similar to those to be found in section 72. We have seen in section 71 that the Nurseries and Child Minders Regulation Act 1948 provided for two registers, one for those persons providing care in their home for reward, now covered by section 72, and another for those providing care in non-domestic premises. This is covered by section 73.

Section 73(1): places a duty upon a local authority to impose reasonable requirements upon registered day care providers. The Nurseries and Child Minders Regulation Act 1948 applied to services for children up to the age of sixteen. This was poorly understood and rarely enforced. The White Paper, "The Law on Child Care and Family Services", felt that there was general agreement that the younger children are the most vulnerable and that there was little support for maintaining the full requirements in respect of the upper age limit of sixteen. It was therefore proposed to reduce this to five. However, at the committee stage of the Bill this was increased to eight.

Section 73(2): mirrors section 71(3). Note that persons need not be registered in respect of day care where children are looked after in certain homes and hospitals and it is provided as part of the establishment's activities by the person who carries on the home or hospital or an authorised employee: see Schedule 9 paragraph 4.

Section 73(3): lists the requirements which a local authority shall impose upon day care providers. These are the same as those defined in section 72(2) in relation to child minders, with the addition that section 73(3)(c)(d) requires the day care providers to notify the local authority of any changes in the facilities provided at the time at which they are provided and to specify the number of persons assisting in looking after children.

Section 73(4): enables the Secretary of State to make regulations providing that certain requirements must, or must not be, imposed by a local authority with regard to day care providers. It was the view of the White Paper, "The Law on Child Care and Family Services", that there should be parallel arrangements for the supervision of private and voluntary accommodation by a local authority; hence there should be included a duty on a local authority to impose appropriate requirements in connection with registration: see also section 72(3).

Section 73(5): defines the term "children looked after". The Nurseries and Child Minders Regulation Act 1948 talked of children "received to be looked after": see the White Paper "The Law on Child Care and Family Services".

Section 73(6): mirrors section 72(4). These requirements should find their way into a certificate of registration to be issued in accordance with Schedule 9 paragraph 6.

Section 73(7): specifies that there should not be any incompatibility between the requirements imposed by virtue of section 72(2) and any other additional requirements imposed by a local authority.

Section 73(8): mirrors section 72(6). Under the prior law, there was no obligation to impose any conditions at all but where a local authority decided to do so it could only apply to those specified in the Nurseries and Child Minders Regulation Act 1948. This was considered far too rigid: see Minister of State, Hansard Col 394 Standing Committee B, 6 June 1989: see also section 72(6).

Section 74. Cancellation of registration

74.—(1) A local authority may at any time cancel the registration of any person under section 71(1)(a) if—

    (a) it appears to them that the circumstances of the case are such that they would be justified in refusing to register that person as a child minder;

    (b) the care provided by that person when looking after any child as a child minder is, in the opinion of the authority, seriously inadequate having regard to the needs of that child; or

    (c) that person has—

        (i) contravened, or failed to comply with, any requirement imposed on him under section 72; or

        (ii) failed to pay any annual fee under paragraph 7 of Schedule 9 within the prescribed time.

(2) A local authority may at any time cancel the registration of any person under section 71(1)(b) with respect to particular premises if—

    (a) it appears to them that the circumstances of the case are such that they would be justified in refusing to register that person with respect to those premises;

    (b) the day care provided by that person on those premises is, in the opinion of the authority, seriously inadequate having regard to the needs of the children concerned; or

(c) that person has—

(i) contravened, or failed to comply with, any requirement imposed on him under section 73; or

(ii) failed to pay any annual fee under paragraph 7 of Schedule 9 within the prescribed time.

(3) A local authority may at any time cancel all registrations of any person under section 71(1)(b) if it appears to them that the circumstances of the case are such that they would be justified in refusing to register that person with respect to any premises.

(4) Where a requirement to carry out repairs or make alterations or additions has been imposed on a registered person under section 72 or 73, his registration shall not be cancelled on the ground that the premises are not fit to be used for looking after children if—

(a) the time set for complying with the requirements has not expired, and

(b) it is shown that the condition of the premises is due to the repairs not having been carried out or the alterations or additions not having been made.

(5) Any cancellation under this section must be in writing.

(6) In considering the needs of any child for the purposes of subsection (1)(b) or (2)(b), a local authority shall, in particular, have regard to the child's religious persuasion, racial origin and cultural and linguistic background.

Annotation

Section 74: provides for the cancellation of the registration of any person registered as a child minder or day care provider on one of several grounds. These include the circumstances which exist that would entitle registration to be declined—that the care which is provided is seriously inadequate for the needs of the children, or where a requirement has been broken or the annual fee unpaid. Payment of the annual inspection fee is a condition of continued registration: see Schedule 9 paragraph 7(2). Section 74 also provides that in considering the needs of the children particular regard should be had to their religious persuasion, racial origin and cultural and linguistic background.

Section 74(1): provides that a local authority may cancel the registration of a child minder in accordance with prescribed conditions. The purpose of Part X of the Act is to replace the Nurseries and Child Minders Regulation Act 1948 in such a way that the registration system is strengthened. It follows that where a local authority is under a duty to attach certain conditions to a person's registration, with powers to add others, and to inspect annually, they should also have power to cancel a person's registration if they consider the care being given to a particular child to be seriously inadequate—hence section 74(1).

Section 74(2): extends the power of cancellation to include day care providers and covers not only inadequacy of the person but also inadequacy of the premises. Inadequacy means what it says in section 74(2)(b) as well as in section 74(1)(b). However, the government recognised that training had an important part to play in improving a person's skills in looking after children but were not convinced it should be a mandatory pre-registration requirement in primary legislation: see the government's response on the second report from the Social Services Committee on the Children Bill H/C 578.

Section 74(3): provides that a local authority may at any time cancel all registrations of a day care provider. Note that section 71(3) requires separate registration for each of the premises in which a person provides day care within the area of a local authority. This was to ensure that requirements could be tailor-made for each premises. Section 74(3) goes to the inadequacy of a person, in all the circumstances of the case, rather than to inadequacy of premises.

Section 74(4): provides time to render inadequate premises adequate. Though section 74(4) refers to alterations or additions imposed on a registered person under sections 72 or 73, alterations or additions may also be required under these sections following inspection. For the provisions on inspection see section 76.

Section 74(5): provides that any cancellation under this section must be in writing. There is always the prospect that any cancellation will lead to a local authority being taken to court to have the cancellation overturned; hence the need to have cancellation in writing and the provision written into the Act under section 74(5) as a legal requirement: see section 77 for the provison on appeals.

Section 74(6): provides that regard should be had for a child's religious persuasion, racial origin and cultural and linguistic background. The purpose of section 74(6) is to encourage a local authority when dealing with child minders and day care providers to take account of the ethnic composition of their areas and to have regard for the different racial groups of children in need: see Minister of State, 23 April 1989, Hansard Col 485. See also sections 61(3) and 64(3).

Section 75. Protection of children in an emergency

75. —(1) If—

(a) a local authority apply to the court for an order—

(i) cancelling a registered person's registration;
(ii) varying any requirement imposed on a registered person under section 72 or 73; or
(iii) removing a requirement or imposing an additional requirement on such a person; and

(b) it appears to the court that a child who is being, or may be, looked after by that person, or (as the case may be) in accordance with the provision for day care made by that person, is suffering, or is likely to suffer, significant harm,

the court may make the order.

(2) any such cancellation, variation, removal or imposition shall have effect from the date on which the order is made.

(3) An application under subsection (1) may be made *ex parte* and shall be supported by a written statement of the authority's reasons for making it.

(4) Where an order is made under this section, the authority shall serve on the registered person, as soon as is reasonably practicable after the making of the order—

(a) notice of the order and of its terms; and
(b) a copy of the statement of the authority's reasons which supported their application for the order.

(5) Where the court imposes or varies any requirement under subsection (1), the requirement, or the requirement as varied, shall be treated for all purposes, other than those of section 77, as if it had been imposed under section 72 or (as the case may be) 73 by the authority concerned.

Annotation

Section 75: deals with the protection of children in an emergency and provides a local authority with a power to have a person's registration cancelled or varied by asking the courts for an order if it appears that the child is suffering or is likely to suffer significant harm. A local authority has no power to remove a child from the care of a child minder or day care provider without a court order.

Section 75(1): provides for the cancellation, variation, removal or imposition of any registration or requirement upon registration. Note that this does not give a local authority the power to remove a child from a child minder or day care provider. That would require an emergency protection order where the court was satisfied that there was reasonable cause to believe that the child was likely to suffer significant harm if not removed to accommodation provided by or on behalf of the local authority: see section 44(1)(a).

Section 75(2): provides that any such cancellation, variation, removal or imposition shall have effect from the date on which the order is made. Notice that an order is to be sought is not required under section 75(2) since it deals with an emergency situation where the child's welfare is paramount.

Section 75(3): provides that any application under section 75(1) may be made *ex parte*. It is the intention under the Children Act that applications should be made to a full court during court hours, although rules which prevent the publication of details of children's cases which are heard in private in the High Court and county courts continue to have effect: see section 12 of the Administration of Justice Act 1960, as amended by Schedule 13, paragraph 14. The Act also enables rules of court to permit a magistrates' court to sit in private in proceedings in which powers under it may be exercised with respect to a child: see section 97(1).

Section 75(4): provides that whilst notice that an order is to be sought need not be given, because the child may be suffering, or is likely to suffer significant harm, nevertheless notice of the order and its terms together with a statement by the local authority shall be served upon the registered person as soon as is reasonably practicable. Contrast the term "reasonably practicable" with the fourteen day period in section 77(1) dealing with appeals within the framework of Part X.

Section 75(5): provides for the incorporation into any registration of any imposition or variation of a requirement by the court so that it conforms with the provisions of section 72. A local authority which has applied to the court thus adopts the modified requirements as their own.

Section 76. Inspection

76. — (1) Any person authorised to do so by a local authority may at any reasonable time enter—

(a) any domestic premises within the authority's area on which child minding is at any time carried on; or

(b) any premises within their area on which day care for children under the age of eight is at any time provided.

(2) Where a local authority have reasonable cause to believe that a child is being looked after on any premises within their area in contravention of this Part, any person authorised to do so by the authority may enter those premises at any reasonable time.

(3) Any person entering premises under this section may inspect—

(a) the premises;
(b) any children being looked after on the premises;
(c) the arrangements made for their welfare; and
(d) any records relating to them which are kept as a result of this Part.

(4) Every local authority shall exercise their power to inspect the premises mentioned in subsection (1) at least once every year.

(5) Any person inspecting any records under this section—

(a) shall be entitled at any reasonable time to have access to, and inspect and check the operation of, any computer and any associated apparatus or material which is, or has been, in use in connection with the records in question; and

(b) may require—

(i) the person by whom or on whose behalf the computer is or has been so used; or
(ii) any person having charge of, or otherwise concerned with the operation of, the computer, apparatus or material,

to afford him such reasonable assistance as he may require.

(6) A person exercising any power conferred by this section shall, if so required, produce some duly authenticated document showing his authority to do so.

(7) Any person who intentionally obstructs another in the exercise of any such power shall be guilty of an offence and liable on summary conviction to a fine not exceeding level 3 on the standard scale.

Annotation

Section 76: replaces the section on inspection in the Nurseries and Child Minders Regulation Act 1948 and enables authorised persons to enter and inspect premises in which child minding is being carried on, or where day care is provided. Open to inspection are the premises, the children being looked after, the arrangements for their welfare, and any records kept relating to the service which registered persons are giving. An important addition to the 1948 Act is the imposition of a duty upon a local authority to carry out an inspection at least once a year. This does not, however, restrict the number of inspections which a local authority may carry out—it is designed to provide a ceiling.

Section 76(1): empowers any person authorised by a local authority to enter premises both domestic and non-domestic within the authority's area where child minding or day care provision takes place. According to the Minister of State, "We know that many local authorities make no inspections, but that is not necessarily because of a shortage of staff. We shall now require them to inspect at least once a year. That is fair. I stress the words 'at least'. It does not mean that they cannot inspect more frequently, if they so wish, and I hope some of them will do so": see Hansard Col 405 Standing Committee B 6 June 1989.

Section 76(2): empowers a local authority to use the full extent of its investigative duties in relation to child minders and day care providers. The full range of such investigative duties available to local authorities in order to protect children are to be found under Part X of the Act. These include applications for an emergency protection order, a child assessment order and a recovery order: see sections 47(1)(b), 47(2) and 47(1)(a).

Section 76(3): enables a person so authorised by a local authority to inspect those premises where children are looked after, the arrangements for their welfare and any records kept relating to the services provided in accordance with Part X of the Act. Note that such inspection powers do not derive from the duty to carry out routine inspections pursuant to section 76(4) but under the investigative duties to be found under Part V.

Section 76(4): imposes a duty on a local authority at least once a year to inspect domestic and non domestic premises in relation to child minding or day care provision. A local authority may perform this inspection duty more often: see section 74(1). Schedule 9, paragraph 7 enables a local authority to charge a fee for annual inspection. The Secretary of State shall fix the fees at a level appropriate to particular organisations: see Minister of State Hansard Col 405 Standing Committee B 6 June 1989.

Section 76(5): enables a person authorised by a local authority to have access to computerised information, access to computers and other hi-tech facilities, and assistance from those persons associated with the computers or hi-tech facilities.

Section 76(6): mirrors section 50(8)(b) and section 67(4) which require an officer to produce identification before seeking to carry out his duties in accordance with section 76.

Section 76(7): provides that a person guilty of an offence of intentionally obstructing an authorised person acting in accordance with his powers under seciton 76, shall be liable to a fine on summary conviction.

Section 77. Appeals

77.—(1) Not less than 14 days before—

(a) refusing an application for registration under section 71;
(b) cancelling any such registration;
(c) refusing consent under paragraph 2 of Schedule 9;
(d) imposing, removing or varying any requirement under section 72 or 73; or
(e) refusing to grant any application for the variation or removal of any such requirement,

the authority concerned shall send to the applicant, or (as the case may be) registered person, notice in writing of their intention to take the step in question ("the step").

(2) Every such notice shall—

(a) give the authority's reasons for proposing to take the step; and
(b) inform the person concerned of his rights under this section.

(3) Where the recipient of such a notice informs the authority in writing of his desire to object to the step being taken, the authority shall afford him an opportunity to do so.

(4) Any objection made under subsection (3) may be made in person or by a representative.

(5) If the authority, after giving the person concerned an opportunity to object to the step being taken, decide nevertheless to take it they shall send him written notice of their decision.

(6) A person aggrieved by the taking of any step mentioned in subsection (1) may appeal against it to the court.

(7) Where the court imposes or varies any requirement under subsection (8) or (9) the requirement, or the requirement as

varied, shall be treated for all purposes (other than this section) as if it had been imposed by the authority concerned.

(8) Where the court allows an appeal against the refusal or cancellation of any registration under section 71 it may impose requirements under section 72 or (as the case may be) 73.

(9) Where the court allows an appeal against such a requirement it may, instead of cancelling the requirement, vary it.

(10) In Scotland, an appeal under subsection (6) shall be by summary application to the sheriff and shall be brought within 21 days from the date of the step to which the appeal relates.

(11) A step of a kind mentioned in subsection (1)(b) or (d) shall not take effect until the expiry of the time within which an appeal may be brought under this section or, where such an appeal is brought, before its determination.

Annotation

Section 77: replaces the section in the Nurseries and Child Minders Regulation Act 1948 which dealt with the right of appeal of a registered person, but extends this right of appeal to registered persons whose applications for variation or removal of any requirement is refused, or where impositions or variations are to be made by a local authority. It is the purpose of the Act to identify a number of arrangements which may be made where children spend time with a child minder or in day care, which require regulation. Also it is designed to provide a local authority with a general duty to take steps to satisfy themselves as to the welfare of the children concerned. It follows that where requirements may be imposed on providers—and where necessary they may be prevented from looking after children by a refusal to admit registration—there must be an appeals procedure; hence section 77.

Section 77(1): introduces the first of a two-tier appeals procedure by imposing a duty on a local authority, fourteen days before action is taken, to so notify the applicant or registered person. Note, however, that in order to permit immediate cancellation or the imposition, removal or variation of requirements, where it appears that a person is suffering, or is likely to suffer, significant harm, a local authority may apply directly to the court without giving notice to the registered person: see section 75(1)(2) and (3).

Section 77(2): provides that a local authority must give their reasons for the action they propose to take and inform the applicant or registered person of the right of appeal under section 77. The response of the applicant or registered person may consist of explaining why it is not appropriate for the local authority to take the action they propose—"appeal against conviction"—or why such action should not be carried out—"appeal against sentence".

Section 77(3): provides an opportunity to an applicant or registered person to give notice in writing to object to the action proposed. A local authority will then afford the opportunity to do so. The objection may be made orally or in writing.

Section 77(4): provides that any objection may be made by the applicant or registered person or by a representative. That is to say he is entitled to legal or any other representation. This would equally apply where the hearing is oral, pursuant to the provisions of section 77(3).

Section 77(5): provides that where a local authority reject the submissions made by an applicant or registered person, either acting on his behalf or through a representative, they shall do so in writing. This would bring to an end the first tier of the appeal procedure between a local authority and an applicant or registered person and open the way to the second: see section 77(6).

Section 77(6): provides that an applicant or registered person aggrieved by any action taken in accordance with section 77(1) may appeal against it to the court. There is no legal obligation upon an applicant or registered person to involve himself in the first tier of the appeal procedure—he may simply await notification of any decision by a local authority. In practice, however, an applicant or registered person would wish both tiers to be brought into play in the hope that resolution within the first-tier procedure might obviate court action.

Section 77(7): mirrors section 75(5) and provides for the incorporation into any registration after allowing an appeal, of any imposition or variation of a requirement of the court so that it conforms with the provisions of sections 72 or 73, as the case may be. Thus, a local authority will be required to adopt as their own any requirements of the court.

Section 77(8): provides that the court may make its own requirements in accordance with the provisions of sections 72 or 73, as the case may be, where it allows an appeal against the refusal or cancellation of a registration.

Section 77(9): provides for the court to exercise its powers by varying rather than cancelling a registration. The court will have before it all the range of options available to a local authority when exercising its regulation-making powers under Part X.

Section 77(10): provides the procedures for appeal in accordance with section 77(6) as these relate to Scotland. Note that whereas section 77(10) provides for a limitation of twenty-one days for an appeal to be brought, no such time limit is imposed for appeals in England and Wales in accordance with the provisions of section 77. This will be covered by regulations or rules of court.

Section 77(11): provides that where the first tier of the appeal procedure is completed, no action can be taken by a local authority until the time for an appeal has passed, or an appeal has been determined. This refers to the cancellation of a registration or the imposition, removal or variation of any requirement.

Section 78. Offences

78.—(1) No person shall provide day care for children under the age of eight on any premises within the area of a local authority unless he is registered by the authority under section 71(1)(b) with respect to those premises.

(2) If any person contravenes subsection (1) without reasonable excuse, he shall be guilty of an offence.

(3) No person shall act as a child minder on domestic premises within the area of a local authority unless he is registered by the authority under section 71(1)(a).

(4) Where it appears to a local authority that a person has contravened subsection (3), they may serve a notice ("an enforcement notice") on him.

(5) An enforcement notice shall have effect for a period of one year beginning with the date on which it is served.

(6) If a person with respect to whom an enforcement notice is in force contravenes subsection (3) without reasonable excuse he shall be guilty of an offence.

(7) Subsection (6) applies whether or not the subsequent contravention occurs within the area of the authority who served the enforcement notice.

(8) Any person who without reasonable excuse contravenes, or otherwise fails to comply with, any requirement imposed on him under section 72 or 73 shall be guilty of an offence.

(9) If any person—

    (a) acts as a child minder on domestic premises at any time when he is disqualified by regulations made under paragraph 2 of Schedule 9; or

  (b) contravenes any of sub-paragraphs (3) to (5) of paragraph
       2,

he shall be guilty of an offence.

(10) Where a person contravenes sub-paragraph (3) of paragraph 2 he shall not be guilty of an offence under this section if
he proves that he did not know, and had no reasonable grounds
for believing, that the person in question was living or employed
in the household.

(11) Where a person contravenes sub-paragraph (5) of paragraph 2 he shall not be guilty of an offence under this section if
he proves that he did not know, and had no reasonable grounds
for believing, that the person whom he was employing was disqualified.

  (12) A person guilty of an offence under this section shall be
        liable on summary conviction—

    (a) in the case of an offence under subsection (8), to a fine
         not exceeding level 4 on the standard scale;
    (b) in the case of an offence under subsection (9), to impris-
         onment for a term not exceeding six months, or to a fine
         not exceeding level 5 on the standard scale, or to both;
         and
    (c) in the case of any other offence, to a fine not exceeding
         level 5 on the standard scale.

Annotation

Section 78: provides that it is an offence to look after children or
provide day care while unregistered. There is no difference to the
prior law under the Nurseries and Child Minders Regulation Act
1948, except in the treatment of the occasional baby sitter or child
minder, who would technically be guilty of an offence if they were
not registered. Section 78 gives a local authority power to issue
an enforcement notice when they discover that an unregistered
person is child minding. This means that occasional child minders
shall not be guilty of an offence unless they continue to child mind
without being registered, after receiving a notice from the local
authority.

Section 78(1): provides that a person must be registered in regard
to specific non-domestic premises in order to provide day care for
children under the age of eight. There is a differentiation between
those persons registering as day care providers under the provisions of section 71(1)(b) and those who are child minders and
registered separately under section 71(1)(a).

Section 78(2): provides that it is an offence to provide day care provision on non-domestic premises without prior registration. Note the defence of reasonable excuse. Where such a defence is pleaded, it will be for the court to decide what is reasonable in all the circumstances.

Section 78(3): provides that a person must be registered in regard to domestic premises in order to child mind within an authority's area. In order to protect the occasional child minder from criminal liability, such a child minder no longer commits an offence simply by a failure to register in accordance with the provisions of section 71(1)(a).

Section 78(4): provides that where it appears to a local authority that a person has contravened section 78(3), that is to say is child minding on domestic premises without registration pursuant to the provisions of section 71(1)(a), the local authority may serve an enforcement notice on such a child minder. Where no such enforcement order is served upon the occasional child minder, this takes such child minder out of the purview of the criminal law.

Section 78(5): provides that any enforcement order served under the provisions of section 78(4) shall be effective for one year beginning with the day on which it is served. That is to say no person can act as a child minder within the year unless registered in accordance with the provisions of 71(1)(a).

Section 78(6): provides that where a person with respect to whom an enforcement order is in force child minds on domestic premises without registration, and without reasonable excuse, such person shall be guilty of an offence.

Section 78(7): provides that an enforcement order is not territorial and is not restricted to the area covered by the issuing local authority.

Section 78(8): makes it an offence to contravene any requirement imposed by sections 72 or 73. Section 72 imposes a duty on a local authority to attach conditions to the registration of child minders and section 73 imposes duties upon a local authority in relation to the requirements to be complied with by those persons providing day care for young children similar to those to be found in section 72.

Section 78(9): provides for it to be an offence for any person to act as a child minder on domestic premises when disqualified by regulations made by the Secretary of State. It applies equally to those classes of persons defined in Schedule 9 paragraph 2(3) to

(5) dealing with disqualification. The Secretary of State has extensive powers under Part XI of the Act which extend and update his functions in connection with children: see sections 80–83.

Section 78(10): mirrors section 70(2) and raises the defence of no guilty intent.

Section 78(11): mirrors section 78(10) and raises the defence of no guilty intent.

Section 78(12): provides a number of different penalties to which a person becomes liable on summary conviction and mirrors the provisions of section 70(3)(4)(5) and (6) in reflecting different levels of penalties to match the different levels of seriousness of the offences.

Section 79. Application of this Part to Scotland

79. —(1) In the application to Scotland of this Part—

    (a) "the court" means the sheriff;
    (b) "day care" means any form of care or of activity supervised by a responsible person provided for children during the day (whether or not it is provided on a regular basis);
    (c) "education authority" has the same meaning as in the Education (Scotland) Act 1980;
    (d) "local authority foster parent" means a foster parent with whom a child is placed by a local authority;
    (e) for references to a person having parental responsibility for a child there shall be substituted references to a person in whom parental rights and duties relating to the child are vested; and
    (f) for references to fostering a child privately there shall be substituted references to maintaining a foster child within the meaning of the Foster Children (Scotland) Act 1984.

Annotation

Section 79: provides for the application of Part X of the Act to Scotland. We have seen that the Act in general applies only to England and Wales but that those provisions relating to child minding and day care for young children apply also to Scotland— hence the need for section 79. For example, the new concept of parental responsibility, summing up as it does a collection of duties, rights and authority which a parent has in respect of his child, is unknown to Scotland—here it is known as the person in whom parental rights and duties relating to the child are vested: see section 79(e). Another example is that the definition of day care pursuant to section 71(2)(b) is where a person does not provide day care for children unless the period, or the total of periods, during which children are looked after exceeds two hours in any day. In Scotland day care means any form of care or of activity supervised by a responsible person provided for children during the day (whether or not it is provided on a regular basis): see section 79(b).

PART XI

SECRETARY OF STATE'S SUPERVISORY FUNCTIONS AND RESPONSIBILITIES

Section 80. Inspection of children's homes etc. by persons authorised by Secretary of State

80.—(1) The Secretary of State may cause to be inspected from time t9po time any—

(a) children's home;

(b) premises in which a child who is being looked after by a local authority is living;

(c) premises in which a child who is being accommodated by or on behalf of a local education authority or voluntary organisation is living;

(d) premises in which a child who is being accommodated by or on behalf of a health authority is living;

(e) premises in which a child is living with a person with whom he has been placed by an adoption agency;

(f) premises in which a child who is a protected child is, or will be, living;

(g) premises in which a privately fostered child, or child who is treated as a foster child by virtue of paragraph 9 of Schedule 8, is living or in which it is proposed that he will live;

(h) premises on which any person is acting as a child minder;

(i) premises with respect to which a person is registered under section 71(1)(b);

(j) residential care home, nursing home or mental nursing home required to be registered under the Registered Homes Act 1984 and used to accommodate children;

(k) premises which are provided by a local authority and in which any service is provided by that authority under Part III;

(l) independent school providing accommodation for any child;

(2) An inspection under this section shall be conducted by a person authorised to do so by the Secretary of State.

(3) An officer of a local authority shall not be so authorised except with the consent of that authority.

(4) The Secretary of State may require any person of a kind mentioned in subsection (5) to furnish him with such information, or allow him to inspect such records (in whatever form they are held), relating to—

(a) any premises to which subsection (1) or, in relation to Scotland, subsection (1)(h) or (i) applies;
(b) any child who is living in any such premises;
(c) the discharge by the Secretary of State of any of his functions under this Act; or
(d) the discharge by any local authority of any of their functions under this Act,

as the Secretary of State may at any time direct.

(5) The persons are any—

(a) local authority;
(b) voluntary organisation;
(c) person carrying on a children's home;
(d) proprietor of an independent school;
(e) person fostering any privately fostered child or providing accommodation for a child on behalf of a local authority, local education authority, health authority or voluntary organisation;
(f) local education authority providing accommodation for any child;
(g) person employed in a teaching or administrative capacity at any educational establishment (whether or not maintained by a local education authority) at which a child is accommodated on behalf of a local authority or local education authority;
(h) person who is the occupier of any premises in which any person acts as a child minder (within the meaning of Part X) or provides day care for young children (within the meaning of that Part);
(i) person carrying on any home of a kind mentioned in subsection (1)(j).

(6) Any person inspecting any home or other premises under this section may—

(a) inspect the children there; and
(b) make such examination into the state and management

of the home or premises and the treatment of the children there as he thinks fit.

(7) Any person authorised by the Secretary of State to exercise the power to inspect records conferred by subsection (4)—

(a) shall be entitled at any reasonable time to have access to, and inspect and check the operation of, any computer and any associated apparatus or material which is or has been in use in connection with the records in question; and

(b) may require—

(i) the person by whom or on whose behalf the computer is or has been so used; or

(ii) any person having charge of, or otherwise concerned with the operation of, the computer, apparatus or material,

to afford him such reasonable assistance as he may require.

(8) A person authorised to inspect any premises under this section shall have a right to enter the premises for that purpose, and for any purpose specified in subsection (4), at any reasonable time.

(9) Any person exercising that power shall, if so required, produce some duly authenticated document showing his authority to do so.

(10) Any person who intentionally obstructs another in the exercise of that power shall be guilty of an offence and liable on summary conviction to a fine not exceeding level 3 on the standard scale.

(11) The Secretary of State may by order provide for subsections (1), (4) and (6) not to apply in relation to such homes, or other premises, as may be specified in the order.

(12) Without prejudice to section 104, any such order may make different provision with respect to each of those subsections.

Annotation

Section 80: introduces Part XI of the Act which provides for inspection, by persons authorised by the Secretary of State, of children's homes and other establishments, for inquiries and financial support by the Secretary of State and for returns of information. Section 80 permits the Secretary of State to cause to be inspected specified classes of establishment in which children are living or are being looked after, and the children in those establishments, and provides a right of entry. Section 80 also provides for the furnishing of information and inspection of records. Obstruction is to be an offence subject to a fine not exceeding level three on the standard scale. Section 80 replaces sections 74 and 75 of the Child Care Act 1980.

Section 80(1): updates and extends those definitions of premises in section 74(1) of the Child Care Act 1980. Note that the provisions of section 80(1)(c)(d) where a child is being accommodated by or on behalf of a local education authority or by or on behalf of a health authority are dealt with in section 85, the provisions of section 80(1)(j) by section 86, and the welfare of children accommodated in independent schools referred to in section 80(1)(l), by section 87. In relation to section 80(1)(c)(f) concerning premises in which a child has been placed by an adoption agency or where a protected child is living, see Part III of the Adoption Act 1976.

Section 80(2): provides for an inspection to be carried out by a person authorised by the Secretary of State. The person so authorised will be empowered to inspect premises and to provide the Secretary of State with information.

Section 80(3): provides that no officer of a local authority may be so authorised without the consent of the local authority. A local authority may also conduct or assist others to conduct research: see section 83(2).

Section 80(4): provides that the Secretary of State may require certain persons to supply him with such records or information as he may direct relating to any premises to which section 80 applies. See also section 80(6).

Section 80(5): defines those persons to whom section 80(4) applies. Note that these persons are generally persons or agencies who are responsible for accommodating children or for the premises to which section 80 applies. Thus the paramountcy principle in relation to children, and the supervision thereof, extends beyond the investigative duties of local authorities back to the Secretary of State himself.

Section 80(6): enables a person acting in accordance with powers conferred upon him by the Secretary of State pursuant to section 80 to inspect the children in the premises, to examine the management of the premises and the treatment of children there, as he thinks fit. Information garnered from such access may be supplied to the Secretary of State in accordance with section 80(4).

Section 80(7): enables an authorised person to have access to data held on computer and to all computer equipment and material, and enables the authorised person to require to render certain person such assistance as he may reasonably require. It mirrors section 76(5) dealing with powers of inspection.

Section 80(8): provides an authorised person a right of entry to premises, access to any child who is living on such premises and to records, in order to fulfil other duties conferred upon him by section 80, at any reasonable time.

Section 80(9): requires such an authorised person to produce evidence of his authority, if asked to do so. It mirrors section 76(6) and other provisions, notably sections 50(8)(b) and section 67(4).

Section 80(10): provides that it shall be an offence to obstruct any authorised person in the exercise of those duties conferred upon him by section 80. Liability on summary conviction is a maximum fine not exceeding level three on the standard scale.

Section 80(11): enables the Secretary of State to order that section 80(1)(4) or (6) do not apply to such accommodation as is specified in the order.

Section 80(12): provides that, without prejudice to section 104, dealing with the powers of the Lord Chancellor or the Secretary of State, any order made under section 80(11) may make different provision with respect to section 80(1)(4) and (6).

Section 81. Inquiries

81.—(1) The Secretary of State may cause an inquiry to be held into any matter connected with—

    (a) the functions of the social services committee of a local authority, in so far as those functions relate to children;

    (b) the functions of an adoption agency;

    (c) the functions of a voluntary organisation, in so far as those functions relate to children;

    (d) a [*registered*] children's home or voluntary home;

    (e) a residential care home, nursing home or mental nursing home, so far as it provides accommodation for children;

    (f) a home provided [in accordance with arrangements made] by the Secretary of State under section 82(5);

    (g) the detention of a child under section 53 of the Children and Young Persons Act 1933.

Note: The words *in italics* within square brackets were deleted by the Courts and Legal Services Act 1990.
Note: The words within square brackets were inserted by the Courts and Legal Services Act 1990.

(2) Before an inquiry is begun, the Secretary of State may direct that it shall be held in private.

(3) Where no direction has been given, the person holding the inquiry may if he thinks fit hold it, or any part of it, in private.

(4) Subsections (2) to (5) of section 250 of the Local Government Act 1972 (powers in relation to local inquiries) shall apply in relation to an inquiry under this section as they apply in relation to a local inquiry under that section.

(5) In this section "functions" includes powers and duties which a person has otherwise than by virtue of any enactment.

Annotation

Section 81: re-enacts section 76 of the Child Care Act 1980 with certain amendments. Section 76 enabled the Secretary of State to cause an inquiry to be held into matters relating to certain authorities, agencies or homes relating to children. Section 81 amends those provisions by extending them to include the functions of a voluntary organisation insofar as they relate to children, not just voluntary homes, registered children's homes and residential care homes, nursing homes and mental nursing homes insofar as these provide accommodation for children.

Section 81(1): enables the Secretary of State to cause an inquiry to be held into any matter connected with certain homes and into the functions of a social services committee of a local authority, insofar as these functions relate to children. Thus, the investigative duty of a local authority and the provisions which it makes for the welfare of children will always be subject to inquiry by the Secretary of State, if the Secretary of State thinks fit. It was under the powers of section 76 of the Child Care Act 1980, now replaced by the provisions of section 81, that a statutory inquiry was established to look into the arrangements for dealing with suspected cases of child abuse in Cleveland from 1 January 1987.

Section 81(2): enables the Secretary of State to cause an enquiry to be held in private. Section 81(2) replaces section 76(2) of the Child Care Act 1980.

Section 81(3): provides that, in the absence of any directions in accordance with section 81(2), the person conducting the inquiry may hold it, or any part of it, in private. Thus the Butler-Sloss enquiry into cases of suspected child abuse in Cleveland was held partly in public and partly in private. The evidence of parents was heard in private and never revealed to the public.

Section 81(4): replaces section 76(3) of the Child Care Act 1980 and provides that section 250(2)(b) of the Local Government Act 1972—powers in relation to local inquiries—shall also apply to inquiries held under section 81(4).

Section 81(5): replaces section 76(4) and defines "functions" for the purposes of section 81.

Section 82. Financial support by Secretary of State

82.—(1) The Secretary of State may (with the consent of the Treasury) defray or contribute towards—

(a) any fees or expenses incurred by any person undergoing approved child care training;

(b) any fees charged, or expenses incurred, by any person providing approved child care training or preparing material for use in connection with such training; or

(c) the cost of maintaining any person undergoing such training.

(2) The Secretary of State may make grants to local authorities in respect of expenditure incurred by them in providing secure accommodation in community homes other than assisted community homes.

(3) Where—

(a) a grant has been made under subsection (2) with respect to any secure accommodation; but

(b) the grant is not used for the purpose for which it was made or the accommodation is not used as, or ceases to be used as, secure accommodation,

the Secretary of State may (with the consent of the Treasury) require the authority concerned to repay the grant, in whole or in part.

(4) The Secretary of State may make grants to voluntary organisations towards—

(a) expenditure incurred by them in connection with the establishment, maintenance or improvement of voluntary homes which, at the time when the expenditure was incurred—

(i) were assisted community homes; or

(ii) were designated as such; or

(b) expenses incurred in respect of the borrowing of money to defray any such expenditure.

(5) The Secretary of State may arrange for the provision, equip-

ment and maintenance of homes for the accommodation of children who are in need of particular facilities and services which—

(a) are or will be provided in those homes; and

(b) in the opinion of the Secretary of State, are unlikely to be readily available in community homes.

(6) In this Part—

"child care training" means training undergone by any person with a view to, or in the course of—

(a) his employment for the purposes of any of the functions mentioned in section 83(9) or in connection with the adoption of children or with the accommodation of children in a residential care home, nursing home or mental nursing home; or

(b) his employment by a voluntary organisation for similar purposes;

"approved child care training" means child care training which is approved by the Secretary of State; and

"secure accommodation" means accommodation provided for the purpose of restricting the liberty of children.

(7) Any grant made under this section shall be of such amount, and shall be subject to such conditions, as the Secretary of State may (with the consent of the Treasury) determine.

Annotation

Section 82: enables the Secretary of State or any local authority to conduct research into various matters relating to children. Section 82 also provides that the Secretary of State, with the consent of the Treasury, may assist with expenditure in relation to training and the provision of secure accommodation and special facilities, and with the expenditure incurred by voluntary organisations in connection with voluntary homes. Section 82 re-enacts with certain minor amendments sections 78, 80, 81 and 82 of the Child Care Act 1980.

Section 82(1): re-enacts section 78 of the Child Care Act 1980 which concerned the power of the Secretary of State to make grants to persons undergoing training in child care. Section 82(1) extends this power to include those persons who are providing such training as well as those who are undergoing training.

Section 82(2): re-enacts section 81(1) of the Child Care Act 1980 relating to powers to make grants towards the expenditure incurred by a local authority in providing secure accommodation.

Section 82(3): re-enacts section 81(2) of the Child Care Act 1980 which concerned the repayment of grants when the grant was not used for the purpose for which it was made or the premise ceased to be used for secure accommodation purposes. The requirement under section 81(2) of the Child Care Act 1980 is extended by section 82(3) of the present Act to cover those cases where the premises are not used for secure accommodation.

Section 82(4): re-enacts section 82 of the Child Care Act 1980, which empowered the Secretary of State to make grants to voluntary homes in respect of expenditure incurred in establishing, maintaining or improving certain assisted community homes.

Section 82(5): re-enacts section 80 of the Child Care Act 1980, which enabled the Secretary of State to provide homes offering specialised facilities which were unlikely to be available elsewhere, for example youth treatment centres. This provision is extended to apply not only in respect of children in care, or accommodated by or on behalf of a local authority, but to include other children, for example children who have been convicted of a serious offence, or children subject to a Scottish supervision order who may need to be so accommodated.

Section 82(6): provides definitions for the purposes of section 82.

Section 82(7): provides that grants made in accordance with section 82 may be subject to such conditions as the Secretary of State, with the consent of the Treasury, may determine.

Section 83. Research and returns of information

83.—(1) The Secretary of State may conduct, or assist other persons in conducting, research into any matter connected with—

(a) his functions, or the functions of local authorities, under the enactments mentioned in subsection (9);
(b) the adoption of children; or
(c) the accommodation of children in a residential care home, nursing home or mental nursing home.

(2) Any local authority may conduct, or assist other persons in conducting, research into any matter connected with—

(a) their functions under the enactments mentioned in subsection (9);
(b) the adoption of children; or
(c) the accommodation of children in a residential care home, nursing home or mental nursing home.

(3) Every local authority shall, at such times and in such form

as the Secretary of State may direct, transmit to him such particulars as he may require with respect to—

(a) the performance by the local authority of all or any of their functions—

(i) under the enactments mentioned in subsection (9); or
(ii) in connection with the accommodation of children in a residential care home, nursing home or mental nursing home; and

(b) the children in relation to whom the authority have exercised those functions.

(4) Every voluntary organisation shall, at such times and in such form as the Secretary of State may direct, transmit to him such particulars as he may require with respect to children accommodated by them or on their behalf.

(5) The Secretary of State may direct the clerk of each magistrates' court to which the direction is expressed to relate to transmit—

(a) to such person as may be specified in the direction; and
(b) at such times and in such form as he may direct,

such particulars as he may require with respect to proceedings of the court which relate to children.

(6) The Secretary of State shall in each year lay before Parliament a consolidated and classified abstract of the information transmitted to him under subsections (3) to (5).

(7) The Secretary of State may institute research designed to provide information on which requests for information under this section may be based.

(8) The Secretary of State shall keep under review the adequacy of the provision of child care training and for that purpose shall receive and consider any information from or representations made by—

(a) the Central Council for Education and Training in Social Work;
(b) such representatives of local authorities as appear to him to be appropriate; or
(c) such other persons or organisations as appear to him to be appropriate,

concerning the provision of such training.

(9) The enactments are —

    (a) this Act;

    (b) the Children and Young Persons Acts 1933 to 1969;

    (c) section 116 of the Mental Health Act 1983 (so far as it relates to children looked after by local authorities);

    (d) section 10 of the Mental Health (Scotland) Act 1984 (so far as it relates to children for whom local authorities have responsibility).

Annotation

Section 83: enables the Secretary of State or any local authority to conduct, or assist others in conducting, research into various matters relating to children. Section 83 requires local authorities, voluntary organisations and clerks of court to make returns of information to the Secretary of State, and requires him to lay before Parliament each year an abstract of the information. Section 83 also requires the Secretary of State to keep under review the adequacy of the provision of child care training. This is a new provision.

Section 83(1): re-enacts section 77(1) of the Child Care Act 1980, extended through the application of section 83(9) to include matters formerly relating to the Nurseries and Child Minders Regulation Act 1948 but which have now been replaced by provisions incorporated into the present Act: see Part X sections 71–79. Also any matter relating to the accommodation of children in residential care, nursing homes or mental nursing homes: see section 86.

Section 83(2): re-enacts section 77(2) of the Child Care Act 1980 and extends its provisions in the same way as section 83(1).

Section 83(3): requires a local authority to provide the Secretary of State with such information as he may require with respect to the performance of the local authority's functions under the enactments described in section 83(5) and in connection with the accommodation of children in residential care homes, nursing or mental homes, and with respect to the children in relation to whom the local authority have exercised these functions.

Section 83(4): replaces section 70 of the Child Care Act 1980 and provides that the Secretary of State shall receive such details as he may require concerning children accommodated by or on behalf of the voluntary organisation.

Section 83(5): re-enacts sections 79(2) and (2A) of the Child Care Act 1980.

Section 83(6): re-enacts section 79(3) of the Child Care Act 1980. Section 79 of the 1980 Act and section 105 of the Children Act 1975 required the Secretary of State to present to Parliament an annual abstract of the information, and to provide every three and five years a report with respect to the various functions and enactments specified in those sections. Section 83(6) maintains the requirement of an annual abstract, as this data is generally regarded as a valuable source of information, but the provision of the triennial and quinquennial reports has been discontinued. It was considered that the usefulness of the report was not sufficient to justify what was required to produce it and that most of the information required can be provided through the Social Services Select Committee, for example.

Section 83(7): replaces section 105 of the Children Act 1975 and enables the Secretary of State to initiate such research as is necessary to provide information on which requests for information under section 83 may be based.

Section 83(8): requires the Secretary of State to keep under review the adequacy of provision of child care training. This is a new provision. The Secretary of State should receive and consider information from the Central Council for Education and Training in Social Work, and any other person or bodies as appear to him to be appropriate.

Section 83(9): lists the various enactments to which section 83 applies.

Section 84. Local authority failure to comply with statutory duty: default power of Secretary of State

84. – (1) If the Secretary of State is satisfied that any local authority has failed, without reasonable excuse, to comply with any of the duties imposed on them by or under this Act he may make an order declaring that authority to be in default with respect to that duty.

(2) An order under subsection (1) shall give the Secretary of State's reasons for making it.

(3) An order under subsection (1) may contain such directions for the purpose of ensuring that the duty is complied with, within such period as may be specified in the order, as appear to the Secretary of State to be necessary.

(4) Any such direction shall, on the application of the Secretary of State, be enforceable by mandamus.

Annotation

Section 84: introduces into the Act a default power in respect of any duties of a local authority. The power is exercisable wherever the Secretary of State is satisfied that a local authority are in default of any duty and the order may contain directions which would ensure that the duty is complied with within a specified period. The power introduced by section 84 should be seen in the context of the various provisions already in the Act which enable persons who may be dissatisfied with a local authority's decision to be heard: see section 22(4)(5) and section 26.

Section 84(1): provides what the Solicitor General has described as a broad power which should almost never be used. The default power has been introduced as a broad power to enable the Secretary of State to intervene in individual cases in extreme circumstances, since individuals would be expected to avail themselves of the powers available to them under section 22(4)(5) and section 26. Section 84(1) is not designed to open the gates to floods of representation: see Solicitor General, Hansard Col 492 Standing Committee B 8 June 1989.

Section 84(2): provides that where an order is made under section 84(1) the Secretary of State shall give the reasons for making it. An example of where the power may be used is where a local authority fail to make requisite provision for a class of children.

Section 84(3): provides that the order may contain directions for the purposes of ensuring that the duty is complied with and within a specified time limit. Again, individual cases are only rarely expected to fall within the default powers of the Secretary of State. For example, where a local authority have a duty to ascertain, so far as is reasonably practicable, and to have regard to the wishes and feelings of a child whom they are looking after, his parents, others with parental responsibility and any other person whose wishes and feelings are relevant, such appropriate people can rely on section 22 to ensure that the local authority give due consideration to their wishes and feelings.

Section 84(4): provides that any such direction shall be enforceable by mandamus on an application by the Secretary of State. No such order is likely to be issued by the Secretary of State, or any enforcement applied for, in cases which are covered by the representation procedure laid down in section 26. This provides the first opportunity for redress in respect of a child who is being looked after, or who, although not looked after, is in need. The procedure relates to any local authority functions under Part III of the Act and is available to the child, his parents, others with parental responsibility, and any other person whom the local authority consider has sufficient interest in the child's welfare. Cases involving individual children are expected to be covered by the representations or complaints procedure and the majority of cases settled at that stage without invoking the powers defined in section 84.

PART XII

MISCELLANEOUS AND GENERAL

Notification of children accommodated in certain establishments

Section 85. Children accommodated by health authorities and local education authorities

85.—(1) Where a child is provided with accommodation by any health authority or local education authority ("the accommodating authority")—

(a) for a consecutive period of at least three months; or
(b) with the intention, on the part of that authority, of accommodating him for such a period,

the accommodating authority shall notify the responsible authority.

(2) Where subsection (1) applies with respect to a child, the accommodating authority shall also notify the responsible authority when they cease to accommodate the child.

(3) In this section "the responsible authority" means—

(a) the local authority appearing to the accommodating authority to be the authority within whose area the child was ordinarily resident immediately before being accommodated; or
(b) where it appears to the accommodating authority that a child was not ordinarily resident within the area of any local authority, the local authority within whose area the accommodation is situated.

(4) Where a local authority have been notified under this section, they shall—

(a) take such steps as are reasonably practicable to enable them to determine whether the child's welfare is adequately safeguarded and promoted while he is accommodated by the accommodating authority; and
(b) consider the extent to which (if at all) they should exer-

cise any of their functions under this Act with respect to the child.

Annotation

Section 85: makes general provisions in respect of children accommodated by a health authority or a local education authority. The purpose of section 85 is to safeguard the welfare of a child who remains for long periods in accommodation where he has been placed by a health authority or a local education authority. Thus a health authority or a local education authority which places a child in accommodation for at least three months, or intends to accommodate him for such a period, will be required to notify the local authority. Note that this is a new duty imposed upon health and education authorities and that the three month period does not include time before the Act was implemented: see Schedule 14 paragraph 35.

Section 85(1): imposes a duty on a health authority or a local education authority who accommodate, or intend to accommodate, a child for a consecutive period of at least three months to notify the responsible authority. Section 85(1) applies to children placed in national health service hospitals or state-maintained special schools, as well as those placed by statutory agencies in private hospitals or care homes, or in schools offering special education.

Section 85(2): imposes the same duty as in section 85(1) upon a health authority or a local education authority, known as the accommodating authority, where they cease to accommodate the child. The duty applies, as in section 85(1), wherever a health authority or a local education authority arranged accommodation for the child.

Section 85(3): defines "responsible authority". Such responsible authority can only be a local authority, though which local authority will depend upon the locus as defined in section 85(3)(a)(b).

Section 85(4): defines the duties upon a local authority designated a responsible authority. The local authority which have been notified have a duty to take such steps as are reasonably practicable to satisfy themselves that the child's welfare is being promoted and safeguarded. For example, they might decide to provide services to the child under Part III in order to promote contact between the child and his family. If a person who is under twenty one leaves accommodation which has been provided by a health or local education authority for at least three months, he may qualify for advice and assistance from the local authority in whose area he is.

Section 86. Children accommodated in residential care, nursing or mental nursing homes

86.—(1) Where a child is provided with accommodation in any residential care home, nursing home or mental nursing home—

(a) for a consecutive period of at least three months; or
(b) with the intention, on the part of the person taking the decision to accommodate him, of accommodating him for such period,

the person carrying on the home shall notify the local authority within whose area the home is carried on.

(2) Where subsection (1) applies with respect to a child, the person carrying on the home shall also notify that authority when he ceases to accommodate the child in the home.

(3) Where a local authority have been notified under this section, they shall—

(a) take such steps as are reasonably practicable to enable them to determine whether the child's welfare is adequately safeguarded and promoted while he is accommodated in the home; and
(b) consider the extent to which (if at all) they should exercise any of their functions under this Act with respect to the child.

(4) If the person carrying on any home fails, without reasonable excuse, to comply with this section he shall be guilty of an offence.

(5) A person authorised by a local authority may enter any residential care home, nursing home or mental nursing home within the authority's area for the purpose of establishing whether the requirements of this section have been complied with.

(6) Any person who intentionally obstructs another in the exercise of the power of entry shall be guilty of an offence.

(7) Any person exercising the power of entry shall, if so required, produce some duly authenticated document showing his authority to do so.

(8) Any person committing an offence under this section shall be liable on summary conviction to a fine not exceeding level 3 on the standard scale.

Annotation

Section 86: provides for children accommodated in residential care, nursing or mental nursing homes.

Children who are handicapped or chronically ill or who have special education needs may be placed in these establishments in order to treat an illness or provide specialised care or education. Section 86 reflects the concern that often such children have little or no contact with their families. Reviews of their situation may be infrequent and insufficient attention paid to their wider welfare needs. Section 86(4)(8) makes it an offence not to comply with this section or to obstruct any person exercising his power of entry.

Section 86(1): imposes a new duty and mirrors section 85(1). The three month period does not include time before the Act was implemented: see Schedule 14 paragraph 35. The homes referred to in section 86(1) shall in general be registered and regulated under the Registered Homes Act 1984.

Section 86(2): mirrors section 85(2). The local authority are the authority for the area where the home is situated. The person carrying on the home must inform the local authority for the area in which the child is going to live, if a child who has reached sixteen leaves the home after living there for three months. Such a child may qualify for advice and assistance from the local authority: see section 24(2).

Section 86(3): mirrors section 85(4). It is intended through notification to ensure that the welfare needs of these children receives attention and that contact and rehabilitation with their families is promoted where that is possible.

Section 86(4): stresses the importance of section 86 by making it an offence not to comply with its terms. It nevertheless provides a defence of reasonable excuse. What is reasonable in all the circumstances will be a matter for the court.

Section 86(5): reinforces those duties upon a local authority by providing a supporting power to enter those premises defined in section 8(1).

Section 86(6): makes it an offence to obstruct a person exercising his power of entry under section 86. It nevertheless provides a defence of no guilty intent.

Section 86(7): mirrors section 67(4) and 50(8)(b) and other provisions, that a person carrying out an inspection pursuant to section 86 shall produce his authority to enter premises, if required to do so.

Section 86(8): provides for a fine on summary conviction for any person committing an offence under section 86.

Section 87. Welfare of children accommodated in independent schools

87. — (1) It shall be the duty of —

(a) the proprietor of any independent school which provides accommodation for any child; and

(b) any person who is not the proprietor of such a school but who is responsible for conducting it,

to safeguard and promote the child's welfare.

(2) Subsection (1) does not apply in relation to a school which is a children's home or a residential care home.

(3) Where accommodation is provided for a child by an independent school within the area of a local authority, the authority shall take such steps as are reasonably practicable to enable them to determine whether the child's welfare is adequately safeguarded and promoted while he is accommodated by the school.

(4) Where a local authority are of the opinion that there has been a failure to comply with subsection (1) in relation to a child provided with accommodation by a school within their area, they shall notify the Secretary of State.

(5) Any person authorised by a local authority may, for the purpose of enabling the authority to discharge their duty under this section, enter at any reasonable time any independent school within their area which provides accommodation for any child.

(6) Any person entering an independent school in exercise of the power conferred by subsection (5) may carry out such inspection of premises, children and records as is prescribed by regulations made by the Secretary of State for the purposes of this section.

(7) Any person exercising that power shall, if asked to do so, produce some duly authenticated document showing his authority to do so.

(8) Any person authorised by the regulations to inspect records —

(a) shall be entitled at any reasonable time to have access to, and inspect and check the operation of, any computer and any associated apparatus or material which is or has been in use in connection with the records in question; and

(b) may require —

(i) the person by whom or on whose behalf the computer is or has been so used; or

(ii) any person having charge of, or otherwise concerned with the operation of, the computer, apparatus or material,

to afford him such assistance as he may reasonably require.

(9) Any person who intentionally obstructs another in the exercise of any power conferred by this section or the regulations shall be guilty of an offence and liable on summary conviction to a fine not exceeding level 3 on the standard scale.

(10) In this section "proprietor" has the same meaning as in the Education Act 1944.

Annotation

Section 87: arose out of media allegations of the sexual abuse of children being accommodated at an independent school. Section 87 represents a new provision containing three main elements. First, a new duty is placed on the proprietor or any other person conducting an independent school which provides accommodation for any child to safeguard the child's welfare; this provision applies to independent schools that are not categorised as children's homes or residential homes. A second duty is upon a local authority within whose area the accommodation is provided to do what is reasonably practicable to determine whether the child's welfare is adequately safeguarded and promoted whilst he is accomodated by the school. The third is that, where a local authority considers that a person or proprietor conducting the school is failing to discharge his welfare duty under section 87(1), the authority must notify the Secretary of State. Section 87 applies to children up to the age of eighteen, so that it corresponds to the usual school leaving age for independent schools.

Section 87(1): imposes a duty on the proprietor and the person responsible for the conduct of an independent school which accommodates a child to safeguard and promote the child's welfare. The Education Act 1944 section 114(1) defines an independent school as "any school at which full-time education is provided for five or more pupils of compulsory school age (whether or not education is also provided for pupils under or over that age), not being a school maintained by a local authority, a grant maintained school, or a special school not maintained by a local education authority."

Section 87(2): ensures that section 87(1) does not apply to independent schools which are also children's homes or residential care homes. These are provided for under Part VIII of the Act: see section 63 for the definition of what constitutes a registered children's home. Note also that section 63(6) extends the definition of a children's home to include all independent schools which provide accommodation for not more than fifty pupils and which are not approved for special education. Section 87 does not extend to children attending schools teaching English as a foreign language, most of which provide short, non-residential courses, but some children boarding out for twenty eight days or more fall within the scope of private fostering provisions in Part IX.

Section 87(3): extends the duties of a local authority in relation to children accommodated by a local education authority and any health authority to those in independent schools: see section 85(4). In the past, a local authority could only intervene at an independent school when an allegation of abuse or ill treatment had been made. A local authority will have a duty to satisfy themselves about the social, as opposed to the educational welfare of the children. The circumstances of individual schools will determine the amount of time a local authority feel they must spend.

Section 87(4): provides for notification to the Secretary of State of any failure in the duty to safeguard and promote a child's welfare. The Education Act 1944 has been amended to ensure that failure to comply with this duty will be a ground on which notice of complaint action can be taken. This could lead in serious cases to the school's being removed from the register of independent schools and having to close: Minister of State Hansard 23 October 1989, Col 615. For the powers of the Secretary of State see sections 71–75 of the Education Act 1944.

Section 87(5): mirrors section 86(5) in relation to children accommodated in residential care, nursing or mental nursing homes. The power is accorded in order to meet genuine fears that abuse may be occurring and so that an emergency protection order may be sought. All the powers falling upon a local authority under the Act also come into play. Where, for example, there is an allegation of abuse, an emergency protection order can be sought *ex parte* and a local authority can intervene at any point. Where action well short of an emergency protection order is required, but an investigation is nevertheless material, a report can be made to the Department of Education and Science. They would then be expected to send inspectors to the school to examine the circumstances.

Section 87(6): provides that, subject to regulations, not only children and records but also premises may be inspected. It mirrors section 62(6) dealing with the duties of a local authority in relation to voluntary organisations providing accommodation. These are new powers under the Act. There was no such power to enter and inspect independent school premises under section 68 of the Child Care Act 1980.

Section 87(7): mirrors section 86(7), which in turn equates with sections 67(4) and 50(8)(b) and other provisions, that a person carrying out an inspection pursuant to section 87 shall produce his authority to enter premises if required to do so.

Section 87(8): mirrors section 80(7) dealing with the inspection of children's homes by persons authorised by the Secretary of State.

Section 87(9): mirrors section 86(6)(8) by making it an offence to obstruct a person exercising his power of entry under section 87, whilst providing a defence of no guilty intent. It also sets the liability on summary conviction.

Section 87(10): provides that "proprietor" has the same meaning as in the Education Act 1944. In the Act, the proprietor of any school is defined as "the person or body of persons responsible for the management of the school".

Adoption

Section 88. Amendments of adoption legislation

88. — (1) The Adoption Act 1976 shall have effect subject to the amendments made by Part I of Schedule 10.

(2) The Adoption (Scotland) Act 1978 shall have effect subject to the amendments made by Part II of Schedule 10.

Annotation

Section 88: introduces changes to the adoption law. The first of these changes comprises amendments to harmonise adoption law within the United Kingdom, meeting needs arising from the introduction of new adoption provisions in Northern Ireland and as a consequence of the changes in child care law contained in the Act. The changes are to enable agencies in different parts of the United Kingdom to work in cooperation for the benefit of children who need to move from one part of the country to another. The second is to update the numerous references in adoption legislation to ensure that they are appropriately carried across to child care legislation and so that the two areas of law interlink. The third of these changes consists of a small number of improvements made outside the context of a general review of adoption law. Described as "piecemeal changes", they are helpful and can be made without needing a full review: Minister of State Standing Committee B Hansard 380, 6 June 1989.

Section 88(1): provides that the Adoption Act 1976 shall have effect subject to the amendments made by Part I of Schedule 10. Part I of Schedule 10 introduces consequential amendments designed to harmonise United Kingdom adoption law. Examples of these amendments are those in Part I and II of Schedule 10 referring to Northern Ireland adoption agencies and to orders made by Northern Irish courts inserted into the Adoption Act 1976 and the Adoption (Scotland) Act 1978 in order to achieve an integrated and mutually compatible adoption law within the United Kingdom.

Section 88(2): provides that the Adoption (Scotland) Act 1978 shall have effect subject to the amendments made by Part II of Schedule 10, the purpose being to harmonise United Kingdom adoption law. Another example of these amendments is the introduction into the Adoption Act 1976 and the Adoption (Scotland) Act 1978 of the concept of parental responsibility to replace parental rights and duties, updating references to legal and actual custody.

Paternity tests

Section 89. Tests to establish paternity

89. In section 20 of the Family Law Reform Act 1969 (power of court to require use of tests to determine paternity), the following subsections shall be inserted after subsection (1)—

> "(1A) Where—
>
> > (a) an application is made for a direction under this section; and
> > (b) the person whose paternity is in issue is under the age of eighteen when the application is made,
>
> the application shall specify who is to carry out the tests.
>
> (1B) In the case of a direction made on an application to which subsection (1A) applies the court shall—
>
> > (a) specify, as the person who is to carry out the tests, the person specified in the application; or
> > (b) where the court considers that it would be inappropriate to specify that person (whether because to

specify him would be incompatible with any provision made by or under regulations made under
section 22 of this Act or for any other reason),
decline to give the direction applied for."

Annotation

Section 89: inserts into section 20 of the Family Law Reform Act
1969 provisions dealing with tests to establish paternity. Note that
the Family Law Reform Act 1987 also deals with evidence of
paternity in civil proceedings. Section 29 of that Act amends
section 12 of the Civil Evidence Act 1968 relating to the admissibility in civil proceedings of evidence of the fact that a person has
been adjudged to be the father of a child in affiliation proceedings.
Section 89 adds to section 20 of the Family Law Reform Act that
where an application is made to a court to require use of tests to
determine paternity it shall specify who is to carry out the tests
and any direction made upon application shall specify the same
person unless the court declines to give the direction applied for.
Reference is made to regulations under section 22 of the Act—
this defines the general duty of a local authority to promote and
safeguard the welfare of children whom they are looking after
and is often described as "a cornerstone duty".

Criminal care and supervision orders

Section 90. Care and supervision orders in criminal proceedings

90. — (1) The power of a court to make an order under subsection (2) of section 1 of the Children and Young Persons Act 1969
(care proceedings in juvenile courts) where it is of the opinion
that the condition mentioned in paragraph (f) of that subsection
("the offence condition") is satisfied is hereby abolished.

(2) The powers of the court to make care orders—

    (a) under section 7(7)(a) of the Children and Young Persons
        Act 1969 (alteration in treatment of young offenders
        etc.); and
    (b) under section 15(1) of that Act, on discharging a super-
        vision order made under section 7(7)(b) of that Act,

are hereby abolished.

(3) The powers given by that Act to include requirements in
supervision orders shall have effect subject to amendments made
by Schedule 12.

Annotation

Section 90: abolishes the power of the court to make a care order in criminal proceedings and provides that the court should have additional powers in relation to supervision orders by amending the Children and Young Persons Act 1969. These amendments are set out in Schedule 12. They allow the court to include in a supervision order the requirement that the child or young person reside in accommodation provided by or on behalf of the local authority and to specify that he may not live with a named person.

Section 90(1): abolishes the power of a court to make a care order under section 1(2)(f) of the Children and Young Persons Act 1969. Under the prior law a care or supervision order could be made in respect of a child who had committed an offence. The former grounds for making care or supervision orders under section 1 of the 1969 Act are replaced with the more general grounds defined in section 31, which relate to harm or likely harm to a child. But if it is intended by the Act that all care orders shall be subject to the same grounds then the making of an order as a consequence of the commission of an offence is not compatible with these revised grounds. Furthermore, there was concern that the indeterminate length of a care order was not appropriate for young persons as a disposal in criminal proceedings and that a care order should not be regarded as a means of punishment.

Section 90(2): removes the power of a court to make a care order in criminal proceedings under section 7(7) of the Children and Young Persons Act 1969 together with the powers of the court to discharge a supervision order under section 7(7)(b) of the 1969 Act. The abolition of care orders in criminal proceedings was suggested in a consultation paper issued in August 1988. There was widespread agreement between the courts, local authorities and other interested parties that this was desirable.

Section 90(3): relates to section 90(2) and provides that in place of care orders in such proceedings defined in section 90, courts have a new power to attach to a supervision order, that is a requirement that the child reside in accommodation provided by or on behalf of a local authority for a maximum of six months, specifying also that the offender should not live with a named person. Section 12 of the 1969 Act is amended accordingly by way of section 90(3) and Schedule 12. Schedule 12 deals with minor amendments, but the grounds to be satisfied for such a requirement to be attached to a supervision order are: (a) that the current offence is one which for an adult aged over twenty one could be punishable by imprisonment; (b) that the circumstances in which the child is living have contributed significantly to his offending behaviour and that a criminal supervision order with requirements is already in force.

Effect and duration of orders etc.

Section 91. Effect and duration of orders etc.

91.—(1) The making of a residence order with respect to a child who is the subject of a care order discharges the care order.

(2) The making of a care order with respect to a child who is the subject of any section 8 order discharges that order.

(3) The making of a care order with respect to a child who is the subject of a supervision order discharges that other order.

(4) The making of a care order with respect to a child who is a ward of court brings that wardship to an end.

(5) The making of a care order with respect to a child who is the subject of a school attendance order made under section 37 of the Education Act 1944 discharges the school attendance order.

(6) Where an emergency protection order is made with respect to a child who is in care, the care order shall have effect subject to the emergency protection order.

(7) Any order made under section 4(1) or 5(1) shall continue in force until the child reaches the age of eighteen, unless it is brought to an end earlier.

(8) Any—

    (a) agreement under section 4; or
    (b) appointment under section 5(3) or (4),

shall continue in force until the child reaches the age of eighteen, unless it is brought to an end earlier.

(9) An order under Schedule 1 has effect as specified in that Schedule.

(10) A section 8 order shall, if it would otherwise still be in force, cease to have effect when the child reaches the age of sixteen, unless it is to have effect beyond that age by virtue of section 9(6).

(11) Where a section 8 order has effect with respect to a child who has reached the age of sixteen, it shall, if it would otherwise still be in force, cease to have effect when he reaches the age of eighteen.

(12) Any care order, other than an interim care order, shall continue in force until the child reaches the age of eighteen, unless it is brought to an end earlier.

(13) Any order made under any other provision of this Act in relation to a child shall, if it would otherwise still be in force, cease to have effect when he reaches the age of eighteen.

(14) On disposing of any application for an order under this Act, the court may (whether or not it makes any other order in response to the application) order that no application for an order under this Act of any specified kind may be made with respect to the child concerned by any person named in the order without leave of the court.

(15) Where an application ("the previous application") has been made for—

  (a) the discharge of a care order;
  (b) the discharge of a supervision order;
  (c) the discharge of an education supervision order;
  (d) the substitution of a supervision order for a care order; or
  (e) a child assessment order,

no further application of a kind mentioned in paragraphs (a) to (e) may be made with respect to the child concerned, without leave of the court, unless the period between the disposal of the previous application and the making of the further application exceeds six months.

(16) Subsection (15) does not apply to applications made in relation to interim orders.

(17) Where—

  (a) a person has made an application for an order under section 34;
  (b) the application has been refused; and
  (c) a period of less than six months has elapsed since the refusal,

that person may not make a further application for such an order with respect to the same child, unless he has obtained the leave of the court.

Annotation

Section 91: provides that the making of a residence order discharges an existing care order and vice-versa. It also provides for the maximum duration of orders, appointments and agreements under the Act. Section 91 empowers the court when determining an application to require that any further applications for an order shall require the court's leave unless, in the case of the discharge of a care or supervision order or the substitution of one for the other, six months have elapsed since the previous application. Thus, section 91 enables the court to prevent repeated applications for orders under Parts I and II of the Act.

Section 91(1): provides that all those persons who are able to apply as of right for residence orders will in effect also be entitled to apply to bring about the discharge of care orders. It gives effect to a recommendation of the Law Commission in its report "Family Law, Review of Child Law, Guardianship and Custody," that since the purpose of a residence order is to determine where the child is to live, such orders clearly should supersede care orders.

Section 91(2): provides that the making of a care order with respect to a child who is the subject of any section 8 order discharges that order, because a care order gives parental responsibility to the local authority, save that the local authority will not thereby have the right to consent to adoption or appoint a guardian. Section 8 orders are contact, prohibited steps, residence or specific issue orders: see section 8(1).

Section 91(3): mirrors section 91(2) and extends the recommendation of the Law Commission that courts should have powers to ensure that a care order shall supersede and discharge a residence, contact, specific issue or prohibited steps order. A supervision order is an order under section 31(1)(b) and, except where express provision to the contrary is made, includes an interim supervision order made under section 38.

Section 91(4): mirrors section 91(2)(3). It is the purpose of section 91 to provide a single system of powers to deal with the upbringing of children built upon the principles, among others, developed in wardship proceedings and adopting them to modern conditions and to proceedings under which the upbringing of children may arise in the courts. See also section 100, which repeals section 7 of the Family Law Reform Act 1969.

Section 91(5): mirrors section 91(2)(3)(4) in relation to school attendance orders. Note that section 36 introduces an education supervision order which, upon a successful application to the court, places a child not being property educated under the supervision of a local education authority. A care order and an education supervision order are mutually exclusive: see section 36(6). Section 91(5) provides for the discharge of a school attendance order by the making of a care order.

J

Section 91(6): subordinates a care order to an emergency protection order. Note that section 45(4) enables a person who, in the first instance, has parental responsibility acquired under an emergency protection order and, in the second, is entitled to apply for a care order under the provisions of section 31(1), to apply to the court for an emergency protection order to be extended. Note also that since an emergency protection order is for a limited period only, it may be that an applicant would apply for a full care order, in which case the full care order may be subordinated to any conditions imposed by section 44(6).

Section 91(7): provides that a parental responsibility order in favour of an unmarried father or an appointment of a guardian by the court shall unless terminated earlier continue in force until the child attains the age of eighteen. Note that section 4(4) also empowers the court to bring parental responsibility orders to an end and that under section 6(7) the court may terminate the appointment of a guardian at any time.

Section 91(8): provides that any parental responsibility agreement under section 4, or appointment of a guardian by an individual, shall continue until the child reaches the age of eighteen, unless terminated earlier. Note the provisos of section 4(4) and 6(7) referred to under section 91(7).

Section 91(9): links the effect and duration of orders under section 91 with the provisions of Schedule 1 dealing with orders for financial relief. An application for a financial order may be made at the same time as an application for a residence order, or any other order where it is necessary to safeguard and promote the child's welfare, without the need for a separate application. In the words of the Law Commission, "if the court makes a residence order it would be wasteful and unnecessary to require a separate application for a financial order".

Section 91(10): reflects the practical approach, bearing in mind that sixteen is the age at which children may leave school and seek full-time employment and become entitled to certain benefits and allowances in their own right. Section 9(6) prohibits the court from making any section 8 order, other than one varying or discharging such an order, in respect of a child who has reached the age of sixteen unless the circumstances are exceptional.

Section 91(11): provides that a section 8 order shall come to an end at the age of eighteen. The former powers of the court enabled it to make custody and access orders last until the child reached eighteen, although the court would rarely, if ever, make a custody order contrary to the wishes of a child who had reached sixteen. In addition, there were powers of direct enforcement of custody orders which operated on the child, and the older a child became the less just it was to attempt to enforce against him an order to which he had never been a party. This applies equally to section 8 orders.

Section 91(12): mirrors section 91(11). Note that no interim care order may last for more than eight weeks: see section 38(5).

Section 91(13): mirrors section 91(11)(12) in relation to other orders, such as assessment orders, not already covered.

Section 91(14): adopts a recommendation of the Law Commission in its report "Family Law, Review of Child Law, Guardianshp and Custody", that the courts should have power to protect children and those looking after them from repeated applications from those who would otherwise have a right to apply whenever they wished to do so. Under the former law there was nothing to prevent either parent from applying for custody or access as often as he liked.

Section 91(15): prevents a vindictive or obsessive harrassment by a parent making an application for an order shortly after a fully argued hearing in which he has been unsuccessful. This can undermine the security and happiness of a child's home or education but was possible under the former law.

Section 91(16): provides that section 91(15) does not apply to applications made in relation to interim care orders. It was the view of the Law Commission that the court should have power to prohibit a named person from making such applications without leave of the court but that an order should only be made where it was the most effective way to safeguard or promote the child's welfare. Note that, in accordance with section 38, in considering the child's welfare as paramount, a court may decide that it is better to make an interim order rather than making no order at all. Hence the exclusion of an application for an interim care order in respect of section 91(15).

Section 91(17): mirrors section 91(14)(15) in respect of a person who has made an application for an order under section 34 which has been unsuccessful. Note that the provision of section 34 is to enable a court to consider contact between a child in care and his parents or other persons. Section 34(1) imposes a duty on a designated local authority to allow the child reasonable contact with his parents or any guardian. A court would be expected to ensure that reasonable contact proposals were before it when considering any applications under section 34.

Jurisdiction and procedure etc.

Section 92. Jurisdiction of courts

92. — (1) The name "domestic proceedings", given to certain proceedings in magistrates' courts, is hereby changed to "family proceedings" and the names "domestic court" and "domestic court panel" are hereby changed to "family proceedings court" and "family panel", respectively.

(2) Proceedings under this Act shall be treated as family proceedings in relation to magistrates' courts.

(3) Subsection (2) is subject to the provisions of section 65(1) and (2) of the Magistrates' Courts Act 1980 (proceedings which may be treated as not being family proceedings), as amended by this Act.

(4) A magistrates' court shall not be competent to entertain any application, or make any order, involving the administration or application of—

(a) any property belonging to or held in trust for a child; or
(b) the income of any such property.

(5) The powers of a magistrates' court under section 63(2) of the Act of 1980 to suspend or rescind orders shall not apply in relation to any order made under this Act.

(6) Part I of Schedule 11 makes provision, including provision for the Lord Chancellor to make orders, with respect to the jurisdiction of courts and justices of the peace in relation to—

(a) proceedings under this Act; and
(b) proceedings under certain other enactments.

(7) For the purposes of this Act "the court" means the High Court, a county court or a magistrates' court.

(8) Subsection (7) is subject to the provision made by or under Part I of Schedule 11 and to any express provision as to the jurisdiction of any court made by any other provision of this Act.

(9) The Lord Chancellor may by order make provision for the principal registry of the Family Division of the High Court to be treated as if it were a county court for such purposes of this Act, or of any provision made under this Act, as may be specified in the order.

(10) Any order under subsection (9) may make such provision as the Lord Chancellor thinks expedient for the purpose of applying (with or without modifications) provisions which apply in

relation to the procedure in county courts to the principal registry when it acts as if it were a county court.

(11) Part II of Schedule 11 makes amendments consequential on this section.

Annotation

Section 92: reflects the purpose of the Act to provide for a substantive child care law and a unified jurisdiction. The significance of a unified jurisdiction is that a case might be heard at whatever level is appropriate, with swift and expert means to determine and adjust that level as circumstances require, and with the same law and the same powers applying at every level: see Solicitor General Col 548 Hansard, 23 October 1989. A unified jurisdiction is an important stage on the way to a full family court. It was the view of the Solicitor General that a great deal of careful review which was under consideration by the Law Commission, among others, would need to be thought through to create a substantive body of law appropriate to all levels, before further steps could be taken in the direction of a family court.

Section 92(1): provides for the unification of language around the concept of family proceedings. One purpose of the Act is to "create, first a single body of law and then a unified jurisdiction that runs through all the courts": Solicitor General Col 547 Hansard, 23 October 1989. The Solicitor General also said: "There is, I believe, widespread acceptance of the need for a properly supported specialist jurisdiction in family matters, encompassing the courts at all relevant levels. That includes the magistrates' courts, the county courts and the High Court": Col 547 Hansard 23 October 1989.

Section 92(3): deals with those proceedings which may be treated as not being family proceedings. Note that whilst one purpose of Section 92 is to move towards the concept of a family court, the Act does not deal with other aspects of family proceedings, such as divorce, domestic violence or access or denial of access to the matrimonial home.

Section 92(4): provides that whilst proceedings in relation to the Act shall be considered as family proceedings, the magistrates' court shall nevertheless not be competent to handle matters in relation to property, which are also excluded from the Act.

Section 92(5): provides that, in conformity with the provisions of the Act and the powers of the court under the Act, section 63(2) of the Magistrates' Court Act 1980 shall not apply. Otherwise, the balance struck in the Act and the applications which may or may not be made, and the variation upon directions of such applications, would be intruded upon by a section of another Act.

Section 92(6): links to Part I of Schedule 11 which makes provision with respect to the jurisdiction of courts and justices of the peace in relation to proceedings under the Act and other enactments. The purpose of section 92 being to create a single concurrent jurisdiction, thus it is for the Lord Chancellor to make the orders so that the single concurrent jursidiction can be brought about.

Section 92(7): extends jurisdiction under the Act to the magistrates' courts, the county courts and the High Court. Consequently, applications seeking care orders which were formerly heard by magistrates may now be heard in the county courts or even the High Court.

Section 92(8): subordinates section 92(7) to Part I of Schedule 11.

Section 92(9): provides that the Lord Chancellor may by order make certain provisions—another step on the road to a unified and concurrent jurisdiction which can come about once there is a substantive body of child care law on which such procedures can be built. In the words of the Solicitor General, "In the county courts, the great majority of orders will be made, as now in the case of divorce proceedings, by divorce county courts. The intention is to concentrate children's and other family proceedings in the hands of selected judges and registrars, many of whom will have had long experience in this area, either as practitioners or on the Bench, and who will have made a special study of such proceedings and built up expertise in family matters": Col 549 Hansard 23 October 1989.

Section 92(10): provides for further orders to be made by the Lord Chancellor. Again it was the view of the Solicitor General that, for example, where there is an application in a county court to adopt a child subject to a care order and the parents are applying to a magistrates' court to discharge that care order, rules will ensure that the two applications can be heard together.

Section 92(11): reflects the power of the Lord Chancellor to order the transfer of cases from one specified level or class of court to another. In the words of the Solicitor General, since the Act creates "a single body of child law, it is possible to give the Lord Chancellor power to provide for the allocation of children's cases and some non-children's family cases with concurrent jurisdiction and to consolidate them with proceedings about a child": Col 549 Hansard, 23 October 1989.

Section 93. Rules of court

93. —(1) An authority having power to make rules of court may make such provision for giving effect to—

(a) this Act;

(b) the provisions of any statutory instrument made under this Act; or

(c) any amendment made by this Act in any other enactment,

as appears to that authority to be necessary or expedient.

(2) The rules may, in particular, make provision—

(a) with respect to the procedure to be followed in any relevant proceedings (including the manner in which any application is to be made or other proceedings commenced);

(b) as to the persons entitled to participate in any relevant proceedings, whether as parties to the proceedings or by being given the opportunity to make representations to the court;

(c) with respect to the documents and information to be furnished, and notices to be given, in connection with any relevant proceedings;

(d) applying (with or without modification) enactments which govern the procedure to be followed with respect to proceedings brought on a complaint made to a magistrates' court to relevant proceedings in such a court brought otherwise than on a complaint;

(e) with respect to preliminary hearings;

(f) for the service outside [*the United Kingdom*] [England and Wales], in such circumstances and in such manner as may be prescribed, of any notice of proceedings in a magistrates' court;

(g) for the exercise by magistrates' courts, in such circumstances as may be prescribed, of such powers as may be prescribed (even though a party to the proceedings in question is [or resides] outside England and Wales);

(h) enabling the court, in such circumstances as may be prescribed, to proceed on any application even though the respondent has not been given notice of the proceedings;

(i) authorising a single justice to discharge the functions of a magistrates' court with respect to such relevant proceedings as may be prescribed;

Note: The words *in italics* within square brackets were deleted by the Courts and Legal Services Act 1990.

Note: The words within square brackets were inserted by the Courts and Legal Services Act 1990.

(j) authorising a magistrates' court to order any of the parties
to such relevant proceedings as may be prescribed, in
such circumstances as may be prescribed, to pay the
whole or part of the costs of all or any of the other
parties.

(3) In subsection (2)—

"notice of proceedings" means a summons or such other
notice of proceedings as is required; and "given", in
relation to a summons, means "served";

"prescribed" means prescribed by the rules; and

"relevant proceedings" means any application made, or proceedings brought, under any of the provisions mentioned
in paragraphs (a) to (c) of subsection (1) and any part
of such proceedings.

(4) This section and any other power in this Act to make rules
of court are not to be taken as in any way limiting any other
power of the authority in question to make rules of court.

(5) When making any rules under this section an authority shall
be subject to the same requirements as to consultation (if any) as
apply when the authority makes rules under its general rule
making power.

Annotation

Section 93: enables rules of court to be made to govern practice
and procedure and therefore puts "flesh and bones" on the principles defined in the Act for dealing with cases involving children:
Solicitor General Col 589 Hansard, 23 October 1989. It is the
purpose of section 90 to ensure that the best use is made of judicial
resources. Cases under the Act may be heard by a magistrates'
or county or the High Court, but rules of court will be made to
ensure that there is an allocation of some types of cases between
the courts. Such rules of court will mean that local authority
proceedings involving the protection of children will start in a
magistrates' court but will be transferrable to a county court or
the High Court where their weight or complexity justifies it.

Section 93(1): provides for the making of provisions to give effect
to the Act, any statutory instrument, or any amendment made by
the Act in any other enactment. One purpose of the rules of court
under section 93(1) is to enable the transfer of cases between
courts in order to avoid unnecessary delay, or to allow cases
involving the same child and his family to be heard together.

Section 93(2): covers those aspects for which rules of court will make provision. Most family cases of a private nature will be heard along with other proceedings dealing with the same family, such as divorce, as they were under the prior law. In the case of magistrates' courts referred to in section 93(2)(g), there is to be much more disclosure of the parties' evidence and cases ahead of the hearing, greater reliance on written material and magistrates reading the papers before the hearing and giving reasons for their decision at the end. Specially trained magistrates will sit as family proceedings courts with powers to hear care-related cases as well as all other magistrates' family and children's cases.

Section 93(3): provides further elaboration of section 93(2). Note that under the Act the courts have an independent duty to do what is best for the child. If the courts are to discharge that duty, often they will have to take an active part in the proceedings rather than simply acting as umpires between the contending parties.

Section 93(4): provides that section 93 does not limit any other powers in the Act to make rules of court. Note that in the county courts and the High Court it is hoped to concentrate the work in the hands of a limited number of specialists, who have made a particular study of children's matters.

Section 93(5): provides for consultation. Note that under the Act the courts have an independent duty to do what is best for the child. If the courts are to discharge that duty often they will have to take an active part in the proceedings. These aims will be taken into account when the authority makes rules under its general rule-making power.

Section 94. Appeals

94.—(1) [Subject to any express provisions to the contrary made by or under this Act] An appeal shall lie to the High Court against—

(a) the making by a magistrates' court of any order under this Act; or
(b) any refusal by a magistrates' court to make such an order.

(2) Where a magistrates' court has power, in relation to any proceedings under this Act, to decline jurisdiction because it considers that the case can more conveniently be dealt with by another court, no appeal shall lie against any exercise by that magistrates' court of that power.

Note: The words within square brackets were inserted by the Courts and Legal Services Act 1990.

(3) Subsection (1) does not apply in relation to an interim order for periodical payments made under Schedule 1.

(4) On an appeal under this section, the High Court may make such orders as may be necessary to give effect to its determination of the appeal.

(5) Where an order is made under subsection (4) the High Court may also make such incidental or consequential orders as appear to it to be just.

(6) Where an appeal from a magistrates' court relates to an order for the making of periodical payments, the High Court may order that its determination of the appeal shall have effect from such date as it thinks fit to specify in the order.

(7) The date so specified must not be earlier than the earliest date allowed in accordance with rules of court made for the purposes of this section.

(8) Where, on an appeal under this section in respect of an order requiring a person to make periodical payments, the High Court reduces the amount of those payments or discharges the order—

(a) it may order the person entitled to the payments to pay to the person making them such sum in respect of payments already made as the High Court thinks fit; and

(b) if any arrears are due under the order for periodical payments, it may remit payment of the whole, or part, of those arrears.

(9) Any order of the High Court made on an appeal under this section (other than one directing that an application be re-heard by a magistrates' court) shall, for the purposes—

(a) of the enforcement of the order; and

(b) of any power to vary, revive or discharge orders,

be treated as if it were an order of the magistrates' court from which the appeal was brought and not an order of the High Court.

(10) The Lord Chancellor may by order make provision as to the circumstances in which appeals may be made against decisions taken by courts on questions arising in connection with the transfer, or proposed transfer, of proceedings by virtue of any order under paragraph 2 of Schedule 11.

(11) Except to the extent provided for in any order made under subsection (10), no appeal may be made against any decision of a kind mentioned in that subsection.

Annotation

Section 94: is designed to put all parties on an even footing with regard to appeals. Note that there is no appeal from the making or refusal of an emergency order and any directions consequential upon such an order: Solicitor General Col 591 Hansard, 23 October 1989. A child and anyone who has parental responsibility for him or with whom he lives will be able to challenge emergency protection orders seventy-two hours after they have been made: see section 39(8) and (9). That will adequately safeguard the position of the child and those close to him. Given the short duration and emergency nature of the orders, no other provision is necessary and none is to be found in section 94. Indeed, a formal appeals procedure, with the added delay that that would necessarily involve, would be singularly inappropriate: Solicitor General Col 591 Hansard, 23 October 1989. Section 94 deals with the question of appeals, particularly from magistrates.

Section 94(1) specifies two important changes to the prior law. Formerly, appeals on the facts in care proceedings went from the magistrates' court to the Crown courts, but by changing the forum of appeal the civil nature of applications for care orders is emphasised. Furthermore, an appeal on the facts was not formerly available to local authorities.

Section 94(2): aims to reduce the hold-ups in relation to children's cases, where delay is prejudicial to the child, and to enable magistrates to recognise the complexities of certain cases and decide to pass them on to the appropriate court without delay. In the Cleveland child abuse crisis in 1987, it took a decision of Lord Justice Watkins, Vice Chancellor, to have cases removed from Cleveland to the High Court sitting in Leeds.

Section 94(3): provides that section 94(1) does not apply in relation to an interim order for periodical payments made under Schedule 1. Thus there are limitations imposed on the matters which may be appealed to the High Court: see sections 94(2), (3), (10), and (11). Schedule 1 deals with the financial provision for children and includes, among other things, orders for financial relief against parents and orders for financial relief for persons over eighteen.

Section 94(4): introduces a series of subsections through section 94(8) setting out the powers of the High Court when hearing an appeal. Clearly, the High Court must have power to make an order which reflects its conclusions after hearing the appeal, together with any consequential orders made necessary by its determination.

Section 94(5): deals with the exercise of the High Court's powers to make such incidental or consequential orders referred to in section 94(4) above.

Section 94(6): provides that on an appeal from a magistrates' court relating to an order for the making of periodical payments, the High Court may order that its determination of the appeal shall have effect from such date as it thinks fit to specify in the order: see section 94(4) above.

Section 94(7): relates to section 94(6).

Section 94(8): completes the series of subsections introduced by section 94(4) above setting out the powers of the High Court when hearing an appeal. It deals also with an order requiring a person to make periodical payments.

Section 94(9): makes clear that an order of the High Court made on appeal shall have the effect of an order made by the original court. The obvious exception to that it is an order for rehearing. Section 94 places limitation upon rights of appeal: see section 94(2), (3), (10) and (11).

Section 94(10): provides that the Lord Chancellor may by order make provision as to the circumstances in which appeals may be made against decisions taken by courts on questions arising in connection with the transfer of proceedings. This deals with the specified level of court in relation to such transfer.

Section 94(11): limits the right of appeal against any decision made under section 94(10): see section 94(9) above in relation to other exceptions to the rights of appeal and limitations placed upon these rights.

Section 95. Attendance of child at hearing under Part IV or V

95.—(1) In any proceedings in which a court is hearing an application for an order under Part IV or V, or is considering whether to make any such order, the court may order the child concerned to attend such stage or stages of the proceedings as may be specified in the order.

(2) The power conferred by subsection (1) shall be exercised in accordance with rules of court.

(3) Subsections (4) to (6) apply where—

    (a) an order under subsection (1) has not been complied with; or

    (b) the court has reasonable cause to believe that it will not be complied with.

(4) The court may make an order authorising a constable, or such person as may be specified in the order—

   (a) to take charge of the child and to bring him to the court; and

   (b) to enter and search any premises specified in the order if he has reasonable cause to believe that the child may be found on the premises.

(5) The court may order any person who is in a position to do so to bring the child to the court.

(6) Where the court has reason to believe that a person has information about the whereabouts of the child it may order him to disclose it to the court.

Annotation

Section 95: enables a court hearing an application for an order under Part IV or Part V of the Act, which relate to care and supervision orders, or education orders or other orders of that kind, to order that the child attend part or all of the proceedings. Such powers must be exercised in accordance with rules of court. The Act's principal reforms on representation of the child and court procedure and practice should make it unnecessary for the child to attend the hearing in many cases.

Section 95(1): provides for the attendance of a child at a hearing under Part IV or V. Section 95 not only gives the court the discretion and the right to exercise the power to require the child to come to court, but there is no reason why the court should not intimate to the child that it would like him to come and that it is open to the child to come. The child as a party is entitled to attend, and that entitlement alone might be brought to his attention: Solicitor General Col 631 Hansard, 23 October 1989.

Section 95(2): relates to rules of court defined in section 93. Note that the purpose of section 95 is to "decriminalise" the provisions of the Children and Young Persons Act 1969. Formerly, care proceedings were brought in juvenile courts by bringing the child before the court. Now care will be sought by an application to the court by the local authority or authorised person.

Section 95(3): introduces section 95(4) to (6) which give the court enforcement powers in the event of non-compliance. This is another addition to the Act in the series on procedure and practice in family proceedings in the courts having concurrent jurisdiction: see section 92.

Section 95(4): provides specific enforcement powers. Formerly, under the Children and Young Persons Act 1969, a child could be arrested and detained for up to seventy-two hours. The Children Act is designed to ensure this is not repeated but there is a power, to be found in section 95(4), to ensure that a child is brought to the court for this purpose should it be necessary. One hopes it would happen only in rare cases: Solicitor General Col 630 Hansard 23 October 1989.

Section 95(5): provides that the court may order any person who is in a position to do so to bring the child to the court. Clearly, the child's attendance will be necessary in some cases. The circumstances of the case may be such that the court would be helped by hearing from the child directly, at first hand, for a number of reasons. There may be contradictions in the arguments that have been put forward either by the legal representatives or by the guardian ad litem which may need to be sorted out. Section 95 gives the court a discretionary power to call the child when hearing such applications.

Section 95(6): does not impose a duty upon the court, only a discretionary power, that where the court has reason to believe that a person has information it may order him to disclose it to the court.

Section 96. Evidence given by, or with respect to, children

96.—(1) Subsection (2) applies where a child who is called as a witness in any civil proceedings does not, in the opinion of the court, understand the nature of an oath.

(2) The child's evidence may be heard by the court if, in its opinion—

    (a) he understands that it is his duty to speak the truth; and
    (b) he has sufficient understanding to justify his evidence being heard.

(3) The Lord Chancellor may by order make provision for the admissibility of evidence which would otherwise be inadmissible under any rule of law relating to hearsay.

(4) An order under subsection (3) may only be made with respect to—

    (a) civil proceedings in general or such civil proceedings, or class of civil proceedings, as may be prescribed; and
    (b) evidence in connection with the upbringing, maintenance or welfare of a child.

(5) An order under subsection (3)—

(a) may, in particular, provide for the admissibility of statements which are made orally or in a prescribed form or which are recorded by any prescribed method of recording;

(b) may make different provision for different purposes and in relation to different descriptions of court; and

(c) may make such amendments and repeals in any enactment relating to evidence (other than in this Act) as the Lord Chancellor considers necessary or expedient in consequence of the provision made by the order.

(6) Subsection (5)(b) is without prejudice to section 104(4).

(7) In this section—

"civil proceedings" and "court" have the same meaning as they have in the Civil Evidence Act 1968 by virtue of section 18 of that Act; and

"prescribed" means prescribed by an order under subsection (3).

Annotation

Section 96: links reform of the law of evidence relating to civil proceedings with clarification of the law in relation to the admissibility of hearsay. Under the prior law, hearsay of children's statements was admitted in evidence, but this became limited by decisions of the Court of Appeal: see annotation to section 96(4). According to the Solicitor General, these court decisions "would effectively remove a source of evidence that was available to the courts and would result in children having to undergo more often the trauma of giving direct oral evidence": Col 770 Hansard, 24 October 1989. Hence section 96(3). Note that section 96(3) to (7) came into force upon the Royal Assent.

Section 96(1): lays the groundwork for section 96(2). Note that section 96(1) deals with *any* civil proceedings where a child is called as a witness and is not limited to proceedings arising from the Children Act only.

Section 96(2): brings about what the Solicitor General described as "a welcome reform" in the law of evidence relating to civil proceedings. Section 96(2) allows the unsworn evidence of a child of tender years to be received in evidence in such proceedings where, in the court's opinion, he does not understand the nature of the oath but is of sufficient understanding to justify the reception of his evidence and understands the duty to tell the truth.

Section 96(3): deals with the power of the Lord Chancellor to make orders overriding rules relating to hearsay: 'We consider it necessary to give the Lord Chancellor that power because until very recently it had been the practice of courts to moderate the strict rules of evidence in civil proceedings concerning children, especially with regard to admitting hearsay evidence of a child's statement": Solicitor General Col 769 Hansard, 24 October 1989.

Section 96(4): limits the use of the power conferred on the Lord Chancellor under section 96(3). The consequence of the moderation of the strict rules of evidence referred to in the annotation to section 96(3) was affected by Court of Appeal decisions in the cases of Re. H and Re. K. These were to the effect that the flexible approach was mistaken and that, except in wardship, hearsay evidence could be admitted only in accordance with the exceptions to the general rule which is recognised by law.

Section 96(5): adds flexibility in that the Lord Chancellor's power will allow the overriding of evidential rules entirely, or in respect of certain types of evidence only—for example, children's statements—or in respect of certain types of case only. It will allow for different provisions to be made for different courts and tiers of courts: see Solicitor General Col 770 Hansard, 24 October 1989.

Section 96(6): links with section 96(5) in the provision of flexibility. Note that section 104(4) deals with the regulations and orders to be made by the Lord Chancellor or the Secretary of State in relation to statutory instruments made under the Act.

Section 96(7): relates the definition of civil proceedings under the Act to the wider scope of the Civil Evidence Act. Note that when section 96(7) defines "prescribed", this also links with the class of civil proceedings under section 96(4)(a).

Section 97. Privacy for children involved in certain proceedings

97.—(1) Rules made under section 144 of the Magistrates' Courts Act 1980 may make provision for a magistrates' court to sit in private in proceedings in which any powers under this Act may be exercised by the court with respect to any child.

(2) No person shall publish any material which is intended, or likely, to identify—

(a) any child as being involved in any proceedings before a magistrates' court in which any power under this Act may be exercised by the court with respect to that or any other child; or

(b) an address or school as being that of a child involved in any such proceedings.

(3) In any proceedings for an offence under this section it shall be a defence for the accused to prove that he did not know, and had no reason to suspect, that the published material was intended, or likely, to identify the child.

(4) The court or the Secretary of State may, if satisfied that the welfare of the child requires it, by order dispense with the requirements of subsection (2) to such extent as may be specified in the order.

(5) For the purposes of this section—

"publish" includes—

(a) broadcast by radio, television or cable television; or
(b) cause to be published; and

"material" includes any picture or representation.

(6) Any person who contravenes this section shall be guilty of an offence and liable, on summary conviction, to a fine not exceeding level 4 on the standard scale.

(7) Subsection (1) is without prejudice to—

(a) the generality of the rule making power in section 144 of the Act of 1980; or
(b) any other power of a magistrates' court to sit in private.

(8) [Sections 69 (sittings of magistrates' courts for family proceedings) and] [*Section*] 71 of the Act of 1980 (newspaper reports of certain proceedings) shall apply in relation to any proceedings to which this section applies subject to the provisions of this section.

Annotation

Section 97: provides for privacy for children involved in certain proceedings. Rules which prevent the publication of details of children's cases which are heard in private in the High Court and county courts continue to have effect: see section 12 of the Administration of Justice Act 1960, as amended by paragraph 14, Schedule 13. Section 97 also creates a new offence to prohibit the publication of material which is likely to identify a child as being involved in such proceedings in a magistrates' court, including his address or school as being that of a child involved in such proceedings: see section 97(2).

Note: The words within square brackets were inserted by the Courts and Legal Services Act 1990.
Note: The words *in italics* within square brackets were deleted by the Courts and Legal Services Act 1990.

Section 97(1): enables rules of court to permit a magistrates' court to sit in private in proceedings in which powers under it may be exercised with respect to a child. In the past the ability of magistrates' courts to sit in private and restrictions on publication of material about children involved in civil cases differed between courts and according to the types of case being heard.

Section 97(2): creates a new offence. Note that previously most cases affecting the custody of or access to children which were heard in magistrates' courts were heard under the Guardianship of Minors Act 1971 in the domestic court. Rules of court will specify when hearings under this Act can be held in private. In the past, rules specified that the court heard applications in private when it considered it expedient in the interests of the minor.

Section 97(3): provides a defence to any action brought under section 97, to wit that there was no guilty intent, nor foresight that the published material was likely to identify the child.

Section 97(4): provides that the Secretary of State shall have power by order to lift restrictions upon identifying a child involved under this Act. This is because it may be in the child's best interests, albeit only in rare cases, for facts to be fully published, rather than have rumour and speculation flourish. Such orders would have to be made quickly. It would be both unwieldy and inappropriate for them to be made under the statutory instrument procedure: Solicitor General Col 634 Hansard, 23 October 1989.

Section 97(5): provides that the offence under section 97 covers radio and television broadcasts as well as printed material. The offence is similar to that in section 49 of the Children and Young Persons Act 1933 regarding juvenile courts.

Section 97(6): provides for a fine on summary conviction not exceeding level 4 on the standard scale. This is in line with fines upon summary conviction in other parts of the Act.

Section 97(7): provides that section 97(1) is not to prejudice the generality of the rule-making power in section 144 of the Act of 1980 and any other power of a magistrates' court to sit in private. Rules of court will set out the circumstances under which a court can sit in private and may take account of whether the protection of secrecy can be afforded to adults as well as children: see Solicitor General Col 634 Hansard 23 October 1989.

Section 97(8): provides that section 97 shall apply equally with section 71 of the Magistrates' Courts Act 1980 dealing with newspaper reports of certain proceedings. The Guardianship of Minors Act 1971 may be repealed by this Act, section 71 of the Magistrates' Court Act 1980 is not.

Section 98. Self-incrimination

98.—(1) In any proceedings in which a court is hearing an application for an order under Part IV or V, no person shall be excused from—

(a) giving evidence on any matter; or
(b) answering any question put to him in the course of his giving evidence,

on the ground that doing so might incriminate him or his spouse in proceedings for an offence other than perjury.

Annotation

Section 98: deals with self-incrimination. It is important that courts hearing applications for care or supervision orders, or for emergency protection orders, should have the benefit of all the evidence available to them. Generally, a witness in proceedings enjoys a privilege against self-incrimination, but courts hearing types of application outlined under parts IV and V of the Act should not be deprived of potentially useful evidence even on this ground—hence section 98.

Section 98(1): relates to those special provisions in respect of care, supervision, emergency protection, child assessment and other orders under Parts IV and V which concern a child who may be at particular risk. Under the Children and Young Persons Act, a witness in equivalent proceedings might refuse to give evidence which would enable the court to decide what steps should be taken to protect the child concerned. In order, however, to encourage witnesses to give evidence and to help avoid delay in children's cases, a person will no longer be able to refuse to give evidence or answer a question put to him while he gives evidence, simply on the ground of incrimination.

Section 98(2): grants a witness an indemnity so that his evidence in proceedings under the Act cannot be relied upon in proceedings against himself or his spouse for any criminal offence other than perjury.

Section 99. Legal aid

99.—(1) The Legal Aid Act 1988 is amended as mentioned in subsections (2) to (4).

(2) In section 15 (availability of, and payment for, representation under provisions relating to civil legal aid), for the words "and (3)" in subsection (1) there shall be substituted "to (3B)":

and the following subsections shall be inserted after subsection (3)—

> "(3A) Representation under this Part shall not be available—
>
> (a) to any local authority; or
> (b) to any other body which falls within a prescribed description,
>
> for the purposes of any proceedings under the Children Act 1989.
>
> (3B) Regardless of subsection (2) or (3), representation under this Part must be granted where a child who is brought before a court under section 25 of the 1989 Act (use of accommodation for restricting liberty) is not, but wishes to be, legally represented before the court."

(3) In section 19(5) (scope of provisions about criminal legal aid), at the end of the definition of "criminal proceedings" there shall be added "and also includes proceedings under section 15 of the Children and Young Persons Act 1969 (variation and discharge of supervision orders) and section 16(8) of that Act (appeals in such proceedings)".

(4) Sections 27, 28 and 30(1) and (2) (provisions about legal aid in care, and other, proceedings in relation to children) shall cease to have effect.

(5) The Lord Chancellor may by order make such further amendments in the Legal Aid Act 1988 as he considers necessary or expedient in consequence of any provision made by or under this Act.

Annotation

Section 99: provides for the amendment of the Legal Aid Act 1988. The purpose of the amendment is to ensure that there will be a different method used for the handling of Children Act legal aid applications. The reason for the different procedures, both administratively and procedurally, is that they will ensure that applications are handled swiftly to reduce delays detrimental to the well-being of a child. In the parlance of the Lord Chancellor's office, these are to be "fast track" applications. Section 99 is to be implemented at the time when the full Act comes into force: October 1991.

Section 99(1): provides for the Legal Aid Act 1988 to be amended in accordance with the provisions of section 99(2) to (4). Schedule

12, paragraph 45 provides for modifications to the Act to ensure that civil legal aid will be available for care proceedings under the Children Act. This will be granted by the Legal Aid Board.

Section 99(2): provides that legal aid will continue to be granted if sought by a child who is to be placed in secure accommodation under section 25 of the Children Act, though now such aid may be granted without a means test. Legal aid will continue to be restricted to individuals and will not be available to local authorities or other bodies such as the National Society for the Prevention of Cruelty to Children.

Section 99(3): provides that since sections 15 and 16(8) of the Children and Young Persons Act 1969 are not repealed by the Children Act, these two sections shall now attract Part V—criminal legal aid.

Section 99(4): provides that Part VI legal aid will cease to have effect as concurrent jurisdiction between magistrates' courts, county courts and the High Court will render it unworkable after the Act comes into force.

Section 99(5): provides that the Legal Aid Act 1988 can also be modified to cater for changes arising from the Children Act in the future: for example, where further transfers of cases between courts are introduced it may be necessary to make special provisions to deal with the change in relations to the legal aid certificates then existing, without the need for the parties to re-apply to the Legal Aid Board.

Section 100. Restrictions on use of wardship jurisdiction

100.—(1) Section 7 of the Family Law Reform Act 1969 (which gives the High Court power to place a ward of court in the care, or under the supervision, of a local authority) shall cease to have effect.

(2) No court shall exercise the High Court's inherent jurisdiction with respect to children—

(a) so as to require a child to be placed in the care, or put under the supervision, of a local authority;

(b) so as to require a child to be accommodated by or on behalf of a local authority;

(c) so as to make a child who is the subject of a care order a ward of court; or

(d) for the purpose of conferring on any local authority power to determine any question which has arisen, or which may arise, in connection with any aspect of parental responsibility for a child.

(3) No application for any exercise of the court's inherent juris-diction with respect to children may be made by a local authority unless the authority have obtained the leave of the court.

(4) The court may only grant leave if it is satisfied that—

    (a) the result which the authority wish to achieve could not be achieved through the making of any order of a kind to which subsection (5) applies; and

    (b) there is reasonable cause to believe that if the court's inherent jurisdiction is not exercised with respect to the child he is likely to suffer significant harm.

(5) this subsection applies to any order—

    (a) made otherwise than in the exercise of the court's inherent jurisdiction; and

    (b) which the local authority is entitled to apply for (assuming, in the case of any application which may only be made with leave, that leave is granted).

Annotation

Section 100: prevents the inherent power of the High Court being used to put a child into local authority care or under its supervision or otherwise to give a local authority compulsory powers in respect of a child. Section 100 also requires that before a local authority may otherwise invoke the inherent jurisdiction they must obtain the leave of the court by showing that the remedy they are seeking is not otherwise available and that in its absence the child will suffer significant harm. Section 100 seeks to protect children and families from compulsory care or supervision, except where the statutory grounds for care exist under the Act and in other cases to preclude intervention by local authorities, unless significant harm to the child is likely.

Section 100(1): repeals section 7 of the Family Law Reform Act 1969 by virtue of which the High Court might when exercising its inherent wardship jurisdiction either (a) commit a ward to the care of a local authority where there were exceptional circumstances making it impracticable or undesirable for a ward of court to be, or continue to be, under the care of either of his parents or of any other individual, or (b) put the child under the supervision of a welfare officer or a local authority where there were exceptional circumstances which made it desirable. Note that it is section 37 which replaces section 7 of the 1969 Act.

Section 100(2): seeks to protect the integrity and independence of families from the risk of unwarranted interventions by the state in the guise of a local authority. Section 100(2) achieves this end by precluding exercise of the High Court's inherent *parens patriae* jurisdiction to achieve compulsory local authority care or supervision of the child, or otherwise to confer powers on a local authority in respect of the child's upbringing.

Section 100(3): provides that where a local authority do not seek compulsory powers over a child, and are not therefore excluded by section 100(2), they can continue to invoke the wardship jurisdiction for other purposes. Thus, for example, they could apply to the High Court where they wished a child subject to a care order to undergo major irreversible medical treatment such as an abortion or sterilisation, but felt that the Court's authority was desirable perhaps because the parents objected. The only restriction which the Act imposes on such cases is a requirement that the local authority obtain the Court's permission under section 100(3).

Section 100(4): provides that if a local authority wanted, for example, permission for a child to receive medical treatment it could apply for an order under the Act and the condition imposed by section 100(4)(a) would prevent the authority using the inherent jurisdiction instead. The purpose of section 100(4)(b) is to retain the likelihood of the risk of "significant harm" as the minimum threshold above which intervention in the upbringing of a child or his family by a public authority is justified and allowable under the Act. It represents a logical follow-through of the protection provided by the conditions for a care or supervision order in section 31(2).

Section 100(5): provides that a local authority is not to be able to resort to the inherent jurisdiction where the statutory application is subject to leave and the local authority either does not expect to obtain that leave or, indeed, has already been refused it. That provision is specifically designed to ensure that the refusal of leave to apply under section 10 for a specific issue or prohibited steps order does not then open the door to the inherent jurisdiction.

Section 101. Effect of orders as between England and Wales and Northern Ireland, the Channel Islands or the Isle of Man

101.—(1) The Secretary of State may make regulations providing—

    (a) for prescribed orders which—

        (i) are made by a court in Northern Ireland; and

        (ii) appear to the Secretary of State to correspond

in their effect to orders which may be made under any provision of this Act,

to have effect in prescribed circumstances, for prescribed purposes of this Act, as if they were orders of a prescribed kind made under this Act;

(b) for prescribed orders which—

    (i) are made by a court in England and Wales; and
    (ii) appear to the Secretary of State to correspond in their effect to orders which may be made under any provision in force in Northern Ireland,

to have effect in prescribed circumstances, for prescribed purposes of the law of Northern Ireland, as if they were orders of a prescribed kind made in Northern Ireland.

(2) Regulations under subsection (1) may provide for the order concerned to cease to have effect for the purposes of the law of Northern Ireland, or (as the case may be) the law of England and Wales, if prescribed conditions are satisfied.

(3) The Secretary of State may make regulations providing for prescribed orders which—

(a) are made by a court in the Isle of Man or in any of the Channel Islands; and
(b) appear to the Secretary of State to correspond in their effect to orders which may be made under this Act,

to have effect in prescribed circumstances for prescribed purposes of this Act, as if they were orders of a prescribed kind made under this Act.

(4) Where a child who is in the care of a local authority is lawfully taken to live in Northern Ireland, the Isle of Man or any of the Channel Islands, the care order in question shall cease to have effect if the conditions prescribed in regulations made by the Secretary of State are satisfied.

(5) Any regulations made under this section may—

(a) make such consequential amendments (including repeals) in—

    (i) section 25 of the Children and Young Persons Act 1969 (transfers between England and Wales and Northern Ireland); or
    (ii) section 26 (transfers between England and Wales and Channel Islands or Isle of Man) of that Act,

as the Secretary of State considers necessary or expedient; and

(b) modify any provision of this Act, in its application (by virtue of the regulations) in relation to an order made otherwise than in England and Wales.

Annotation

Section 101: provides for the effect of orders as between England and Wales and Northern Ireland, the Channel Islands or the Isle of Man, and vice versa in the case of Northern Ireland. The intention is to provide for transfers across borders of children subject to such orders, or to prescribe that such orders shall cease to have effect.

Section 101(1): provides for the Secretary of State to prescribe by regulation those orders which, having been made by a court in Northern Ireland, shall have effect as if they had been made under specified provisions in this Act and vice versa. Sections 25 and 26 of the Children and Young Persons Act 1969 provided for children who were subject to certain orders to be transferred from Northern Ireland, the Channel Islands or the Isle of Man to England or Wales subject to the authorisation of the Secretary of State. Section 25 also enabled a child to be similarly transferred to Northern Ireland.

Section 101(2): specifies that regulations made under section 101(1) may provide for the orders to cease to have effect. Under the former law, the order to which the child had been subjected would take effect as if it were the equivalent order made in the place to which he had moved. The purpose of regulations referred to in section 101(2), and others to be prescribed under section 101, is to provide for a singular updated framework for the identification of those orders which may be transferred, or cease to have effect.

Section 101(3): provides for the Secretary of State to make similar regulations in respect of orders made in the Channel Islands or the Isle of Man. The Secretary of State will be able to specify by regulation which orders are capable of being transferred. Such regulations throughout section 101 will be capable of making the necessary consequential amendments to sections 25 and 26 of the Children and Young Persons Act 1969.

Section 101(4): mirrors section 101(2) in relation to a child who is in the care of a local authority and is lawfully taken to live in Northern Ireland, the Isle of Man or any of the Channel Islands.

Section 101(5): provides for regulations made under section 101 to make necessary consequential amendments to sections 25 and 26 of the Children and Young Persons Act 1969 and to modify any provisions of this Act in its application to an order made somewhere other than in England and Wales.

Search warrants

Section 102. Power of constable to assist in exercise of certain powers to search for children or inspect premises

102. —(1) Where, on an application made by any person for a warrant under this section, it appears to the court—

(a) that a person attempting to exercise powers under any enactment mentioned in subsection (6) has been prevented from doing so by being refused entry to the premises concerned or refused access to the child concerned; or

(b) that any such person is likely to be so prevented from exercising any such powers,

it may issue a warrant authorising any constable to assist that person in the exercise of those powers, using reasonable force if necessary.

(2) Every warrant issued under this section shall be addressed to, and executed by, a constable who shall be accompanied by the person applying for the warrant if—

(a) that person so desires; and

(b) the court by whom the warrant is issued does not direct otherwise.

(3) A court granting an application for a warrant under this section may direct that the constable concerned may, in executing the warrant, be accompanied by a registered medical practitioner, registered nurse or registered health visitor if he so chooses.

(4) An application for a warrant under this section shall be made in the manner and form prescribed by rules of court.

(5) Where—

(a) an application for a warrant under this section relates to a particular child; and

(b) it is reasonably practicable to do so,

the application and any warrant granted on the application shall name the child; and where it does not name him it shall describe him as clearly as possible.

(6) The enactments are—

    (a) sections 62, 64, 67, 76, 80, 86 and 87;

    (b) paragraph 8(1)(b) and (2)(b) of Schedule 3;

    (c) section 33 of the Adoption Act 1976 (duty of local authority to secure that protected children are visited from time to time).

Annotation

Section 102: provides that a court may issue a warrant authorising a constable to assist a person attempting to exercise powers under certain specified enactments who has been, or is likely to be, prevented from exercising those powers by being refused entry to the premises concerned. The only power of entry in this Act which is not supported by this warrant provision is that dealt with in section 48. This is because section 48 deals with powers to assist in discovery of children who may be in need of emergency protection.

Section 102(1): mirrors section 48(9). It was felt in relation to section 48(9) that with the addition of the warrant powers, an applicant should have sufficient legal powers to do what is necessary to protect a child in need of emergency protection. By extending section 48(9) through section 102(1) legal strength is added to powers of entry in relation to those enactments covered by section 102(6).

Section 102(2): mirrors section 48(10). In relation to section 48(10) extended through section 102(2) any applicant will be acting in concert with the police. Note that, in part, section 102 replaces the effect of section 40 of the Children and Young Persons Act 1969.

Section 102(3): mirrors section 48(11). The decision that a constable may be accompanied by a registered medical practitioner, registered nurse or registered health visitor, is one for the constable—it is the power of direction that rests with the court.

Section 102(4): mirrors section 48(12): See section 93 for the provisions dealing with rules of court.

Section 102(5): mirrors section 48(13). Rules which prevent the publication of details of children's cases which are heard in private in the High Court and county courts continue to have effect: see section 12 of the Administration of Justice Act 1960 as amended by Schedule 13, paragraph 14.

Section 102(6): defines the enactments covered by section 102. Remember, section 102 is a new provision which relates to powers of entry in respect of private fostering, community, voluntary and registered children's homes, the Secretary of State's inspection powers, supervision orders, the power to inspect premises used for the reception of children under the Nurseries and Child Minders Regulation Act 1948 and the duty of a local authority to visit protected children under the Adoption Act 1976.

General

Section 103. Offences by bodies corporate

103. — (1) This section applies where any offence under this Act is committed by a body corporate.

(2) If the offence is proved to have been committed with the consent or connivance of or to be attributable to any neglect on the part of any director, manager, secretary or other similar officer of the body corporate, or any person who was purporting to act in any such capacity, he (as well as the body corporate) shall be guilty of the offence and shall be liable to be proceeded against and punished accordingly.

Annotation

Section 103: makes provision under the Act in relation to the commission of any offence by a body corporate. Thus the negligence of any inividual may lead to an offence having been committed by the body corporate. It also imposes a duty on such body corporate to introduce and enact procedures that will hold accountable those directors, managers, secretaries or others acting on its behalf.

Section 103(1): applies where any offence under this Act has been committed by a body corporate. A body corporate is a body of persons having in law an existence and rights and duties distinct from those of the individual persons who from time to time form it.

Section 103(2): provides that it is an offence by a body corporate where such offence has been committed with the consent or connivance, or may be attributable to any neglect on the part of officials or officers of the body corporate. Bodies corporate were not originally liable for crime, but now a body corporate can be indicted, and fines may be imposed upon it. A body corporate is liable criminally for acts of omission and for the acts of its officials and officers in the course of their employment.

Section 104. Regulations and orders

104.—(1) Any power of the Lord Chancellor or the Secretary of State under this Act to make an order, regulations, or rules, except an order under section 54(2), 56(4)(a), 57(3), 84 or 97(4) or paragraph 1(1) of Schedule 4, shall be exercisable by statutory instrument.

(2) Any such statutory instrument, except one made under section 17(4), 107 or 108(2), shall be subject to annulment in pursuance of a resolution of either House of Parliament.

(3) an order under section 17(4) shall not be made unless a draft of it has been laid before, and approved by a resolution of, each House of Parliament.

(4) Any statutory instrument made under this Act may—

- (a) make different provision for different cases;
- (b) provide for exemptions from any of its provisions; and
- (c) contain such incidental, supplemental and transitional provisions as the person making it considers expedient.

Annotation

Section 104: provides that the specified power to make regulations or orders under the Act shall be exercisable by statutory instrument and thus imposes a requirement that any such regulations or orders shall be laid before Parliament. They may then become the subject of debate and render the Lord Chancellor and the Secretary of State accountable.

Section 104(1): provides that any order shall be exercisable by statutory instrument, except an order revoking the instrument of management of a community home or a controlled or assisted home, the revocation of an instrument of management of a controlled or assisted community home, the revocation of a home's instrument of management under section 57(3), in relation to the default power in respect of any duty of a local authority, powers in relation to the privacy of children involved in certain proceedings, or in relation to instruments of management for controlled and assisted community homes under paragraph 1(1) of Schedule 4.

Section 104(2): provides for such statutory instruments to be subject to annulment pursuant to a resolution of either House of Parliament. Exceptions are made for any statutory instruments made in relation to the provision of services for families to be found in Part I of Schedule 2, the extension of provisions in the

Act to the Channel Islands, or in relation to the date on which the Act is to come into force: see sections 17(4), 107 or 108(2).

Section (3): ensures that any statutory instruments made under section 17(4) shall be by the draft affirmative resolution procedure. Section 17(4) covers statutory instruments made in relation to the provision of services for families to be found in Part 1 of Schedule 2. They deal with the Secretary of State's power to amend or add to the list of local authority services.

Section 104(4): provides that statutory instruments made under the Act shall make different provisions in different cases, provide for exceptions, and contain incidental, supplemental and transitional provisions. Section 104(4) is designed to ensure flexibility in the wording of statutory instruments in order to get the best out of the Act and its regulatory provisions.

Section 105. Interpretation

105. — (1) In this Act —

"adoption agency" means a body which may be referred to as an adoption agency by virtue of section 1 of the Adoption Act 1976;

"bank holiday" means a day which is a bank holiday under the Banking and Financial Dealings Act 1971;

"care order" has the meaning given by section 31(11) and also includes any order which by or under any enactment has the effect of, or is deemed to be, a care order for the purposes of this Act; and any reference to a child who is in the care of an authority is a reference to a child who is in their care by virtue of a care order;

"child" means, subject to paragraph 16 of Schedule 1, a person under the age of eighteen;

"child assessment order" has the meaning given by section 43(2);

"child minder" has the meaning given by section 71;

"child of the family", in relation to the parties to a marriage, means —

(a) a child of both of those parties;

(b) any other child, not being a child who is placed with those parties as foster parents by a local authority or voluntary organisation, who has been treated by both of those parties as a child of their family;

"children's home" has the same meaning as in section 63;

"community home" has the meaning given by section 53;

"contact order" has the meaning given by section 8(1);

"day care" has the same meaning as in section 18;

"disabled", in relation to a child, has the same meaning as in section 17(11);

"district health authority" has the same meaning as in the National Health Service Act 1977;

"domestic premises" has the meaning given by section 71(12);

"education supervision order" has the meaning given in section 36;

"emergency protection order" means an order under section 44;

"family assistance order" has the meaning given in section 16(2);

"family proceedings" has the meaning given by section 8(3);

"functions" includes powers and duties;

"guardian of a child" means a guardian (other than a guardian of the estate of a child) appointed in accordance with the provisions of section 5;

"harm" has the same meaning as in section 31(9) and the question of whether harm is significant shall be determined in accordance with section 31(10);

"health authority" means any district health authority and any special health authority established under the National Health Service Act 1977;

"health service hospital" has the same meaning as in the National Health Service Act 1977;

"hospital" has the same meaning as in the Mental Health Act 1983, except that it does not include a special hospital within the meaning of that Act;

"ill-treatment" has the same meaning as in section 31(9);

"independent school" has the same meaning as in the Education Act 1944;

"local authority" means, in relation to England and Wales, the council of a county, a metropolitan district, a London

Borough or the Common Council of the City of London and, in relation to Scotland, a local authority within the meaning of section 1(2) of the Social Work (Scotland) Act 1968;

"local authority foster parent" has the same meaning as in section 23(3);

"local education authority" has the same meaning as in the Education Act 1944;

"local housing authority" has the same meaning as in the Housing Act 1985;

"mental nursing home" has the same meaning as in the Registered Homes Act 1984;

"nursing home" has the same meaning as in the Act of 1984;

"parental responsibility" has the meaning given in section 3;

"parental responsibility agreement" has the meaning given in section 4(1);

"prescribed" means prescribed by regulations made under this Act;

"privately fostered child" and "to foster a child privately" have the same meaning as in section 66;

"prohibited steps order" has the meaning given by section 8(1);

"protected child" has the same meaning as in Part III of the Adoption Act 1976;

"registered children's home" has the same meaning as in section 63;

"registered pupil" has the same meaning as in the Education Act 1944;

"relative", in relation to a child, means a grandparent, brother, sister, uncle or aunt (whether of the full blood or half blood or by affinity) or step-parent;

"residence order" has the meaning given by section 8(1);

"residential care home" has the same meaning as in the Registered Homes Act 1984;

"responsible person", in relation to a child who is the subject of a supervision order, has the meaning given in paragraph 1 of Schedule 3;

"school" has the same meaning as in the Education Act 1944 or, in relation to Scotland, in the Education (Scotland) Act 1980;

"service", in relation to any provision made under Part III, includes any facility;

"signed", in relation to any person, includes the making by that person of his mark;

"special educational needs" has the same meaning as in the Education Act 1981;

"special health authority" has the same meaning as in the National Health Service Act 1977;

"specific issue order" has the meaning given by section 8(1);

"supervision order" has the meaning given by section 31(11);

"supervised child" and "supervisor", in relation to a supervision order or an education supervision order, mean respectively the child who is (or is to be) under supervision and the person under whose supervision he is (or is to be) by virtue of the order;

"upbringing", in relation to any child, includes the care of the child but not his maintenance;

"voluntary home" has the meaning given by section 60;

"voluntary organisation" means a body (other than a public or local authority) whose activities are not carried on for profit.

(2) References in this Act to a child whose father and mother were, or (as the case may be) were not, married to each other at the time of his birth must be read with section 1 of the Family Law Reform Act 1987 (which extends the meaning of such references).

(3) References in this Act to—

(a) a person with whom a child lives, or is to live, as the result of a residence order; or
(b) a person in whose favour a residence order is in force,

shall be construed as references to the person named in the order as the person with whom the child is to live.

(4) References in this Act to a child who is looked after by a local authority have the same meaning as they have (by virtue of section 22) in Part III.

(5) References in this Act to accommodation provided by or

on behalf of a local authority are references to accommodation so provided in the exercise of functions which stand referred to the social services committee of that or any other local authority under the Local Authority Social Services Act 1970.

(6) In determining the "ordinary residence" of a child for any purpose of this Act, there shall be disregarded any period in which he lives in any place—

(a) which is a school or other institution;
(b) in accordance with the requirements of a supervision order under this Act or an order under section 7(7)(b) of the Children and Young Persons Act 1969; or
(c) while he is being provided with accommodation by or on behalf of a local authority.

(7) References in this Act to children who are in need shall be construed in accordance with section 17.

(8) Any notice or other document required under this Act to be served on any person may be served on him by being delivered personally to him, or being sent by post to him in a registered letter or by the recorded delivery service at his proper address.

(9) Any such notice or other document required to be served on a body corporate or a firm shall be duly served if it is served on the secretary or clerk of that body or a partner of that firm.

(10) For the purposes of this section, and of section 7 of the Interpretation Act 1978 in its application to this section, the proper address of a person—

(a) in the case of a secretary or clerk of a body corporate, shall be that of the registered or principal office of that body;
(b) in the case of a partner of a firm, shall be that of the principal office of the firm; and
(c) in any other case, shall be the last known address of the person to be served.

Annotation

Section 105: provides definitions for various terms used throughout the Act and contains certain explanatory and interpretative provisions. These relate to the Family Law Reform Act 1987, the Local Authority Social Services Act 1970 and the Interpretation Act 1978. Section 7(7)(b) of the Children and Young Persons Act 1969 is referred to in relation to the determination of the "ordinary residence" of a child, and the status of a person named in a residence order is also defined. So, too, is the definition of service in relation to documentation and the mode of delivery for such service to be legally valid.

Section 105(1): provides the definition of terms used throughout the Act and confirms that where the definitions are given in certain sections they hold good throughout the Act. Note that any reference to a child who is in the care of an authority is a reference to a child who is in their care by virtue of a care order. Thus "care" no longer indicates a child who is accommodated by a local authority on a voluntary basis. Under the Act, children who are accommodated by or on behalf of a local authority are referred to as "looked after" by a local authority, whether the accommodation is provided voluntarily or compulsorily.

Section 105(2): relates to section 1 of the Family Law Reform Act 1987. Section 1 of the Act defined a general principle that in enactments passed and instruments made after the coming into force of that section, references (however expressed) to any relationship between two persons should, unless the contrary intention appeared, be construed without regard to whether or not the father and mother or either of them, or the father and mother of any person through whom the relationship was deduced, had been married to each other at any time.

Section 105(3): defines the person named in the residence order as the person with whom the child lives, or is to live. Note that it is section 12 that deals with residence orders and parental responsibility. It is a principle of the Act that it is the person with whom the child lives who has the primary role for his care and upbringing.

Section 105(4): relates to section 22 and the "cornerstone duty" of the Act, that it is the general duty of a local authority to promote and safeguard the welfare of children whom they are looking after. A local authority must have regard to the wishes and feelings of the child, any parent or other person with parental responsibility, and any other person whose wishes and feelings they consider relevant.

Section 105(5): relates a local authority to its social services committee. Notwithstanding it is social services and social workers who must deal with children in need, a fact recognised by public and specialists alike, the onus of responsibility for acts or omissions always falls upon a local authority, which is why they are referred to so punctiliously throughout the Act. Section 105(6) makes it clear that responsibility within the authority is clearly devolved upon social service departments.

Section 105(6): provides for the determination of "ordinary residence". Note that it is section 8(1) that defines residence, contact and other orders with respect to children. Residence and contact orders resemble and replace the former custody and access orders but avoid the confusion as to differing degrees of custody.

Section 105(7): refers to the definition of children in need in section 17, which applies to all children, including those who are disabled or handicapped within the meaning of section 29 of the National Assistance Act 1948. Note that in section 105(1) a child means, subject to paragraph 16 of Schedule 1, a person under the age of eighteen.

Section 105(8): provides for the method of service of any notice or document required under the Act. It requires service to be made personally to any person who may be served or by registered or recorded delivery. Simply posting a letter will not constitute service, nor will any communication hand delivered but simply dropped through a letterbox.

Section 105(9): provides that notice is served on a body corporate or a firm if it is served upon the secretary or a partner, as the case may be. Note the provisions of section 105(8) as to what constitutes service.

Section 105(10): relates to section 7 of the Interpretation Act 1978. Note with regard to section 105(10)(a) the contents of section 103 dealing with offences by bodies corporate. Section 105(10)(c) will fulfil requirements imposed upon a local authority when, for example, dealing with the protection of children: see section 43(11).

Section 106. Financial provisions

106. —(1) Any—

(a) grants made by the Secretary of State under this Act; and

(b) any other expenses incurred by the Secretary of State under this Act,

shall be payable out of money provided by Parliament.

(2) Any sums received by the Secretary of State under section 58, or by way of the repayment of any grant made under section 82(2) or (4) shall be paid into the Consolidated Fund.

Annotation

Section 106: provides that any grants made or expenses incurred by the Secretary of State under provisions of the Act are payable out of money provided by Parliament. It also provides that monies received by the Secretary of State under section 58, or by way of repayment of any grant, shall be paid into the consolidated fund. In general, it was the contention of the government that none of the provisions of the Act was likely to have a substantial impact upon the Treasury. Nevertheless the sponsoring departments might have to make modest provision for monitoring the effect of the changes brought about by the Act. Section 106 deals solely with the specific involvement of the Secretary of State to disburse monies and to receive grant or other repayment.

Section 106(1): ensures that any grants made by the Secretary of State and any other expenses incurred shall be provided for by Parliament and will be drawn from the budget allocated to his department.

Section 106(2): provides for repayment into the consolidated fund. Note that under section 58, when premises or parts of premises used for the purposes of a controlled or assisted community home are disposed of or put to alternative use before the home's designation as a community home has been withdrawn, that proportion of the value of the premises or parts disposed of, or put to alternative use, which is attributable to the expenditure of public money, will fall to be repaid by the voluntary organisation providing the home. Where the home is vested in trustees, repayment will fall upon them. Section 106(2) provides for any monies thus received to revert into the consolidated fund.

Section 107. Application to Channel Islands

107. Her Majesty may by Order in Council direct that any of the provisions of this Act shall extend to any of the Channel Islands with such exceptions and modifications as may be specified in the Order.

Annotation

Section 107: provides for the extension of the Act to the Channel Islands. Note that the Act in general applies only to England and Wales, with the important exception that Part X dealing with child minding and day care for young children applies also in Scotland. There are also a number of consequential amendments which have been made to the law in Scotland and Northern Ireland: see also section 101 for the effect of orders as between England and Wales and Northern Ireland, the Channel Islands or the Isle of Man.

Section 108. Short title, commencement extent etc.

108.—(1) This Act may be cited as the Children Act 1989.

(2) Sections 89 and 96(3) to (7), and paragraph 35 of Schedule 12, shall come into force on the passing of this Act and paragraph 36 of Schedule 12 shall come into force at the end of the period of two months beginning with the day on which this Act is passed but otherwise this Act shall come into force on such date as may be appointed by order made by the Lord Chancellor or the Secretary of State, or by both acting jointly.

(3) Different dates may be appointed for different provisions of this Act and in relation to different cases.

(4) The minor amendments set out in Schedule 12 shall have effect.

(5) The consequential amendments set out in Schedule 13 shall have effect.

(6) The transitional provisions and savings set out in Schedule 14 shall have effect.

(7) The repeals set out in Schedule 15 shall have effect.

(8) An order under subsection (2) may make such transitional provisions or savings as appear to the person making the order to be necessary or expedient in connection with the provisions brought into force by the order, including—

    (a) provisions adding to or modifying the provisions of Schedule 14; and

    (b) such adaptations—

        (i) of the provisions brought into force by the order; and

        (ii) of any provisions of this Act then in force,

      as appear to him necessary or expedient in consequence of the partial operation of this Act.

(9) The Lord Chancellor may by order make such amendments or repeals, in such enactments as may be specified in the order, as appear to him to be necessary or expedient in consequence of any provision of this Act.

(10) This Act shall, in its application to the Isles of Scilly, have effect subject to such exceptions, adaptations and modifications as the Secretary of State may by order prescribe.

(11) The following provisions of this Act extend to Scotland—

section 19;

section 25(8)

section 50(13);

Part X;

section 80(1)(h) and (i), (2) to (4), (5)(a), (b) and (h) and (6) to (12);

section 88;

section 104 (so far as necessary);

section 105 (so far as necessary);

subsections (1) to (3), (8) and (9) and this subsection;

in Schedule 2, paragraph 24;

in Schedule 12, paragraphs 1, 7 to 10, 18, 27, 30(a) and 41 to 44;

in Schedule 13, paragraphs 18 to 23, 32, 46, 47, 50, 57, 62, 63, 68(a) and (b) and 71;

in Schedule 14, paragraphs 1, 33 and 34;

in Schedule 15, the entries relating to—

> (a) the Custody of Children Act 1891;
> (b) the Nurseries and Child Minders Regulation Act 1948;
> (c) section 53(3) of the Children and Young Persons Act 1963;
> (d) section 60 of the Health Services and Public Health Act 1968;
> (e) the Social Work (Scotland) Act 1968;
> (f) the Adoption (Scotland) Act 1978;
> (g) the Child Care Act 1980;
> (h) the Foster Children (Scotland) Act 1984;
> (i) the Child Abduction and Custody Act 1985; and
> (j) the Family Law Act 1986.

(12) The following provisions of this Act extend to Northern Ireland—

section 50;

section 101(1)(b), (2) and (5)(a)(i);

subsections (1) to (3), (8) and (9) and this subsection;

in Schedule 2, paragraph 24;

in Schedule 12, paragraphs 7 to 10, 18 and 27;

in Schedule 13, paragraphs 21, 22, 46, 47, 57, 62, 63, 68(c) to (e) and 69 to 71;

in Schedule 14, paragraphs [*18*], 28 to 30 and 38(a); and

in Schedule 15, the entries relating to the Guardianship of Minors Act 1971, the Children Act 1975, the Child Care Act 1980, and the Family Law Act 1986.

Annotation

Section 108: provides for the short title, the commencement and the extent of the Act. The Act is designed to be a comprehensive reform of the private and public law in relation to children. It has been described as "a major undertaking which has required the codification of a significant body of statute law and major reforms to that law to produce very substantial advances": The Minister of State, Hansard Col 1339, 27 October 1989. Fundamental changes have been made to court procedure and other issues of law.

Section 108(1): gives the Act its name—the Children Act 1989.

Section 108(2): provides that section 89 dealing with tests to establish paternity and section 96(3) to (7) relating to changes in the admissibility of evidence should come into force upon the Royal Assent 16 November 1989: See annotation to section 96. Also that paragraph 36 of Schedule 12 relating to insertions into the Education Act 1981 should come into force 16 January 1990, and that the remainder of the Act shall come into force on a day appointed by order made by the Secretary of State or the Lord Chancellor or by both acting jointly.

Section 108(3): provides that the Act will be immplemented on different dates for different provisions. Note that the whole of the Act is to come into force in October 1991.

Section 108(4): gives effect to those minor amendments set out in Schedule 12 dealing with amendments to other Acts of Parliament consequent upon the passage of the Children Act.

Section 108(5): gives effect to those consequential amendments set out in Schedule 13 dealing with the Wills Act 1937, the Children and Young Persons Act 1933 and other important Acts.

Section 108(6): deals with the transitional provisions and savings

Note: The figures *in italics* within square brackets were deleted by the Courts and Legal Services Act 1990.

set out in Schedule 14 relating, inter alia, to pending proceedings, cessation of declaration of unfitness, and parental responsibility of parents.

Section 108(7): gives effect to those repeals set out in Schedule 15. Since the Children Act is itself a major piece of legislation it follows that it has a considerable impact on other items of legislation already on the statute book.

Section 108(8): relates to orders made under section 108(2) in relation to Schedule 14 which deals with transitionals and savings.

Section 108(9): confers an enabling power upon the Lord Chancellor to effect such orders under the Act as he deems necessary or expedient in relation to its operation.

Section 108(10): prescribes that the Act shall have effect in the Scilly Isles, subject to any exceptions, adaptations and modifications which may be prescribed by the Secretary of State. Note that it will not be for the Lord Chancellor, or the Lord Chancellor and the Secretary of State to prescribe jointly—such powers of prescription are conferred upon the Secretary of State only.

Section 108(11): defines those provisions of the Act which extend to Scotland. Note that the Act generally applies to England and Wales but that Part X dealing with child minding and day care for young children applies to Scotland, as do a number of consequential amendments made to the law in Scotland.

Section 108(12): defines those provisions of the Act that apply to Northern Ireland. Note that there are a number of consequential amendments made to the law in Northern Ireland.

SCHEDULES

Orders for financial relief against parents

1.—(1) On an application made by a parent or guardian of a child, or by any person in whose favour a residence order is in force with respect to a child, the court may—

- (a) in the case of an application to the High Court or a county court, make one or more of the orders mentioned in sub-paragraph (2);
- (b) in the case of an application to a magistrates' court, make one or both of the orders mentioned in paragraphs (a) and (c) of that sub-paragraph.

(2) The orders referred to in sub-paragraph (1) are—

- (a) an order requiring either or both parents of a child—

    (i) to make to the applicant for the benefit of the child; or
    (ii) to make to the child himself,

    such periodical payments, for such term, as may be specified in the order;

- (b) an order requiring either or both parents of a child—

    (i) to secure to the applicant for the benefit of the child; or
    (ii) to secure to the child himself,

    such periodical payments, for such term, as may be so specified;

- (c) an order requiring either or both parents of a child—

    (i) to pay to the applicant for the benefit of the child; or
    (ii) to pay to the child himself,

    such lump sum as may be so specified;

- (d) an order requiring a settlement to be made for the benefit of the child, and to the satisfaction of the court, of property—

    (i) to which either parent is entitled (either in possession or in reversion); and

(ii) which is specified in the order;

(e) an order requiring either or both parents of a child—

(i) to transfer to the applicant, for the benefit of the child; or

(ii) to transfer to the child himself,

such property to which the parent is, or the parents are, entitled (either in possession or in reversion) as may be specified in the order.

(3) The powers conferred by this paragraph may be exercised at any time.

(4) An order under sub-paragraph (2)(a) or (b) may be varied or discharged by a subsequent order made on the application of any person by or to whom payments were required to be made under the previous order.

(5) Where a court makes an order under this paragraph—

(a) it may at any time make a further such order under sub-paragraph (2)(a), (b) or (c) with respect to the child concerned if he has not reached the age of eighteen;

(b) it may not make more than one order under sub-paragraph (2)(d) or (e) against the same person in respect of the same child.

(6) On making, varying or discharging a residence order the court may exercise any of its powers under this Schedule even though no application has been made to it under this Schedule.

[(7) Where a child is a ward of court, the court may exercise any of its powers under ths Schedule even though no application has been made to it.]

Orders for financial relief for persons over eighteen

2.—(1) If, on an application by a person who has reached the age of eighteen, it appears to the court—

(a) that the applicant is, will be or (if an order were made under this paragraph) would be receiving instruction at an educational establishment or undergoing training for a trade, profession or vocation, whether or not while in gainful employment; or

Note: The words within square brackets were inserted by the Courts and Legal Services Act 1990.

(b) that there are special circumstances which justify the making of an order under this paragraph,

the court may make one or both of the orders mentioned in sub-paragraph (2).

(2) The orders are —

(a) an order requiring either or both of the applicant's parents to pay to the applicant such periodical payments, for such term, as may be specified in the order;

(b) an order enquiring either or both of the applicant's parents to pay to the applicant such lump sum as may be so specified.

(3) an application may not be made under this paragraph by any person if, immediately before he reached the age of sixteen, a periodical payments order was in force with respect to him.

(4) No order shall be made under this paragraph at a time when the parents of the applicant are living with each other in the same household.

(5) An order under sub-paragraph (2)(a) may be varied or discharged by a subsequent order made on the application of any person by or to whom payments were required to be made under the previous order.

(6) In sub-paragraph (3) "periodical payments order" means an order made under —

(a) this Schedule;

(b) section 6(3) of the Family Law Reform Act 1969;

(c) section 23 or 27 of the Matrimonial Causes Act 1973;

(d) Part I of the Domestic Proceedings and Magistrates' Courts Act 1978,

for the making or securing of periodical payments.

(7) The powers conferred by this paragraph shall be exercisable at any time.

(8) Where the court makes an order under this paragraph it may from time to time while that order remains in force make a further such order.

Duration of orders for financial relief

3. —(1) the term to be specified in an order for periodical payments made under paragraph 1(2)(a) or (b) in favour of a child

may begin with the date of the making of an application for the order in question or any later date but—

> (a) shall not in the first instance extend beyond the child's seventeenth birthday unless the court thinks it right in the circumstances of the case to specify a later date; and
> (b) shall not in any event extend beyond the child's eighteenth birthday.

(2) Paragraph (b) of sub-paragraph (1) shall not apply in the case of a child if it appears to the court that—

> (a) the child is, or will be or (if an order were made without complying with that paragraph) would be receiving instruction at an educational establishment or undergoing training for a trade, profession or vocation, whether or not while in gainful employment; or
> (b) there are special circumstances which justify the making of an order without complying with that paragraph.

(3) An order for periodical payments made under paragraph 1(2)(a) or 2(2)(a) shall, notwithstanding anything in the order, cease to have effect on the death of the person liable to make payments under the order.

(4) Where an order is made under paragraph 1(2)(a) or (b) requiring periodical payments to be made or secured to the parent of a child, the order shall cease to have effect if—

> (a) any parent making or securing the payments; and
> (b) any parent to whom the payments are made or secured,

live together for a period of more than six months.

Matters to which court is to have regard in making orders for financial relief

4.—(1) In deciding whether to exercise its powers under paragraph 1 or 2, and if so in what manner, the court shall have regard to all the circumstances including—

> (a) the income, earning capacity, property and other financial resources which each person mentioned in sub-paragraph (3) has or is likely to have in the foreseeable future;
> (b) the financial needs, obligations and responsibilities which each person mentioned in sub-paragraph (3) has or is likely to have in the foreseeable future;
> (c) the financial needs of the child;
> (d) the income, earning capacity (if any), property and other financial resources of the child;

(e) any physical or mental disability of the child;

(f) the manner in which the child was being, or was expected to be, educated or trained.

(2) In deciding whether to exercise its powers under paragraph 1 against a person who is not the mother or father of the child, and if so in what manner, the court shall in addition have regard to—

(a) whether that person had assumed responsibility for the maintenance of the child and, if so, the extent to which and basis on which he assumed that responsibility and the length of the period during which he met that responsibility;

(b) whether he did so knowing that the child was not his child;

(c) the liability of any other person to maintain the child.

(3) Where the court makes an order under paragraph 1 against a person who is not the father of the child, it shall record in the order that the order is made on the basis that the person against whom the order is made is not the child's father.

(4) The persons mentioned in sub-paragraph (1) are—

(a) in relation to a decision whether to exercise its powers under paragraph 1, any parent of the child;

(b) in relation to a decision whether to exercise its powers under paragraph 2, the mother and father of the child;

(c) the applicant for the order;

(d) any other person in whose favour the court proposes to make the order.

Provisions relating to lump sums

5.—(1) Without prejudice to the generality of paragraph 1, an order under that paragraph for the payment of a lump sum may be made for the purpose of enabling any liabilities or expenses—

(a) incurred in connection with the birth of the child or in maintaining the child; and

(b) reasonably incurred before the making of the order,

to be met.

(2) The amount of any lump sum required to be paid by an order made by a magistrates' court under paragraph 1 or 2 shall not exceed £1000 or such larger amount as the Secretary of State may from time to time by order fix for the purposes of this sub-paragraph.

(3) The power of the court under paragraph 1 or 2 to vary or discharge an order for the making or securing of periodical payments by a parent shall include power to make an order under that provision for the payment of a lump sum by that parent.

(4) The amount of any lump sum which a parent may be required to pay by virtue of sub-paragraph (3) shall not, in the case of an order made by a magistrates' court, exceed the maximum amount that may at the time of the making of the order be required to be paid under sub-paragraph (2), but a magistrates' court may make an order for the payment of a lump sum not exceeding that amount even though the parent was required to pay a lump sum by a previous order under this Act.

(5) An order made under paragraph 1 or 2 for the payment of a lump sum may provide for the payment of that sum by instalments.

(6) Where the court provides for the payment of a lump sum by instalments the court, on an application made either by the person liable to pay or the person entitled to receive that sum, shall have power to vary that order by varying—

(a) the number of instalments payable;
(b) the amount of any instalment payable;
(c) the date on which any instalment becomes payable.

Variation etc. of orders for periodical payments

6. — (1) In exercising its powers under paragraph 1 or 2 to vary or discharge an order for the making or securing of periodical payments the court shall have regard to all the circumstances of the case, including any change in any of the matters to which the court was required to have regard when making the order.

(2) The power of the court under paragraph 1 or 2 to vary an order for the making or securing of periodical payments shall include power to suspend any provision of the order temporarily and to revive any provision so suspended.

(3) Where on an application under paragraph 1 or 2 for the variation or discharge of an order for the making or securing of periodical payments the court varies the payments required to be made under that order, the court may provide that the payments as so varied shall be made from such date as the court may specify, not being earlier than the date of the making of the application.

(4) An application for the variation of an order made under paragraph 1 for the making or securing of periodical payments to

or for the benefit of a child may, if the child has reached the age of sixteen, be made by the child himself.

(5) When an order for the making or securing of periodical payments made under paragraph 1 ceases to have effect on the date on which the child reaches the age of sixteen, or at any time after that date but before or on the date on which he reaches the age of eighteen, the child may apply to the court which made the order for an order for its revival.

(6) If on such an application it appears to the court that—

    (a) the child is, will be or (if an order were made under this sub-paragraph) would be receiving instruction at an educational establishment or undergoing training for a trade, profession or vocation, whether or not while in gainful employment; or

    (b) there are special circumstances which justify the making of an order under this paragraph,

the court shall have power by order to revive the order from such date as the court may specify, not being earlier than the date of the making of the application.

(7) Any order which is revived by an order under sub-paragraph (5) may be varied or discharged under that provision, on the application of any person by whom or to whom payments are required to be made under the revived order.

(8) An order for the making or securing of periodical payments made under paragraph 1 may be varied or discharged, after the death of either parent, on the application of a guardian of the child concerned.

Variation of orders for secured periodical payments after death of parent

7.—(1) Where the parent liable to make payments under a secured periodical payments order has died, the persons who may apply for the variation or discharge of the order shall include the personal representatives of the deceased parent.

(2) No application for the variation of the order shall, except with the permission of the court, be made after the end of the period of six months from the date on which representation in regard to the estate of that parent is first taken out.

(3) The personal representatives of a deceased person against whom a secured periodical payments order was made shall not be liable for having distributed any part of the estate of the deceased

after the end of the period of six months referred to in sub-paragraph (2) on the ground that they ought to have taken into account the possibility that the court might permit an application for variation to be made after that period by the person entitled to payments under the order.

(4) Sub-paragraph (3) shall not prejudice any power to recover any part of the estate so distributed arising by virtue of the variation of an order in accordance with this paragraph.

(5) Where an application to vary a secured periodical payments order is made after the death of the parent liable to make payments under the order, the circumstances to which the court is required to have regard under paragraph 6(1) shall include the changed circumstances resulting from the death of the parent.

(6) In considering for the purposes of sub-paragraph (2) the question when representation was first taken out, a grant limited to settled land or to trust property shall be left out of account and a grant limited to real estate or to personal estate shall be left out of account unless a grant limited to the remainder of the estate has previously been made or is made at the same time.

(7) In this paragraph "secured periodical payments order" means an order for secured periodical payments under paragraph 1(2)(b).

Financial relief under other enactments

8. —(1) This paragraph applies where a residence order is made with respect to a child at a time when there is in force an order ("the financial relief order") made under any enactment other than this Act and requiring a person to contribute to the child's maintenance.

(2) Where this paragraph applies, the court may, on the application of—

(a) any person, required by the financial relief order to contribute to the child's maintenance; or
(b) any person in whose favour a residence order with respect to the child is in force,

make an order revoking the financial relief order, or varying it by altering the amount of any sum payable under that order or by substituting the applicant for the person to whom any such sum is otherwise payable under that order.

Interim orders

9.—(1) Where an application is made under paragraph 1 or 2 the court may, at any time before it disposes of the application, make an interim order—

    (a) requiring either or both parents to make such periodical payments, at such times and for such term as the court thinks fit; and

    (b) giving any direction which the court thinks fit.

(2) An interim order made under this paragraph may provide for payments to be made from such date as the court may specify, not being earlier than the date of the making of the application under paragraph 1 or 2.

(3) An interim order made under this paragraph shall cease to have effect when the application is disposed of or, if earlier, on the date specified for the purposes of this paragraph in the interim order.

(4) An interim order in which a date has been specified for the purposes of sub-paragraph (3) may be varied by substituting a later date.

Alteration of maintenance agreements

10.—(1) In this paragraph and in paragraph 11 "maintenance agreement" means any agreement in writing made with respect to a child, whether before or after the commencement of this paragraph, which—

    (a) is or was made between the father and mother of the child; and

    (b) contains provision with respect to the making or securing of payments, or the disposition or use of any property, for the maintenance or education of the child,

and any such provisions are in this paragraph, and paragraph 11, referred to as "financial arrangements".

(2) Where a maintenance agreement is for the time being subsisting and each of the parties to the agreement is for the time being either domiciled or resident in England and Wales, then, either party may apply to the court for an order under this paragraph.

(3) If the court to which the application is made is satisfied either—

    (a) that, by reason of a change in the circumstances in the

light of which any financial arrangements contained in the agreement were made (including a change foreseen by the parties when making the agreement), the agreement should be altered so as to make different financial arrangements; or

(b) that the agreement does not contain proper financial arrangements with respect to the child,

then that court may by order make such alterations in the agreement by varying or revoking any financial arrangements contained in it as may appear to it to be just having regard to all the circumstances.

(4) If the maintenance agreement is altered by an order under this paragraph, the agreement shall have effect thereafter as if the alteration had been made by agreement between the parties and for valuable consideration.

(5) Where a court decides to make an order under this paragraph altering the maintenance agreement—

(a) by inserting provision for the making or securing by one of the parties to the agreement of periodical payments for the maintenance of the child; or

(b) by increasing the rate of periodical payments required to be made or secured by one of the parties for the maintenance of the child,

then, in deciding the term for which under the agreement as altered by the order the payments or (as the case may be) the additional payments attributable to the increase are to be made or secured for the benefit of the child, the court shall apply the provisions of sub-paragraphs (1) and (2) of paragraph 3 as if the order were an order under paragraph 1(2)(a) or (b).

(6) A magistrates' court shall not entertain an application under sub-paragraph (2) unless both the parties to the agreement are resident in England and Wales and at least one of the parties is resident in the commission area (within the meaning of the Justices of the Peace Act 1979) for which the court is appointed, and shall not have power to make any order on such an application except—

(a) in a case where the agreement contains no provision for periodical payments by either of the parties, an order inserting provision for the making by one of the parties of periodical payments for the maintenance of the child;

(b) in a case where the agreement includes provision for the making by one of the parties of periodical payments, an order increasing or reducing the rate of, or terminating, any of those payments.

(7) For the avoidance of doubt it is hereby declared that nothing in this paragraph affects any power of a court before which any proceedings between the parties to a maintenance agreement are brought under any other enactment to make an order containing financial arrangements or any right of either party to apply for such an order in such proceedings.

11. — (1) Where a maintenance agreement provides for the continuation, after the death of one of the parties, of payments for the maintenance of a child and that party dies domiciled in England and Wales, the surviving party or the personal representatives of the deceased party may apply to the High court or a county court for an order under paragraph 10.

(2) If a maintenance agreement is altered by a court on an application under this paragraph, the agreement shall have effect thereafter as if the alteration had been made, immediately before the death, by agreement between the parties and for valuable consideration.

(3) An application under this paragraph shall not, except with leave of the High Court or a county court, be made after the end of the period of six months beginning with the day on which representation in regard to the estate of the deceased is first taken out.

(4) In considering for the purposes of sub-paragraph (3) the question when presentation was first taken out, a grant limited to settled land or to trust property shall be left out of account and a grant limited to real estate or to personal estate shall be left out of account unless a grant limited to the remainder of the estate has previously been made or is made at the same time.

(5) A county court shall not entertain an application under this paragraph, or an application for leave to make an application under this paragraph, unless it would have jurisdiction to hear and determine proceedings for an order under section 2 of the Inheritance (Provision for Family and Dependants) Act 1975 in relation to the deceased's estate by virtue of section 25 of the County Courts Act 1984 (jurisdiction under the Act of 1975).

(6) The provisions of this paragraph shall not render the personal representatives of the deceased liable for having distributed any part of the estate of the deceased after the expiry of the period of six months referred to in sub-paragraph (3) on the ground that they ought to have taken into account the possibility

that a court might grant leave for an application by virtue of this paragraph to be made by the surviving party after that period.

(7) Sub-paragraph (6) shall not prejudice any power to recover any part of the estate so distributed arising by virtue of the making of an order in pursuance of this paragraph.

Enforcement of orders for maintenance

12.—(1) Any person for the time being under an obligation to make payments in pursuance of any order for the payment of money made by a magistrates' court under this Act shall give notice of any change of address to such person (if any) as may be specified in the order.

(2) Any person failing without reasonable excuse to give such a notice shall be guilty of an offence and liable on summary conviction to a fine not exceeding level 2 on the standard scale.

(3) An order for the payment of money made by a magistrates' court under this Act shall be enforceable as a magistrates' court maintenance order within the meaning of section 150(1) of the Magistrates' Courts Act 1980.

Direction for settlement of instrument by conveyancing counsel

13. Where the High Court or a county court decides to make an order under this Act for the securing of periodical payments or for the transfer or settlement of property, it may direct that the matter be referred to one of the conveyancing counsel of the court to settle a proper instrument to be executed by all necessary parties.

Financial provision for child resident in country outside England and Wales

14.—(1) Where one parent of a child lives in England and Wales and the child lives outside England and Wales with—

  (a) another parent of his;
  (b) a guardian of his; or
  (c) a person in whose favour a residence order is in force with respect to the child,

the court shall have power, on an application made by any of the persons mentioned in paragraphs (a) to (c), to make one or both of the orders mentioned in paragraph 1(2)(a) and (b) against the parent living in England and Wales.

(2) Any reference in this Act to the powers of the court under paragraph 1(2) or to an order made under paragraph 1(2) shall include a reference to the powers which the court has by virtue of sub-paragraph (1) or (as the case may be) to an order made by virtue of sub-paragraph (1).

Local authority contribution to child's maintenance

15.—(1) Where a child lives, or is to live, with a person as the result of a residence order, a local authority may make contributions to that person towards the cost of the accommodation and maintenance of the child.

(2) Sub-paragraph (1) does not apply where the person with whom the child lives, or is to live, is a parent of the child or the husband or wife of a parent of the child.

Interpretation

16.—(1) In this Schedule "child" includes, in any case where an application is made under paragraph 2 or 6 in relation to a person who has reached the age of eighteen, that person.

(2) In this Schedule, except paragraphs 2 and 15, "parent" includes any party to a marriage (whether or not subsisting) in relation to whom the child concerned is a child of the family; and for this purpose any reference to either parent or both parents shall be construed as references to any parent of his and to all of his parents.

Annotation

Schedule 1: deals with financial provision for children. Note that all courts may make periodical payments and lump sum orders, though magistrates' powers to order lump sums is restricted to £1,000 to take account of the Magistrates' Courts (Increase of Lump Sums) Order 1988. Section 1 deals with applications made by parents, guardians or persons in whose favour a residence order is in force and empowers the court to make one or more of the financial orders specified in Paragraph 1(2). Note that sections 34(1)(b) and (c) of the Children Act 1975 provided for the court to make orders for periodical payments and lump sums on the application of custodians and that in Schedule 1 "parents" includes any party to a marriage, subsisting or not, in relation to whom the child concerned is a child of the family: see Paragraph 16. Such persons are already in the same position as parents if there are proceedings under the Matrimonial Causes Act 1973, the Domestic Proceedings and Magistrates' Courts Act 1978 and section 34(2) of the Children Act 1975.

Paragraph 1: enables the court at any time to order either or both parents, whether or not they have parental responsibility, to make financial provision for a child. The court's powers are exercisable on the application of a parent, a guardian or any person in whose favour a residence order is in force, or of its own motion when making, varying or discharging a residence order. All courts may make periodical payments and lump sum orders. Secured periodical payments orders, property transfer and settlement of property orders will be available where proceedings have been brought in the High Court or a county court.

Paragraph 1(1): empowers the court, on the application of parents, guardians or persons in whose favour a residence order is in force to make one or more of the financial orders specified in Paragraph 1(2). As to parents, Paragraph 1(1) corresponds to, and replaces, section 11B(i) of the Guardianship of Minors Act 1971 which was inserted by the Family Law Reform Act 1987. Paragraph 1(1) extends to guardians because, although under the provisions of the Act they will not usually take office during the lifetime of a surviving parent, where they do they should clearly have the same rights of application as do parents. Persons with the benefit of a residence order are the equivalent, under the provisions of the Act, of custodians under the Children Act 1975.

Paragraph 1(2): sets out the financial orders that can be made under Paragraph 1(1). The orders may be in favour of the child himself or in favour of the applicant for the benefit of the child. The provisions of Paragraph 1(2) correspond with section 11B(2) of the Guardianship of Minors Act 1971, which was inserted by the Family Law Reform Act 1987 and which in turn extended the existing provisions of that Act to correspond with sections 23(1)(d)(e) and (f) and 24(1)(a) and (b) of the Matrimonial Causes Act 1973. The object is to enable all children to have the benefit of the same range of powers as was already available to the children of married parents when their parents divorced.

Paragraph 1(3): enables the court to exercise its powers under Paragraph 1(1) at any time.

Paragraph 1(4): provides for the variation and discharge of periodical payments and secured periodical payments orders on the application of the payer or payee. Paragraph 1(1) should be read in particular with Paragraph 5(3) which enables the court to make a lump sum order when varying or discharging a periodical payments or secured periodical payments order, and with paragraphs

6 and 7, which contain supplemental provisions relating to the variation of orders. Note that paragraph 1(4) does not allow for the variation of lump sum, transfer of property or settlement of property orders. The court can, however, order payment of further lump sums: see paragraph 1(5).

Paragraph 1(5): enables the court to make further periodical payments, secured periodical payments and lump sum orders at any time before the child reaches eighteen. This recognises that all orders for financial relief are only the best that the court can make at any one time, as circumstances may change and create the need for a further order. Property adjustment orders, however, are intended as a once-and-for-all settlement when a relationship ends. Note that it is not possible for the court to make a further order or to vary an existing order under the Matrimonial Causes Act 1973. Paragraph 1(5)(b) reflects the recommendation of the Law Commission prohibiting the court from making more than one transfer or settlement of property order under Paragraph 1(2)(d) or (e) against the same person in respect of the same child.

Paragraph 1(6): enables the court to exercise any of its powers under Schedule 1 of its own motion when making or dealing with a residence order. If the court decides to make a residence order it would be wasteful and unnecessary to require a separate application for a financial order. This provision has the effect of extending the court's powers to make orders for maintenance of wards of court under section 6 of the Family Law Reform Act 1969.

Paragraph 2: provides that a child of eighteen or over whose parents are not living together in the same household may apply in certain circumstances for an order that unsecured periodical payments and/or a lump sum payment be made to him.

Paragraph 2(1): in combination with Paragraph 2(2) provides that the court may, on the application of a child over eighteen and in certain circumstances, order either or both parents to make financial provision for him. Note also that the criteria defined in Paragraph 2(1)(a)(b) reproduce the effect of section 12(2) of the Guardianship of Minors Act 1971.

Paragraph 2(2): sets out the orders (unsecured periodical payments or lump sums) which may be made against either or both of the child's parents. Payments are to be made to the child himself.

Paragraph 2(3): prevents a child over eighteen from applying under Paragraph 2 if immediately before the age of sixteen there was a periodical payments order as defined in Paragraph 2(6) in force with respect to him. In such a situation a child may apply to vary or revive the earlier order: see Paragraphs 6(4) and 6(5). The child over eighteen is not, however, prevented from applying for an order under Paragraph 2 by reason of a lump sum or property adjustment order having been previously made with respect to him.

Paragraph 2(4): provides that an order cannot be made under Paragraph 2 at a time when the parents are living together in the same household. It therefore applies to the situation where cohabitation is resumed between the application and order.

Paragraph 2(5): provides for the variation and discharge of orders for periodical payments, but not lump sums, on the application of the child or parent.

Paragraph 2(6): is supplemental to Paragraph 2(3) which prevents a child of eighteen or over from applying for financial provision under Paragraph 2 if a periodical payments order was in force when he attained sixteen. "Periodical payments order", which includes for this purpose a secured periodical payments order, is defined by reference to the proceedings in which a periodical payments order or secured periodical payments order was made, and includes proceedings under Schedule 1.

Paragraph 2(7): enables the court to exercise its powers under Paragraph 2 at any time.

Paragraph 2(8): enables the court where it makes an order under Paragraph 2 to make further orders from time to time while the original order remains in force.

Paragraph 3: contains provisions governing the duration of orders for periodical payments or secured periodical payments, which the court may make under Paragraphs 1 and 2 of the Schedule corresponding to section 12 of the Guardianship of Minors Act 1971 and section 34B of the Children Act 1975. It further provides that such orders made under paragraph 1 of Schedule 1 shall cease if the parents live together for more than six months.

Paragraph 3(1): provides that orders for periodical payments or secured periodical payments may begin with the date the application for the order is made, but may not in the first instance extend beyond the child's seventeenth birthday unless the court thinks the circumstances require it. Orders must in any event end when the child attains eighteen years of age, unless Paragraph 3(2) applies.

Paragraph 3(2): provides that if it appears to the court that the child's education or training in a trade, profession or vocation would extend beyond the age of eighteen, or if there are other special circumstances—for example those which will prevent the child becoming financially independent until a later age, or disability—then the upper limit of eighteen years referred to in Paragraph 3(1)(b) will not apply. The court may therefore exercise its discretion to order payments to continue beyond that age.

Paragraph 3(3): provides that unsecured periodical payments orders under Paragraphs 1 and 2 shall end on the death of the payer, whether or not the order so provides.

Paragraph 3(4): provides that orders under Paragraph 1 directing periodical payments or secure periodical payments to be made to the parent of the child shall cease if any parent making or securing the payments, and any parent to whom the payments are made or secured, live together for a period of more than six months.

Paragraph 4: specifies the criteria to which the court is to have regard in exercising its powers under Paragraphs 1 and 2 and includes additional matters for the court's consideration when deciding to make orders against a person who is not the mother or father of the child, for example a step parent. Note that the paramountcy principle in Section 1 of the Act does not apply when deciding questions of financial relief.

Paragraph 4(1): provides that the court in deciding whether to exercise its powers under paragraphs 1 or 2, and if so in what manner, shall have regard to all the circumstances, including certain specific matters which are set out in a list. They include the financial resources and obligations of any parent of the child, the applicant for the order or anyone else in whose favour the court proposes to make an order. The list corresponds to that contained in section 12A of the Guardianship of Minors Act 1971, as amended by the Family Law Reform Act 1987 and section 34(A) of the Children Act 1975. The list also includes, in Paragraph 4(1)(f) "the manner in which the child was being, or was expected to be, educated or trained". A corresponding provision is contained in section 25(3)(d) of the Matrimonial Causes Act 1973, but not in other legislation. The Law Commission felt that its omission from this Act would savour of discrimination against the children of unmarried parents.

Paragraph 4(2): lists the additional matters to which the court is to have regard when considering the exercise of its powers against someone who is not the mother or father of the child, for example a step parent. It is thus consistent with section 25(4) of the Matrimonial Causes Act 1973.

Paragraph 4(3): provides that where the court makes an order under Paragraph 1 against a person who is not the father of the child, it shall record this fact in the order. (This was added at the report stage in the passage of the Act.)

Paragraph 4(4): specifies the persons whose resources and obligations set out in Paragraph 4(1) shall be considered by the court in relation to the exercise of its powers under Paragraphs 1 and 2.

Paragraph 5: contains provisions supplemental to the court's powers to order lump sum payments under Paragraphs 1 and 2 and provides, amongst other things, for sums under such orders to be paid by instalments.

Paragraph 5(1): provides that, without prejudice to the generality of Paragraph 1, a lump sum order under that paragraph may be made for the purpose of enabling any liabilities or expenses reasonably incurred before the making of the order to be met, being liabilities incurred in connection with the birth of the child or in maintaining the child. This provision reproduces section 12B(1) of the Guardianship of Minors Act 1971 which is necessarily wider than the corresponding provision contained in section 35A(1) of the Children Act 1975, because of the abolition of affiliation proceedings effected by the Family Law Reform Act 1987 and their replacement by action under the Guardianship of Minors Act 1971.

Paragraph 5(2) limits magistrates' courts' powers to order lump sum payments to such amounts as may be fixed by order.

Paragraph 5(3): empowers the court to make a lump sum order against a parent when varying or discharging an order under which that parent is required to make periodical payments or secured periodical payments. In the case of magistrates' courts, the power is subject to Paragraph 5(4).

Paragraph 5(4): supplements Paragraph 5(3) and provides that any lump sum order which a magistrates' court makes under Paragraph 5(3), on varying or discharging a periodical payments order, shall be limited to such amounts as may be fixed by order as in paragraph 5(2). However, it empowers a magistrates' court to make such orders even though the parent has already been required to pay a lump sum by a previous order under the Act.

Paragraph 5(5): provides that any lump sum payment orders under Paragraphs 1 or 2 may provide for payment by instalments.

Paragraph 5(6): provides for the court, where an order has been made for the payment of a lump sum by instalments, to vary the number or amount of instalments or the date on which any instalment becomes payable: this can be done on the application of the payer or payee.

Paragraph 6: is confined to periodical payments and secured periodical payments orders and contains supplementary provisions concerning the court's power to vary such orders made under Paragraphs 1 and 2. It also contains provisions concerning the suspension, revival and discharge of such orders.

Paragraph 6(1): supplements Paragraphs 1(4) and 2(5) and requires the court, when considering an application for variation, to have regard to all the circumstances, including any change in any of the matters to which the court was to have regard when making the original order. This corresponds to the provisions of section 12C(1) of the Guardianship of Minors Act 1971 and section 35(8) of the Children Act 1975.

Paragraph 6(2): includes in the court's powers of variation power also to suspend any provision of the order temporarily and to revive any provisions so suspended. This corresponds to the provisions of section 12C(2) of the Guardianship of Minors Act 1971.

Paragraph 6(3): enables the court to backdate any variation. The court may provide for the variation to run from any date, not being one before the date of the application for variation. This corresponds to section 12C(3) of the Guardianship of Minors Act 1971 and section 35(9) of the Children Act 1975.

Paragraph 6(4): enables a child for whose benefit the periodical payments or secured periodical payments order was made to apply himself for variation if he has attained sixteen.

Paragraph 6(5): provides that where an order ceases on the child's attaining sixteen, or on a later date between his sixteenth and eighteenth birthdays, the child himself may apply for its revival. The court can grant the application if the circumstances set out in Paragraph 6(6) exist: see also Paragraph 6(7). This provision restores the powers of magistrates' courts to deal with such applications, which they had under section 12C(5) of the Guardianship of Minors Act 1971 until a new subsection (5) was substituted by Schedule 2, Paragraph 34(4), Family Law Reform Act 1987, and thus gives effect to the Law Commission's recommendation in its report "Family Law, Review of Child Law and Guardianship and Custody".

Paragraph 6(6): is supplemental to Paragraph 6(5) and allows the court to revive the order if the child is, or if an order were made would be, undergoing further education or training, or there are other special circumstances such as ill health. Paragraph 6(6) also enables the court to backdate any such order to a date not earlier than the date of the making of such application.

Paragraph 6(7): provides that any order revived by order under Paragraph 6(5) above may be discharged under that provision on the application of the payer or payee.

Paragraph 6(8): provides for the court to vary or discharge an order made under Paragraph 1 after the death of either parent on the application of the child's guardian.

Paragraph 7: contains further supplemental provisions concerning the powers of the court to vary orders for secured periodical payments where the parent liable to make those payments has died. Paragraph 7 applies only to secured periodical payments orders made by the court under paragraph 1 of Schedule 1. These provisions correspond to those in section 12D of The Guardianship of Minors Act 1971, added to that Act by the Family Law Reform Act 1987, Schedule 2.

Paragraph 7(1): provides that where the parent liable to make payments under a secured periodical payments order dies, the persons eligible to apply for variation or discharge of that order shall include that deceased parent's personal representatives. They represent the person "by whom" payments were to be made referred to in Paragraph 1(4).

Paragraph 7(2): precludes applications for variation being made after six months from the date on which a grant of representation in regard to the deceased's estate is taken out, unless the High Court or a county court gives leave.

Paragraph 7(3): protects personal representatives who distribute property after the six month period referred to in paragraph 7(2). The provision is designed to facilitate speedy administration of the deceased's estate.

Paragraph 7(4): preserves the right of the applicant for variation to recover from beneficiaries that property distributed by the personal representatives after the six month period referred to in paragraph 7(2) above, when leave is given to make an application outside that period.

Paragraph 7(5): adds another matter to those set out in Paragraph 6(1) which is to be taken into account when the court considers applications for variation or discharge. Paragraph 7(5) provides that on applications under the Paragraph the court shall also have regard to the changed circumstances resulting from the death of the parent liable to make payments.

Paragraph 7(6): is supplemental to paragraph 7(2). Paragraph

7(6) clarifies the purpose of applying the six month time limit when a grant of representation is to be regarded as having been taken out. Paragraph 7(6) provides that certain limited grants of representation be disregarded for this purpose.

Paragraph 7(7): makes it clear that the provisions of Paragraph 7 only relate to secured periodical payments orders made by the court under Paragraph 1(2)(b) of this Schedule.

Paragraph 8: empowers a court to revoke or vary an order for financial relief made in respect of a child under another Act where a residence order is made in respect of the same child.

Paragraph 8(1): is stated to apply where the court makes a residence order at a time when there is already in force an order under some other enactment, for these purposes referred to as a "financial relief" order, requiring a person to contribute to the child's maintenance.

Paragraph 8(2): empowers the court to vary or revoke a "financial relief order" referred to in Paragraph 8(1). On the application of any person liable to pay under the order, or any person in whose favour a residence order is in force, the court may revoke the financial relief order, alter the amount payable under it, or substitute the person with the benefit of the residence order for the person to whom money is otherwise payable under the order.

Paragraph 9: enables the court, pending disposal of applications for financial relief under Paragraphs 1 and 2 of Schedule 1, to make interim orders requiring parents to make periodical payments for a child. Paragraph 9 also contains provisions governing the duration of such orders.

Paragraph 9(1): provides the court with power (a) at any time before the full hearing of an application for financial relief under Paragraphs 1 and 2 to make an interim order requiring either or both parents to make such periodical payments as it thinks fit, and (b) to give any direction it thinks fit. Its purpose, and the purpose of Paragraph 9(2) to (4) is to replace the provisions of section 2(4) (5B–E) of the Guardianship Act 1973 and to simplify the position. Although it may be necessary to set out the court's powers to grant emergency relief before the full hearing of an application, it is considered unnecessary to impose strict time limits on their use, as the Guardianship of Minors Act 1971 formerly did. It is possible that orders will be made at the same time as temporary orders for residence and contact, and the court may wish to specify the same timetable so that all matters can be decided together: see section 10.

Paragraph 9(2): enables the court to order that payments under an order begin to run from any date not being a date earlier than the making of the application under Paragraphs 1 or 2.

Paragraph 9(3): enables the court to specify for how long the interim order is to run. The order will then terminate on the specified date. If no such date is specified, the interim order will cease to have effect when the application under Paragraph 1 or 2 is disposed of.

Paragraph 9(4): provides that if the court does specify under Paragraph 9(3) that the interim order will last until a certain date, then the order may be subsequently varied by the substitution of a later date.

Paragraph 10: empowers courts, including magistrates' courts, to vary written maintenance agreements with respect to children during the lifetime of either party to the agreement, though the powers of magistrates' courts are confined to dealing with unsecured periodical payments. Paragraph 10 reproduces the effect of section 15 of the Family Law Reform Act 1987 which in turn contains provisions similar to those in sections 35 and 36 of the Matrimonial Causes Act 1973.

Paragraph 10(1): defines "management agreement" and "financial arrangements" for the purposes of paragraphs 10 and 11. The agreement must be in writing, made between the child's father and mother, and contain provision for the child's education or maintenance.

Paragraph 10(2): provides for application to the court to vary a maintenance agreement, provided that each of the parties to the agreement is, for the time being, domiciled or resident in England and Wales.

Paragraph 10(3): enables the court to vary or revoke any financial arrangements in the agreement if it is satisfied that there has been a change of circumstances, not necessarily an unforeseen change, or that the agreement does not contain proper financial arrangements for the child.

Paragraph 10(4): provides that an agreement altered by court order shall have effect thereafter as if the alteration had been made by binding agreement between the parties, so that either party to whom money is due or property is to be transferred under the amended agreement has the normal remedies for breach of contract.

Paragraph 10(5): is to ensure that the same rules apply to the duration of payments under maintenance agreements altered by order as apply to orders for periodical payments under Paragraph

1(2)(a) or (b) of Schedule 1, that is to say usually they will last until the child's seventeenth birthday: see also Paragraph 3(1) and (2).

Paragraph 10(6): provides that magistrates' courts may only exercise jurisdiction under Paragraph 10 to deal with unsecured periodical payments and where the parties are resident in England and Wales, and one resides in the relevant commission area. Magistrates may insert a provision for unsecured periodical payments where no such provision is contained, or may increase or reduce the rate of any such payments provided for, or terminate them altogether.

Paragraph 10(7): ensures that any other financial proceedings between parties to a maintenance agreement should not be prejudiced by the powers conferred by Paragraph 10, nor the right of either party to apply for an order in such proceedings.

Paragraph 11: is supplementary to Paragraph 10 and provides for cases where it is desired to alter a maintenance agreement after one of the parties to it has died. Its provisions follow closely those of section 16 of the Family Law Reform Act 1987.

Paragraph 11(1): provides that where a maintenance agreement makes provision for payments to continue after the death of a party, Paragraph 11 allows the surviving party or the personal representatives of the deceased party to apply to the High Court or a county court for an order under Paragraph 10 varying the agreement.

Paragraph 11(2): provides that the alteration of an agreement by the court is to take effect as if it had been made for valuable consideration immediately before the death, so either party to whom money is due under the amended agreement may pursue his or her normal remedies for breach of contract.

Paragraph 11(3): precludes applications being made under Paragraph 11 after six months from the date on which a grant of representation to the deceased's estate is taken out, unless the High Court or a county court gives leave.

Paragraph 11(4): is supplementary to Paragraph 11(3) and explains when a grant of representation is to be regarded as being taken out. Paragraph 11(4) provides that certain limited grants of representation shall be disregarded for this purpose.

Paragraph 11(5): limits the jurisdiction of the county court under Paragraph 11, including jurisdiction to give leave to make an application, in line with that court's power to deal with an application for financial provision out of the deceased's estate under section 2 of the Inheritance (Provision for Family and Dependants) Act 1975.

Paragraph 11(6): protects personal representatives who distribute property after the six month period referred to in Paragraph 11(3) where leave is subsequently given for an application for variation to be made outside that period.

Paragraph 11(7): preserves the right of an applicant for variation to recover from beneficiaries that property distributed by the personal representatives after the six month period referred to in Paragraph 11(3) where leave is given to make an application outside that period.

Paragraph 12: contains provisions to facilitate enforcement of orders for payment of money made by magistrates' courts. Paragraph 12 reproduces the provisions of sections 13(2) and (3) of the Guardianship of Minors Act 1971 and sections 43(2) and (3) of the Children Act 1975.

Paragraph 12(1): obliges any person liable to make payments under an order made by a magistrates' court under the provisions of this Act to give notice of any change of his or her address to any specified person.

Paragraph 12(2): makes it a summary offence to fail to give notice of change of address as required in Paragraph 12(1) above and makes the penalty a fine. The fine is well within the range of fines upon summary conviction which are provided for throughout the Act.

Paragraph 12(3): provides that an order for payment of money made by a magistrates' court under the provisions of this Act shall be enforceable as a magistrates' court maintenance order within the meaning of section 150(1) of the Magistrates' Courts Act 1980.

Paragraph 13: provides that where the High Court or a county court decides to make an order under this Act for the securing of periodical payments or the transfer or settlement of property it may direct that the matter be referred to conveyancing counsel for him to settle a proper instrument to be executed by all the necessary parties. Paragraph 13 reproduces Section 13B of the Guardianship of Minors Act 1971, added by the Family Law Reform Act 1987.

Paragraph 14: enables a court to make a periodical payments or secured periodical payments order against a parent living in England and Wales when the child resides outside England and Wales. Paragraph 14 corresponds to section 15A of the Guardianship of Minors Act 1971, inserted by the Family Law Reform Act 1986.

Paragraph 14(1): provides that the court can make such an order for periodical payments or secured periodical payments against a parent residing in England and Wales when the child lives outside England and Wales with the other parent, which term includes any party to a marriage—subsisting or not—in relation to whom the child is a child of the family, for example a step-parent, guardian or person in whose favour a residence order is in force with respect to the child.

Paragraph 14(2): provides that any reference in this Act to the powers of, or to an order of, the court under Paragraph 1(2) shall include the power or order referred to in Paragraph 14(1).

Paragraph 15: gives a local authority a discretion to contribute towards the cost of accommodation and maintenance of a child where a residence order is made in favour of any person other than the child's parent, or the spouse of such a parent. Paragraph 15 reproduces the effect of section 34(6) of the Children Act 1975, which permitted a local authority to make contributions to custodians of children formerly boarded out with those custodians, who stood to lose a boarding-out allowance on the making of such an order.

Paragraph 15(1): provides that a local authority may make contributions to the cost of accommodation and maintenance of a child where that child lives, or is to live, with a person other than a parent or the spouse of such a parent, as the result of a residence order. The power to make such contributions is entirely within the discretion of a local authority. Payments may begin at any time a residence order is in force. The provision will enable contributions by a local authority to be made where, for example, the child has been in long-term care, or where the arrangement is a means of preventing the child having to be taken into care. This will encourage people to make applications for residence orders and thus assume responsibility for children where, without financial assistance, they could not otherwise have done so.

Paragraph 15(2): provides that the discretionary power of a local authority to make contributions in accordance with Paragraph 15(1) does not apply where the person with whom the child is to live is the child's parent, or the spouse of such a parent. The absence of this exclusion might possibly lead to some erosion of the court's practice of ordering maintenance payments against a parent when the child is to live with the other parent.

Paragraph 16: confirms that in Schedule 1 where the word "child" is used it includes a person over the age of eighteen in respect of whom an application is made under Paragraphs 2 or 6. Paragraph 16(2) provides that in this Schedule, except Paragraphs 2 and 15, the word "parent" includes any party to a marriage, whether or not subsisting, and for this purpose any reference to either parent or both shall be construed as references to any and to all parents. (Added at report stage.)

SCHEDULE 2: LOCAL AUTHORITY SUPPORT FOR CHILDREN AND FAMILIES

PART I

PROVISION OF SERVICES FOR FAMILIES

Identification of children in need and provision of information

1.—(1) Every local authority shall take reasonable steps to identify the extent to which there are children in need within their area.

(2) Every local authority shall—

(a) publish information—

(i) about services provided by them under sections 17, 18, 20 and 24; and

(ii) where they consider it appropriate, about the provision by others (including, in particular, voluntary organisations) of services which the authority have power to provide under those sections; and

(b) take such steps as are reasonably practicable to ensure that those who might benefit from the services receive the information relevant to them.

Maintenance of a register of disabled children

2.—(1) Every local authority shall open and maintain a register of disabled children within their area.

(2) The register may be kept by means of a computer.

Assessment of children's needs

3. Where it appears to a local authority that a child within their area is in need, the authority may assess his needs for the purposes

of this Act at the same time as any assessment of his needs is made under—

(a) the Chronically Sick and Disabled Persons Act 1970;
(b) the Education Act 1981;
(c) the Disabled Persons (Services, Consultation and Representation) Act 1986; or
(d) any other enactment.

Prevention of neglect and abuse

4.—(1) Every local authority shall take reasonable steps, through the provision of services under Part III of this Act, to prevent children within their area suffering ill-treatment or neglect.

(2) Where a local authority believe that a child who is at any time within their area—

(a) is likely to suffer harm; but
(b) lives or proposes to live in the area of another local authority

they shall inform that other local authority.

(3) When informing that other local authority they shall specify—

(a) the harm that they believe he is likely to suffer; and
(b) (if they can) where the child lives or proposes to live.

Provision of accommodation in order to protect child

5.—(1) Where—

(a) it appears to a local authority that a child who is living on particular premises is suffering, or is likely to suffer, ill treatment at the hands of another person who is living on those premises; and
(b) that other person proposes to move from the premises,

the authority may assist that other person to obtain alternative accommodation.

(2) Assistance given under this paragraph may be in cash.

(3) Subsections (7) to (9) of section 17 shall apply in relation to assistance given under this paragraph as they apply in relation to assistance given under that section.

Provision for disabled children

6. Every local authority shall provide services designed—

    (a) to minimise the effect on disabled children within their area of their disabilities; and

    (b) to give such children the opportunity to lead lives which are as normal as possible.

Provision to reduce need for care proceedings etc.

7. Every local authority shall take reasonable steps designed—

    (a) to reduce the need to bring—

        (i) proceedings for care or supervision orders with respect to children within their area;

        (ii) criminal proceedings against such children;

        (iii) any family or other proceedings with respect to such children which might lead to them being placed in the authority's care; or

        (iv) proceedings under the inherent jurisdiction of the High Court with respect to children;

    (b) to encourage children within their area not to commit criminal offences; and

    (c) to avoid the need for children within their area to be placed in secure accommodation.

Provision for children living with their families

8. Every local authority shall make such provision as they consider appropriate for the following services to be available with respect to children in need within their area while they are living with their families—

    (a) advice, guidance and counselling;

    (b) occupational, social, cultural or recreational activities;

    (c) home help (which may include laundry facilities);

    (d) facilities for, or assistance with, travelling to and from home for the purpose of taking advantage of any other service provided under this Act or of any similar service;

    (e) assistance to enable the child concerned and his family to have a holiday.

Family centres

9.—(1) Every local authority shall provide such family centres as they consider appropriate in relation to children within their area.

(2) "Family centre" means a centre at which any of the persons mentioned in sub-paragraph (3) may—

    (a) attend for occupational, social, cultural or recreational activities;

    (b) attend for advice, guidance or counselling; or

    (c) be provided with accommodation while he is receiving advice, guidance or counselling.

    (3) The persons are—

    (a) a child;

    (b) his parents;

    (c) any person who is not a parent of his but who has parental responsibility for him;

    (d) any other person who is looking after him.

Maintenance of the family home

10. Every local authority shall take such steps as are reasonably practicable, where any child within their area who is in need and whom they are not looking after is living apart from his family—

    (a) to enable him to live with his family; or

    (b) to promote contact between him and his family,

if, in their opinion, it is necessary to do so in order to safeguard or promote his welfare.

Duty to consider racial groups to which children in need belong

11. Every local authority shall, in making any arrangements—

    (a) for the provision of day care within their area; or

    (b) designed to encourage persons to act as local authority foster parents,

have regard to the different racial groups to which children within their area who are in need belong.

PART II

CHILDREN LOOKED AFTER BY LOCAL AUTHORITIES

Regulations as to placing of children with local authority foster parents

12. Regulations under section 23(2)(a) may, in particular, make provision—

    (a) with regard to the welfare of children placed with local authority foster parents;

    (b) as to the arrangements to be made by local authorities in connection with the health and education of such children;

    (c) as to the records to be kept by local authorities;

    (d) for securing that a child is not placed with a local authority foster parent unless that person is for the time being approved as a local authority foster parent by such local authority as may be prescribed;

    (e) for securing that where possible the local authority foster parent with whom a child is to be placed is—

        (i) of the same religious persuasion as the child; or
        (ii) gives an undertaking that the child will be brought up in that religious persuasion;

    (f) for securing that children placed with local authority foster parents, and the premises in which they are accommodated, will be supervised and inspected by a local authority and that the children will be removed from those premises if their welfare appears to require it;

    (g) as to the circumstances in which local authorities may make arrangements for duties imposed on them by the regulations to be discharged, on their behalf.

Regulations as to arrangements under section 23(2)(f)

13. Regulations under section 23(2)(f) may, in particular, make provision as to—

    (a) the persons to be notified of any proposed arrangements;

    (b) the opportunities such persons are to have to make representations in relation to the arrangements proposed;

    (c) the persons to be notified of any proposed changes in arrangements;

    (d) the records to be kept by local authorities;

    (e) the supervision by local authorities of any arrangements made.

Regulations as to conditions under which child in care is allowed to live with parent, etc.

14. Regulations under section 23(5) may, in particular, impose requirements on a local authority as to—

    (a) the making of any decision by a local authority to allow a child to live with any person falling within section 23(4) (including requirements as to those who must be consulted before the decision is made, and those who must be notified when it has been made);

(b) the supervision or medical examination of the child concerned;

(c) the removal of the child, in such circumstances as may be prescribed, from the care of the person with whom he has been allowed to live.

[(d) the records to be maintained by local authorities]

Promotion and maintenance of contact between child and family

15. — (1) Where a child is being looked after by a local authority, the authority shall, unless it is not reasonably practicable or consistent with his welfare, endeavour to promote contact between the child and —

(a) his parents;

(b) any person who is not a parent of his but who has parental responsibility for him; and

(c) any relative, friend or other person connected with him.

[(d) the records to be maintained by local authority]

(2) Where a child is being looked after by a local authority —

(a) the authority shall take such steps as are reasonably practicable to secure that —

(i) his parents; and

(ii) any person who is not a parent of his but who has parental responsibility for him,

are kept informed of where he is being accommodated; and

(b) every such person shall secure that the authority are kept informed of his or her address.

(3) Where a local authority ("the receiving authority") take over the provision of accommodation for a child from another local authority ("the transferring authority") under section 20(2) —

(a) the receiving authority shall (where reasonably practicable) inform —

(i) the child's parents; and

(ii) any person who is not a parent of his but who has parental responsibility for him;

Note: The words within square brackets were inserted by the Courts and Legal Services Act 1990.

    (b) sub-paragraph (2)(a) shall apply to the transferring authority, as well as the receiving authority, until at least one such person has been informed of the change; and

    (c) sub-paragraph (2)(b) shall not require any person to inform the receiving authority of his address until he has been so informed.

(4) Nothing in this paragraph requires a local authority to inform any person of the whereabouts of a child if—

    (a) the child is in the care of the authority; and

    (b) the authority has reasonable cause to believe that informing the person would prejudice the child's welfare.

(5) Any person who fails (without reasonable excuse) to comply with sub-paragraph (2)(b) shall be guilty of an offence and liable on summary conviction to a fine not exceeding level 2 on the standard scale.

(6) It shall be a defence in any proceedings under sub-paragraph (5) to prove that the defendant was residing at the same address as another person who was the child's parent or had parental responsibility for the child and had reasonable cause to believe that the other person had informed the appropriate authority that both of them were residing at that address.

Visits to or by children: expenses

16.—(1) This paragraph applies where—

    (a) a child is being looked after by a local authority; and

    (b) the conditions mentioned in sub-paragraph (3) are satisfied.

(2) The authority may—

    (a) make payments to—

        (i) a parent of the child;

        (ii) any person who is not a parent of his but who has parental responsibility for him; or

        (iii) any relative, friend or other person connected with him,

    in respect of travelling, subsistence or other expenses incurred by that person in visiting the child; or

    (b) make payments to the child, or to any person on his behalf, in respect of travelling, subsistence or other expenses incurred by or on behalf of the child in his visiting—

      (i) a parent of his;
      (ii) any person who is not a parent of his but who has parental responsibility for him; or
      (iii) any relative, friend or other person connected with him.

(3) The conditions are that—

  (a) it appears to the authority, that the visit in question could not otherwise be made without undue financial hardship; and

  (b) the circumstances warrant the making of the payments.

Appointment of visitor for child who is not being visited

17.—(1) Where it appears to a local authority in relation to any child that they are looking after that—

  (a) communication between the child and—

      (i) a parent of his, or
      (ii) any person who is not a parent of his but who has parental responsibility for him,

  has been infrequent; or

  (b) he has not visited or been visited by (or lived with) any such person during the preceding twelve months,

and that it would be in the child's best interests for an independent person to be appointed to be his visitor for the purposes of this paragraph, they shall appoint such a visitor.

(2) A person so appointed shall—

  (a) have the duty of visiting, advising and befriending the child; and

  (b) be entitled to recover from the authority who appointed him any reasonable expenses incurred by him for the purposes of his functions under this paragraph.

(3) A person's appointment as a visitor in pursuance of this paragraph shall be determined if—

  (a) he gives notice in writing to the authority who appointed him that he resigns the appointment; or

  (b) the authority give him notice in writing that they have terminated it.

(4) The determination of such an appointment shall not prejudice any duty under this paragraph to make a further appointment.

(5) Where a local authority propose to appoint a visitor for a child under this paragraph, the appointment shall not be made if—

    (a) the child objects to it; and

    (b) the authority are satisfied that he has sufficient understanding to make an informed decision.

(6) Where a visitor has been appointed for a child under this paragraph, the local authority shall determine the appointment if—

    (a) the child objects to its continuing; and

    (b) the authority are satisfied that he has sufficient understanding to make an informed decision.

(7) The Secretary of State may make regulations as to the circumstances in which a person appointed as a visitor under this paragraph is to be regarded as independent of the local authority appointing him.

Power to guarantee apprenticeship deeds etc.

18.—(1) While a child is being looked after by a local authority, or is a person qualifying for advice and assistance, the authority may undertake any obligation by way of guarantee under any deed of apprenticeship or articles of clerkship which he enters into.

(2) Where a local authority have undertaken any such obligation under any deed or articles they may at any time (whether or not they are still looking after the person concerned) undertake the like obligation under any supplemental deed or articles.

Arrangements to assist children to live abroad

19.—(1) A local authority may only arrange for, or assist in arranging for, any child in their care to live outside England and Wales with the approval of the court.

(2) A local authority may, with the approval of every person who has parental responsibility for the child arrange for, or assist in arranging for, any other child looked after by them to live outside England and Wales.

(3) The court shall not give its approval under sub-paragraph (1) unless it is satisfied that—

    (a) living outside England and Wales would be in the child's best interests;

(b) suitable arrangements have been, or will be, made for his reception and welfare in the country in which he will live;

(c) the child has consented to living in that country; and

(d) every person who has parental responsibility for the child has consented to his living in that country.

(4) Where the court is satisfied that the child does not have sufficient understanding to give or withhold his consent, it may disregard sub-paragraph (3)(c) and give its approval if the child is to live in the country concerned with a parent, guardian, or other suitable person.

(5) Where a person whose consent is required by sub-paragraph (3)(d) fails to give his consent, the court may disregard that provision and give its approval if it is satisfied that that person—

(a) cannot be found;

(b) is incapable of consenting; or

(c) is withholding his consent unreasonably.

(6) Section 56 of the Adoption Act 1976 (which requires authority for the taking or sending abroad for adoption of a child who is a British subject) shall not apply in the case of any child who is to live outside England and Wales with the approval of the court given under this paragraph.

(7) Where a court decides to give its approval under this paragraph it may order that its decision is not to have effect during the appeal period.

(8) In sub-paragraph (7) "the appeal period" means—

(a) where an appeal is made against the decision, the period between the making of the decision and the determination of the appeal; and

(b) otherwise, the period during which an appeal may be made against the decision.

Death of children being looked after by local authorities

20.—(1) If a child who is being looked after by a local authority dies, the authority—

(a) shall notify the Secretary of State;

(b) shall, so far as is reasonably practicable, notify the child's parents and every person who is not a parent of his but who has parental responsibility for him;

(c) may, with the consent (so far as it is reasonably practicable to obtain it) of every person who has parental responsibility for the child, arrange for the child's body to be buried or cremated; and

(d) may, if the conditions mentioned in sub-paragraph (2) are satisfied, make payments to any person who has parental responsibility for the child, or any relative, friend or other person connected with the child, in respect of travelling, subsistence or other expenses incurred by that person in attending the child's funeral.

(2) The conditions are that—

(a) it appears to the authority that the person concerned could not otherwise attend the child's funeral without undue financial hardship; and

(b) that the circumstances warrant the making of the payments.

(3) Sub-paragraph (1) does not authorise cremation where it does not accord with the practice of the child's religious persuasion.

(4) Where a local authority have exercised their power under sub-paragraph (1)(c) with respect to a child who was under sixteen when he died, they may recover from any parent of the child any expenses incurred by them.

(5) Any sums so recoverable shall, without prejudice to any other method of recovery, be recoverable summarily as a civil debt.

(6) Nothing in this paragraph affects any enactment regulating or authorising the burial, cremation or anatomical examination of the body of a deceased person.

Part III

Contributions Towards Maintenance of Children Looked After by Local Authorities

Liability to contribute

21.—(1) Where a local authority are looking after a child (other than in the cases mentioned in sub-paragraph (7)) they shall consider whether they should recover contributions towards the child's maintenance from any person liable to contribute ("a contributor").

(2) An authority may only recover contributions from a contributor if they consider it reasonable to do so.

(3) The persons liable to contribute are—

  (a) where the child is under sixteen, each of his parents;
  (b) where he has reached the age of sixteen, the child himself.

(4) A parent is not liable to contribute during any period when he is in receipt of income support or family credit under the Social Security Act 1986.

(5) A person is not liable to contribute towards the maintenance of a child in the care of a local authority in respect of any period during which the child is allowed by the authority (under section 23(5)) to live with a parent of his.

(6) A contributor is not obliged to make any contribution towards a child's maintenance except as agreed or determined in accordance with this Part of this Schedule.

(7) The cases are where the child is looked after by a local authority under—

  (a) section 21;
  (b) an interim care order;
  (c) section 53 of the Children and Young Persons Act 1933.

Agreed contributions

22.—(1) Contributions towards a child's maintenance may only be recovered if the local authority have served a notice ("a contribution notice") on the contributor specifying—

  (a) the weekly sum which they consider that he should contribute; and
  (b) arrangements for payment.

(2) The contribution notice must be in writing and dated.

(3) Arrangements for payment shall, in particular, include—

  (a) the date on which liability to contribute begins (which must not be earlier than the date of the notice);
  (b) the date on which liability under the notice will end (if the child has not before that date ceased to be looked after by the authority); and
  (c) the date on which the first payment is to be made.

(4) The authority may specify in a contribution notice a weekly sum which is a standard contribution determined by them for all children looked after by them.

(5) The authority may not specify in a contribution notice a weekly sum greater than that which they consider—

(a) they would normally be prepared to pay if they had placed a similar child with local authority foster parents; and

(b) it is reasonably practicable for the contributor to pay (having regard to his means).

(6) An authority may at any time withdraw a contribution notice (without prejudice to their power to serve another).

(7) Where the authority and the contributor agree—

(a) the sum which the contributor is to contribute; and
(b) arrangements for payment,

(whether as specified in the contribution notice or otherwise) and the contributor notifies the authority in writing that he so agrees, the authority may recover summarily as a civil debt any contribution which is overdue and unpaid.

(8) A contributor may, by serving a notice in writing on the authority, withdraw his agreement in relation to any period of liability falling after the date of service of the notice.

(9) Sub-paragraph (7) is without prejudice to any other method of recovery.

Contribution orders

23.—(1) Where a contributor has been served with a contribution notice and has—

(a) failed to reach any agreement with the local authority as mentioned in paragraph 22(7) within the period of one month beginning with the day on which the contribution notice was served; or

(b) served a notice under paragraph 22(8) withdrawing his agreement,

the authority may apply to the court for an order under this paragraph.

(2) On such an application the court may make an order ("a contribution order") requiring the contributor to contribute a weekly sum towards the child's maintenance in accordance with arrangements for payment specified by the court.

(3) A contribution order—

(a) shall not specify a weekly sum greater than that specified in the contribution notice; and

(b) shall be made with due regard to the contributor's means.

(4) A contribution order shall not—

(a) take effect before the date specified in the contribution notice; or

(b) have effect while the contributor is not liable to contribute (by virtue of paragraph 21); or

(c) remain in force after the child has ceased to be looked after by the authority who obtained the order.

(5) An authority may not apply to the court under sub-paragraph (1) in relation to a contribution notice which they have withdrawn.

(6) Where—

(a) a contribution order is in force;

(b) the authority serve another contribution notice; and

(c) the contributor and the authority reach an agreement under paragraph 22(7) in respect of that other contribution notice,

the effect of the agreement shall be to discharge the order from the date on which it is agreed that the agreement shall take effect.

(7) Where an agreement is reached under sub-paragraph (6) the authority shall notify the court—

(a) of the agreement; and

(b) of the date on which it took effect.

(8) A contribution order may be varied or revoked on the application of the contributor or the authority.

(9) In proceedings for the variation of a contribution order, the authority shall specify—

(a) the weekly sum which, having regard to paragraph 22, they propose that the contributor should contribute under the order as varied; and

(b) the proposed arrangements for payment.

(10) Where a contribution order is varied, the order—

(a) shall not specify a weekly sum greater than that specified by the authority in the proceedings for variation; and

(b) shall be made with due regard to the contributor's means.

(11) An appeal shall lie in accordance with rules of court from any order made under this paragraph.

Enforcement of contribution orders etc.

24.—(1) A contribution order made by a magistrates' court shall be enforceable as a magistrates' court maintenance order (within the meaning of section 150(1) of the Magistrates' Courts Act 1980).

(2) Where a contributor has agreed, or has been ordered, to make contributions to a local authority, any other local authority within whose area the contributor is for the time being living may—

    (a) at the request of the local authority who served the contribution notice; and

    (b) subject to agreement as to any sum to be deducted in respect of services rendered,

collect from the contributor any contributions due on behalf of the authority who served the notice.

(3) In sub-paragraph (2) the reference to any other local authority includes a reference to—

    (a) a local authority within the meaning of section 1(2) of the Social Work (Scotland) Act 1968; and

    (b) a Health and Social Services Board established under Article 16 of the Health and Personal Social Services (Northern Ireland) Order 1972.

(4) The power to collect sums under sub-paragraph (2) includes the power to—

    (a) receive and give a discharge for any contributions due; and

    (b) (if necessary) enforce payment of any contributions,

even though those contributions may have fallen due at a time when the contributor was living elsewhere.

(5) Any contribution collected under sub-paragraph (2) shall be paid (subject to any agreed deduction) to the local authority who served the contribution notice.

(6) In any proceedings under this paragraph, a document which purports to be—

    (a) a copy of an order made by a court under or by virtue of paragraph 23; and

    (b) certified as a true copy by the clerk of the court,

shall be evidence of the order.

(7) In any proceedings under this paragraph, a certificate which—

(a) purports to be signed by the clerk or some other duly authorised officer of the local authority who obtained the contribution order; and

(b) states that any sum due to the authority under the order is overdue and unpaid,

shall be evidence that the sum is overdue and unpaid.

Regulations

25. The Secretary of State may make regulations—

(a) as to the considerations which a local authority must take into account in deciding—

(i) whether it is reasonable to recover contributions; and

(ii) what the arrangements for payment should be;

(b) as to the procedures they must follow in reaching agreements with—

(i) contributors (under paragraphs 22 and 23); and

(ii) any other local authority (under paragraph 23).

Annotation

Schedule 2: supplements Part III of the Act and makes further detailed provisions in respect of local authority support for children and families. **Part I** deals with the provision of services for families and is introduced by section 17. Section 17 imposes a general duty on a local authority to provide an appropriate range and level of services to safeguard and promote the welfare of children in need in their area and to promote the upbringing of such children by their families. Children in need are defined in section 17(10).

Part I of Schedule 2 consists of a number of powers and duties which a local authority shall have to consider in order to carry out those functions in relation to children in need. In accordance with section 17(4) the Secretary of State may modify, repeal or add to these provisions. In many cases these will be services which many or most local authorities already provided under section 1 of the Child Care Act 1980, sections 21 or 29 of the National Assistance Act 1948 and Schedule 8 to the National Health Service Act 1977, which are replaced by section 17 and Part III of this Act.

Paragraph 1: requires a local authority to take reasonable steps to identify the extent to which children in their area are in need.

They should publicise the services provided to children and their families and take reasonable steps to ensure that anyone who might benefit from such services receives the relevant information. Paragraph 1 enables a local authority to assess the range and level of services that may be available to them. It repeats, in the case of disabled children, the effect of section 1 of the Chronically Sick and Disabled Persons Act 1970.

Paragraph 2: requires a local authority to maintain a register of disabled children within their area. The provision is necessary since disabled children are being removed under the Act from existing provisions in respect of disabled persons generally, which include a duty to inform themselves of the persons to whom section 29 of the National Assistance Act 1948 applies.

Paragraph 3: enables a local authority to assess a child's needs under Part III of the Act at the same time as his needs are assessed under certain other specified enactments. This allows a single process of assessment when this is practicable to embrace all local authority responsibilities towards children. The intention is to ensure that comprehensive assessments are carried out rather than separate assessments being made under this Act and under, for example, disablement or education legislation.

Paragraph 4: requires a local authority to take reasonable steps to prevent children suffering ill treatment or neglect. This duty is one aspect of the preventative role of local authority social work. The intention is to secure that children may wherever possible remain within their famiily with such local authority support as is appropriate: see also Paragraph 6.

Paragraph 5: provides that, in order to protect a child who is suffering or is likely to suffer ill treatment at the hands of another person and that other person proposes to move from the premises, a local authority may assist him make the move by helping him find an alternative accommodation or with cash, or both. Paragraph 5 thus provides a legal framework for a local authority to assist with removal of an alleged perpetrator of abuse from the family home where such alleged perpetrator agrees to leave. It links to section 17 which deals with the provision of services for children in need, their families and others.

Paragraph 6: requires a local authority to attempt to minimise the effect of a disabled child's disability through the provision of services, and to give him the opportunity to lead as normal a life as possible.

Paragraph 7: requires a local authority to take steps to reduce the need to bring care, wardship or criminal proceedings or any other proceedings which might result in a child being placed in local authority care. They are also to take steps to encourage children in their area not to commit criminal offences. This updates and makes more comprehensive the preventative duty under section 1 of the Child Care Act 1980 which is repealed in its entirety by this Act.

Paragraph 8: requires a local authority to make appropriate provision of certain services in respect of children in need who live with their families. These services will form a part of the preventative work referred to above and include advice, guidance and counselling; home helps; assistance with travelling; occupational, social, cultural or recreational facilities and assistance to enable the child and his family to have a holiday.

Paragraph 9: is a new provision requiring the local authority to provide such family centres as the authority consider appropriate for children of all ages within their area. Such a facility may include providing accommodation whilst persons are receiving advice, guidance or counselling. Persons for the purpose of this paragraph are the child, the parents, someone with parental responsibility, or any other carer.

Paragraph 10: requires a local authority to take reasonable steps to enable a child to live with his family or to have contact with his family where he lives away from them, whether or not he is being looked after by the authority. This is another provision building on the experience of the Code of Practice—"Access to Children in Care", stressing the importance of maintaining family links.

Paragraph 11: deals with a duty to consider racial groups to which children in need belong when making decisions as to day care or with regard to local authority foster parents. Paragraph 11 is in keeping with the thrust of the Act that a local authority must give due consideration to the child's religious persuasion, racial origin and cultural and linguistic background: see section 22(5)(c). These factors must be taken into account even if there has been insufficient time to investigate the wishes and feelings of the child and others.

Part II deals with children looked after by local authorities and is given effect by section 23(9). It makes detailed provisions in respect of the duties of local authorities towards children whom they look after, whether under voluntary arrangements or by virtue of a court order. In part, it covers the matters that were formerly found in Part III of the Child Care Act 1980, which specified local authority powers and duties towards children in care. In particular, Part II contains regulation-making powers in respect of children placed with local authority foster parents, children placed with a parent or other person with parental responsibility, and children who are looked after under other, unspecified, arrangements.

Paragraph 12: replaces section 22 of the Child Care Act 1980. It enables the Secretary of State to make regulations governing the placement of children by local authorities with local authority foster parents. Under section 22 these were referred to as "boarding out regulations". The term "local authority fostering" will replace "boarding out". This paragraph additionally enables the regulations to provide for the arrangements to be made by the local authority in respect of the child's health and education and the circumstances in which they can arrange for duties under these regulations to be discharged by a voluntary organisation.

Paragraph 13: creates a new regulation-making power in respect of children accommodated by local authorities under arrangements not otherwise specified under section 23(2) but which are appropriate in the particular case: see section 23(2)(f). This provision ensures that there are regulations governing all types of placement which the local authority may make in respect of a child whom they are looking after.

Paragraph 14: provides for the making of regulations governing the conditions under which a child is allowed to live with his parents or other person with parental responsibility whilst subject to a care order. Paragraph 14 replaces with updated terminology the provisions of section 22A of the Child Care Act 1980 which was inserted by the Children and Young Persons (Amendment) Act 1986. The Charge and Control Regulations under section 22A were expected to be implemented during 1989. An important change is that the regulations will only govern placements with parents and others with parental responsibility. Placements with relatives and friends who do not have parental responsibility will in future be regulated by fostering control.

Paragraph 15: concerns the responsibilities of a local authority in relation to the promotion and maintenance of contact beween a child whom they are looking after and his family. Sections 12A and 12G of the Child Care Act 1980 formerly made provisions regarding access to children who are in care subject to a court order, and under Section 12G enabled the Secretary of State to issue a code of practice on access to children in care. This was published in December 1983. Paragraph 15 extends to children who are looked after by the local authority whether or not under a care order, and makes minor changes to the former statutory provisions regarding access.

Paragraph 16: replaces section 26 of the Child Care Act 1980 enabling a local authority to make payments to parents and others in respect of expenses incurred in visiting a child whom they look after. This provision is extended to include payments to the child for expenses incurred in visiting his parents or other persons.

Paragraph 17: requires a local authority to appoint an independent person to visit, advise and befriend any child who has not been visited by a parent or others in the previous twelve months, or who receives such visits only infrequently. This replaces section 11 of the Child Care Act 1980 and extends it to all children who are looked after by a local authority, not just those who are subject to a care order. Regulations may be made by the Secretary of State regarding which persons may be regarded as independent of the local authority for the purposes of Paragraph 17. Note the right of a child to object: see Paragraph 15(5)(6).

Paragraph 18: replaces section 23 of the Child Care Act 1980, empowering the local authority to guarantee apprenticeship deeds or articles of clerkship in respect of a child whom they looked after. This is extended to include all children looked after by the local authority.

Paragraph 19: replaces section 24 of the Child Care Act 1980. Section 24 enabled the local authority to arrange for a child in their care to live abroad, subject to the consent of the Secretary of State. Paragraph 19 distinguishes between those children who are accommodated under voluntary arrangements and those who are subject to a care order. In respect of the former, the local authority is able to arrange for a child to live abroad provided they have the approval of the child's parents and every person who has parental responsibility for him. Where the child is subject to a care order, Paragraph 19 will allow him to live abroad only with the consent of the court. Paragraph 19 sets out the considerations of which the court must take account in deciding whether or not to give consent. Note the provisions as to appeal: see Paragraph 19(7)(8).

Paragraph 20: replaces section 25 of the Child Care Act 1980. Paragraph 20 enables a local authority to bury or have cremated the body of any child who dies while being looked after by them, and to recover expenses for this from the child's parents if he was under sixteen. Paragraph 20 also requires a local authority to notify the Secretary of State and the child's parents and other persons who had parental responsibility for him at his death.

Part III of Schedule 2 replaces Part V of the Child Care Act 1980 as amended by the Family Law Reform Act 1987, which includes the repeal of sections 49 and 50 dealing with affiliation orders. Part III ties in with the provisions on charging for other services in section 29. References to children being "in the care of" a local authority are updated to refer to children "looked after" by a local authority and the power to charge is amended. This is so that it can be aligned with that in section 17 of the Health and Social Services and Social Security Adjudications Act 1983 in respect of services provided under section 29 of the National Assistance Act 1948 and Schedule 8 of the National Health Service Act 1977. These are no longer to apply to children as they are now provided with such services under the Act. Part III considerably simplifies the old Part V of the Child Care Act 1980 and places greater emphasis on a local authority agreeing contributions with parents.

Paragraph 21: sets out which people are liable to contribute towards the maintenance of a child looked after by the local authority and under what circumstances. It replaces section 45 of the Child Care Act 1980.

Paragraph 21(1): imposes a new duty on a local authority when looking after children to *consider whether they should recover* such contributions.

Paragraph 21(2): provides that a local authority may only recover contributions *if they consider it reasonable* to do so.

Paragraph 21(3): provides that the child, if he has reached sixteen, or his parents if he is under sixteen, are liable to contribute.

Paragraph 21(4): updates the reference in section 45(1A) of the 1980 Act and provides that persons in receipt of income support or family credit are not liable. Paragraph 21(3) and (4) repeat the former law.

Paragraph 21(5): provides that there is no liability to contribute while the child is living with a parent or other person with parental responsibility, which reflects the former law with updated terminology.

Paragraph 21(6): is a new provision which makes clear that no person who is a contributor under Part III is liable to contribute to maintenance of a child other than under Part III of Schedule 2.

Paragraph 21(7): defines the cases where the child is looked after by a local authority.

Paragraph 22: replaces section 46 of the Child Care Act 1980.

Paragraph 22 requires a local authority who wish to receive contributions to serve a contribution notice on a person liable to contribute, stating the weekly sum to be contributed, together with arrangements for payment. It is hoped that the specification of arrangements for payment will help clarify liability and encourage agreement.

Paragraph 23: makes provision concerning the enforcement of contribution orders and the power to collect contributions. This replaces sections 47, 48, 51 and 53 of the Child Care Act 1980: see also Paragraph 24.

Paragraph 24: puts on a statutory basis arrangements between local authorities for recovery and enforcement of contributions within the United Kingdom.

Paragraph 25: is a new provision enabling the Secretary of State to make regulations concerning procedures and the factors which a local authority should consider when making decisions regarding contributions.

SCHEDULE 3: SUPERVISION ORDERS

PART I

GENERAL

Meaning of "responsible person"

1. In this Schedule, "the responsible person", in relation to a supervised child, means—

(a) any person who has parental responsibility for the child; and
(b) any other person with whom the child is living.

Power of supervisor to give directions to supervised child

2.—(1) A supervision order may require the supervised child to comply with any directions given from time to time by the supervisor which require him to do all or any of the following things—

(a) to live at a place or places specified in the directions for a period or periods so specified;
(b) to present himself to a person or persons specified in the directions at a place or places and on a day or days so specified;

(c) to participate in activities specified in the directions on a day or days so specified.

(2) It shall be for the supervisor to decide whether, and to what extent, he exercises his power to give directions and to decide the form of any directions which he gives.

(3) Sub-paragraph (1) does not confer on a supervisor power to give directions in respect of any medical or psychiatric examination or treatment (which are matters dealt with in paragraphs 4 and 5).

Imposition of obligations on responsible person

3. —(1) With the consent of any responsible person, a supervision order may include a requirement—

(a) that he take all reasonable steps to ensure that the supervised child complies with any direction given by the supervisor under paragraph 2;
(b) that he take all reasonable steps to ensure that the supervised child complies with any requirement included in the order under paragraph 4 or 5;
(c) that he comply with any directions given by the supervisor requiring him to attend at a place specified in the directions for the purpose of taking part in activities so specified.

(2) A direction given under sub-paragraph (1)(c) may specify the time at which the responsible person is to attend and whether or not the supervised child is required to attend with him.

(3) A supervision order may require any person who is a responsible person in relation to the supervised child to keep the supervisor informed of his address, if it differs from the child's.

Psychiatric and medical examinations

4. —(1) A supervision order may require the supervised child—

(a) to submit to a medical or psychiatric examination; or
(b) to submit to any such examination from time to time as directed by the supervisor.

(2) Any such examination shall be required to be conducted—

(a) by, or under the direction of, such registered medical practitioner as may be specified in the order;
(b) at a place specified in the order and at which the supervised child is to attend as a non-resident patient; or

(c) at—

> (i) a health service hospital; or
> (ii) in the case of a psychiatric examination, a hospital or mental nursing home,

at which the supervised child is, or is to attend as, a resident patient.

(3) A requirement of a kind mentioned in sub-paragraph (2)(c) shall not be included unless the court is satisfied, on the evidence of a registered medical practitioner, that—

(a) the child may be suffering from a physical or mental condition that requires, and may be susceptible to, treatment; and

(b) a period as a resident patient is necessary if the examination is to be carried out properly.

(4) No court shall include a requirement under this paragraph in a supervision order unless it is satisfied that—

(a) where the child has sufficient understanding to make an informed decision, he consents to its inclusion; and

(b) satisfactory arrangements have been, or can be, made for the examination.

Psychiatric and medical treatment

5.—(1) Where a court which proposes to make or vary a supervision order is satisfied, on the evidence of a registered medical practitioner approved for the purposes of section 12 of the Mental Health Act 1983, that the mental condition of the supervised child—

(a) is such as requires, and may be susceptible to, treatment; but

(b) is not such as to warrant his detention in pursuance of a hospital order under Part III of that Act,

the court may include in the order a requirement that the supervised child shall, for a period specified in the order, submit to such treatment as is so specified.

(2) The treatment specified in accordance with sub-paragraph (1) must be—

(a) by, or under the direction of, such registered medical practitioner as may be specified in the order;

(b) as a non-resident patient at such a place as may be so specified; or

(c) as a resident patient in a hospital or mental nursing home.

(3) Where a court which proposes to make or vary a supervision order is satisfied, on the evidence of a registered medical practitioner, that the physical condition of the supervised child is such as requires, and may be susceptible to, treatment, the court may include in the order a requirement that the supervised child shall, for a period specified in the order, submit to such treatment as is to specified.

(4) The treatment specified in accordance with sub-paragraph (3) must be—

(a) by, or under the direction of, such registered medical practitioner as may be specified in the order;
(b) as a non-resident patient at such place as may be so specified; or
(c) as a resident patient in a health service hospital.

(5) No court shall include a requirement under this paragraph in a supervision order unless it is satisfied—

(a) where the child has sufficient understanding to make an informed decision, that he consents to its inclusion; and
(b) that satisfactory arrangements have been, or can be, made for the treatment.

(6) If a medical practitioner by whom or under whose direction a supervised person is being treated in pursuance of a requirement included in a supervision order by virtue of this paragraph is unwilling to continue to treat or direct the treatment of the supervised child or is of the opinion that—

(a) the treatment should be continued beyond the period specified in the order;
(b) the supervised child needs different treatment;
(c) he is not susceptible to treatment; or
(d) he does not require further treatment,

the practitioner shall make a report in writing to that effect to the supervisor.

(7) On receiving a report under this paragraph the supervisor shall refer it to the court, and on such a reference the court may make an order cancelling or varying the requirement.

PART II

MISCELLANEOUS

Life of supervision order

6. — (1) Subject to sub-paragraph (2) and section 91, a supervision order shall cease to have effect at the end of the period of one year beginning with the date on which it was made.

(2) A supervision order shall also cease to have effect if an event mentioned in section 25(1)(a) or (b) of the Child Abduction and Custody Act 1985 (termination of existing orders) occurs with respect to the child.

(3) Where the supervisor applies to the court to extend, or further extend, a supervision order the court may extend the order for such period as it may specify.

(4) A supervision order may not be extended so as to run beyond the end of the period of three years beginning with the date on which it was made.

[Limited life of directions

7. — (1) The total number of days in respect of which a supervised child or (as the case may be) responsible person may be required to comply with directions given under paragraph 2 or 3 shall not exceed 90 or such lesser number (if any) as the supervision order may specify.

(2) For the purpose of calculating that total number of days, the supervisor may disregard any day in respect of which directions previously given in pursuance of the order were not complied with.]

Information to be given to supervisor etc.

8. — (1) A supervision order may require the supervised child—

- (a) to keep the supervisor informed of any change in his address; and
- (b) to allow the supervisor to visit him at the place where he is living.

(2) The responsible person in relation to any child with respect to whom a supervision order is made shall—

Note: The words *in italics* within square brackets were deleted by the Courts and Legal Services Act 1990.

(a) if asked by the supervisor, inform him of the child's address (if it is known to him); and

(b) if he is living with the child, allow the supervisor reasonable contact with the child.

Selection of supervisor

9.—(1) A supervision order shall not designate a local authority as the supervisor unless—

(a) the authority agree; or

(b) the supervised child lives or will live within their area.

(2) A court shall not place a child under the supervision of a probation officer unless—

(a) the appropriate authority so request; and

(b) a probation officer is already exercising or has exercised, in relation to another member of the household to which the child belongs, duties imposed on probation officers—

(i) by paragraph 8 of Schedule 3 to the Powers of Criminal Courts Act 1973; or

(ii) by rules under paragraph 18(1)(b) of that Schedule.

(3) In sub-paragraph (2) "the appropriate authority" means the local authority appearing to the court to be the authority in whose area the supervised child lives or will live.

(4) Where a supervision order places a person under the supervision of a probation officer, the officer shall be selected in accordance with arrangements made by the probation committee for the area in question.

(5) If the selected probation officer is unable to carry out his duties, or dies, another probation officer shall be selected in the same manner.

Effect of supervision order on earlier orders

10. The making of a supervision order with respect to any child brings to an end any earlier care or supervision order which—

(a) was made with respect to that child; and

(b) would otherwise continue in force.

Local authority functions and expenditure

11.—(1) The Secretary of State may make regulations with respect to the exercise by a local authority of their functions where a child has been placed under their supervision by a supervision order.

(2) Where a supervision order requires compliance with directions given by virtue of this section, any expenditure incurred by the supervisor for the purposes of the directions shall be defrayed by the local authority designated in the order.

Part III

Education supervision orders

Effect of orders

12.—(1) Where an education supervision order is in force with respect to a child, it shall be the duty of the supervisor—

  (a) to advise, assist and befriend, and give directions to—

>   (i) the supervised child; and
>   (ii) his parents,

  in such a way as will, in the opinion of the supervisor, secure that he is properly educated;

  (b) where any such directions given to—

>   (i) the supervised child; or
>   (ii) a parent of his,

  have not been complied with, to consider what further steps to take in the exercise of the supervisor's powers under this Act.

(2) Before giving any directions under sub-paragraph (1) the supervisor shall, so far as is reasonably practicable, ascertain the wishes and feelings of—

  (a) the child; and
  (b) his parents,

including, in particular, their wishes as to the place at which the child should be educated.

(3) When settling the terms of any such directions, the supervisor shall give due consideration—

  (a) having regard to the child's age and understanding, to such wishes and feelings of his as the supervisor has been able to ascertain; and
  (b) to such wishes and feelings of the child's parents as he has been able to ascertain.

(4) Directions may be given under this paragraph at any time while the education supervision order is in force.

13.—(1) Where an education supervision order is in force with respect to a child, the duties of the child's parents under sections 36 and 39 of the Education Act 1944 (duty to secure education of children and to secure regular attendance of registered pupils) shall be superseded by their duty to comply with any directions in force under the education supervision order.

(2) Where an education supervision order is made with respect to a child—

    (a) any school attendance order—

        (i) made under section 37 of the Act of 1944 with respect to the child; and
        (ii) in force immediately before the making of the education supervision order,

    shall cease to have effect; and

    (b) while the education supervision order remains in force, the following provisions shall not apply with respect to the child—

        (i) section 37 of that Act (school attendance orders);
        (ii) section 76 of that Act (pupils to be educated in accordance with wishes of their parents);
        (iii) sections 6 and 7 of the Education Act 1980 (parental preference and appeals against admission decisions);

    (c) a supervision order made with respect to the child in criminal proceedings, while the education supervision order is in force, may not include an education requirement of the kind which could otherwise be included under section 12C of the Children and Young Persons Act 1969;
    (d) any education requirement of a kind mentioned in paragraph (c), which was in force with respect to the child immediately before the making of the education supervision order, shall cease to have effect.

Effect where child also subject to supervision order

14.—(1) This paragraph applies where an education supervision order and a supervision order, or order under section 7(7)(b) of the Children and Young Persons Act 1969, are in force at the same time with respect to the same child.

(2) Any failure to comply with a direction given by the supervisor under the education supervision order shall be disregarded if it would not have been reasonably practicable to comply with it without failing to comply with a direction given under the other order.

Duration of orders

15. — (1) An education supervision order shall have effect for a period of one year, beginning with the date on which it is made.

(2) An education supervision order shall not expire if, before it would otherwise have expired, the court has (on the application of the authority in whose favour the order was made) extended the period during which it is in force.

(3) Such an application may not be made earlier than three months before the date on which the order would otherwise expire.

(4) The period during which an education supervision order is in force may be extended under sub-paragraph (2) on more than one occasion.

(5) No one extension may be for a period of more than three years.

(6) An education supervision order shall cease to have effect on—

    (a) the child's ceasing to be of compulsory school age; or
    (b) the making of a care order with respect to the child;

and sub-paragraphs (1) to (4) are subject to this sub-paragraph.

Information to be given to supervisor etc.

16. — (1) An education supervision order may require the child—

    (a) to keep the supervisor informed of any change in his address; and
    (b) to allow the supervisor to visit him at the place where he is living.

(2) A person who is the parent of a child with respect to whom an education supervision order has been made shall—

    (a) if asked by the supervisor, inform him of the child's address (if it is known to him); and

M

(b) if he is living with the child, allow the supervisor reasonable contact with the child.

Discharge of orders

17.—(1) The court may discharge any education supervision order on the application of—

(a) the child concerned;
(b) a parent of his; or
(c) the local education authority concerned.

(2) On discharging an education supervision order, the court may direct the local authority within whose area the child lives, or will live, to investigate the circumstances of the child.

Offences

18.—(1) If a parent of a child with respect to whom an education supervision order is in force persistently fails to comply with a direction given under the order he shall be guilty of an offence.

(2) It shall be a defence for any person charged with such an offence to prove that—

(a) he took all reasonable steps to ensure that the direction was complied with;
(b) the direction was unreasonable; or
(c) he had complied with—

(i) a requirement included in a supervision order made with respect to the child; or
(ii) directions given under such a requirement,

and that it was not reasonably practicable to comply both with the direction and with the requirement or directions mentioned in this paragraph.

(3) A person guilty of an offence under this paragraph shall be liable on summary conviction to a fine not exceeding level 3 on the standard scale.

Persistent failure of child to comply with directions

19.—(1) Where a child with respect to whom an education supervision order is in force persistently fails to comply with any direction given under the order, the local education authority concerned shall notify the appropriate local authority.

(2) Where a local authority have been notified under sub-paragraph (1) they shall investigate the circumstances of the child.

(3) In this paragraph "the appropriate local authority" has the same meaning as in section 36.

Miscellaneous

20. The Secretary of State may by regulations make provision modifying, or displacing, the provisions of any enactment about education in relation to any child with respect to whom an education supervision order is in force to such extent as appears to the Secretary of State to be necessary or expedient in consequence of the provision made by this Act with respect to such orders.

Interpretation

21. In this Part of this Schedule "parent" has the same meaning as in the Education Act 1944 (as amended by Schedule 13).

Annotation

Schedule 3: makes various detailed provisions in respect of supervision orders and education supervision orders. These are supplementary to Part IV of the Act. Many of these were formerly dealt with under sections 12 to 19 of the Children and Young Persons Act 1969. However, that Act now applies only to those orders made in criminal proceedings. Schedule 3 repeats some of the former law but also introduces a number of changes designed to make supervision a more effective alternative to a care order.

Paragraph 1: defines "responsible person" in relation to supervision orders: see Paragraph 3.

Paragraph 2: concerns the power of a supervisor to give direction to the child. It emphasises that intermediate treatment may be used in respect of children who are not offenders, which hitherto has been insufficiently appreciated. Section 12(2) of the Children and Young Persons Act 1969 is re-enacted, giving the supervisor certain powers relating to intermediate treatment, but these do not extend to giving directions in respect of medical or psychiatric examination or treatment: see in relation to paragraphs 4 and 5 below.

Paragraph 3: is a new provision and enables the court, with the consent of the responsible person, to include in a supervision order certain requirements. The thinking behind Paragraph 3 is that parents and others will be encouraged to play a positive role in making supervision orders work.

Paragraph 4: deals with psychiatric and medical examinations and linked to paragraph 5 concerns the power of a court to require that a child be medically or psychiatrically examined or treated, or to enable the supervisor to give directions concerning such examinations.

Paragraph 5: links to Paragraph 4, which means that the two Paragraphs set out the circumstances under which directions may be given and are in all cases subject to the condition that the child, if he has sufficient understanding to make an informed decision, consents to it being included in the order, and that satisfactory arrangements have been or can be made for treatment or examination. Paragraphs 4 and 5 substantially repeat the former law: see section 12(4) and (5) of the Children and Young Persons Act 1969.

Paragraph 6: provides for the duration of supervision orders. An order may last for a period of up to one year. This is a substantial change from the Children and Young Persons Act 1969, under which an order lasted for three years unless the court specified that it should be for less. It may be extended so as to last more than three years. In any event, under section 91, it ceases to have effect when the child reaches eighteen.

Paragraph 7: replaces section 12(3) of the Children and Young Persons Act 1969 in relation to supervision orders under the Act, limiting directions given under Paragraphs 2 or 3 to ninety days duration.

Paragraph 8: empowers the supervisor to require the child and the responsible person to keep him informed of the child's address and to allow him contact with the child.

Paragraph 9: replaces section 13(1) of the Children and Young Persons Act 1969 and, in relation to supervision orders under the Act, concerns the selection of a supervisor.

Paragraph 10: provides that the making of a supervision order brings to an end any existing care or supervision order whether or not made under this Act in respect of that child.

Paragraph 11: enables the Secretary of State to make regulations regarding the functions of a local authority where they are the supervisor. Paragraph 11 requires them to defray certain expenses incurred by the supervisor.

Paragraph 12: sets out the effects of an education supervision order. Note that section 36 enables the court to make an education supervision order where it is satisfied that the child concerned is of compulsory school age and is not being properly educated. This is a new order and its detailed provisions are set out in Part III of Schedule 3 beginning with Paragraph 12, which supplements section 36. The power of a court to make a supervision order on education grounds under section 1(2)(e) of the Children and Young Persons Act 1969 is replaced. Paragraph 12 also provides for the effect of a supervision order on certain provisions of the Education Act 1944 and on education requirements which may otherwise be included in criminal supervision orders under section 12A of the Children and Young Persons Act 1969. Note Paragraph 12(4) relating to the giving of directions at any time while the education supervision order is in force.

Paragraph 13: links the new education supervision order with sections 36 and 39 of the Education Act 1944. It also links the new supervision order with section 12C of the Children and Young Persons Act 1969 in relation to a supervision order made with respect to the child in criminal proceedings.

Paragraph 14: provides that a person need not comply with a direction given under an education supervision order if this would result in a failure to comply with a direction given under a supervision order. It links to section 7(7)(b) of the Children and Young Persons Act 1969.

Paragraph 15: provides for the duration of an order, which lasts until the child ceases to be of compulsory school age or until a care order is made. Subject to this, it may last for one year but may be extended, on application, for up to three years.

Paragraph 16: places an obligation upon the child to keep the supervisor informed of any change in his address and to allow the supervisor to visit him at the place where he is living. There is an additional obligation upon the parent of a child to cooperate with the supervisor if called upon to do so, that is to say, inform the supervisor of the child's address and allow reasonable contact.

Paragraph 17: enables the court to discharge an order on application by the local education authority, the child, his parents or any other person with parental responsibility.

Paragraph 18: was added at report stage and defines offences in relation to a supervision order, where the parent of a child persistently fails to comply with a direction given under the order. Paragraph 18(2) nevertheless provides a defence based on reasonableness—that the parent took all reasonable steps to ensure that the direction was complied with, that the direction itself was unreasonable, or that it was not reasonably practicable to comply both with the direction and the requirement. The liability on summary conviction is well within the scale of fines which may be imposed under the Act.

Paragraph 19: provides that where there has been a persistent failure of a child to comply with directions a local authority shall be notified. The local authority to be notified shall be the appropriate local authority defined in section 36. Thus, a child who persistently fails to comply with directions will find the circumstances of his life subject to investigation as one of the duties of a local authority and will be liable to one of the other orders for which the Act makes provision.

Paragraph 20: enables the Secretary of State to make regulations concerning the application of enactments about education to any child who is subject to an education supervision order.

Paragraph 21: provides an interpretation of the word "parent", which has the same meaning as in the Education Act 1944, as amended by Schedule 13.

SCHEDULE 4: MANAGEMENT AND CONDUCT OF COMMUNITY HOMES

PART I

INSTRUMENTS OF MANAGEMENT

Instruments of management for controlled and assisted community homes

1.—(1) The Secretary of State may by order make an instrument of management providing for the constitution of a body of managers for any [*voluntary*] home which is designated as a controlled or assisted community home.

(2) Sub-paragraph (3) applies where two or more [*voluntary*] homes are designated as controlled community homes or as assisted community homes.

(3) If—

(a) those homes are, or are to be, provided by the same voluntary organisation; and

Note: The words *in italics* within square brackets were deleted by the Courts and Legal Services Act 1990.

(b) the same local authority is to be represented on the body of managers for those homes,

a single instrument of management may be made by the Secretary of State under this paragraph constituting one body of managers for those homes or for any two or more of them.

(4) The number of persons who, in accordance with an instrument of management, constitute the body of managers for a [*voluntary*] home shall be such number (which must be a multiple of three) as may be specified in the instrument.

.(5) The instrument shall provide that the local authority specified in the instrument shall appoint—

(a) in the case of a [*voluntary*] home which is designated as a controlled community home, two-thirds of the managers; and

(b) in the case of a [*voluntary*] home which is designated as an assisted community home, one-third of them.

(6) An instrument of management shall provide that the foundation managers shall be appointed, in such manner and by such persons as may be specified in the instrument—

(a) so as to represent the interests of the voluntary organisation by which the home is, or is to be, provided; and

(b) for the purpose of securing that—

(i) so far as is a practicable, the character of the home as a [*voluntary*] home will be preserved; and
(ii) subject to paragraph 2(3), the terms of any trust deed relating to the home are observed.

(7) An instrument of management shall come into force on such date as it may specify.

(8) If an instrument of management is in force in relation to a [*voluntary*] home the home shall be (and be known as) a controlled community home or an assisted community home, according to its designation.

(9) In this paragraph—

"foundation managers", in relation to a [*voluntary*] home, means those of the managers of the home who are not appointed by a local authority in accordance with subparagraph (5); and

Note: The words *in italics* within square brackets were deleted by the Courts and Legal Services Act 1990.

"designated" means designated in accordance with section 53.

2.—(1) An instrument of management shall contain such provisions as the Secretary of State considers appropriate.

(2) Nothing in the instrument of management shall affect the purposes for which the premises comprising the home are held.

(3) Without prejudice to the generality of sub-paragraph (1), an instrument of management may contain provisions—

(a) specifying the nature and purpose of the home (or each of the homes) to which it relates;

(b) requiring a specified number or proportion of the places in that home (or those homes) to be made available to local authorities and to any other body specified in the instrument; and

(c) relating to the management of that home (or those homes) and the charging of fees with respect to—

(i) children placed there; or

(ii) places made available to any local authority or other body.

(4) Subject to sub-paragraphs (1) and (2), in the event of any inconsistency between the provisions of any trust deed and an instrument of management, the instrument of management shall prevail over the provisions of the trust deed in so far as they relate to the home concerned.

(5) After consultation with the voluntary organisation concerned and with the local authority specified in its instrument of management, the Secretary of State may by order vary or revoke any provisions of the instrument.

Part II

Management of Controlled and Assisted Community Homes

3.—(1) The management, equipment and maintenance of a controlled community home shall be the responsibility of the local authority specified in its instrument of management.

(2) The management, equipment and maintenance of an assisted community home shall be the responsibility of the voluntary organisation by which the home is provided.

(3) In this paragraph—

"home" means a controlled community home or (as the case may be) assisted community home; and

"the managers", in relation to a home, means the managers constituted by its instrument of management; and

"the responsible body", in relation to a home, means the local authority or (as the case may be) voluntary organisation responsible for its management, equipment and maintenance.

(4) The functions of a home's responsible body shall be exercised through the managers.

(5) Anything done, liability incurred or property acquired by a home's managers shall be done, incurred or acquired by them as agents of the responsible body.

(6) In so far as any matter is reserved for the decision of a home's responsible body by—

    (a) sub-paragraph (8);
    (b) the instrument of management;
    (c) the service by the body on the managers, or any of them, of a notice reserving any matter,

that matter shall be dealt with by the body and not by the managers.

(7) In dealing with any matter so reserved, the responsible body shall have regard to any representations made to the body by the managers.

(8) The employment of persons at a home shall be a matter reserved for the decision of the responsible body.

(9) Where the instrument of management of a controlled community home so provides, the responsible body may enter into arrangements with the voluntary organisation by which that home is provided whereby, in accordance with such terms as may be agreed between them and the voluntary organisation, persons who are not in the employment of the responsible body shall undertake duties at that home.

(10) Subject to sub-paragraph (11)—

    (a) where the responsible body for an assisted community home proposes to engage any person to work at that home or to terminate without notice the employment of any person at that home, it shall consult the local authority specified in the instrument of management and, if that authority so direct, the responsible body shall not carry out its proposal without their consent; and

    (b) that local authority may, after consultation with the responsible body, require that body to terminate the employment of any person at that home.

(11) Paragraphs (a) and (b) of sub-paragraph (10) shall not apply —

    (a) in such cases or circumstances as may be specified by notice in writing given by the local authority to the responsible body; and

    (b) in relation to the employment of any persons or class of persons specified in the home's instrument of management.

(12) The accounting year of the managers of a home shall be such as may be specified by the responsible body.

(13) Before such date in each accounting year as may be so specified, the managers of a home shall submit to the responsible body estimates, in such form as the body may require, of expenditure and receipts in respect of the next accounting year.

(14) Any expenses incurred by the managers of a home with the approval of the responsible body shall be defrayed by that body.

(15) The managers of a home shall keep —

    (a) proper accounts with respect to the home; and

    (b) proper records in relation to the accounts.

(16) Where an instrument of management relates to more than one home, one set of accounts and records may be kept in respect of all the homes to which it relates.

Part III

Regulations

4. —(1) The Secretary of State may make regulations —

    (a) as to the placing of children in community homes;

    (b) as to the conduct of such homes; and

    (c) for securing the welfare of children in such homes.

(2) The regulations may, in particular —

    (a) prescribe standards to which the premises used for such homes are to conform;

(b) impose requirements as to the accommodation, staff and equipment to be provided in such homes, and as to the arrangements to be made for protecting the health of children in such homes;

(c) provide for the control and discipline of children in such homes;

(d) impose requirements as to the keeping of records and giving of notices in respect of children in such homes;

(e) impose requirements as to the facilities which are to be provided for giving religious instruction to children in such homes;

(f) authorise the Secretary of State to give and revoke directions requiring—

(i). the local authority by whom a home is provided or who are specified in the instrument of management for a controlled community home, or

(ii) the voluntary organisation by which an assisted community home is provided,

to accommodate in the home a child looked after by a local authority for whom no places are made available in that home or to take such action in relation to a child accommodated in the home as may be specified in the directions;

(g) provide for consultation with the Secretary of State as to applicants for appointment to the charge of a home;

(h) empower the Secretary of State to prohibit the appointment of any particular applicant except in the cases (if any) in which the regulations dispense with such consultation by reason that the person to be appointed possesses such qualifications as may be prescribed;

(i) require the approval of the Secretary of State for the provision and use of accommodation for the purpose of restricting the liberty of children in such homes and impose other requirements (in addition to those imposed by section 25) as to the placing of a child in accommodation provided for that purpose, including a requirement to obtain the permission of any local authority who are looking after the child;

(j) provide that, to such extent as may be provided for in the regulations, the Secretary of State may direct that any provision of regulations under this paragraph which is specified in the direction and makes any such provision as is referred to in paragraph (a) or (b) shall not apply in relation to a particular home or the premises used for it, and may provide for the variation or revocation of any such direction by the Secretary of State.

(3) Without prejudice to the power to make regulations under this paragraph conferring functions on—

    (a) the local authority or voluntary organisation by which a community home is provided; or

    (b) the managers of a controlled or assisted community home,

regulations under this paragraph may confer functions in relation to a controlled or assisted community home on the local authority named in the instrument of management for the home.

Annotation

Schedule 4: supplements the provisions of Part VI of the Act concerning the management, conduct, registration and regulation of community homes, including those provided by voluntary organisations, that is to say community homes and assisted community homes. Part VI and Schedule 4 together represent the re-enactment, with certain amendments, of Part IV of the Child Care Act 1980. Schedule 4 replaces sections 35 to 39 of the Act dealing with instruments of management for controlled and assisted community homes, the management arrangements for such homes, and the regulation-making power governing community homes. This regulation-making power is amended to provide greater alignment with those governing voluntary homes and registered children's homes. The regulations are to provide for the control and discipline of children and to impose requirements concerning the keeping of records. They will also provide for the Secretary of State to be consulted as to applications for appointment to the charge of a home. The remaining provisions of sections 35 to 39 of the Child Care Act 1980 are re-enacted with substantive amendment, although sections 37 and 38, which provided separately for the management arrangements of controlled and assisted community homes, are now combined in Paragraph 3 of Part II of Schedule 4.

Paragraph 1: replaces section 35 of the Child Care Act 1980.

Paragraph 1(1): enables the Secretary of State to make by order an instrument of management for any voluntary home which is designated as a controlled or assisted community home.

Paragraph 1(2)(3): replaces section 35(2) of the Child Care Act 1980, enabling a single instrument of management to be made in respect of two or more such homes in specified circumstances.

Paragraph 1(4)(5): replaces section 35(3) of the Child Care Act 1980. Paragraph 1(4) and (5) provides for the body of managers to consist of the number of persons specified in the instrument of management, and for the number of local authority managers to consist of two thirds of that body in the case of a controlled community home and one third in the case of an assisted community home.

Paragraph 1(6): replaces section 35(4) of the Child Care Act 1980 and provides for the appointment and function of the foundation managers.

Paragraph 1(7) (8): re-enacts section 35(5) of the Child Care Act 1980, providing for the instrument of management to come into force on such a date as it may specify and for homes to become controlled or assisted community homes according to their designation.

Paragraph 1(9): provides certain definitions for the purposes of Paragraph 1.

Paragraph 2: re-enacts section 36 of the Child Care Act 1980.

Paragraph 2(1)(2): replaces section 36(1) of the Child Care Act 1980, providing for an instrument of management to contain such provisions as the Secretary of State considers appropriate.

Paragraph 2(3): replaces section 36(2) of the Child Care Act 1980. It enables the instrument of management to contain particular provisions concerning the nature and purpose of the home, the number of places to be available to local authorities, the management of the home and the charging of fees.

Paragraph 2(4): re-enacts section 36(3) of the Child Care Act 1980, providing that where there is any inconsistency between the two, the instrument of management shall prevail over any trust deed relating to the home.

Paragraph 2(5): replaces section 36(4), enabling the Secretary of State, after consultation, to revoke all or any provisions of the instrument of management.

Paragraph 3: deals with the management of controlled and assisted community homes and replaces sections 37 and 38 of the Child Care Act 1980. Whereas sections 37 and 38 dealt separately with controlled and assisted community homes respectively, Paragraph 3 makes provision for the management of both of these types of community home.

Paragraph 3(1)(2)(3): replaces sections 37(1) and 38(1) of the Child Care Act 1980. It makes provisions regarding who shall manage, equip and maintain a controlled or assisted community home, and provides certain definitions which apply to this Paragraph.

Paragraph 3(4)(5): replaces sections 37(2) and 38(2) of the Child Care Act 1980. It provides for the functions of the responsible body to be exercised by the managers as agents of the body.

Paragraph 3(6)(7): replaces sections 37(7) and 38(3) of the Child Care Act 1980, providing for certain matters to be the responsibility of the responsible body and not the managers.

Paragraph 3(8)(9)(10)(11): replaces sections 37(4) and 38(4) and (5) of the Child Care Act 1980 and deals with the employment of persons in controlled or assisted community homes.

Paragraph 3(12)(13)(14)(15)(16): replaces sections 37(5), 37(6), 38(6) and 38(7) of the Child Care Act 1980. It makes certain requirements regarding the keeping of accounts and records with respect to the home and the defrayment of expenses.

Paragraph 4: enables the Secretary of State to make regulations governing community homes, including controlled or assisted community homes. Paragraph 4 replaces section 39 of the Child Care Act 1980. Similar regulations are covered by Schedule 5 and 6 dealing with voluntary homes and registered children's homes. Whilst these regulations are not identical, they have each been updated and amended to introduce a greater degree of alignment. In this Paragraph 4 provisions are made enabling the regulations to include directions regarding the control and discipline of children, the keeping of records and the appointment of persons to take charge of the home.

Paragraph 4(1): enables the Secretary of State to make regulations governing the conduct of community homes, the placing of children in such homes, and the securing of the welfare of children in them. The reference to the placing of children in community homes is in addition to the provisions currently contained in section 39(1) of the Child Care Act 1980.

Paragraph 4(2): specifies particular matters which may be provided for in regulations. These effectively re-enact section 39(2) of the Child Care Act 1980 but include new references at Paragraph 4(2)(c)(d)(g)(h) to the control and discipline of children, the keeping of records and consultation with, and powers of, the Secretary of State in respect of applications for appointment of persons to take charge of the home.

Paragraph 4(3): replaces section 39(3) of the Child Care Act 1980 and enables regulations under Paragraph 4 to confer functions relating to a controlled or assisted community home on the appropriate local authority.

SCHEDULE 5: VOLUNTARY HOMES AND VOLUNTARY ORGANISATIONS

PART I

REGISTRATION OF VOLUNTARY HOMES

General

1.—(1) An application for registration under this paragraph shall—

(a) be made by the persons intending to carry on the home to which the application relates; and

(b) be made in such manner, and be accompanied by such particulars, as the Secretary of State may prescribe.

(2) On an application duly made under sub-paragraph (1) the Secretary of State may—

(a) grant or refuse the application, as he thinks fit; or

(b) grant the application subject to such conditions as he considers appropriate.

(3) The Secretary of State may from time to time—

(a) vary any condition for the time being in force with respect to a voluntary home by virtue of this paragraph; or

(b) impose an additional condition,

either on the application of the person carrying on the home or without such an application.

(4) Where at any time it appears to the Secretary of State that the conduct of any voluntary home—

(a) is not in accordance with regulations made under paragraph 7; or

(b) is otherwise unsatisfactory,

he may cancel the registration of the home and remove it from the register.

(5) Any person who, without reasonable excuse, carries on a voluntary home in contravention of—

(a) section 60; or

(b) a condition to which the registration of the home is for the time being subject by virtue of this Part, shall be guilty of an offence.

(6) Any person guilty of such an offence shall be liable on summary conviction to a fine not exceeding—

    (a) level 5 on the standard scale, if his offence is under sub-paragraph (5)(a); or

    (b) level 4, if it is under sub-paragraph (5)(b).

(7) Where the Secretary of State registers a home under this paragraph, or cancels the registration of a home, he shall notify the local authority within whose area the home is situated.

Procedure

2.—(1) Where—

    (a) a person applies for registration of a voluntary home; and

    (b) the Secretary of State proposes to grant his application,

the Secretary of State shall give him written notice of his proposal and of the conditions subject to which he proposes to grant the application.

(2) The Secretary of State need not give notice if he proposes to grant the application subject only to conditions which—

    (a) the applicant specified in the application; or

    (b) the Secretary of State and the applicant have subsequently agreed.

(3) Where the Secretary of State proposes to refuse such an application he shall give notice of his proposal to the applicant.

(4) The Secretary of State shall give any person carrying on a voluntary home notice of a proposal to—

    (a) cancel the registration of the home;

    (b) vary any condition for the time being in force with respect to the home by virtue of paragraph 1; or

    (c) impose any additional condition.

(5) A notice under this paragraph shall give the Secretary of State's reasons for his proposal.

Right to make representations

3.—(1) A notice under paragraph 2 shall state that within 14 days of service of the notice any person on whom it is served may (in writing) require the Secretary of State to give him an opportunity to make representations to the Secretary of State concerning the matter.

(2) Where a notice has been served under paragraph 2, the Secretary of State shall not determine the matter until either—

  (a) any person on whom the notice was served has made representations to him concerning the matter; or
  (b) the period during which any such person could have required the Secretary of State to give him an opportunity to make representations has elapsed without the Secretary of State being required to give such an opportunity; or
  (c) the conditions specified in sub-paragraph (3) are satisfied.

(3) The conditions are that—

  (a) a person on whom the notice was served has required the Secretary of State to give him an opportunity to make representations to the Secretary of State;
  (b) the Secretary of State has allowed him a reasonable period to make his representations; and
  (c) he has failed to make them within that period.

(4) The representations may be made, at the option of the person making them, either in writing or orally.

(5) If he informs the Secretary of State that he desires to make oral representations, the Secretary of State shall give him an opportunity of appearing before, and of being heard by, a person appointed by the Secretary of State.

Decision of Secretary of State

4.—(1) If the Secretary of State decides to adopt the proposal, he shall serve notice in writing of his decision on any person on whom he was required to serve notice of his proposal.

(2) A notice under this paragraph shall be accompanied by a notice explaining the right of appeal conferred by paragraph 5.

(3) A decision of the Secretary of State, other than a decision to grant an application for registration subject only to such conditions as are mentioned in paragraph 2(2) or to refuse an application for registration, shall not take effect—

  (a) if no appeal is brought, until the end of the period of 28 days referred to in paragraph 5(3); and
  (b) if an appeal is brought, until it is determined or abandoned.

Appeals

5.—(1) An appeal against a decision of the Secretary of State under Part VII shall lie to a Registered Homes Tribunal.

(2) An appeal shall be brought by notice in writing given to the Secretary of State.

(3) No appeal may be brought by a person more than 28 days after service on him of notice of the decision.

(4) On an appeal, the Tribunal may confirm the Secretary of State's decision or direct that it shall not have effect.

(5) A Tribunal shall also have power on an appeal to—

    (a) vary any condition for the time being in force by virtue of Part VII with respect to the home to which the appeal relates;

    (b) direct that any such condition shall cease to have effect; or

    (c) direct that any such condition as it thinks fit shall have effect with respect to the home.

Notification of particulars with respect to voluntary homes

6.—(1) It shall be the duty of the person in charge of any voluntary home established after the commencement of this Act to send to the Secretary of State within three months from the establishment of the home such particulars with respect to the home as the Secretary of State may prescribe.

(2) It shall be the duty of the person in charge of any voluntary home (whether established before or after the commencement of this Act) to send to the Secretary of State such particulars with respect to the home as may be prescribed.

(3) The particulars must be sent—

    (a) in the case of a home established before the commencement of this Act, in every year, or

    (b) in the case of a home established after the commencement of this Act, in every year subsequent to the year in which particulars are sent under sub-paragraph (1),

by such date as the Secretary of State may prescribe.

(4) Where the Secretary of State by regulations varies the particulars which are to be sent to him under sub-paragraph (1) or (2) by the person in charge of a voluntary home—

    (a) that person shall send to the Secretary of State the prescribed particulars within three months from the date of the making of the regulations;

(b) where any such home was established before, but not more than three months before, the making of the regulations, compliance with paragraph (a) shall be sufficient compliance with the requirement of sub-paragraph (1) to send the prescribed particulars within three months from the establishment of the home;

(c) in the year in which the particulars are varied, compliance with paragraph (a) by the person in charge of any voluntary home shall be sufficient compliance with the requirement of sub-paragraph (2) to send the prescribed particulars before the prescribed date in that year.

(5) If the person in charge of a voluntary home fails, without reasonable excuse, to comply with any of the requirements of this paragraph he shall be guilty of an offence.

(6) Any person guilty of such an offence shall be liable on summary conviction to a fine not exceeding level 2 on the standard scale.

Part II

Regulations as to Voluntary Homes

Regulations as to conduct of voluntary homes

7.—(1) The Secretary of State may make regulations—

(a) as to the placing of children in voluntary homes;
(b) as to the conduct of such homes; and
(c) for securing the welfare of children in such homes.

(2) The regulations may, in particular—

(a) prescribe standards to which the premises used for such homes are to conform;

(b) impose requirements as to the accommodation, staff and equipment to be provided in such homes, and as to the arrangements to be made for protecting the health of children in such homes;

(c) provide for the control and discipline of children in such homes;

(d) require the furnishing to the Secretary of State of information as to the facilities provided for—

      (i) the parents of children in the homes; and

    (ii) persons who are not parents of such children but who have parental responsibility for them; and

    (iii) other persons connected with such children,

to visit and communicate with the children;

(e) authorise the Secretary of State to limit the number of children who may be accommodated in any particular voluntary home;

(f) prohibit the use of accommodation for the purpose of restricting the liberty of children in such homes;

(g) impose requirements as to the keeping of records and giving of notices with respect to children in such homes;

(h) impose requirements as to the facilities which are to be provided for giving religious instruction to children in such homes;

(i) require notice to be given to the Secretary of State of any change of the person carrying on or in charge of a voluntary home or of the premises used by such a home.

(3) The regulations may provide that a contravention of, or failure to comply with, any specified provision of the regulations without reasonable excuse shall be an offence against the regulations.

(4) Any person guilty of such an offence shall be liable to a fine not exceeding level 4 on the standard scale.

Disqualification

8. The Secretary of State may by regulation make provision with respect to the disqualification of persons in relation to voluntary homes of a kind similar to that made in relation to children's homes by section 65.

Annotation

Schedule 5: deals with voluntary homes and voluntary organisations, supplements the provisions in Part VII of the Act and concerns the registration and regulation of voluntary homes. Schedule 5 re-enacts, with certain amendments, sections 57, 57A, 57B, 57C, 57D, 59, 60 and 61 of the Child Care Act 1980. Amendments to the former legislation are mostly in Paragraph 7 of Part II of Schedule 5, which concerns the regulation-making power in respect of voluntary homes. The particular provisions which the regulations may make are aligned with the regulation-making powers in respect of community homes and registered children's homes. Note that section 62 already places a duty on local authorities to satisfy themselves that voluntary organisations which provide accommodation for children satisfactorily safeguard and promote the children's welfare. They are required to visit the children and have a duty to intervene if they are not satisfied with provisions for the children's welfare. Such intervention may involve the local authority's providing accommodation on a voluntary basis or taking compulsory measures under Parts IV and V. Local authorities are provided with a right of entry to premises to enable them to discharge their duties.

Paragraph 1: re-enacts section 57 of the Child Care Act 1980.

Paragraph 1(1): requires a person intending to carry on a voluntary home to make an application for registration in a manner prescribed by the Secretary of State.

Paragraph 1(2): empowers the Secretary of State to grant or refuse the application, or to grant the application subject to such conditions as he thinks fit.

Paragraph 1(3): empowers the Secretary of State to vary such conditions or to impose additional conditions.

Paragraph 1(4): enables the Secretary of State to cancel the registration if the conduct of a home does not comply with the regulations under Paragraph 7, or is otherwise unsatisfactory.

Paragraph 1(5): provides that it is an offence to carry on a voluntary home either (a) without being registered or (b) in contravention of a condition imposed under this Part.

Paragraph 1(6): provides the penalties for these offences under Paragraph 1(5) as fines not exceeding levels 5 and 4 respectively. Note that such scale of fines is well within those provided for throughout the Act.

Paragraph 1(7): requires the Secretary of State to notify a local authority of the registration, or cancellation of registration, of a home in their area.

Paragraph 2: deals with the procedure whereby the Secretary of State shall give notice of his intention to grant or refuse an application. Paragraph 2 replaces section 57A of the Child Care Act 1980. It requires the Secretary of State to give written notice, with reasons, of any intention to grant an application, and of any conditions, to refuse an application or to vary conditions, to cancel a registration, or to impose additional conditions. Notice need not be given if he proposes to grant an application subject to conditions which were specified in the application or which were subsequently agreed.

Paragraph 3: re-enacts section 57B of the Child Care Act 1980. It concerns the right of a person on whom notice has been served under Paragraph 2 to make representations concerning the matter.

Paragraph 3(1): requires that the notice should state that the person may, within fourteen days, require the Secretary of State to give him an opportunity to make representations.

Paragraph 3(2)(3): provides that the Secretary of State may only determine the matter if the person did not require the Secretary of State to allow him to make representations, or he has made such representations, or, having been allowed to make representations, he has failed to do so within a reasonable time.

Paragraph 3(4)(5): allows for representations to be made orally or in writing and, when orally, for this to be before a person appointed by the Secretary of State.

Paragraph 4: replaces section 57C of the Child Care Act 1980. It provides for the Secretary of State to give notice of any decision to adopt certain proposals, but for them not to take effect if no appeal is brought, until twenty eight days after the notice, or if an appeal has been brought, until it is determined or abandoned.

Paragraph 5: replaces section 57D of the Child Care Act 1980. It provides for appeals to be heard by a Registered Homes Tribunal. Notice of appeal should be given in writing to the Secretary of State within twenty eight days of the service of notice of his decision. The Tribunal can confirm or reverse a decision of the Secretary of State, and may impose or vary any condition that has been imposed, or direct that such a condition should cease to have effect, or impose any condition.

Paragraph 6: re-enacts section 59 of the Child Care Act 1980. It concerns the duty of the person in charge of a voluntary home to provide such details to the Secretary of State as he may prescribe.

Paragraph 6(1): requires such details to be sent within three months of the establishment of a home after the commencement of this Act.

Paragraph 6(2): requires, in respect of any voluntary home, such details to be sent as the Secretary of State prescribes.

Paragraph 6(3): concerns the requirement for such particulars to be sent every year.

Paragraph 6(4): enables the Secretary of State by regulations to vary the particulars which are to be sent to him and provide for the duties or the person in charge of a voluntary home when the Secretary of State does vary the requirements.

Paragraph 6(5)(6): provides for an offence of failing without reasonable excuse to comply with these requirements, subject to a penalty of a fine not exceeding level 2 on the standard scale. The "without reasonable excuse" condition is additional to the provisions of section 59(4) of the Child Care Act 1980 and the fine is amended from the former level 1 on the standard scale plus £1 for each day after conviction that the person failed to send the particulars.

Paragraph 7: introduces Part III of Schedule 5 dealing with regulations as to voluntary homes and organisations. It replaces section 60 of the Child Care Act 1980. It enables the Secretary of State to make regulations governing the conduct of voluntary homes and gives details of those provisions which the regulations may include. The current provisions are updated and amended and are aligned with regulations for community homes and registered children's homes.

Paragraph 7(1): enables regulations to be made as to placing of children in voluntary homes, the conduct of such homes and for securing the welfare of children in them.

Paragraph 7(2): lists the particular provisions which the regulations may include. These replace the provisions of section 60(1)(a) to (f) of the Child Care Act 1980. Certain new provisions are included to align with community homes regulations under Schedule 4 paragraph 4. Note Paragraph 7(2)(f), added at report stage, that the Secretary of State's power to approve the provision of secure accommodation be replaced by a regulation-making power to prohibit the use of such accommodation in relation to voluntary homes.

Paragraph 7(3)(4): provides that it is an offence to fail to comply with any such regulation, subject to a fine not exceeding level 4. This re-enacts section 60(2) of the Child Care Act 1980 but adds the qualification that the contravention should be "without reasonable excuse". We have seen throughout the Act the test of reasonableness added where an offence might have been comitted.

Paragraph 8: was added at report stage and brings into line the Secretary of State's powers in relation to voluntary homes with those in relation to children's homes referred to in section 65.

Schedule 6: Registered Children's Homes

Part I

Registration

Application for registration

1.—(1) An application for the registration of a children's home shall be made—

    (a) by the person carrying on, or intending to carry on, the home; and

    (b) to the local authority for the area in which the home is, or is to be, situated.

(2) The application shall be made in the prescribed manner and shall be accompanied by—

    (a) such particulars as may be prescribed; and

    (b) such reasonable fee as the local authority may determine.

(3) In this Schedule "prescribed" means prescribed by regulations made by the Secretary of State.

(4) If a local authority are satisfied that a children's home with respect to which an application has been made in accordance with this Schedule complies or (as the case may be) will comply—

    (a) with such requirements as may be prescribed, and

    (b) with such other requirements (if any) as appear to them to be appropriate,

they shall grant the application, either unconditionally or subject to conditions imposed under paragraph 2.

(5) Before deciding whether or not to grant an application a local authority shall comply with any prescribed requirements.

(6) Regulations made for the purposes of sub-paragraph (5) may, in particular, make provision as to the inspection of the home in question.

(7) Where an application is granted, the authority shall notify the applicant that the home has been registered under this Act as from such date as may be specified in the notice.

(8) If the authority are not satisfied as mentioned in sub-paragraph (4), they shall refuse the application.

(9) For the purposes of this Act, an application which has not been granted or refused within the period of twelve months beginning with the date when it is served on the authority shall

be deemed to have been refused by them, and the applicant shall be deemed to have been notified of their refusal at the end of that period.

(10) Where a school to which section 63(1) applies is registered it shall not cease to be a registered children's home by reason only of a subsequent change in the number of children for whom it provides accommodation.

Conditions imposed on registration

2.—(1) A local authority may grant an application for registration subject to such conditions relating to the conduct of the home as they think fit.

(2) A local authority may from time to time—

(a) vary any condition for the time being in force with respect to a home by virtue of this paragraph; or
(b) impose an additional condition,

either on the application of the person carrying on the home or without such an application.

(3) If any condition imposed or varied under this paragraph is not complied with, the person carrying on the home shall, if he has no reasonable excuse, be guilty of an offence and liable on summary conviction to a fine not exceeding level 4 on the standard scale.

Annual review of registration

3.—(1) In this [*Part*] [section] "the responsible authority", in relation to a registered children's home means the local authority who registered it.

(2) The responsible authority for a registered children's home shall, at the end of the period of twelve months beginning with the date of registration, and annually thereafter, review its registration for the purpose of determining whether the registration should continue in force or be cancelled under paragraph 4(3).

(3) If on any such annual review the responsible authority are satisfied that the home is being carried on in accordance with the

Note: The words in *italics* within square brackets were deleted by the Courts and Legal Services Act 1990.
Note: The words within square brackets were inserted by the Courts and Legal Services Act 1990.

relevant requirements they shall determine that, subject to sub-paragraph (4), the registration should continue in force.

(4) The responsible authority shall give to the person carrying on the home notice of their determination under sub-paragraph (3) and the notice shall require him to pay to the authority with respect to the review such reasonable fee as the authority may determine.

(5) It shall be a condition of the home's continued registration that the fee is so paid before the expiry of the period of twenty-eight days beginning with the date on which the notice is received by the person carrying on the home.

(6) In this Schedule "the relevant requirements" means any requirements of Part VIII and of any regulations made under paragraph 10, and any conditions imposed under paragraph 2.

Cancellation of registration

4.—(1) The person carrying on a registered children's home may at any time make an application, in such manner and including such particulars as may be prescribed, for the cancellation by the responsible authority of the registration of the home.

(2) If the authority are satisfied, in the case of a school registered by virtue of section 63(6), that it is no longer a school to which that provision applies, the authority shall give to the person carrying on the home notice that the registration of the home has been cancelled as from the date of the notice.

(3) If on any annual review under paragraph 3, or at any other time, it appears to the responsible authority that a registered home is being carried on otherwise than in accordance with the relevant requirements, they may determine that the registration of the home should be cancelled.

(4) The responsible authority may at any time determine that the registration of a home should be cancelled on the ground—

    (a) that the person carrying on the home has been convicted of an offence under this Part or any regulations made under paragraph 10; or

    (b) that any other person has been convicted of such an offence in relation to the home.

Procedure

5. —(1) Where—

(a) a person applies for the registration of a children's home; and

(b) the local authority propose to grant his application,

they shall give him written notice of their proposal and of the conditions (if any) subject to which they propose to grant his application.

(2) The authority need not give notice if they propose to grant the application subject only to conditions which—

(a) the applicant specified in the application; or

(b) the authority and the applicant have subsequently agreed.

(3) The authority shall give an applicant notice of a proposal to refuse his application.

(4) The authority shall give any person carrying on a registered children's home notice of a proposal—

(a) to cancel the registration;

(b) to vary any condition for the time being in force with respect to the home by virtue of Part VIII; or

(c) to impose any additional condition.

(5) A notice under this paragraph shall give the local authority's reasons for their proposal.

Right to make representations

6. —(1) A notice under paragraph 5 shall state that within 14 days of service of the notice any person on whom it is served may in writing require the local authority to give him an opportunity to make representations to them concerning the matter.

(2) Where a notice has been served under paragraph 5, the local authority shall not determine the matter until—

(a) any person on whom the notice was served has made representations to them concerning the matter;

(b) the period during which any such person could have required the local authority to give him an opportunity to make representations has elapsed without their being required to give such an opportunity; or

(c) the conditions specified in sub-paragraph (3) below are satisfied.

(3) The conditions are—

(a) that a person on whom the notice was served has required the local authority to give him an opportunity to make representations to them concerning the matter;

(b) that the authority have allowed him a reasonable period to make his representations; and

(c) that he has failed to make them within that period.

(4) The representations may be made, at the option of the person making them, either in writing or orally.

(5) If he informs the local authority that he desires to make oral representations, the authority shall give him an opportunity of appearing before and of being heard by a committee or sub-committee of theirs.

Decision of local authority

7.—(1) If the local authority decide to adopt a proposal of theirs to grant an application, they shall serve notice in writing of their decision on any person on whom they were required to serve notice of their proposal.

(2) A notice under this paragraph shall be accompanied by an explanation of the right of appeal conferred by paragraph 8.

(3) A decision of a local authority, other than a decision to grant an application for registration subject only to such conditions as are mentioned in paragraph 5(2) or to refuse an application for registration, shall not take effect—

(a) if no appeal is brought, until the end of the period of 28 days referred to in paragraph 8(3); and

(b) if an appeal is brought, until it is determined or abandoned.

Appeals

8.—(1) An appeal against a decision of a local authority under Part VIII shall lie to a Registered Homes Tribunal.

(2) An appeal shall be brought by notice in writing given to the local authority.

(3) No appeal shall be brought by a person more than 28 days after service on him of notice of the decision.

(4) On an appeal the Tribunal may confirm the local authority's decision or direct that it shall not have effect.

(5) A Tribunal shall also have power on an appeal—

    (a) to vary any condition in force with respect to the home to which the appeal relates by virtue of paragraph 2;

    (b) to direct that any such condition shall cease to have effect; or

    (c) to direct that any such condition as it thinks fit shall have effect with respect to the home.

(6) A local authority shall comply with any direction given by a Tribunal under this paragraph.

Prohibition on further applications

9.—(1) Where an application for the registration of a home is refused, no further application may be made within the period of six months beginning with the date when the applicant is notified of the refusal.

(2) Sub-paragraph (1) shall have effect, where an appeal against the refusal of an application is determined or abandoned, as if the reference to the date when the applicant is notified of the refusal were a reference to the date on which the appeal is determined or abandoned.

(3) Where the registration of a home is cancelled, no application for the registration of the home shall be made within the period of six months beginning with the date of cancellation.

(4) Sub-paragraph (3) shall have effect, where an appeal against the cancellation of the registration of a home is determined or abandoned, as if the reference to the date of cancellation were a reference to the date on which the appeal is determined or abandoned.

Part II

Regulations

10.—(1) The Secretary of State may make regulations—

    (a) as to the placing of children in registered children's homes;

    (b) as to the conduct of such homes; and

    (c) for securing the welfare of the children in such homes.

(2) The regulations may in particular—

    (a) prescribe standards to which the premises used for such homes are to conform;

(b) impose requirements as to the accommodation, staff and equipment to be provided in such homes;

(c) impose requirements as to the arrangements to be made for protecting the health of children in such homes;

(d) provide for the control and discipline of children in such homes;

(e) require the furnishing to the responsible authority of information as to the facilities provided for—

(i) the parents of children in such homes;

(ii) persons who are not parents of such children but who have parental responsibility for them; and

(iii) other persons connected with such children,

to visit and communicate with the children;

(f) impose requirements as to the keeping of records and giving of notices with respect to children in such homes;

(g) impose requirements as to the facilities which are to be provided for giving religious instruction to children in such homes;

(h) make provision as to the carrying out of annual reviews under paragraph 3;

(i) authorise the responsible authority to limit the number of children who may be accommodated in any particular registered home;

(j) prohibit the use of accommodation for the purpose of restricting the liberty of children in such homes;

(k) require notice to be given to the responsible authority of any change of the person carrying on or in charge of a registered home or of the premises used by such a home;

(l) make provision similar to that made by regulations under section 26.

(3) The regulations may provide that a contravention of or failure to comply with any specified provision of the regulations, without reasonable excuse, shall be an offence against the regulations.

(4) Any person guilty of such an offence shall be liable on summary conviction to a fine not exceeding level 4 on the standard scale.

Annotation

Schedule 6: replaces sections 3 to 8 of the Children's Homes Act 1982, including those added by the Health and Social Services and Social Security Adjudications Act 1983, known as "HASSASSA". The replacement is with provisions of equivalent effect, with certain amendments. Apart from updated references, including those required by amendments in sections 63 to 65, the main change in the provisions in Schedule 6 is in the power of the Secretary of State to make regulations as to the conduct of registered children's homes. As with the equivalent powers to make regulations in respect of community and voluntary homes, this has been amended in order that the regulations for each of these types of home may be more closely aligned.

Paragraph 1: replaces section 3 of the Children's Homes Act 1982. It includes provisions concerning the manner in which an application shall be made, including provision for a fee to be charged, the local authority's powers and duties in respect of granting or refusing an application and the period within which the local authority should grant or refuse the application. Note also Paragraph 1(5)(6), added at report stage, which provides specifically for regulations that make provision as to the inspection of the home in question. Although it was unlikely that any authority would register a home without first inspecting it, the Bill as drafted did not require a pre-registration inspection. Hence the addition of Paragraph 1(5)(6) at report stage.

Paragraph 2: replaces section 4 of the Children's Homes Act 1982. Paragraph 2 enables the local authority on granting an application to attach such conditions as they think fit. They may also vary such conditions or impose additional ones. Failure to comply without reasonable excuse is an offence subject to a fine not exceeding level 4. The qualification of "without reasonable excuse" is new and follows the introduction of the test of reasonableness in relation to any alleged offences that may be committed in regard to the Act.

Paragraph 3: replaces section 5 of the Children's Homes Act 1982. Paragraph 3 provides for the local authority to review annually the registration of each registered children's home. Only if they are satisfied that the home is being conducted in accordance with all necessary requirements would the registration continue in force. Paragraph 3 provides for the local authority to charge a fee for the annual review and requires them to give notice of their decision as to whether the registration shall continue.

Paragraph 4: replaces section 6 of the Children's Homes Act 1982. It makes provision enabling the person carrying on a registered children's home to apply to the local authority for registration to be cancelled. It also enables the local authority to decide, in the case of a school registered by virtue of section 63(6), that the provision no longer applies, to cancel a registration, or to cancel a registration if they consider that a home is not being conducted in accordance with the necessary requirements, or where any person carrying on the home or any other person in relation to the home has been convicted of an offence under Part I Schedule 6 or any regulation made under Paragraph 10.

Paragraph 5: replaces section 6A of the Children's Homes Act 1982. It sets out the procedure to be followed wherever an application is made for registration. It requires the local authority to give notice to the applicant, including their reasons, of any proposal in respect of granting or refusing an application, unless they propose to grant the application subject only to conditions which were specified in the application or were subsequently agreed.

Paragraph 6: replaces section 6B of the Children's Homes Act 1982. It enables the person on whom notice has been served under Paragraph 5 to require the local authority to give him an opportunity to make representations concerning the matter. These provisions are identical to those which apply in respect of voluntary homes in Paragraph 3 of Schedule 5.

Paragraph 7: replaces section 6C of the Children's Homes Act 1982. It concerns the duty of a local authority to give notice of any decision which they propose to make, and provides that such a decision should not take effect until the applicant has appealed or has had the opportunity to appeal. This reflects Paragraph 4 of Schedule 5 in respect of voluntary homes.

Paragraph 8: replaces section 6D of the Children's Homes Act 1982. It provides for appeals against decisions of the local authority regarding registration of homes to be made to a Registered Homes Tribunal. An appeal must be brought within twenty eight days of notice being served and the Tribunal will be able to confirm or reverse the local authority decision, or confirm, reverse or amend any conditions which have been imposed, and may impose any new condition. This provision reflects Paragraph 5 of Schedule 5 which applies in respect of voluntary homes.

Paragraph 9: replaces section 6E of the Children's Homes Act 1982. It makes provisions prohibiting applications for registration from being made within a period of six months of a similar application being refused or of a registration being cancelled.

Paragraph 10: replaces section 8 of the Children's Homes Act 1982. It contains the power of the Secretary of State to make regulations governing the conduct of registered children's homes. The detailed provisions which may be included in the regulations are in some respects changed from those in section 8 of the 1982 Act in order to align them with the voluntary and community homes regulation-making powers under the Act insofar as this is practicable.

Paragraph 10(1): enables the Secretary of State to make regulations as to the placement of children in registered children's homes, the conduct of such homes and the securing of the welfare of the children in the homes.

Paragraph 10(2): replaces section 8(2) of the Children's Homes Act 1982. It makes certain additional provisions which the regulations may include. These are to provide for the control and discipline of children and cover the use of secure accommodation in the home.

Paragraph 10(3)(4): re-enacts section 8(4) of the Children's Homes Act 1982. This provides for an offence of failing to comply with regulations without reasonable excuse, subject to a penalty of a fine not exceeding level 4 on the standard scale. The qualification of "without reasonable excuse" is additional to the offence formerly defined in section 8(4) of the 1982 Act and is in line with the test of reasonableness introduced in this Act as a defence against alleged offences.

SCHEDULE 7: FOSTER PARENTS: LIMITS ON NUMBER OF FOSTER CHILDREN

Interpretation

1. For the purposes of this Schedule, a person fosters a child if—

   (a) he is a local authority foster parent in relation to the child;
   (b) he is a foster parent with whom the child has been placed by a voluntary organisation; or
   (c) he fosters the child privately.

The usual fostering limit

2. Subject to what follows, a person may not foster more than three children ("the usual fostering limit").

Siblings

3. A person may exceed the usual fostering limit if the children concerned are all siblings with respect to each other.

N

Exemption by local authority

4. —(1) A person may exceed the usual fostering limit if he is exempted from it by the local authority within whose area he lives.

(2) In considering whether to exempt a person, a local authority shall have regard, in particular, to—

    (a) the number of children whom the person proposes to foster;

    (b) the arrangements which the person proposes for the care and accommodation of the fostered children;

    (c) the intended and likely relationship between the person and the fostered children;

    (d) the period of time for which he proposes to foster the children; and

    (e) whether the welfare of the fostered children (and of any other children who are or will be living in the accommodation) will be safeguarded and promoted.

(3) Where a local authority exempt a person, they shall inform him by notice in writing—

    (a) that he is so exempted;

    (b) of the children, described by name, whom he may foster; and

    (c) of any condition to which the exemption is subject.

(4) A local authority may at any time by notice in writing—

    (a) vary or cancel an exemption; or

    (b) impose, vary or cancel a condition to which the exemption is subject,

and, in considering whether to do so, they shall have regard in particular to the considerations mentioned in sub-paragraph (2).

(5) The Secretary of State may make regulations amplifying or modifying the provisions of this paragraph in order to provide for cases where children need to be placed with foster parents as a matter of urgency.

Effect of exceeding fostering limit

5. —(1) A person shall cease to be treated as fostering and shall be treated as carrying on a children's home if—

    (a) he exceeds the usual fostering limit; or

    (b) where he is exempted under paragraph 4,—

      (i) he fosters any child not named in the exemption; and

      (ii) in so doing, he exceeds the usual fostering limit.

(2) Sub-paragraph (1) does not apply if the children concerned are all siblings in respect of each other.

Complaints etc.

6. —(1) Every local authority shall establish a procedure for considering any representations (including any complaint) made to them about the discharge of their functions under paragraph 4 by a person exempted or seeking to be exempted under that paragraph.

(2) In carrying out any consideration of representations under sub-paragraph (1), a local authority shall comply with any regulations made by the Secretary of State for the purposes of this paragraph.

Annotation

Schedule 7 deals with foster parents and the limitation on the number of foster children. Part IX of the Children Act replaces the Foster Children Act 1980. Local authority functions in respect of privately fostered children are similar to those under the 1980 Act. However, a number of changes have been made to come into line with local authority functions in respect of other children away from home. For example, the "usual fostering limit" of three children will apply and, unless exemption from the limit has been granted by the local authority, the arrangement will be classed as a children's home. Secondly, the welfare duty which is now owed to privately fostered children is the same as that owed to children living in children's homes and voluntary homes. Note that the power to remove a foster child from his placement has been repealed, given that emergency procedures cover such children.

Paragraph 1: interprets "foster parent" in relation both to a local authority, a private placement, or a placement by a voluntary organisation. Note that a local authority are required to satisfy themselves that the welfare of privately fostered children in their area is being satisfactorily safeguarded and promoted. They must also secure that private foster parents are given advice where it seems to be needed: see section 67(1).

Paragraph 2: imposes a requirement on private foster parents that they may not foster more than three children—the usual fostering limit. Note that a local authority may also prohibit a person from privately fostering, or from fostering a particular child, or from fostering in particular premises. Prohibitions may be imposed if a person is not suitable to foster a child, the premises are not suitable for fostering, or if it would be prejudicial to the welfare of the child for him to be fostered by the person in the premises concerned: see section 69(1)(2)(3).

Paragraph 3: provides that a person may exceed the usual fostering limit if the children concerned are all siblings with respect to each other. Note that regulations will also specify the circumstances in which a person is disqualified from privately fostering a child without the consent of the local authority: see section 68.

Paragraph 4: deals with exemption by a local authority and provides that an exempted person shall be informed by notice in writing and that the Secretary of State may make regulations amplifying or modifying the provisions in order to provide for cases where children need to be placed with foster parents as a matter of urgency. Note that, generally speaking, private foster children are those whose parents place them for more than twenty eight days by private arrangement with a family which is not related to the child. Unlike the situation under the Foster Children Act 1980, placements for less than a month will not be classed as private fostering, even if the person caring for the child is a "regular foster parent".

Paragraph 5: provides that a person shall cease to be treated as fostering and shall be treated as carrying on a children's home if he exceeds the usual fostering limit. Siblings make for an exemption. Note that the definition of "children's home" comes into play if more than three children are cared for and accommodated there, except that an independent school may be a children's home even though it provides for less than three children. See section 63(3).

Paragraph 6: provides for a complaints procedure. Note that if a local authority are not satisfied about the welfare of a child who is privately fostered they must consider whether they should exercise any of their functions under the Act: see section 67(5). They may decide to impose requirements or even a prohibition on a foster parent. The purpose of Paragraph 6, however, is to give foster parents the right to appeal against any decisions made in their regard which are covered by Paragraph 4(4) of Schedule 7.

Schedule 8: Privately Fostered Children

Exemptions

1. A child is not a privately fostered child while he is being looked after by a local authority.

2. —(1) A child is not a privately fostered child while he is in the care of any person—

(a) in premises in which any—

(i) parent of his;
(ii) person who is not a parent of his but who has parental responsibility for him; or
(iii) person who is a relative of his and who has assumed responsibility for his care,

is for the time being living;

(b) in any children's home;
(c) in accommodation provided by or on behalf of any voluntary organisation;
(d) in any school in which he is receiving full-time education;
(e) in any health service hospital;
(f) in any residential care home, nursing home or mental nursing home; or
(g) in any home or institution not specified in this paragraph but provided, equipped and maintained by the Secretary of State.

(2) Sub-paragraph (1)(b) to (g) does not apply where the person caring for the child is doing so in his personal capacity and not in the course of carrying out his duties in relation to the establishment mentioned in the paragraph in question.

3. A child is not a privately fostered child while he is in the care of any person in compliance with—

(a) an order under section 7(7)(b) of the Children and Young Persons Act 1969; or
(b) a supervision requirement within the meaning of the Social Work (Scotland) Act 1968.

4. A child is not a privately fostered child while he is liable to be detained, or subject to guardianship, under the Mental Health Act 1983.

5. A child is not a privately fostered child while—

(a) he is placed in the care of a person who proposes to

adopt him under arrangements made by an adoption agency within the meaning of —

(i) section 1 of the Adoption Act 1976;
(ii) section 1 of the Adoption (Scotland) Act 1978; or
(iii) Article 3 of the Adoption (Northern Ireland) Order 1987; or

(b) he is a protected child.

Power of local authority to impose requirements

6. —(1) Where a person is fostering any child privately, or proposes to foster any child privately, the appropriate local authority may impose on him requirements as to —

(a) the number, age and sex of the children who may be privately fostered by him;
(b) the standard of the accommodation and equipment to be provided for them;
(c) the arrangements to be made with respect to their health and safety; and
(d) particular arrangements which must be made with respect to the provision of care for them,

and it shall be his duty to comply with any such requirement before the end of such period as the authority may specify unless, in the case of a proposal, the proposal is not carried out.

(2) A requirement may be limited to a particular child, or class of child.

(3) A requirement (other than one imposed under sub-paragraph (1)(a)) may be limited by the authority so as to apply only when the number of children fostered by the person exceeds a specified number.

(4) A requirement shall be imposed by notice in writing addressed to the person on whom it is imposed and informing him of —

(a) the reason for imposing the requirement;
(b) his right under paragraph 8 to appeal against it; and
(c) the time within which he may do so.

(5) a local authority may at any time vary any requirement, impose any additional requirement or remove any requirement.

(6) In this Schedule —

(a) "the appropriate local authority" means —

(i) the local authority within whose area the child is being fostered; or

(ii) in the case of a proposal to foster a child, the local authority within whose area it is proposed that he will be fostered; and

(b) "requirement", in relation to any person, means a requirement imposed on him under this paragraph.

Regulations requiring notification of fostering etc.

7.—(1) The Secretary of State may by regulations make provision as to—

(a) the circumstances in which notification is required to be given in connection with children who are, have been or are proposed to be fostered privately; and

(b) the manner and form in which such notification is to be given.

(2) The regulations may, in particular—

(a) require any person who is, or proposes to be, involved (whether or not directly) in arranging for a child to be fostered privately to notify the appropriate authority;

(b) require any person who is—

(i) a parent of a child; or

(ii) a person who is not a parent of his but who has parental responsibility for a child,

and who knows that it is proposed that the child should be fostered privately, to notify the appropriate authority;

(c) require any parent of a privately fostered child, or person who is not a parent of such a child but who has parental responsibility for him, to notify the appropriate authority of any change in his address;

(d) require any person who proposes to foster a child privately, to notify the appropriate authority of his proposal;

(e) require any person who is fostering a child privately, or proposes to do so, to notify the appropriate authority of—

(i) any offence of which he has been convicted;

(ii) any disqualification imposed on him under section 68; or

(iii) any prohibition imposed on him under section 69;

    (f) require any person who is fostering a child privately, to notify the appropriate authority of any change in his address;

    (g) require any person who is fostering a child privately to notify the appropriate authority in writing of any person who begins, or ceases, to be part of his household;

    (h) require any person who has been fostering a child privately, but has ceased to do so, to notify the appropriate authority (indicating, where the child has died, that that is the reason).

Appeals

8.—(1) A person aggrieved by—

    (a) a requirement imposed under paragraph 6;

    (b) a refusal of consent under section 68;

    (c) a prohibition imposed under section 69;

    (d) a refusal to cancel such a prohibition;

    (e) a refusal to make an exemption under paragraph 4 of Schedule 7;

    (f) a condition imposed in such an exemption; or

    (g) a variation or cancellation of such an exemption,

may appeal to the court.

(2) The appeal must be made within fourteen days from the date on which the person appealing is notified of the requirement, refusal, prohibition, condition, variation or cancellation.

(3) Where the appeal is against—

    (a) a requirement imposed under paragraph 6;

    (b) a condition of an exemption imposed under paragraph 4 of Schedule 7; or

    (c) a variation or cancellation of such an exemption,

the requirement, condition, variation or cancellation shall not have effect while the appeal is pending.

(4) Where it allows an appeal against a requirement or prohibition, the court may, instead of cancelling the requirement or prohibition—

    (a) vary the requirement, or allow more time for compliance with it; or

    (b) if an absolute prohibition has been imposed, substitute for it a prohibition on using the premises after such time as the court may specify unless such specified requirements as the local authority had power to impose under paragraph 6 are complied with.

(5) Any requirement or prohibition specified or substituted by a court under this paragraph shall be deemed for the purposes of Part IX (other than this paragraph) to have been imposed by the local authority under paragraph 6 or (as the case may be) section 69.

(6) Where it allows an appeal against a refusal to make an exemption, a condition imposed in such an exemption or a variation or cancellation of such an exemption, the court may—

(a) make an exemption;
(b) impose a condition; or
(c) vary the exemption.

(7) Any exemption made or varied under sub-paragraph (6), or any condition imposed under that sub-paragraph, shall be deemed for the purposes of Schedule 7 (but not for the purposes of this paragraph) to have been made, varied or imposed under that Schedule.

(8) Nothing in sub-paragraph (1)(e) to (g) confers any right of appeal on—

(a) a person who is, or would be if exempted under Schedule 7, a local authority foster parent; or
(b) a person who is, or would be if so exempted, a person with whom a child is placed by a voluntary organisation.

Extension of Part IX to certain school children during holidays

9.—(1) Where a child under sixteen who is a pupil at a school which is not maintained by a local education authority lives at the school during school holidays for a period of more than two weeks, Part IX shall apply in relation to the child as if—

(a) while living at the school, he were a privately fostered child; and
(b) paragraphs 2(1)(d) and 6 were omitted.

(2) Sub-paragraph (3) applies to any person who proposes to care for and accommodate one or more children at a school in circumstances in which some or all of them will be treated as private foster children by virtue of this paragraph.

(3) That person shall, not less than two weeks before the first of those children is treated as a private foster child by virtue of this paragraph during the holiday in question, give written notice

of his proposal to the local authority within whose area the child is ordinarily resident ("the appropriate authority"), stating the estimated number of the children.

(4) A local authority may exempt any person from the duty of giving notice under sub-paragraph (3).

(5) Any such exemption may be granted for a special period or indefinitely and may be revoked at any time by notice in writing given to the person exempted.

(6) Where a child who is treated as a private foster child by virtue of this paragraph dies, the person caring for him at the school shall, not later than 48 hours after the death, give written notice of it—

(a) to the appropriate local authority; and
(b) where reasonably practicable, to each parent of the child and to every person who is not a parent of his but who has parental responsibility for him.

(7) Where a child who is treated as a foster child by virtue of this paragraph ceases for any other reason to be such a child, the person caring for him at the school shall give written notice of the fact to the appropriate local authority.

Prohibition of advertisements relating to fostering

10. No advertisement indicating that a person will undertake, or will arrange for, a child to be privately fostered shall be published, unless it states that person's name and address.

Avoidance of insurances on lives of privately fostered children

11. A person who fosters a child privately and for reward shall be deemed for the purposes of the Life Assurance Act 1774 to have no interest in the life of the child.

Annotation

Schedule 8: adds to Schedule 7 and deals with privately fostered children. Schedule 8 supplements the provisions of Part IX of the Act. Part IX and Schedules 7 and 8 represent the re-enactment, with amendments, of the Foster Children Act 1980: see also sections 66 to 70. Section 12 of the 1980 Act is not re-enacted, as removal of children is possible where there is a likelihood of significant harm. Note that there is no concept of a regular foster parent. To be privately fostered a child must not be looked after by a local authority, in which case a family placement will usually be with a local authority foster parent, or on behalf of a voluntary organisation: see Schedule 8 paragraph 1 and 2(c). Also a proposal to foster a child privately must be notified to the local authority in whose area the fostering will take place. The detailed requirements of notification will be set down in regulations: see Schedule 8 paragraph 7.

Paragraphs 1–5: provide for exceptions to the definition of a privately fostered child given in section 66. Paragraphs 1–5 replace with equivalent effect, and with updated references, section 1 of the Foster Children Act 1980. In particular, a child who is looked after by a local authority is not a privately fostered child. Such children will be covered by regulations governing local authority fostering.

Paragraph 6: enables a local authority to impose requirements on any person who is keeping, or intends to keep, a private foster child. Paragraph 6 replaces section 9 of the Foster Children Act 1980, taking into account that institutional placements are generally to be covered by Part VIII dealing with registered children's homes. Paragraph 7 of Schedule 8 now reflects the situation of a private family household and provides for requirements generally including the standard of accommodation, arrangements for the care of the child, as well as requirements in respect of the number, age and sex of the children who may be privately fostered.

Paragraph 7: provides for the Secretary of State to make regulations in respect of notification requirements for privately fostered children. Regulations can be made currently under section 4 of the Foster Children Act 1980 in respect of notification to the local authority by parents who arrange, or who intend to arrange, for their children to be privately fostered. The regulations under Paragraph 7 will include notification by parents as well as the provisions formerly in sections 5 and 6 of the Act: notification by persons keeping, or intending to keep, a privately fostered child, and by persons ceasing to keep such a child. The extent of the regulation-making power will be equivalent to the combined effect of the former sections 4 to 6.

Paragraph 8: replaces with equivalent effect section 11 of the Foster Children Act 1980. This deals with appeals against a requirement or prohibition imposed upon a person by a local authority in respect of private fostering or disqualification. Paragraph 8 extends section 11 to refusals to consent to fostering by disqualified persons. Rules of court will provide for the court in which an appeal will be heard.

Paragraph 9: replaces, with some amendments, the provisions of section 17 of the Foster Children Act 1980 regarding certain children who remain in school during school holidays. This applies in respect of independent schools where the school continues to accommodate a child who is a pupil at the school during school holidays for over two weeks. In such circumstances the child is treated as a privately fostered child but subject to the provisions of Paragraph 9. Paragraph 9 amends the former section 17 of the 1980 Act.

Paragraph 10: replaces section 15 of the Foster Children Act 1980 which prohibits people from advertising themselves as prospective foster parents. The power to make regulations prohibiting parents from advertising for a person to care for a child is not replaced; regulations have not been made under this power which it is considered could unnecessarily interfere with a parent's capacity to make the most appropriate arrangements for the care of a child.

Paragraph 11: replaces with equivalent effect section 19 of the Foster Children Act 1980, which provides that a person who privately fosters a child for reward shall have no interest in the life of the child for the purposes of the Life Assurance Act 1774.

SCHEDULE 9: CHILD MINDING AND DAY CARE FOR YOUNG CHILDREN

Applications for registration

1.—(1) An application for registration under section 71 shall be of no effect unless it contains—

    (a) a statement with respect to the applicant which complies with the requirements of regulations made for the purposes of this paragraph by the Secretary of State; and

    (b) a statement with respect to any person assisting or likely to be assisting in looking after children on the premises in question, or living or likely to be living there, which complies with the requirements of such regulations.

(2) Where a person provides, or proposes to provide, day care for children under the age of eight on different premises situated within the area of the same local authority, he shall make a separate application with respect to each of those premises.

(3) An application under section 71 shall be accompanied by such fee as may be prescribed.

(4) On receipt of an application for registration under section

71 from any person who is acting, or proposes to act, in any way which requires him to be registered under that section, a local authority shall register him if the application is properly made and they are not otherwise entitled to refuse to do so.

Disqualification from registration

2.—(1) A person may not be registered under section 71 if he is disqualified by regulations made by the Secretary of State for the purposes of this paragraph [unless—

(a) he has disclosed the fact to the appropriate local authority; and

(b) obtained their written consent]

(2) The regulations may, in particular, provide for a person to be disqualified where—

(a) an order of a prescribed kind has been made at any time with respect to him;

(b) any order of a prescribed kind has been made at any time with respect to any child who has been in his care;

(c) a requirement of a prescribed kind has been imposed at any time with respect to such a child, under or by virtue of any enactment;

(d) he has at any time been refused registration under Part X or any other prescribed enactment or had any such registration cancelled;

(e) he has been convicted of any offence of a prescribed kind, or has been placed on probation or discharged absolutely or conditionally for any such offence;

(f) he has at any time been disqualified from fostering a child privately;

(g) a prohibition has been imposed on him at any time under section [*61*], [69] section 10 of the Foster Children (Scotland) Act 1984 or any other prescribed enactment;

(h) his rights and powers with respect to a child have at any time been vested in a prescribed authority under a prescribed enactment.

(3) A person who lives—

(a) in the same household as a person who is himself disqualified by the regulations; or

Note: The words within square brackets were inserted by the Courts and Legal Services Act 1990.
Note: The figures *in italics* within square brackets were deleted by the Courts and Legal Services Act 1990.

(b) in a household at which any such person is employed,

shall be disqualified unless he has disclosed the fact to the appropriate local authority and obtained their written consent.

(4) A person who is disqualified shall not provide day care, or be concerned in the management of, or have any financial interest in, any provision of day care unless he has—

(a) disclosed the fact to the appropriate local authority; and
(b) obtained their written consent.

(5) No person shall employ, in connection with the provision of day care, a person who is disqualified, unless he has—

(a) disclosed to the appropriate local authority the fact that that person is so disqualified; and
(b) obtained their written consent.

(6) In this paragraph "enactment" means any enactment having effect, at any time, in any part of the United Kingdom.

Exemption of certain schools

3.—(1) Section 71 does not apply in relation to any child looked after in any—

(a) school maintained or assistedby a local education authority;
(b) school under the management of an education authority;
(c) school in respect of which payments are made by the Secretary of State under section 100 of the Education Act 1944;
(d) independent school;
(e) grant-aided school;
(f) grant maintained school;
(g) self-governing school;
(h) play centre maintained or assisted by a local education authority under section 53 of the Act of 1944, or by an education authority under section 6 of the Education (Scotland) Act 1980.

(2) The exemption provided by sub-paragraph (1) only applies where the child concerned is being looked after in accordance with provision for day care made by—

(a) the person carrying on the establishment in question as part of the establishment's activities; or
(b) a person employed to work at that establishment and authorised to make that provision as part of the establishment's activities.

(3) In sub-paragraph (1)—

"assisted" and "maintained" have the same meanings as in the Education Act 1944;

"grant maintained" has the same meaning as in section 52(3) of the Education Reform Act 1988; and

"grant-aided school", "self-governing school" and (in relation to Scotland) "independent school" have the same meaning as in the Education (Scotland) Act 1980.

Exemption for other establishments

4.—(1) Section 71(1)(b) does not apply in relation to any child looked after in—

(a) a registered children's home;

(b) a voluntary home;

(c) a community home;

(d) a residential care home, nursing home or mental nursing home required to be registered under the Registered Homes Act 1984;

(e) a health service hospital;

(f) a home provided, equipped and maintained by the Secretary of State; or

(g) an establishment which is required to be registered under section 61 of the Social Work (Scotland) Act 1968.

(2) The exemption provided by sub-paragraph (1) only applies where the child concerned is being looked after in accordance with provision for day care made by—

(a) the department, authority or other person carrying on the establishment in question as part of the establishment's activities; or

(b) a person employed to work at that establishment and authorised to make that provision as part of the establishment's activities.

(3) In this paragraph "a health service hospital" includes a health service hospital within the meaning of the National Health Service (Scotland) Act 1978.

Exemption for occasional facilities

5.—(1) Where day care for children under the age of eight is provided in particular premises on less than six days in any year, that provision shall be disregarded for the purposes of section 71 if the person making it has notified the appropriate local authority in writing before the first occasion on which the premises concerned are so used in that year.

(2) In sub-paragraph (1) "year" means the year beginning with the day on which the day care in question is (after the commencement of this paragraph) first provided in the premises concerned and any subsequent year.

Certificates of registration

6. —(1) Where a local authority register a person under section 71 they shall issue him with a certificate of registration.

(2) The certificate shall specify—

  (a) the registered person's name and address;
  (b) in a case falling within section 71(1)(b), the address or situation of the premises concerned; and
  (c) any requirements imposed under section 72 or 73.

(3) Where, due to a change of circumstances, any part of the certificate requires to be amended, the authority shall issue an amended certificate.

(4) Where the authority are satisfied that the certificate has been lost or destroyed, they shall issue a copy, on payment by the registered person of such fee as may be prescribed.

Fees for annual inspection of premises

7. —(1) Where—

  (a) a person is registered under section 71, and
  (b) the local authority concerned make an annual inspection of the premises in question under section 76,

they shall serve on that person a notice informing him that the inspection is to be carried out and requiring him to pay to them such fee as may be prescribed.

(2) It shall be a condition of the continued registration of that person under section 71 that the fee is so paid before the expiry of the period of twenty-eight days beginning with the date on which the inspection is carried out.

Co-operation between authorities

8. —(1) Where it appears to a local authority that any local education authority or, in Scotland, education authority could, by

taking any specified action, help in the exercise of any of their functions under Part X, they may request the help of that local education authority, or education authority, specifying the action in question.

(2) An authority whose help is so requested shall comply with the request if it is compatible with their own statutory or other duties and obligations and does not unduly prejudice the discharge of any of their functions.

Annotation

Schedule 9: deals with child minding and day care for young children and links with section 71 and Part X of the Act, which modifies and updates the Nurseries and Child Minders Regulation Act 1948, which is repealed. The purpose behind the changes was that the private and voluntary sectors were showing considerable interest in developing day care services. It was the view of the government that private and voluntary provision are complementary to a local authority's own provision, both for children under five and in the developing field of out-of-school and holiday schemes for school-aged children: see Minister of State, Hansard 6 June 1989, Standing Committee B.

Paragraph 1: deals with applications for registration. A new registration system is introduced and the law makes clear who should and should not be registered. The registration system is designed to ensure that independent people provide particular services to an acceptable standard. Thus, applications for registration will have to contain a statement about the applicant and those who are likely to look after children or live on the premises in question.

Paragraph 2: deals with disqualification from registration and provides that it will be for a local authority to check whether any persons are disqualified from being registered. Disqualification arises if one of the circumstances prescribed in regulations apply to them, such as that they have committed certain offences or previously had registration cancelled.

Paragraph 3: deals with the exemption of certain schools. Pursuant to Schedule 9 people do not need to be registered in respect of child minding or day care if the children concerned are being looked after in a school, except in respect of any independent nursery school which operates as a day nursery as part of the school's activities.

Paragraph 4: provides that persons need not be registered in respect of day care where children are looked after in certain homes and hospitals, and it is provided as part of the establishment's activities by the person who carries on the home or hospital or an authorised employee. The exemptions under Paragraph 3 and 4 are similar to those under the former law. They do not apply if the premises are used to provide day care or child minding by an outside agent, that is to say someone who neither runs the establishment in question nor is an authorised employee. There is a new exemption from registration in favour of occasional facilities such as *crèches*.

Paragraph 5: provides that where day care is provided on particular premises for less than six days a year registration is not required, provided that the local authority are notified in writing before the first time the premises are used in that year.

Paragraph 6: deals with certificates of registration. If registration is granted, a certificate must be issued. This certificate should specify any requirements which have been imposed on the applicant.

Paragraph 7: deals with fees for annual inspection of premises. A person authorised by the local authority may enter premises in which child minding is being carried on or day care is provided. A fee may be charged for annual inspection.

Paragraph 8: deals with cooperation between authorities. Thus, local education authorities are placed under a new duty to assist a local authority which so requests with respect to their functions under Part X, provided that the assistance requested is compatible with their own obligations and does not unduly prejudice the discharge of their functions.

Schedule 10: Amendments of Adoption Legislation

Part I

Amendments of Adoption Act 1976 (c. 36)

1. In section 2 (local authorities' social services) for the words from "relating to" to the end there shall be substituted—

> "(a) under the Children Act 1989, relating to family assistance orders, local authority support for children and families, care and supervision and emergency protection of children, community homes, voluntary homes and organisations, registered children's homes, private arrangements for fostering children, child minding and day care for young children and children accommodated by health author-

ities and local education authorities or in residential care, nursing or mental nursing homesor in independent schools; and

(b) under the National Health Service Act 1977, relating to the provision of care for expectant and nursing mothers."

2. In section 11 (restrictions on arranging adoptions and placing of children) for subsection (2) there shall be substituted—

"(2) An adoption society which is—

(a) approved as respects Scotland under section 3 of the Adoption (Scotland) Act 1978; or

(b) registered as respects Northern Ireland under Article 4 of the Adoption (Northern Ireland) Order 1987,

but which is not approved under section 3 of this Act, shall not act as an adoption society in England and Wales except to the extent that the society considers it necessary to do so in the interests of a person mentioned in section 1 of the Act of 1978 or Article 3 of the Order of 1987."

3.—(1) In section 12 (adoption orders), in subsection (1) for the words "vesting the parental rights and duties relating to a child in" there shall be substituted "giving parental responsibility for a child to".

(2) In subsection (2) of that section for the words "the parental rights and duties so far as they relate" there shall be substituted "parental responsibility so far as it relates".

(3) In subsection (3) of that section for paragraph (a) there shall be substituted—

"(a) the parental responsibility which any person has for the child immediately before the making of the order;

(aa) any order under the Children Act 1989";

and in paragraph (b) for the words from "for any period" to the end there shall be substituted "or upbringing for any period after the making of the order."

4. For section 14(1) (adoption by married couple) there shall be substituted—

"(1) an adoption order shall not be made on the application of more than one person except in the circumstances specified in subsections (1A) and (1B).

(1A) An adoption order may be made on the application

of a married couple where both the husband and the wife have attained the age of 21 years.

(1B) An adoption order may be made on the application of a married couple where—

(a) the husband or the wife—

(i) is the father or mother of the child; and
(ii) has attained the age of 18 years;

and

(b) his or her spouse has attained the age of 21 years."

5.—(1) In section 16 (parental agreement), in subsection (1) for the words from "in England" to "Scotland)" there shall be substituted—

"(i) in England and Wales, under section 18;
(ii) in Scotland, under section 18 of the Adoption (Scotland) Act 1978; or
(iii) in Northern Ireland, under Article 17(1) or 18(1) of the Adoption (Northern Ireland) Order 1987."

(2) In subsection (2)(c) of that section for the words "the parental duties in relation to" there shall be substituted "his parental responsibility for".

6.—(1) In section 18 (freeing child for adoption), after subsection (2) there shall be inserted—

"(2A) For the purposes of subsection (2) a child is in the care of an adoption agency if the adoption agency is a local authority and he is in their care."

(2) In subsection (5) of that section, for the words from "the parental rights" to "vest in" there shall be substituted "parental responsibility for the child is given to", and for the words "and (3)" there shall be substituted "to (4)".

(3) For subsections (7) and (8) of that section there shall be substituted—

"(7) Before making an order under this section in the case of a child whose father does not have parental responsibility for him, the court shall satisfy itself in relation to any person claiming to be the father that—

(a) he has no intention of applying for—

(i) an order under section 4(1) of the Children Act 1989, or

(ii) a residence order under section 10 of that Act, or

(b) if he did make any such application, it would be likely to be refused.

(8) Subsections (5) and (7) of section 12 apply in relation to the making of an order under this section as they apply in relation to the making of an order under that section."

7. In section 19(1) (progress reports to former parents) for the words "in which the parental rights and duties were vested" there shall be substituted "to which parental responsibility was given".

8.—(1) In section 20 (revocation of section 18 order), in subsections (1) and (2) for the words "the parental rights and duties", in both places where they occur, there shall be substituted "parental responsibility".

(2) For subsection (3) of that section there shall be substituted—

"(3) the revocation of an order under section 18 ("a section 18 order") operates—

(a) to extinguish the parental responsibility given to the adoption agency under the section 18 order;

(b) to give parental responsibility for the child to—

(i) the child's mother; and
(ii) where the child's father and mother were married to each other at the time of his birth, the father; and

(c) to revive—

(i) any parental responsibility agreement,
(ii) any order under section 4(1) of the Children Act 1989, and
(iii) any appointment of a guardian in respect of the child (whether made by a court or otherwise),

extinguished by the making of the section 18 order.

(3A) Subject to subsection (3)(c), the revocation does not—

(a) operate to revive—

(i) any order under the Children Act 1989, or
(ii) any duty referred to in section 12(3)(b),

extinguished by the making of the section 18 order; or

(b) affect any person's parental responsibility so far as it relates to the period between the making of the section 18 order and the date of revocation of that order."

9. For section 21 (transfer of parental rights and duties between adoption agencies) there shall be substituted—

"Variation of section 18 order so as to substitute one adoption agency for another.

21.—(1) On an application to which this section applies, an authorised court may vary an order under section 18 so as to give parental responsibility for the child to another adoption agency ("the substitute agency') in place of the agency for the time being having parental responsibility for the child under the order ('the existing agency').

(2) This section applies to any application made jointly by—

(a) the existing agency; and
(b) the would-be substitute agency.

(3) Where an order under section 18 is varied under this section, section 19 shall apply as if the substitute agency had been given responsibility for the child on the making of the order."

10.—(1) In section 22 (notification to local authority of adoption application), after subsection (1) there shall be inserted the following subsections

"(1A) An application for such an adoption order shall not be made unless the person wishing to make the application has, within the period of two years preceding the making of the application, given notice as mentioned in subsection (1).—

(1B) In subsections (1) and (1A) the references to the area in which the applicant or person has his home are references to the area in which he has his home at the time of giving the notice."

(2) In subsection (4) of that section for the word "receives" there shall be substituted "receive" and for the words "in the care of" there shall be substituted "looked after by".

11. In section 25(1) (interim orders) for the words "vesting the legal custody of the child in" there shall be substituted "giving parental responsibility for the child to".

12. In—

    (a) section 27(1) and (2) (restrictions on removal where adoption agreed or application made under section 18); and

    (b) section 28(1) and (2) (restrictions on removal where applicant has provided home for 5 years),

for the words "actual custody", in each place where they occur, there shall be substituted "home".

13. After section 27(2) there shall be inserted—

    "(2A) For the purposes of subsection (2) a child is in the care of an adoption agency if the adoption agency is a local authority and he is in their care."

14.—(1) After section 28(2) there shall be inserted—

    "(2A) The reference in subsections (1) and (2) to any enactment does not include a reference to section 20(8) of the Children Act 1989".

(2) For subsection (3) of that section there shall be substituted—

    "(3) In any case where subsection (1) or (2) applies and—

        (a) the child was being looked after by a local authority before he began to have his home with the applicant or, as the case may be, the prospective adopter, and

        (b) the child is still being looked after by a local authority,

the authority which are looking after the child shall not remove him from the home of the applicant or the prospective adopter except in accordance with section 30 or 31 or with the leave of a court."

(3) In subsection (5) of that section—

    (a) for the word "receives" there shall be substituted "receive"; and

    (b) for the words "in the care of another local authority or of a voluntary organisation" there shall be substituted "looked after by another local authority".

15. In section 29 (return of child taken away in breach of section 27 or 28) for subsections (1) and (2) there shall be substituted—

    "(1) An authorised court may, on the application of a

person from whose home a child has been removed in breach of —

    (a) section 27 or 28,

    (b) section 27 or 28 of the Adoption (Scotland) Act 1978, or

    (c) Article 28 or 29 of the Adoption (Northern Ireland) Order 1987,

order the person who has so removed the child to return the child to the applicant.

(2) An authorised court may, on the application of a person who has reasonable grounds for believing that another person is intending to remove a child from his home in breach of —

    (a) section 27 or 28,

    (b) section 27 or 28 of the Adoption (Scotland) Act 1978, or

    (c) Article 28 or 29 of the Adoption (Northern Ireland) Order 1987,

by order direct that other person not to remove the child from the applicant's home in breach of any of those provisions.'

16. —(1) In section 30 (return of children placed for adoption by adoption agencies), in subsection (1) there shall be substituted —

    (a) for the words "delivered into the actual custody of" the words "placed with";

    (b) in paragraph (a) for the words "retain the actual custody of the child" the words "give the child a home"; and

    (c) in paragraph (b) for the words "actual custody" the word "home".

(2) In subsection (3) of that section for the words "in his actual custody" there shall be substituted "with him".

17. —(1) In section 31 (application of section 30 where child not placed for adoption), in subsection (1) for the words from "child", where it first occurs, to "except" there shall be substituted "child —

    (a) who is (when the notice is given) being looked after by a local authority; but

    (b) who was placed with that person otherwise than in pursuance of such arrangements as are mentioned in section 30(1),

that section shall apply as if the child had been placed in pursuance of such arrangements".

(2) In subsection (2) of that section for the words "for the time being in the care of" there shall be substituted "(when the notice is given) being looked after by".

(3) In subsection (3) of that section—

(a) for the words "remains in the actual custody of" there shall be substituted "has his home with"; and

(b) for the words "section 45 of the Child Care Act 1980" there shall be substituted "Part III of Schedule 2 to the Children Act 1989".

(4) At the end of that section there shall be added—

"(4) Nothing in this section affects the right of any person who has parental responsibility for a child to remove him under section 20(8) of the Children Act 1989".

18.—(1) In section 32 (meaning of "protected child"), in subsection (2) for the words "section 37 of the Adoption Act 1958" there shall be substituted—

"(a) section 32 of the Adoption (Scotland) Act 1978; or

(b) Article 33 of the Adoption (Northern Ireland) Order 1987."

(2) In subsection (3) of that section for paragraph (a) there shall be substituted—

"(a) he is in the care of any person—

(i) in any community home, voluntary home or registered children's home;

(ii) in any school in which he is receiving full-time education;

(iii) in any health service hospital";

and at the end of that subsection there shall be added—

"(d) he is in the care of any person in any home or institution not specified in this subsection but provided, equipped and maintained by the Secretary of State."

(3) After that subsection there shall be inserted—

"(3A) In subsection (3) 'community home', 'voluntary home', 'registered children's home', 'school' and 'health service hospital' have the same meaning as in the Children Act 1989."

(4) For subsection (4) of that section there shall be substituted—

"(4) A protected child ceases to be a protected child—

(a) on the grant or refusal of the application for an adoption order;

(b) on the notification to the local authority for the area where the child has his home that the application for an adoption order has been withdrawn;

(c) in a case where no application is made for an adoption order, on the expiry of the period of two years from the giving of the notice;

(d) on the making of a residence order, a care order or a supervision order under the Children Act 1989 in respect of the child;

(e) on the appointment of a guardian for him under that Act;

(f) on his attaining the age of 18 years; or

(g) on his marriage,

whichever first occurs.

(5) In subsection (4)(d) the references to a care order and a supervision order do not include references to an interim care order or interim supervision order."

19.—(1) In section 35 (notices and information to be given to local authorities), in subsection (1) for the words "who has a protected child in his actual custody" there shall be substituted "with whom a protected child has his home".

(2) In subsection (2) of that section for the words "in whose actual custody he was" there shall be substituted "with whom he had his home".

20.—(1) In section 51 (disclosure of birth records of adopted children), in subsection (1) for the words "subsections (4) and (6)" there shall be substituted "what follows".

(2) For subsections (3) to (7) of that section there shall be substituted—

"(3) Before supplying any information to an applicant under subsection (1), the Registrar General shall inform the applicant that counselling services are available to him—

(a) if he is in England and Wales—

(i) at the General Register Office;

(ii) from the local authority in whose area he is living;

(iii) where the adoption order relating to him was made in England and Wales, from the local author-

ity in whose area the court which made the order
sat; or

(iv) from any other local authority;

(b) if he is in Scotland —

(i) from the regional or islands council in whose
area he is living;

(ii) where the adoption order relating to him was
made in Scotland, from the council in whose area
the court which made the order sat; or

(iii) from any other regional or islands council;

(c) if he is in Northern Ireland —

(i) from the Board in whose area he is living;

(ii) where the adoption order relating to him was
made in Northern Ireland, from the Board in whose
area the court which made the order sat; or

(iii) from any other Board;

(d) if he is in the United Kingdom and his adoption was
arranged by an adoption society —

(i) approved under section 3,

(ii) approved under section 3 of the Adoption
(Scotland) Act 1978,

(iii) registered under Article 4, of the Adoption
(Northern Ireland) Order 1987,

from that society.

(4) Where an adopted person who is in England and
Wales —

(a) applies for information under —

(i) subsection (1), or

(ii) Article 54 of the Adoption (Northern Ireland)
Order 1987, or

(b) is supplied with information under section 45 of the
Adoption (Scotland) Act 1978,

it shall be the duty of the persons and bodies mentioned in
subsection (5) to provide counselling for him if asked by him
to do so.

(5) The persons and bodies are —

(a) the Registrar General;

(b) any local authority falling within subsection (3)(a)(ii)
to (iv);

(c) any adoption society falling within subsection (3)(d) in so far as it is acting as an adoption society in England and Wales.

(6) If the applicant chooses to receive counselling from a person or body falling within subsection (3), the Registrar General shall send to the person or body the information to which the applicant is entitled under subsection (1).

(7) Where a person—

(a) was adopted before 12th November 1975, and
(b) applies for information under subsection (1),

the Registrar General shall not supply the information to him unless he has attended an interview with a counsellor arranged by a person or body from whom counselling services are available as mentioned in subsection (3).

(8) Where the Registrar General is prevented by subsection (7) from supplying information to a person who is not living in the United Kingdom, he may supply the information to any body which—

(a) the Registrar General is satisfied is suitable to provide counselling to that person, and
(b) has notified the Registrar General that it is prepared to provide such counselling.

(9) In this section—

"a Board" means a Health and Social Services Board established under Article 16 of the Health and Personal Social Services (Northern Ireland) Order 1972; and

"prescribed" means prescribed by regulations made by the Registrar General."

21. After section 51 there shall be inserted—

"Adoption Contact Register.

51A.—(1) The Registrar General shall maintain at the General Register Office a register to be called the Adoption Contact Register.

(2) The register shall be in two parts—

(a) Part I: Adopted Persons; and
(b) Part II: Relatives.

(3) The Registrar General shall, on payment of such fee as may be prescribed, enter in Part I of the register the name and address of any adopted person who fulfils

the conditions in subsection (4) and who gives notice that he wishes to contact any relative of his.

(4) The conditions are that—

    (a) a record of the adopted person's birth is kept by the Registrar General; and

    (b) the adopted person has attained the age of 18 years and—

        (i) has been supplied by the Registrar General with information under section 51; or

        (ii) has satisfied the Registrar General that he has such information as is necessary to enable him to obtain a certified copy of the record of his birth.

(5) The Registrar General shall, on payment of such fee as may be prescribed, enter in Part II of the register the name and address of any person who fulfils the conditions in subsection (6) and who gives notice that he wishes to contact an adopted person.

(6) The conditions are that—

    (a) a record of the adopted person's birth is kept by the Registrar General; and

    (b) the person giving notice under subsection (5) has attained the age of 18 years and has satisfied the Registrar General that—

        (i) he is a relative of the adopted person; and

        (ii) he has such information as is necessary to enable him to obtain a certified copy of the record of the adopted person's birth.

(7) The Registrar General shall, on receiving notice from any person named in an entry in the register that he wishes the entry to be cancelled, cancel the entry.

(8) Any notice given under this section must be in such form as may be determined by the Registrar General.

(9) The Registrar General shall transmit to an adopted person whose name is entered in Part I of the register the name and address of any relative in respect of whom there is an entry in Part II of the register.

(10) Any entry cancelled under subsection (7) ceases from the time of cancellation to be an entry for the purposes of subsection (9).

(11) The register shall not be open to public inspection or search and the Registrar General shall not supply any person with information entered in the register (whether in an uncancelled or a cancelled entry) except in accordance with this section.

(12) The register may be kept by means of a computer.

(13) In this section—

    (a) "relative" means any person (other than an adoptive relative) who is related to the adopted person by blood (including half-blood) or marriage;

    (b) "address" includes any address at or through which the person concerned may be contacted; and

    (c) "prescribed" means prescribed by the Secretary of State."

21.—(1) In section 55 (adoption of children abroad), in subsection (1) after the word "Scotland" there shall be inserted "or Northern Ireland" and for the words "vesting in him the parental rights and duties relating to the child" there shall be substituted "giving him parental responsibility for the child".

(2) In subsection (3) of that section for the words "word '(Scotland)'" there shall be substituted "words '(Scotland)' or '(Northern Ireland)'."

23.—(1) In section 56 (restriction on removal of children for adoption outside Great Britain),—

    (a) in subsections (1) and (3) for the words "transferring the actual custody of a child to", in both places where they occur, there shall be substituted "placing a child with"; and

    (b) in subsection (3)(a) for the words "in the actual custody of" there shall be substituted "with".

(2) In subsection (1) of that section—

    (a) for the words from "or under" to "abroad)" there shall be substituted "section 49 of the Adoption (Scotland) Act 1978 or Article 57 of the Adoption (Northern Ireland) Order 1987"; and

(b) for the words "British Islands" there shall be substituted "United Kingdom, the Channel Islands and the Isle of Man".

24.—(1) In section 57 (prohibition on certain payments) in subsection (1)(c), for the words "transfer by that person of the actual custody of a child" there shall be substituted "handing over of a child by that person".

(2) In subsection (3A)(b) of that section, for the words "in the actual custody of" there shall be substituted "with".

25. After section 57 there shall be inserted—

"Permitted allowances.

57A.—(1) The Secretary of State may make regulations for the purpose of enabling adoption agencies to pay allowances to persons who have adopted, or intend to adopt, children in pursuance of arrangements made by the agencies.

(2) Section 57(1) shall not apply to any payment made by an adoption agency in accordance with the regulations.

(3) The regulations may, in particular, make provision as to—

(a) the procedure to be followed by any agency in determining whether a person should be paid an allowance;

(b) the circumstances in which an allowance may be paid;

(c) the factors to be taken into account in determining the amount of an allowance;

(d) the procedure for review, variation and termination of allowances; and

(e) the information about allowances to be supplied by any agency to any person who is intending to adopt a child.

(4) Any scheme approved under section 57(4) shall be revoked as from the coming into force of this section.

(5) Section 57(1) shall not apply in relation to any payment made—

> (a) in accordance with a scheme revoked under subsection (4) or section 57(5)(b); and
> (b) to a person to whom such payments were made before the revocation of the scheme.

> (6) Subsection (5) shall not apply where any person to whom any payments may lawfully be made by virtue of subsection (5) agrees to receive (instead of such payments) payments complying with regulations made under this section."

26.—(1) In section 59 (effect of determination and orders made in Scotland and overseas in adoption proceedings), in subsection (1) for the words "Great Britain" there shall be substituted "the United Kingdom".

(2) For subsection (2) of that section there shall be substituted—

> "(2) Subsections (2) to (4) of section 12 shall apply in relation to an order freeing a child for adoption (other than an order under section 18) as if it were an adoption order; and, on the revocation in Scotland or Northern Ireland of an order freeing a child for adoption, subsections (3) and (3A) of section 20 shall apply as if the order had been revoked under that section."

27. In section 60 (evidence of adoption in Scotland and Northern Ireland), in paragraph (a) for the words "section 22(2) of the Adoption Act 1958" there shall be substituted "section 45(2) of the Adoption (Scotland) Act 1978" and in paragraph (b) for the words from "section 23(4)" to "in force" there shall be substituted "Article 63(1) of the Adoption (Northern Ireland) Order 1987".

28. In section 62(5)(b) (courts), for the words from "section 8" to "child)" there shall be substituted—

> "(i) section 12 or 18 of the Adoption (Scotland) Act 1978; or
> (ii) Article 12, 17 or 18 of the Adoption (Northern Ireland) Order 1987".

29. After section 65 (guardians ad litem and reporting officers) there shall be inserted—

65A. — (1) The Secretary of State may by regulations provide for the establishment of panels of persons from whom guardians ad litem and reporting officers appointed under rules made under section 65 must be selected.

"Panels for selection of guardians ad litem and reporting officers.

(2) The regulations may, in particular, make provision —

(a) as to the constitution, administration and procedures of panels;

(b) requiring two or more specified local authorities to make arrangements for the joint management of a panel;

(c) for the defrayment by local authorities of expenses incurred by members of panels;

(d) for the payment by local authorities of fees and allowances for members of panels;

(e) as to the qualifications for membership of a panel;

(f) as to the training to be given to members of panels;

(g) as to the co-operation required of specified local authorities in the provision of panels in specified areas; and

(h) for monitoring the work of guardians ad litem and reporting officers.

(3) Rules of court may make provision as to the assistance which any guardian ad litem or reporting officer may be required by the court to give to it."

30. — (1) Section 72(1) (interpretation) shall be amended as follows.

(2) In the definition of "adoption agency" for the words from "section 1" to the end there shall be substituted " —

(a) section 1 of the Adoption (Scotland) Act 1978; and

(b) Article 3 of the Adoption (Northern Ireland) Order 1987."

(3) For the definition of "adoption order" there shall be substituted

"adoption order' —

(a) means an order under section 12(1); and

P

(b) in sections 12(3) and (4), 18 to 20, 27, 28 and 30 to 32 and in the definition of 'British adoption order' in this subsection includes an order under section 12 of the Adoption (Scotland) Act 1978 and Article 12 of the Adoption (Northern Ireland) Order 1987 (adoption orders in Scotland and Northern Ireland respectively); and

(c) in sections 27, 28 and 30 to 32 includes an order under section 55, section 49 of the Adoption (Scotland) Act 1978 and Article 57 of the Adoption (Northern Ireland) Order 1987 (orders in relation to children being adopted abroad)."

(4) For the definition of "British adoption order" there shall be substituted—

" 'British adoption order' means—

(a) an adoption order as defined in this subsection, and

(b) an order under any provision for the adoption of a child effected under the law of any British territory outside the United Kingdom."

(5) For the definition of "guardian" there shall be substituted—

" 'guardian' has the same meaning as in the Children Act 1989."

(6) In the definition of "order freeing a child for adoption" for the words from "section 27(2)" to the end there shall be substituted "sections 27(2) and 59 includes an order under—

(a) section 18 of the Adoption (Scotland) Act 1978; and

(b) Article 17 or 18 of the Adoption (Northern Ireland) Order 1987".

(7) After the definition of "overseas adoption" there shall be inserted—

" 'parent' means, in relation to a child, any parent who has parental responsibility for the child under the Children Act 1989;

'parental responsibility' and 'parental responsibility agreement' have the same meaning as in the Children Act 1989."

(8) After the definition of "United Kingdom national" there shall be inserted—

" 'upbringing' has the same meaning as in the Children Act 1989."

(9) For section 72(1A) there shall be substituted the following subsections —

"(1A) In this Act, in determining with what person, or where, a child has his home, any absence of the child at a hospital or boarding school and any other temporary absence shall be disregarded.

(1B) In this Act, references to a child who is in the care of or looked after by a local authority have the same meaning as in the Children Act 1989."

31. For section 74(3) and (4) (extent) there shall be substituted —

"(3) This Act extends to England and Wales only."

Part II

Amendments of Adoption (Scotland) Act 1978 (c. 28)

32. In section 11 (restrictions on arranging of adoptions and placing of children) for subsection (2) there shall be substituted —

"(2) An adoption society which is —

(a) approved as respects England and Wales under section 3 of the Adoption Act 1976; or
(b) registered as respects Northern Ireland under Article 4 of the Adoption (Northern Ireland) Order 1987,

but which is not approved under section 3 of this Act, shall not act as an adoption society in Scotland except to the extent that the society considers it necessary to do so in the interests of a person mentioned in section 1 of that Act or, as the case may be, Article 3 of that Order."

33. For section 14(1) (adoption by married couple) there shall be substituted —

"(1) Subject to section 53(1) of the Children Act 1975 (which provides for the making of a custody order instead of an adoption order in certain cases), an adoption order shall not be made on the application of more than one person except in the circumstances specified in subsections (1A) and (1B).

(1A) An adoption order may be made on the application

of a married couple where both the husband and the wife have attained the age of 21 years.

(1B) An adoption order may be made on the application of a married couple where—

(a) the husbanbd or the wife—

(i) is the father or mother of the child; and
(ii) has attained the age of 18 years; and
(b) his or her spouse has attained the age of 21 years."

34. In section 16(1)(a) (parental agreement) for the words from "in England" to "revoked", in the second place where it occurs there shall be substituted—

"(i) in Scotland under section 18;
(ii) in England and Wales under section 18 of the Adoption Act 1976; or
(iii) in Northern Ireland under Article 17(1) or 18(1) of the Adoption (Northern Ireland) Order 1987,

and not revoked".

35. In section 18(5) (effect of order freeing child for adoption) for the words "and (3)" there shall be substituted "to (4)".

36. In section 20(3)(c) (revocation of section 18 order) the words "section 12(3)(b) of the Adoption Act 1976 or of" shall cease to have effect.

37. For section 21 (transfer of parental rights and duties between adoption agencies) there shall be substituted—

"Variation of section 18 order so as to substitute one adoption agency for another.

21.—(1) On an application to which this section applies an authorised court may vary an order under section 18 so as to transfer the parental rights and duties relating to the child from the adoption agency in which they are vested under the order ('the existing agency') to another adoption agency ('the substitute agency').

(2) This section applies to any application made jointly by the existing agency and the would-be substitute agency.

(3) Where an order under section 18 is varied under this section, section 19 shall apply as if the parental rights and duties relating to the child had

vested in the substitute agency on the making of the order."

38. In section 22(4) (notification to local authority of adoption application) for the word "receives" there shall be substituted "receive".

39. In section 29 (return of child taken away in breach of section 27 or 28) after the word "1976" in each place where it occurs there shall be inserted "or Article 28 or 29 of the Adoption (Northern Ireland) Order 1987".

40. In section 32 (meaning of "protected child"), at the end of subsection (2) there shall be added "or Article 33 of the Adoption (Northern Ireland) Order 1987".

41. In section 45 (adopted children register)—

(a) for the words from "or an approved" in subsection (5) to the end of subsection (6) there shall be substituted—

"Board or adoption society falling within subsection (6) which is providing counselling for that adopted person.

(6) Where the Registrar General for Scotland furnishes an adopted person with information under subsection (5), he shall advise that person that counselling services are available—

(a) if the person is in Scotland—

(i) from the local authority in whose area he is living;
(ii) where the adoption order relating to him was made in Scotland, from the local authority in whose area the court which made the order sat; or
(iii) from any other local authority in Scotland;

(b) if the person is in England and Wales—

(i) from the local authority in whose area he is living;
(ii) where the adoption order relating to him was made in England and Wales, from the local authority in whose area the court which made the order sat; or
(iii) from any other local authority in England and Wales;

(c) if the person is in Northern Ireland—

(i) from the Board in whose area he is living;

(ii) where the adoption order relating to him was made in Northern Ireland, from the Board in whose area the court which made the order sat; or

(iii) from any other Board;

(d) if the person is in the United Kingdom and his adoption was arranged by an adoption society—

(i) approved under section 3;

(ii) approved under section 3 of the Adoption Act 1976; or

(iii) registered under Article 4 of the Adoption (Northern Ireland) Order 1987,

from that society.

(6A) Where an adopted person who is in Scotland—

(a) is furnished with information under subsection (5); or

(b) applies for information under—

(i) section 51(1) of the Adoption Act 1976; or

(ii) Article 54 of the Adoption (Northern Ireland) Order 1987,

any body mentioned in subsection (6B) to which the adopted person applies for counselling shall have a duty to provide counselling for him.

(6B) The bodies referred to in subsection (6A) are—

(a) any local authority falling within subsection (6)(a); and

(b) any adoption society falling within subsection (6)(d) so far as it is acting as an adoption society in Scotland.";

(b) in subsection (7)—

(i) for the word "under" there shall be substituted "from a local authority, Board or adoption society falling within";

(ii) for the words "or adoption society which is providing that counselling" there shall be substituted ", Board or adoption society"; and

(iii) after the word "authority" where it second occurs there shall be inserted ", Board"; and

(c) after subsection (9) there shall be inserted the following subsection—

"(10) In this section—

"Board" means a Health and Social Services Board
established under Article 16 of the Health and
Personal Social Services (Northern Ireland)
Order 1972; and

"local authority", in relation to England and Wales,
means the council of a county (other than a
metropolitan county), a metropolitan district, a
London borough or the Common Council of
the City of London."

42. In section 49 (adoption of children abroad)—

(a) in subsection (1) after the word "Scotland" there shall
be inserted "or Northern Ireland"; and

(b) in subsection (3) for the words "word 'England'' ' there
shall be substituted "words '(England)' or '(Northern
Ireland)'' '.

43. In section 50(1) (restriction on removal of children for
adoption outside Great Britain) after the word "1976" there shall
be inserted "or Article 57 of the Adoption (Northern Ireland)
Order 1987".

44. In section 53(1) (effect of determination and orders made
in England and Wales and overseas in adoption proceedings)—

(a) in subsection (1) for the words "Great Britain" there
shall be substituted "the United Kingdom"; and

(b) for subsection (2) there shall be substituted

"(2) Subsections (2) to (4) of section 12 shall apply in
relation to an order freeing a child for adoption (other than
an order under section 18) as if it were an adoption order;
and on the revocation in England and Wales or Northern
Ireland of an order freeing a child for adoption subsection
(3) of section 20 shall apply as if the order had been revoked
under that section."

45. In section 54(b) (evidence of adoption in Northern Ireland)
for the words from "section 23(4)" to "in force" there shall be
substituted "Article 63(1) of the Adoption (Northern Ireland)
Order 1987".

46. In section 65(1) (interpretation)—

(a) in the definition of "adoption agency", at the end there
shall be added "and an adoption agency within the meaning of Article 3 of the Adoption (Northern Ireland) Order
1987 (adoption agencies in Northern Ireland)";

(b) for the definition of "adoption order" there shall be substituted—

" 'adoption order' —

    (a) means an order under section 12(1); and

    (b) in sections 12(3) and (4), 18 to 20, 27, 28 and 30 to 32 and in the definition of "British adoption order" in this subsection includes an order under section 12 of the Adoption Act 1976 and Article 12 of the Adoption (Northern Ireland) Order 1987 (adoption orders in England and Wales and Northern Ireland respectively); and

    (c) in sections 27, 28 and 30 to 32 includes an order under section 49, section 55 of the Adoption Act 1976 and Article 57 of the Adoption (Northern Ireland) Order 1987 (orders in relation to children being adopted abroad;";

(c) for the definition of "British adoption order" there shall be substituted—

" 'British adoption order' means—

    (a) an adoption order as defined in this subsection; and

    (b) an order under any provision for the adoption of a child effected under the law of any British territory outside the United Kingdom;";

(d) in the definition of "order freeing a child for adoption" for the words from "section 27(2)" to the end there shall be substituted "sections 27(2) and 53 includes an order under—

    (a) section 18 of the Adoption Act 1976; and

    (b) Article 17 or 18 of the Adoption (Northern Ireland) Order 1987;".

Annotation

Schedule 10: covers an additional aspect of child law which is affected by the Act, namely adoption. The Minister of State pointed out that the Lord Chancellor intended to embark upon a full review of adoption law, a review that would provide an opportunity for detailed consideration of all matters relating to adoption. This was to be in the light of the changes that have taken place since the last major review and the introduction of the Children Act 1975. This was subsequently consolidated into the Adoption Act 1976. One object of the Children Act 1975 was to enable and encourage courts to make custody rather than adoption orders where these would be more appropriate. This would usually be the case in applications by relatives or step-parents. The relevant provisions caused difficulty for two reasons. First, they were so worded that they appeared to add little to the requirement to choose whichever order would be best for the child. Secondly, the court might always make a custody order instead of an adoption order if the required agreements to adoption had been given or could be dispensed with. This meant that the court could not of its own motion make a custody order when the parent was reasonably withholding agreement to adoption because custodianship would be better. It was the view of the Law Commission in its report on Guardianship and Custody (Law Com 172) that this difficulty would disappear if adoption proceedings became family proceedings for the purpose of this legislation. All proceedings are family proceedings within the Children Act.

In the words of the Minister of State, the changes to the adoption law in Schedule 10 "do not constitute major changes but are nevertheless important": Minister of State, Hansard 6 June, Col 380, Standing Committee B. They may be categorised in three groups. First are amendments that are intended to harmonise adoption law within the United Kingdom, thus meeting needs arising from the introduction of new adoption provisions in Northern Ireland and as a consequence of the changes in child care law contained in the Act. The changes will enable agencies in the different parts of the United Kingdom to work in cooperation for the benefit of children who need to move from one part of the country to another. Secondly, other consequential amendments update the numerous references in adoption legislation to ensure that they are appropriately carried across to child care legislation, so that the two areas of law interlink. Thirdly, a small number of improvements, made outside the context of a general review of adoption law, meets the needs of particular groups. They are "piecemeal" changes, but they are helpful and can be made without awaiting the full review of adoption law promised by the Lord Chancellor.

Part I: deals with amendments to the Adoption Act 1976. Note that some important repeals, such as those of sections 14(3) and 15(4) of the Adoption Act 1976, are also to be found in Schedule 15. Note also that under prior law, an application could be made without the consent of a parent or guardian if the child was "in the care of" an adoption agency. This phrase was not defined in the 1976 Act but was taken to include a child in voluntary care. In future, however, an adoption agency will not be able to apply for a freeing order without the consent of a parent or guardian, unless the agency is a local authority in whose care the child may be under a care order: see Paragraphs 6(1) and 30(9), which insert sections 18(2A) and 72(1B) into the 1976 Act.

Note that the Registrar General is required to set up an Adoption Contact Register to enable adopted people to contact their birth parents and other relatives: see Paragraph 21, which inserts a new section 51A into the Adoption Act 1976. This register builds upon the informal contact service which the Registrar General has operated in recent years. A further amendment to the 1976 Act assists people to obtain information about their birth records. A person who was adopted before 1975 is required to attend a counselling interview before he may be given information as to his birth records: see section 51 Adoption Act 1976. Under the former law the counselling interview had to take place in England, Wales or Scotland. The amendments permit counselling to be obtained either anywhere within the United Kingdom or from a body outside the United Kingdom which has notified the Registrar General that it is willing to provide counselling and satisfies the Registrar that it is suitable to do so: see Paragraph 20, which amends section 51 of the 1976 Act.

Part II: amends the Adoption (Scotland) Act 1978 in relation to the Adoption Act 1976, to ensure that the work of adoption agencies and court orders made under the equivalent legislation in Northern Ireland is required: see Paragraphs 2, 20, 30, 32, 41 and 46. Also, in future, individual schemes for the payment of adoption allowances to adopters and those who intend to adopt will not need to be approved by the Secretary of State. Instead they will be subject to regulations made by him. Existing schemes will be replaced by arrangements for payments made under the regulations: see Paragrah 25, which inserts section 57A into the 1976 Act.

SCHEDULE 11: JURISDICTION

PART I

GENERAL

Commencement of proceedings

1.—(1) The Lord Chancellor may by order specify proceedings under this Act or the Adoption Act 1976 which may only be commenced in—

(a) a specified level of court;
(b) a court which falls within a specified class of court; or

(c) a particular court determined in accordance with, or specified in, the order.

(2) The Lord Chancellor may by order specify circumstances in which specified proceedings under this Act or the Adoption Act 1976 (which might otherwise be commenced elsewhere) may only be commenced in—

(a) a specified level of court;
(b) a court which falls within a specified class of court; or
(c) a particular court determined in accordance with, or specified in, the order.

(3) The Lord Chancellor may by order make provision by virtue of which, where specified proceedings with respect to a child under—

(a) this Act;
(b) the Adoption Act 1976; or
(c) the High Court's inherent jurisdiction with respect to children,

have been commenced in or transferred to any court (whether or not by virtue of an order under this Schedule), any other specified family proceedings which may affect, or are otherwise connected with, the child may, in specified circumstances, only be commenced in that court.

(4) A class of court specified in an order under this Schedule may be described by reference to a description of proceedings and may include different levels of court.

Transfer of proceedings

2.—(1) The Lord Chancellor may by order provide that in specified circumstances the whole, or any specified part of, specified proceedings to which this paragraph applies shall be transferred to—

(a) a specified level of court;
(b) a court which falls within a specified class of court; or
(c) a particular court determined in accordance with, or specified in, the order.

(2) Any order under this paragraph may provide for the transfer to be made at any stage, or specified stage, of the proceedings and whether or not the proceedings, or any part of them, have already been transferred.

(3) The proceedings to which this paragraph applies are—

(a) any proceedings under this Act;

(b) any proceedings under the Adoption Act 1976;

(c) any other proceedings which—

> (i) are family proceedings for the purposes of this Act, other than proceedings under the inherent jurisdiction of the High Court; and
>
> (ii) may affect, or are otherwise connected with, the child concerned.

(4) Proceedings to which this paragraph applies by virtue of sub-paragraph (3)(c) may only be transferred in accordance with the provisions of an order made under this paragraph for the purpose of consolidating them with proceedings under—

(a) this Act;

(b) the Adoption Act 1976; or

(c) the High Court's inherent jurisdiction with respect to children.

(5) An order under this paragraph may make such provision as the Lord Chancellor thinks appropriate for excluding proceedings to which this paragraph applies from the operation of any enactment which would otherwise govern the transfer of those proceedings, or any part of them.

Hearings by single justice

3.—(1) In such circumstances as the Lord Chancellor may by order specify—

(a) the jurisdiction of a magistrates' court to make an emergency protection order;

(b) any specified question with respect to the transfer of specified proceedings to or from a magistrates' court in accordance with the provisions of an order under paragraph 2,

may be exercised by a single justice.

(2) Any provision made under this paragraph shall be without prejudice to any other enactment or rule of law relating to the functions which may be performed by a single justice of the peace.

General

4.—(1) For the purposes of this Schedule—

(a) the commencement of proceedings under this Act includes the making of any application under this Act in the course of proceedings (whether or not those proceedings are proceedings under this act); and

(b) there are three levels of court, that is to say the High Court, any county court and any magistrates' court.

(2) In this Schedule "specified" means specified by an order made under this Schedule.

(3) Any order under paragraph 1 may make provision as to the effect of commencing proceedings in contravention of any of the provisions of the order.

(4) An order under paragraph 2 may make provision as to the effect of a failure to comply with any of the provisions of the order.

(5) An order under this Schedule may—

(a) make such consequential, incidental or transitional provision as the Lord Chancellor considers expedient, including provision amending any other enactment so far as it concerns the jurisdiction of any court or justice of the peace;

(b) make provision for treating proceedings which are—

(i) in part proceedings of a kind mentioned in paragraph (a) or (b) of paragraph 2(3); and
(ii) in part proceedings of a kind mentioned in paragraph (c) of paragraph 2(3),

as consisting entirely of proceedings of one or other of those kinds, for the purposes of the application of any order made under paragraph 2.

PART II

CONSEQUENTIAL AMENDMENTS

The Administration of Justice Act 1964 (c. 42)

5. In section 38 of the Administration of Justice Act 1964 (interpretation), the definition of "domestic court", which is spent, shall be omitted.

The Domestic Proceedings and Magistrates' Courts Act 1978 (c. 22)

6. In the Domestic Proceedings and Magistrates' Courts Act 1978—

(a) for the words "domestic proceedings", wherever they occur in sections 16(5)(c) and 88(1), there shall be substituted "family proceedings";

(b) for the words "domestic court panel", wherever they occur in section 16(4)(b), there shall be substituted "family panel".

The Justices of the Peace Act 1979 (c. 55)

7. In the Justices of the Peace Act 1979—

(a) for the words "domestic proceedings", wherever they occur in section 16(5), there shall be substituted "family proceedings";

(b) for the words "domestic court", wherever they occur in section 17(3), there shall be substituted "family proceedings court";

(c) for the words "domestic courts", wherever they occur in sections 38(2) and 58(1) and (5), there shall be substituted "family proceedings courts".

The Magistrates' Courts Act 1980 (c. 43)

8. In the Magistrates' Courts Act 1980—

(a) in section 65(1) (meaning of family proceedings), the following paragraph shall be inserted after paragraph (m)—

"(n) the Children Act 1989";

(b) in section 65(2)(a) for the words "and (m)" there shall be substituted "(m) and (n)";

(c) for the words "domestic proceedings", wherever they occur in sections 65(1), (2) and (3), 66(1) and (2), 67(1), (2) and (7), 69(1), (2), (3) and (4), 70(2) and (3), 71(1) and (2), 72(1), 73, 74(1), 121(8) and 150(1), there shall be substituted "family proceedings";

(d) for the words "domestic court panel", wherever they occur in section 67(3), (4), (5) and (6), there shall be substituted "family panels";

(f) for the words "domestic courts", wherever they occur in sections 67(1) and (3) and 68(1), there shall be substituted "family proceedings courts";

(g) for the words "domestic court", wherever they occur in section 67(2) and (5), there shall be substituted "family proceedings court".

The Supreme Court Act 1981 (c. 54)

9. In paragraph 3 of Schedule 1 to the Supreme Court Act 1981 (distribution of business to the Family Division of the High Court), the following sub-paragraph shall be added at the end—

"(e) proceedings under the Children Act 1989".

The Matrimonial and Family Proceedings Act 1984 (c. 42)

10. In section 44 of the Matrimonial and Family Proceedings Act 1984 (domestic proceedings in magistrates' courts to include applications to alter maintenance agreements) for the words "domestic proceedings", wherever they occur, there shall be substituted "family proceedings".

The Insolvency Act 1986 (c. 45)

11.—(1) In section 281(5)(b) of the Insolvency Act 1986 (discharge not to release bankrupt from bankruptcy debt arising under any order made in family proceedings or in domestic proceedings), the words "or in domestic proceedings" shall be omitted.

(2) In section 281(8) of that Act (interpretation), for the definitions of "domestic proceedings" and "family proceedings" there shall be substituted—

"family proceedings" means—

(a) family proceedings within the meaning of the Magistrates' Courts Act 1980 and any proceedings which would be such proceedings but for section 65(1)(ii) of that Act (proceedings for variation of order for periodical payments); and
(b) family proceedings within the meaning of Part V of the Matrimonial and Family Proceedings Act 1984."

Annotation

Schedule 11: deals with jurisdiction.

Part I: deals with the commencement of proceedings. Note that while jurisdiction is generally concurrent, the Lord Chancellor may order that certain proceedings must start in specified courts: see Paragraph 1. The exercise of this power is to be determined, but it is likely that proceedings under the Act in county and magistrates' courts will have to start in a court which is local to where the child usually lives. An exception to this rule is likely to be that, where the child is the subject of family proceedings in one court, proceedings under the Act should also start in that court. The converse could also be achieved; an order may require that any family proceedings which may affect the child should start in a court in which proceedings under the Act are already pending. The start rules will be complemented by rules for the transfer of proceedings between courts. The Lord Chancellor may order that proceedings under the Act and other family proceedings which may affect the child, other than proceedings under the inherent jurisdiction of the High Court, should be transferred to specified courts: see Paragraph 2.

The intention is that by a combination of start and transfer rules cases will be directed to the best possible venue. Guidance will be supplied for the operation of these rules: in proceedings relating to care and supervision orders, decisions about the complexity of the case, its likely duration, the availability of court time and the number of expert witnesses who may be involved. It is hoped that in this way cases will be matched with the most appropriate level of court. In all proceedings under the Act it should be possible to avoid delays which may otherwise build up in certain courts. In particular, it should be possible to consolidate proceedings which relate to the same child in one court, which should reduce the stress and cost of multiple proceedings.

Part II: deals with consequential amendments to a number of Acts: see also Schedule 12 dealing with minor amendments, Schedule 13 with consequential amendments, and Schedule 15 for a list of the extent to which other Acts are repealed.

Schedule 12: Minor Amendments

The Custody of Children Act 1891 (c. 3)

1. The Custody of Children Act 1891 (which contains miscellaneous obsolete provisions with respect to the custody of children) shall cease to have effect.

The Children and Young Persons Act 1933 (c. 12)

2. In section 2(2)(a) of the Children and Young Persons Act 1933 (cruelty to persons under sixteen), after the words "young person" there shall be inserted ", or the legal guardian of a child or young person,".

3. Section 40 of that Act shall cease to have effect.

The Education Act 1944 (c. 31)

4. In section 40(1) of the Education Act 1944 (enforcement of school attendance), the words from "or to imprisonment" to the end shall cease to have effect.

The Marriage Act 1949 (c. 76)

5.—(1) In section 3 of the Marriage Act 1949 (consent required to the marriage of a child by common licence or superintendent registrar's certificate), in subsection (1) for the words "the Second Schedule to this Act" there shall be substituted "subsection (1A) of this section".

(2) After that subsection there shall be inserted—

"(1A) The consents are—

(a) subject to paragraphs (b) to (d) of this subsection, the consent of—

(i) each parent (if any) of the child who has parental responsibility for him; and
(ii) each guardian (if any) of the child;

(b) where a residence order is in force with respect to the child, the consent of the person or persons with whom he lives, or is to live, as a result of the order (in substitution for the consents mentioned in paragraph (a) of this subsection);

(c) where a care order is in force with respect to the child, the consent of the local authority designated in the order (in addition to the consents mentioned in paragraph (a) of this subsection);

(d) where neither paragraph (b) nor (c) of this subsection applies but a residence order was in force with respect to the child immediately before he reached the age of sixteen, the consent of the person or persons with whom he lived, or was to live, as a result of the order (in substitution for the consents mentioned in paragraph (a) of this subsection).

(1B) In this section 'guardian of a child', 'parental responsibility', 'residence order' and 'care order' have the same meaning as in the Children Act 1989."

The Births and Deaths Registration Act 1953 (c. 20)

6.—(1) Sections 10 and 10A of the Births and Deaths Registration Act 1953 (registration of father, and re-registration, where parents not married) shall be amended as follows.

(2) In sections 10(1) and 10A(1) for paragraph (d) there shall be substituted—

"(d) at the request of the mother or that person on production of—
    (i) a copy of a parental responsibility agreement made between them in relation to the child; and
    (ii) a declaration in the prescribed form by the person making the request stating that the agreement was made in compliance with section 4 of the Children Act 1989 and has not been brought to an end by an order of a court; or

(e) at the request of the mother or that person on production of—
    (i) a certified copy of an order under section 4 of the Children Act 1989 giving that person parental responsibility for the child; and
    (ii) a declaration in the prescribed form by the person making the request stating that the order has not been brought to an end by an order of a court; or

(f) at the request of the mother or that person on production of—
    (i) a certified copy of an order under paragraph 1 of Schedule 1 to the Children Act 1989 which requires that person to make any financial provision for the child and which is not an order falling within paragraph 4(3) of that Schedule; and
    (ii) a declaration in the prescribed form by the person making the request stating that the order has not been discharged by an order of a court; or

(g) at the request of the mother or that person on production of—
    (i) a certified copy of any of the orders which are mentioned in subsection (1A) of this section which has been made in relation to the child; and
    (ii) a declaration in the prescribed form by the person making the request stating that the order has

not been brought to an end or discharged by an order of a court."

(3) After sections 10(1) and 10A(1) there shall be inserted—

"(1A) The orders are—

(a) an order under section 4 of the Family Law Reform Act 1987 that that person shall have all the parental rights and duties with respect to the child;

(b) an order that that person shall have custody or care and control or legal custody of the child made under section 9 of the Guardianship of Minors Act 1971 at a time when such an order could only be made in favour of a parent;

(c) an order under section 9 or 11B of that Act which requires that person to make any financial provision in relation to the child;

(d) an order under section 4 of the Affiliation Proceedings Act 1957 naming that person as putative father of the child."

(4) In section 10(2) for the words "or (d)" there shall be substituted "to (g)".

(5) In section 10(3) for the words from ' "relevant order" ' to the end there shall be substituted ' "parental responsibility agreement' has the same meaning as in the Children Act 1989".

(6) In section 10A(2) in paragraphs (b) and (c) for the words "paragraph (d)" in both places where they occur there shall be substituted "any of paragraphs (d) to (g)".

The Army Act 1955 (c. 18)

7. In section 151 of the Army Act 1955 (deductions from pay for maintenance of wife or child), in subsection (1A)(a) for the words "in the care of a local authority in England or Wales" there shall be substituted "being looked after by a local authority in England or Wales (within the meaning of the Children Act 1989)".

8.—(1) Schedule 5A to that Act (powers of court on trial of civilian) shall be amended as follows.

(2) For paragraphs 7(3) and (4) there shall be substituted—

"(3) While an authorisation under a reception order is in force the order shall (subject to sub-paragraph (4) below) be deemed to be a care order for the purposes of the Children Act 1989, and the authorised authority shall be deemed to be the authority designated in that deemed care order.

(3A) In sub-paragraph (3) above "care order" means a care order which is not an interim care order under section 38 of the Children Act 1989.

(4) The Children Act 1989 shall apply to a reception order which is deemed to be a care order by virtue of sub-paragraph (3) above as if sections 31(8) (designated local authority), 91 (duration of care order etc.) and 101 (effect of orders as between different jurisdictions) were omitted."

(3) In sub-paragraph (5)(c) for the words from "attains" to the end there shall be substituted "attains 18 years of age".

(4) In paragraph 8(1) for the words "Children and Young Persons Act 1969" there shall be substituted "Children Act 1989".

The Air Force Act 1955 (c. 19)

9. Section 151(1A) of the Air Force Act 1955 (deductions from pay for maintenance of wife or child) shall have effect subject to the amendment that is set out in paragraph 7 in relation to section 151(1A) of the Army Act 1955.

10, Schedule 5A to that Act (powers of court on trial of civilian) shall have effect subject to the amendments that are set out in paragraph 8(2) to (4) in relation to Schedule 5A to the Army Act 1955.

The Sexual Offences Act 1956 (c. 69)

11. In section 19(3) of the Sexual Offences Act 1956 (abduction of unmarried girl under eighteen from the parent or guardian) for the words "the lawful care or charge of" there shall be substituted "parental responsibility for or care of".

12. In section 20(2) of that Act (abduction of unmarried girl under sixteen from parent or guardian) for the words "the lawful care or charge of" there shall be substituted "parental responsibility for or care of".

13. In section 21(3) of that Act (abduction of defective from parent or guardian) for the words "the lawful care or charge of" there shall be substituted "parental responsibility for or care of".

14. In section 28 of that Act (causing or encouraging prostitution of, intercourse with, or indecent assault on, girl under sixteen) for subsections (3) and (4) there shall be substituted—

"(3) The persons who are to be treated for the purposes

of this section as responsible for a girl are (subject to subsection (4) of this section) —

(a) her parents;
(b) any person who is not a parent of hers but who has parental responsibility for her; and
(c) any person who has care of her.

(4) An individual falling within subsection (3)(a) or (b) of this section is not to be treated as responsible for a girl if —

(a) a residence order under the Children Act 1989 is in force with respect to her and he is not named in the order as the person with shom she is to live; or
(b) a care order under that Act is in force with respect to her."

15. Section 38 of that Act (power of court to divest person of authority over girl or boy in case of incest) shall cease to have effect.

16.—(1) In section 43 of that Act (power to search for and recover woman detained for immoral purposes), in subsection (5) for the words "the lawful care of charge of" there shall be substituted "parental responsibility for or care of".

(2) In subsection (6) of that section, for the words "section forty of the Children and Young Persons Act 1933" there shall be substituted "Part V of the Children Act 1989".

17. After section 46 of that Act there shall be inserted —

"Meaning of 'parental responsibility'.   46A. In this Act 'parental responsibility' has the same meaning as in the Children Act 1989."

The Naval Discipline Act 1957 (c. 53)

18. Schedule 4A to the Naval Discipline Act 1957 (powers of court on trial of civilian) shall have effect subject to the amendments that are set out in paragraph 8(2) to (4) in relation to Schedule 5A to the Army Act 1955.

The Children and Young Persons Act 1963 (c. 37)

19. Section 3 of the Children and Young Persons Act 1963 (children and young persons beyond control) shall cease to have effect.

The Children and Young Persons Act 1969 (c. 54)

20. In section 5 of the Children and Young Persons Act 1969 (restrictions on criminal proceedings for offences by young persons), in subsection (2), for the words "section 1 of this Act" there shall be substituted "Part IV of the Children Act 1989".

21. After section 7(7) of that Act (alteration in treatment of young offenders, etc.) there shall be inserted—

"(7B) An order under subsection (7)(c) of this section shall not require a person to enter into a recognisance—

(a) for an amount exceeding £1,000; or
(b) for a period exceeding—

(i) three years; or
(ii) where the young person concerned will attain the age of eighteen in a period shorter than three years, that shorter period.

(7C) Section 120 of the Magistrates' Courts Act 1980 shall apply to a recognisance entered into in pursuance of an order under subsection (7)(c) of this section as it applies to a recognisance to keep the peace."

22. In section 12A of that Act (young offenders) for subsections (1) and (2) there shall be substituted—

"(1) This subsection applies to any supervision order made under section 7(7) of this Act unless it requires the supervised person to comply with directions given by the supervisor under section 12(2) of this Act."

23. After that section there shall be inserted—

"Requirement for young offender to live in local authority accommodation.

12AA.—(1) Where the conditions mentioned in subsection (6) of this section are satisfied, a supervision order may impose a requirement ('a residence requirement') that a child or young person shall live for a specified period in local authority accommodation.

(2) A residence requirement shall designate the local authority who are to receive the child or young person and that authority shall be the authority in whose area the child or young person resides.

(3) The court shall not impose a residence requirement without first consulting the designated authority.

(4) A residence requirement may stipulate that the child or young person shall not live with a named person.

(5) The maximum period which may be specified in a residence requirement is six months.

(6) The conditions are that—

(a) a supervision order has previously been made in respect of the child or young person;

(b) that order imposed—
(i) a requirement under section 12A(3) of this Act; or
(ii) a residence requirement;

(c) he is found guilty of an offence which—
(i) was committed while that order was in force;
(ii) if it had been committed by a person over the age of twenty-one, would have been punishable with imprisonment; and
(iii) in the opinion of the court is serious; and

(d) the court is satisfied that the behaviour which constituted the offence was due, to a significant extent, to the circumstances in which he was living,

except that the condition in paragraph (d) of this subsection does not apply where the condition in paragraph (b)(ii) is satisfied.

(6) For the purposes of satisfying itself as mentioned in subsection (6)(d) of this section, the court shall obtain a social inquiry report which makes particular reference to the circumstances in which the child or young person was living.

(8) Subsection (7) of this section does not apply if the court already has before it a social inquiry report which contains sufficient information about the circumstances in which the child or young person was living.

(9) A court shall not include a residence requirement in respect of a child or young person who is not legally represented at the relevant time in that court unless—

    (a) he has applied for legal aid for the purposes of the proceedings and the application was refused on the ground that it did not appear that his resources were such that he required assistance; or

    (b) he has been informed of his right to apply for legal aid for the purposes of the proceedings and has had the opportunity to do so, but nevertheless refused or failed to apply.

(10) In subsection (9) of this section—

    (a) 'the relevant time' means the time when the court is considering whether or not to impose the requirement; and

    (b) 'the proceedings' means—

        (i) the whole proceedings; or

        (ii) the part of the proceedings relating to the imposition of the requirement.

(11) A supervision order imposing a residence requirement may also impose any of the requirements mentioned in sections 12, 12A, 12B or 12C of this Act.

(12) In this section 'social inquiry report' has the same meaning as in section 2 of the Criminal Justice Act 1982."

24.—(1) In section 15 of that Act (variation and discharge of supervision orders), in subsections (1)(a), (2A), (3)(e) and (4) after the word "12A", in each place where it occurs, there shall be inserted "12AA".

(2) In subsection (4) of that section for the words "(not being a juvenile court)" there shall be substituted "other than a juvenile court".

[25.—*(1) In section 16 of that Act (provisions supplementary to section 15), in subsection (3) for the words "either direct" to the end there shall be substituted—*

    "(i) direct that he be released forthwith; or
    (ii) remand him."

(2) In subsection (4) of that section—

    (a) in paragraph (a) for the words "an interim order made by virtue of" there shall be substituted "a remand under";

(b) in paragraph (b) for the words "*makes an interim order in respect of*" there shall be substituted "remands", and

(c) for the words "*make an interim order in respect of*" there shall be substituted "remand".

(3) *In subsections (5)(b) and (c) and (6)(a) after the word "12A", in each place where it occurs, there shall be inserted "12AA".*]

26. For section 23 of that Act (remand to care of local authorities etc.) there shall be substituted—

"Remand to local authority accommodation, committal of young persons of unruly character, etc.

23.—(1) Where a court—

(a) remands or commits for trial a child charged with homicide or remands a child convicted of homicide; or

(b) remands a young person charged with or convicted of one or more offences or commits him for trial or sentence,

and he is not released on bail, then, unless he is a young person who is certified by the court to be of unruly character, the court shall remand him to local authority accommodation.

(2) A court remanding a person to local authority accommodation shall designate the authority who are to receive him and that authority shall be the authority in whose area it appears to the court that—

(a) he resides; or

(b) the offence or one of the offences was committed.

(3) Where a person is remanded to local authority accommodation, it shall be lawful for any person acting on behalf of the designated authority to detail him.

(4) The court shall not certify a young person as being of unruly character unless—

(a) he cannot safely be remanded to local authority accommodation; and

(b) the conditions prescribed by order made by the Secretary of State under this subsection are satisfied in relation to him.

Note: The words *in italics* within square brackets were deleted by the Courts and Legal Services Act 1990.

(5) Where the court certifies that a young person is of unruly character, it shall commit him—

    (a) to a remand centre, if it has been notified that such a centre is available for the reception from the court of such persons; and

    (b) to a prison, if it has not been so notified.

(6) Where a young person is remanded to local authority accommodation, a court may, on the application of the designated authority, certify him to be of unruly character in accordance with subsection (4) of this section (and on so doing he shall cease to be remanded to local authority accommodation and subsection (5) of this section shall apply).

(7) For the purposes of subsection (6) of this section, "a court" means—

    (a) the court which remanded the young person; or

    (b) any magistrates' court having jurisdiction in the place where that person is for the time being,

and in this section "court" and "magistrates' court" include a justice.

(8) This section has effect subject to—

    (a) section 37 of the Magistrates' Courts Act 1980 (committal to the Crown Court with a view to a sentence of detention in a young offender institution); and

    (b) section 128(7) of that Act (remands to the custody of a constable for periods of not more than three days),

but section 128(7) shall have effect in relation to a child or young person as if for the reference to three clear days there were substituted a reference to twenty-four hours.''

27.—(1) In section 32 of that Act (detention of absentees), for subsection (1A) there shall be substituted the following subsections—

"(1A) If a child or young person is absent, without the consent of the responsible person—

(a) from a place of safety to which he has been taken under section 16(3) of this Act; or
(b) from local authority accommodation—

(i) in which he is required to live under section 12AA of this Act; or
(ii) to which he has been remanded under section 23(1) of this Act,

he may be arrested by a constable anywhere in the United Kingdom or Channel Islands without a warrant.

(1B) A person so arrested shall be conducted to—

(a) the place of safety;
(b) the local authority accommodation; or
(c) such other place as the responsible person may direct,

at the responsible person's expense.

(1C) In this section 'the responsible person' means the person who made the arrangements under section 16(3) of this Act or, as the case may be, the authority designated under section 12AA or 23 of this Act."

(2) In subsection (2B) of that section for the words "person referred to in subsection (1A)(a) or (b) (as the case may be) of this section" there shall be substituted "responsible person".

28. In section 34(1) of that Act (transitional modifications of Part I for persons of specified ages)—

(a) after the definition of "local authority" there shall be inserted—

" 'local authority accommodation' means accommodation provided by or on behalf of a local authority (within the meaning of the Children Act 1989)"; and

(b) in the definition of "reside" for "12(4) and (5)" there shall be substituted "12B(1) and (2)".

30. In section 73 of that Act (extent, etc.)—

(a) in subsection (4)(a) for "32(1), (3) and (4)" there shall be substituted "32(1) to (1C) and (2A) to (4)"; and
(b) in subsection (6) for "32(1), (1A)" there shall be substituted "32(1) to (1C)".

The Matrimonial Causes Act 1973 (c. 18)

31. For section 41 of the Matrimonial Causes Act 1973 (restrictions on decrees for dissolution, annulment or separation affecting children) there shall be substituted—

"Restrictions on decrees for dissolution, annulment or separation affecting children.

41.—(1) In any proceedings for a decree of divorce or nullity of marriage, or a decree of judicial separation, the court shall consider—

(a) whether there are any children of the family to whom this section applies; and

(b) where there are any such children, whether (in the light of the arrangements which have been, or are proposed to be, made for their upbringing and welfare) it should exercise any of its powers under the Children Act 1989 with respect to any of them.

(2) Where, in any case to which this section applies, it appears to the court that—

(a) the circumstances of the case require it, or are likely to require it, to exercise any of its powers under the Act of 1989 with respect to any such child;

(b) it is not in a position to exercise that power or (as the case may be) those powers without giving further consideration to the case; and

(c) there are exceptional circumstances which make it desirable in the interests of the child that the court should give a direction under this section,

it may direct that the decree of divorce or nullity is not to be made absolute, or that the decree of judicial separation is not to be granted, until the court orders otherwise.

(3) This section applies to—

(a) any child of the family who has not reached the age of sixteen at the date when the court considers the case in accordance with the requirements of this section; and

(b) any child of the family who has reached that age at that date and in relation to whom the court directs that this section shall apply."

32. In section 42 of that Act, subsection (3) (declaration by court that party to marriage unfit to have custody of children of family) shall cease to have effect.

33. In section 52(1) of that Act (interpretation), in the definition of "child of the family", for the words "has been boarded-out with those parties" there shall be substituted "is placed with those parties as foster parents".

The National Health Service Act 1977 (c. 49)

34. In Schedule 8 to the National Health Service Act 1977 (functions of local social services authorities), the following sub-paragraph shall be added at the end of paragraph 2—

"(4A) This paragraph does not apply in relation to persons under the age of 18."

The Child Care Act 1980 (c. 5)

35. Until the repeal of the Child Care Act 1980 by this Act takes effect, the definition of "parent" in section 87 of that Act shall have effect as if it applied only in relation to Part I and sections 13, 24, 64 and 65 of that Act (provisions excluded by section 2(1)(f) of the Family Law Reform Act 1987 from the application of the general rule in that Act governing the meaning of references to relationships between persons).

The Education Act 1981 (c. 60)

36. The following section shall be inserted in the Education Act 1981, after section 3—

"Provision outside England and Wales for certain children.

3A.—(1) A local authority may make such arrangements as they think fit to enable any child in respect of whom they maintain a statement under section 7 to attend an establishment outside England and Wales which specialises in providing for children with special needs.

(2) In subsection (1) above "children with special needs" means children who have particular needs which would be special educational needs if those children were in England and Wales.

(3) Where an authority make arrangements under this section with respect to a child, those arrangements may, in particular, include contributing to or paying—

(a) fees charged by the establishment;
(b) expenses reasonably incurred in maintaining him while he is at the establishment or travelling to or from it;
(c) those travelling expenses;
(d) expenses reasonably incurred by any person accompanying him while he is travelling or staying at the establishment.

(4) This section is not to be taken as in any way limiting any other powers of a local education authority."

The Child Abduction Act 1984 (c. 37)

37.—(1) Section 1 of the Child Abduction Act 1984 (offence of abduction by parent, etc.) shall be amended as follows.

(2) For subsections (2) to (4) there shall be substituted—

"(2) A person is connected with a child for the purposes of this section if—

(a) he is a parent of the child; or
(b) in the case of a child whose parents were not married to each other at the time of his birth, there are reasonable grounds for believing that he is the father of the child; or
(c) he is a guardian of the child; or
(d) he is a person in whose favour a residence order is in force with respect to the child; or
(e) he has custody of the child.

(3) In this section 'the appropriate consent', in relation to a child, means—

(a) the consent of each of the following—

    (i) the child's mother;

    (ii) the child's father, if he has parental responsibility for him;

    (iii) any guardian of the child;

    (iv) any person in whose favour a residence order is in force with respect to the child;

    (v) any person who has custody of the child; or

(b) the leave of the court granted under or by virtue of any provision of Part II of the Children Act 1989; or

(c) if any person has custody of the child, the leave of the court which awarded custody to him.

   (4) A person does not commit an offence under this section by taking or sending a child out of the United Kingdom without obtaining the appropriate consent if—

(a) he is a person in whose favour there is a residence order in force with respect to the child, and

(b) he takes or sends him out of the United Kingdom for a period of less than one month.

   (4A) Subsection (4) above does not apply if the person taking or sending the child out of the United Kingdom does so in breach of an order under Part II of the Children Act 1989."

   (3) In subsection (5) for the words from "but" to the end there shall be substituted—

   "(5A) Subsection (5)(c) above does not apply if—

(a) the person who refused to consent is a person—

    (i) in whose favour there is a residence order in force with respect to the child; or

    (ii) who has custody of the child; or

(b) the person taking or sending the child out of the United Kingdom is, by so acting, in breach of an order made by a court in the United Kingdom."

   (4) For subsection (7) there shall be substituted—

   "(7) For the purposes of this section—

(a) 'guardian of a child', 'residence order' and 'parental responsibility' have the same meaning as in the Children Act 1989; and

(b) a person shall be treated as having custody of a child if there is in force an order of a court in the United

Kingdom awarding him (whether solely or jointly with another person) custody, legal custody or care and control of the child."

(5) In subsection (8) for the words from "or voluntary organisation" to "custodianship proceedings or" there shall be substituted "detained in a place of safety, remanded to a local authority accommodation or the subject of".

38.—(1) In section 2 of that Act (offence of abduction of child by other persons), in subsection (1) for the words from "Subject" to "above" there shall be substituted "Subject to subsection (3) below, a person, other than one mentioned in subsection (2) below."

(2) For subsection (2) of that section there shall be substituted—

"(2) The persons are—

(a) where the father and mother of the child in question were married to each other at the time of his birth, the child's father and mother;

(b) where the father and mother of the child in question were not married to each other at the time of his birth, the child's mother; and

(c) any other person mentioned in section 1(2)(c) to (e) above.

(3) In proceedings against any person for an offence under this section, it shall be a defence for that person to prove—

(a) where the father and mother of the child in question were not married to each other at the time of his birth—

(i) that he is the child's father; or

(ii) that, at the time of the alleged offence, he believed, on reasonable grounds, that he was the child's father; or

(b) that, at the time of the alleged offence, he believed that the child had attained the age of sixteen."

39. At the end of section 3 of that Act (construction of references to taking, sending and detaining) there shall be added "and

(d) references to a child's parents and to a child whose parents were (or were not) married to each other at the time of his birth shall be construed in accordance with section 1 of the Family Law Reform Act 1987 (which extends their meaning)."

40.—(1) The Schedule to that Act (modifications of section 1 for children in certain cases) shall be amended as follows.

(2) In paragraph 1(1) for the words "or voluntary organisation" there shall be substituted "within the meaning of the Children Act 1989".

(3) For paragraph 2(1) there shall be substituted—

"(1) This paragraph applies in the case of a child who is—

(a) detained in a place of safety under section 16(3) of the Children and Young Persons Act 1969; or

(b) remanded to local authority accommodation under section 23 of that Act."

(4) In paragraph 3(1)—

(a) in paragraph (a) for the words "section 14 of the Children Act 1975" there shall be substituted "section 18 of the Adoption Act 1976"; and

(b) in paragraph (d) for the words "section 25 of the Children Act 1975 or section 53 of the Adoption Act 1958" there shall be substituted "section 55 of the Adoption Act 1976".

(5) In paragraph 3(2)(a)—

(a) in sub-paragraph (i), for the words from "order or," to "Children Act 1975" there shall be substituted "section 18 order or, if the section 18 order has been varied under section 21 of that Act so as to give parental responsibility to another agency", and

(b) in sub-paragraph (ii), for the words "(c) or (e)" there shall be substituted "or (c)".

(6) At the end of paragraph 3 there shall be added—

"(3) Sub-paragraph (2) above shall be construed as if the references to the court included, in any case where the court is a magistrates' court, a reference to any magistrates' court acting for the same area as that court".

(7) For paragraph 5 there shall be substituted—

"5. In this Schedule—

(a) 'adoption agency' and 'adoption order' have the same meaning as in the Adoption Act 1976; and

(b) 'area', in relation to a magistrates' court, means the petty sessions area (within the meaning of the Justices of the Peace Act 1979) for which the court is appointed."

Q

The Foster Children (Scotland) Act 1984 (c. 56)

41. In section 1 of the Foster Children (Scotland) Act 1984 (definition of foster child) —

  (a) for the words "he is— (a)" there shall be substituted "(a) he is"; and
  (b) the words "for a period of more than 6 days" and the words from "The period" to the end shall cease to have effect.

42. In section 2(2) of that Act (exceptions to section 1), for paragraph (f) there shall be substituted—

  "(f) if he has been in that person's care for a period of less than 28 days and that person does not intend to undertake his care for any longer period."

43. In section 7(1) of that Act (persons disqualified from keeping foster children) —

  (a) the word "or" at the end of paragraph (e) shall be omitted; and
  (b) after paragraph (f) there shall be inserted "or

  (g) he is disqualified from fostering a child privately (within the meaning of the Children Act 1989) by regulations made under section 68 of that Act,".

The Disabled Persons (Services, Consultation and Representation) Act 1986 (c. 33)

44. In section 2(5) of the Disabled Persons (Services, Consultation and Representation) Act 1986 (circumstances in which authorised representative has right to visit etc. disabled person), after paragraph (d) there shall be inserted—

"(dd) in accommodation provided by any educational establishment."

The Legal Aid Act 1988 (c. 34)

45. In paragraph 2 of Part I of Schedule 2 to the Legal Aid Act 1988 (proceedings in magistrates' courts to which the civil legal aid provisions of Part IV of the Act apply), the following sub-paragraph shall be added at the end—

"(g) proceedings under the Children Act 1989."

Annotation

Schedule 12: deals with minor amendments to a series of Acts.

Paragraph 1: deals with the Custody of Children Act 1891 and provides that it shall cease to have effect. The Law Commission in its report dealing with the Guardianship and Custody of Children (Law Com No. 172) concluded that the 1891 Act had no place in a modern scheme of child law—it had been passed in response to a number of cases in which parents successfully brought *habeas corpus* proceedings against the homes of Dr Barnardo where the children had been placed or taken in after being abandoned by their parents. The Law Commission concluded that as the law had developed and a greater recognition had been given to the interests of children, the provisions of the 1891 Act had been superseded.

Paragraph 2: amends section 1(2)(a) of the Children and Young Persons Act 1933 by extending its scope to include the legal guardian of a child or young person. The purpose of section 1(2)(a) was to provide that a certain class of person was to be deemed to have neglected a child or young person in a manner likely to cause injury to his health; for this to be deemed certain criteria needed to be fulfilled. This was relevant to the question of whether an offence had been committed under section 1(1). The relevant class of person was formerly defined as a parent or other person legally liable to maintain the child or young person concerned. However, this would not necessarily cover legal guardians because they would not automatically be liable to maintain the children of whom they were guardians. The purpose of Paragraph 2 is to reflect the fact that legal guardians will be expected to look after children with the same degree of care as that which parents are expected to exercise in similar circumstances.

Paragraph 3: repeals section 40 of the Children and Young Persons Act 1933 which enabled a justice of the peace to issue a warrant authorising a police constable to search for and remove a child in certain circumstances. This provision was used to enforce place of safety orders made under section 28 of that Act. Emergency protection orders under Part V of this Act confer upon the holder of an order the power to obtain information and to enter premises and remove a child. Section 48 provides for a warrant to be issued to enforce those powers and section 102 provides for similar enforcement of powers of entry under various other enactments. These provisions replace section 40 of the 1933 Act, which is repealed.

Paragraph 4: deals with an amendment to the Education Act 1944 in relation to the enforcement of school attendance. Note that this Act creates a new kind of supervision order which may be made on the application of a local education authority. Education supervision orders appoint a designated local education authority to secure that the child receives proper education: see section 36(1) and (7). They may only be made where the condition in section 36(3) is satisfied, namely that the child is of compulsory school age and is not being properly educated: see section 36(4).

Paragraph 5: deals with the Marriage Act 1949. Note that the Children Act substitutes in the Marriage Act 1949 a simpler and more coherent set of rules about whose consent is required to the marriage of a child who is sixteen or seventeen. Unless there is a residence or a care order in force with respect to the child, the consent of each parent who has parental responsibility for the child and each guardian, if any, is needed. Note that the court has power to permit marriage in the face of parental opposition: section 3 Marriage Act 1949.

Paragraph 6: deals with amendments to the Births and Deaths Registration Act 1953. The amendments take into account the concept of parental responsibility and parental responsibility agreements. The Act uses the phrase "parental responsibility" to sum up the collection of duties, rights and authority which a parent has in respect of his child. The choice of words emphasises that the duty to care for the child and to raise him to moral, physical and emotional health is the fundamental task of parenthood and the only justification for the authority it confers. The concept nevertheless requires these amendments to the 1953 Act.

Paragraphs 7–8: make minor amendments to the Army Act 1955 to bring it into line with the Children Act. Note the change in terminology from a child being in the care of a local authority in England or Wales to that of "being looked after by a local authority in England or Wales" (within the meaning of the Children Act 1989). Under the Act, where a child is said to be in local authority "care" he is under a care order. "Care" no longer indicates a child who is accommodated by a local authority on a voluntary basis. In the Act children who are accommodated by or on behalf of a local authority are referred to as "looked after" by a local authority, whether the accommodation is provided voluntarily or compulsorily.

Paragraphs 9 and 10: deal with the Air Force Act 1955 and relate this to Paragraphs 7 and 8 thus bringing the air force into line with the army for the purposes of the Children Act.

Paragraph 11: introduces changes to the Sexual Offences Act

1956. Paragraph 6 amends section 19(3) of the 1956 Act by altering the definition of "guardian" for the purpose of the section which creates an offence of taking an unmarried girl out of the possession of her parent or guardian in certain circumstances. "Guardian" was formerly defined as any person having "the lawful care or charge of" the girl. Paragraph 10 redefines "guardian" as any person having "parental responsibility for or care of" the girl. The concept of parental responsibility created by the Act and the reference to "care" refer to circumstances where a person lawfully has the girl in his actual care.

Paragraph 12: amends section 20(2) of the Sexual Offences Act 1956 by altering the definition of "guardian" for the purpose of section 20(1) which creates an offence of taking an unmarried girl out of the possession of her "parent or guardian" under certain circumstances. The former definition and amendment in Paragraph 7 are the same as those in respect of section 19(3): see Paragraph 10.

Paragraph 13: amends section 21(3) of the Sexual Offences Act 1956 by altering the definition of "guardian" for the purposes of the section which creates an offence of taking a woman who is a defective out of the possession of her parent or guardian in certain circumstances.

Paragraph 14: amends the definition of responsible person for the purpose of section 28 of the Sexual Offences Act 1956, which creates an offence of encouraging, by a person responsible for a girl under the age of sixteen, the prostitution of, or the commission of unlawful sexual intercourse with, or of an indecent assault on, the girl.

Paragraph 15: provides that section 38 of the Sexual Offences Act 1956 shall cease to have effect. The effect of section 38 was to enable a court convicting a person of incest with a child to divest that person of all authority over that child. The Law Commission recommended the repeal of this provision.

Paragraph 16: makes amendments to update certain references in section 43 of the 1956 Act to bring them into line with the provisions of this Act.

Paragraph 17: ensures that the phrase "parental responsibility" when used in the 1956 Act has the meaning ascribed by this Act: see Paragraph 6.

Paragraph 18: deals with the Naval Discipline Act 1957 and incorporates the amendments in relation to Schedule 5A of the Army Act referred to under Paragraph 8. Linked to Paragraphs 9–10 dealing with the air force, it brings all three armed services into line for the purposes of the Children Act.

Paragraph 19: provides for the repeal of section 3 of the Children and Young Persons Act 1963, which enables parents to seek an order directing a local authority to investigate the circumstances of a child. Section 3 of the 1963 Act is not to be replaced and the duty of a local authority to investigate is set out in section 47.

Paragraph 20: introduces amendments to the Children and Young Persons Act 1969. The provisions of this Act which apply to young offenders are preserved, but certain of these require amendment consequential upon the repeal of care provisions in the 1969 Act and their re-enactment in this Act. Paragraph 14 inserts a reference to Part IV of this Act into section 5 of the 1969 Act. Note that Section 5, which places restrictions on the prosecution of juveniles, has not been implemented.

Paragraph 21: inserts new subsections relating to recognisances into section 7 of the 1969 Act, which gives courts certain powers in respect of juvenile offenders. The new subsections preserve the effect of section 2(13) of the 1969 Act in its application to juvenile offenders.

Paragraph 22: deals with a substitution in section 12A of the Children and Young Persons Act 1969. This substitution applies to supervision orders made under section 7(7) of the 1969 Act. (To be read in conjunction with Paragraph 23.)

Paragraph 23: inserts new subsections relating to residence requirements into section 12 of the 1969 Act (which gives power to include requirements in supervision orders). Note that new subsection 1(1) gives the court a power to attach to supervision orders made in criminal proceedings a requirement that the juvenile must live in accommodation provided by or on behalf of the local authority. Note also the power given to a court to specify people with whom the juvenile must not be accommodated and to limit the duration of the residence requirements to six months.

Paragraph 24: deals with further amendments to the Children and Young Persons Act 1969 relating to the variation and discharge of supervision orders. Supervision orders may still be made in criminal proceedings. In recent years these orders have become dissimilar to supervision orders which are made in care proceedings under the Children and Young Persons Act 1969. The difference between criminal and civil supervision orders increase under the Children Act.

Paragraph 25: makes provision for changes in section 16 in relation to remand and an interim order. Note that section 38 provides that interim care or supervision orders stand alongside section 8 orders as means of promoting a child's welfare and that care orders may no longer be imposed as a sentence in criminal proceedings. Section 7(7)(a) of the Children and Young Persons Act 1969 is repealed by Schedule 15.

Paragraph 26: deals with the power to remand a child or young person to the care of a local authority, which is replaced by remand to accommodation provided by a local authority. The intention is that a remanded child should no longer be treated as if he were under a care order. This is to be linked to the introduction of a requirement which may be imposed under a criminal supervision order, that the child or young person will live in accommodation provided by or on behalf of the local authority for up to six months: see Paragraph 23.

Paragraph 27: deals with substitutions to be made in section 32 of the Children and Young Persons Act 1969 in relation to the detention of absentees. The intention is that a child on remand will be looked after by the local authority, who will not have parental responsibility for him, but Paragraph 27 provides that a constable may lawfully detain the remanded person.

Paragraphs 28, 29 and 30: deal with technical amendments to section 34(1), section 70(1) and section 73 of the Children and Young Persons Act 1969.

Paragraph 31: introduces amendments to the Matrimonial Causes Act 1973 and implements the recommendation of the Law Commission in its report "Family Law, Review of Child Law and Guardianship and Custody" (Law Com.No.172). Formerly, the court had a duty under section 41 of the Matrimonial Causes Act 1973 to declare itself satisfied as to the arrangements for children of the family before making absolute a decree of divorce or nullity, or making a decree of judicial separation. The original aims of the procedure were to ensure that divorcing parents made the best possible arrangements for their children and to identify cases of particular concern where protective measures might be needed. The amendment in Paragraph 31 does away with the need for "satisfaction hearings" in every case.

Paragraph 32: gives effect to the recommendation of the Law Commission in its report "Family Law, Review of Child Law and Guardianship and Custody" (Law Com.No.172) and repeals section 42(3) of the Matrimonial Causes Act 1973. That section empowered the court to declare in a decree absolute of divorce or a decree of judicial separation that one spouse was unfit to have custody of the children of the family. This meant that if he was a parent of any child of the family he was not entitled as of right to the custody or guardianship on the death of the other parent. The Law Commission observed that such declarations were hardly ever made today. Indeed, the power has already been repealed in Scotland: Law Reform (Parent and Child) (Scotland) Act 1986, section 10(2) and Schedule 2.

Paragraph 33: modifies section 52(1) of the Children and Young Persons Act 1969 to take into account that under the Children Act children are no longer considered to be boarded out; rather they are placed with foster parents.

Paragraph 34: makes an amendment to the National Health Service Act 1977 in relation to the functions of local social service authorities.

Paragraph 35: deals with the repeal of the Child Care Act 1980. While awaiting repeal of the Act and the subsequent guidelines to accompany the Children Act, social services departments have set up implementation groups to relate the Act upon implementation to the Child Care Act 1980.

Paragraph 36: amends the Education Act 1981 and empowers a local authority to make such arrangements as they think fit to enable any child in respect of whom they maintain a section 7 statement to attend an establishment outside England and Wales which specialises in providing for children with special needs. Note that section 28 provides for consultation between a local authority and a local education authority where it is proposed to place a child in an establishment where education is provided for children who live there. Section 28(4) defines the appropriate local education authority as one covering the area of the local authority, or where a child has special educational needs and the local education authority maintaining the statement of educational needs is situated elsewhere than in the area of the local authority.

Paragraph 37: amends section 1 of the Child Abduction Act 1984 dealing with the offence of abduction by a parent. Note that section 49 deals with the abduction of children in care and makes this an offence liable on summary conviction to imprisonment not exceeding six months or to a fine, or to both. It replaces similar offences under the Child Care Act 1980.

Paragraph 38: amends section 2 of the Child Abduction Act 1984 dealing with the abduction of a child not by a parent but by other persons. Note the test of reasonableness in Paragraph 38(3)(ii). The White Paper, "The Law on Child Care and Family Services", proposed that there should be a single offence consisting of knowingly and without reasonable excuse or lawful authority taking the child or detaining or harbouring him or assisting, inducing or inciting him to run away.

Paragraph 39: amends section 3 of the Child Abduction Act 1984 and relates this to section 1 of the Family Law Reform Act 1987.

Paragraph 40: amends the Schedule to the Child Abduction Act 1984 and makes a number of consequential amendments.

Paragraph 41: deals with amendments to the Foster Children (Scotland) Act 1984 which are of a technical nature.

Paragraph 42: relates to a period of care of less than twenty eight days. Note that, generally speaking, private foster children are those whose parents place them for more than twenty eight days by private arrangement with a family which is not related to the child.

Paragraph 43: relates to persons disqualified from fostering a child privately within the meaning of the Children Act 1989 by regulations under section 68. Note that section 68 prohibits a person from fostering children privately if he is disqualified by regulations made by the Secretary of State referred to in Paragraph 43, or lives in a household in which a disqualified person lives or is employed, unless he obtains the consent of the local authority.

Paragraph 44: extends the provisions of section 2(5) of the Disabled Persons (Services, Consultation and Representation) Act 1986 so that an authorised representative will have the right to visit a disabled child living in any educational establishment.

Paragraph 45: deals with the Legal Aid Act 1988 and provides that civil legal aid is available for all civil proceedings under the Act in a magistrates' court. Proceedings in the High Court and the county court, including those under the Act, automatically attract civil legal aid without the need for specific provision to be made.

Schedule 13: Consequential Amendments

The Wills Act 1837 (c. 26)

1. In section 1 of the Wills Act 1837 (interpretation), in the definition of "will", for the words "and also to a disposition by will and testament or devise of the custody and tuition of any child" there shall be substituted "and also to an appointment by will of a guardian of a child".

The Children and Young Persons Act 1933 (c. 12)

2. In section 1(1) of the Children and Young Persons Act 1933 (cruelty to persons under sixteen) for the words "has the custody, charge or care of" there shall be substituted "has responsibility for".

3. In the following sections of that Act—

(a) 3(1) (allowing persons under sixteen to be in brothels);

(b) 4(1) and (2) (causing or allowing persons under sixteen to be used for begging);

(c) 11 (exposing children under twelve to risk of burning); and

(d) 25(1) (restrictions on persons under eighteen going abroad for the purpose of performing for profit),

for the words "the custody, charge or care of" there shall, in each case, be substituted "responsibility for".

4. In section 10(1A) of that Act (vagrants preventing children from receiving education), for the words from "to bring the child" to the end there shall be substituted "to make an application in respect of the child or young person for an education supervision order under section 36 of the Children Act 1989".

5. For section 17 of that Act (interpretation of Part I) there shall be substituted the following section—

"Interpretation of Part I.

17.—(1) For the purposes of this Part of this Act, the following shall be presumed to have responsibility for a child or young person—

(a) any person who—

(i) has parental responsibility for him (within the meaning of the Children Act 1989); or

(ii) is otherwise legally liable to maintain him; and

(b) any person who has care of him.

(2) A person who is presumed to be responsible for a child or young person by virtue of subsection (1)(a) shall not be taken to have ceased to be responsible for him by reason only that he does not have care of him."

6.—(1) In section 34 of that Act (attendance at court of parent of child or young person charged with an offence etc.), in subsection (1) after the word "offence" there shall be inserted "is the subject of an application for a care or supervision order under Part IV of the Children Act 1989".

(2) In subsection (7) of that section after the words "Children and Young Persons Act 1969" there shall be inserted "or Part IV of the Children Act 1989".

(3) After subsection (7) of that section there shall be inserted—

"(7A) If it appears that at the time of his arrest the child or young person is being provided with accommodation by or on behalf of a local authority under section 20 of the Children Act 1989, the local authority shall also be informed as described in subsection (3) above as soon as it is reasonably practicable to do so."

7. In section 107(1) of that Act (interpretation)—

(a) in the definition of "guardian", for the words "charge of or control over" there shall be substituted "care of";

(b) for the definition of legal guardian there shall be substituted—

' "legal guardian', in relation to a child or young person, means a guardian of a child as defined in the Children Act 1989".

The Education Act 1944 (c. 31)

8.—(1) Section 40 of the Education Act 1944 (enforcement of school attendance) shall be amended as follows.

(2) For subsection (2) there shall be substituted—

"(2) Proceedings for such offences shall not be instituted except by a local education authority.

(2A) Before instituting such proceedings the local education authority shall consider whether it would be appropriate, instead of or as well as instituting the proceedings, to apply for an education supervision order with respect to the child."

(3) For subsections (3) and (4) there shall be substituted—

"(3) The court—

(a) by which a person is convicted of an offence against section 37 of this Act; or

(b) before which a person is charged with an offence under section 39 of this Act, may direct the local education authority instituting the proceedings to apply for an education supervision order with respect to the child unless the authority, having consulted the appropriate local authority, decide that the child's welfare will be satisfactorily safeguarded even though no education supervision order is made.

(3A) Where, following such a direction, a local education authority decide not to apply for an education supervision order they shall inform the court of the reasons for their decision.

(3B) Unless the court has directed otherwise, the information required under subsection (3A) shall be given to the court before the end of the period of eight weeks beginning with the date on which the direction was given.

(4) Where—

    (a) a local education authority apply for an education supervision order with respect to a child who is the subject of a school attendance order; and

    (b) the court decides that section 36(3) of the Children Act 1989 prevents it from making the order;

the court may direct that the school attendance order shall cease to be in force."

(4) After subsection (4) there shall be inserted—

    "(5) In this section—

        'appropriate local authority' has the same meaning as in section 36(9) of the Children Act 1989; and

        'education supervision order' means an education supervision order under that Act."

9. In section 71 of that Act (complaints with respect to independent schools), the following paragraph shall be added after paragraph (d), in subsection (1)—

        "(e) there has been a failure, in relation to a child provided with accommodation by the school, to comply with the duty imposed by section 87 of the Children Act 1989 (welfare of children accommodated in independent schools);".

10. After section 114(1C) of that Act (interpretation) there shall be inserted the following subsections—

    "(1D) In this Act, unless the context otherwise requires,

'parent', in relation to a child or young person, includes any person—

    (a) who is not a parent of his but who has parental responsibility for him, or

    (b) who has care of him,

except for the purposes of the enactments mentioned in subsection (1E) of this section, where it only includes such a person if he is an individual.

    (1E) The enactments are—

    (a) sections 5(4), 15(2) and (6), 31 and 65(1) of, and paragraph 7(6) of Schedule 2 to, the Education (No. 2) Act 1986; and

    (b) sections 53(8), 54(2), 58(5)(k), 60 and 61 of the Education Reform Act 1988.

    (1F) For the purposes of subsection (1D) of this section—

    (a) 'parental responsibility' has the same meaning as in the Children Act 1989; and

    (b) in determining whether an individual has care of a child or young person any absence of the child or young person at a hospital or boarding school and any other temporary absence shall be disregarded."

The National Assistance Act 1948 (c. 29)

11.—(1) In section 21(1)(a) of the National Assistance Act 1948 (persons for whom local authority is to provide residential accommodation) after the word "persons" there shall be inserted "aged eighteen or over".

(2) In section 29(1) of that Act (welfare arrangements for blind, deaf, dumb and crippled persons) after the words "that is to say persons" and after the words "and other persons" there shall, in each case, be inserted "aged eighteen or over".

The Reserve and Auxiliary Forces (Protection of Civil Interests) Act 1951 (c. 65)

12. For section 2(1)(d) of the Reserve and Auxiliary Forces (Protection of Civil Interests) Act 1951 (cases in which leave of the appropriate court is required before enforcing certain orders for the payment of money), there shall be substituted—

    "(d) an order for alimony, maintenance or other payment made under sections 21 to 33 of the Matrimonial Causes

Act 1973 or made, or having effect as if made, under Schedule 1 to the Children Act 1989."

The Mines and Quarries Act 1954 (c. 70)

13. In section 182(1) of the Mines and Quarries Act 1954 (interpretation), in the definition of "parent", for the words from "or guardian" to first "young person" there shall be substituted "of a young person or any person who is not a parent of his but who has parental responsibility for him (within the meaning of the Children Act 1989)".

The Administration of Justice Act 1960 (c. 65)

14. In section 12 of the Administration of Justice Act 1960 (publication of information relating to proceedings in private), in subsection (1) for paragraph (a) there shall be substituted—

"(a) where the proceedings—

(i) relate to the exercise of the inherent jurisdiction of the High Court with respect to minors;
(ii) are brought under the Children Act 1989; or
(iii) otherwise relate wholly or mainly to the maintenance or upbringing of a minor;".

The Factories Act 1961 (c. 34)

15. In section 176(1) of the Factories Act 1961 (interpretation), in the definition of "parent", for the words from "or guardian" to first "young person" there shall be substituted "of a child or young person or any person who is not a parent of his but who has parental responsibility for him (within the meaning of the Children Act 1989)".

The Criminal Justice Act 1967 (c. 80)

16. In section 67(1A)(c) of the Criminal Justice Act 1967 (computation of sentences of imprisonment passed in England and Wales) for the words "in the care of a local authority" there shall be substituted "remanded to local authority accommodation."

The Health Services and Public Health Act 1968 (c. 46)

17.—(1) In section 64(3)(a) of the Health Services and Public Health Act 1968 (meaning of "relevant enactments" in relation to power of Minister of Health or Secretary of State to provide financial assistance), for sub-paragraph (xix) inserted by paragraph 19 of Schedule 5 to the Child Care Act 1980 there shall be substituted—

"(xx) the Children Act 1989."

(2) In section 65(3)(b) of that Act (meaning of "relevant enactments" in relation to power of local authority to provide financial and other assistance), for sub-paragraph (xx) inserted by paragraph 20 of Schedule 5 to the Child Care Act 1980 there shall be substituted—

"(xxi) the Children Act 1989,".

The Social Work (Scotland) Act 1968 (c. 49)

18. In section 2(2) of the Social Work (Scotland) Act 1968 (matters referred to social work committee) after paragraph (j) there shall be inserted—

"(k) section 19 and Part X of the Children Act 1989,".

19. In section 5(2)(c) of that Act (power of Secretary of State to make regulations) for the words "and (j)" there shall be substituted "to (k)".

20. In section 21(3) of that Act (mode of provision of accommodation and maintenance) for the words "section 21 of the Child Care Act 1980" there shall be substituted "section 23 of the Children Act 1989".

21. In section 74(6) of that Act (parent of child in residential establishment moving to England or Wales) for the words from "Children and Young Persons Act 1969" to the end there shall be substituted "Children Act 1989, but as if section 31(8) were omitted".

22. In section 75(2) of that Act (parent of child subject to care order etc. moving to Scotland), for the words "Children and Young Persons Act 1969" there shall be substituted "Children Act 1989".

23. In section 86(3) of that Act (meaning of ordinary residence for purpose of adjustments between authority providing accommodation and authority of area of residence), the words "the Child Care Act 1980 or" shall be omitted and after the words "education authority" there shall be inserted "or placed with local authority foster parents under the Children Act 1989".

24. In section 12(5)(b) of the Civil Evidence Act 1968 (findings of paternity etc. as evidence in civil proceedings—meaning of "relevant proceedings") for sub-paragraph (iv) there shall be substituted—

> *"(iv) paragraph 23 of Schedule 2 to the Children Act 1989."*

The Administration of Justice Act 1970 (c. 31)

25. In Schedule 8 to the Administration of Justice Act 1970 (maintenance orders for purposes of Maintenance Orders Act 1958 and the 1970 Act), in paragraph 6 for the words "section 47 or 51 of the Child Care Act 1980" there shall be substituted "paragraph 23 of Schedule 2 to the Children Act 1989".]

The Local Authority Social Services Act 1970 (c. 42)

26.—(1) In Schedule 1 to the Local Authority Social Services Act 1970 (enactments conferring functions assigned to social service committee)—

(a) in the entry relating to the Mental Health Act 1959, for the words "sections 8 and 9" there shall be substituted "section 8"; and

(b) in the entry relating to the Children and Young Persons Act 1969 for the words "sections 1, 2 and 9" there shall be substituted "section 9".

(2) At the end of that Schedule there shall be added—

"Children Act 1989.	Welfare reports.
The whole Act, in so far as it confers functions on a local authority within the meaning of that Act.	Consent to application for residence order in respect of child in care.
	Family assistance orders.
	Functions under Part III of the Act (local authority support for children and families).
	Care and supervision.
	Protection of children.

Note: The words *in italics* within square brackets were deleted by the Courts and Legal Services Act 1990.

Functions in relation to community homes, voluntary
homes and voluntary organisations, registered children's homes, private
arrangements for fostering
children, child minding and
day care for young children.

Inspection of children's homes
on behalf of Secretary of
State.

Research and returns of information.

Functions in relation to children accommodated by
health authorities and local
education authorities or in
residential care, nursing or
mental nursing homes or in
independent schools."

The Chronically Sick and Disabled Persons Act 1970 (c. 44)

27. After section 28 of the Chronically Sick and Disabled Persons Act 1970 there shall be inserted—

"Application of Act to authorities having functions under the Children Act 1989.

28A. This Act applies with respect to disabled children in relation to whom a local authority have functions under Part III of the Children Act 1989 as it applies in relation to persons to whom section 29 of the National Assistance Act 1948 applies."

The Courts Act 1971 (c. 23)

28. In Part I of Schedule 9 to the Courts Act 1971 (substitution of references to Crown Court), in the entry relating to the Children and Young Persons Act 1969, for the words "Sections 2(12), 3(8), 16(8), 21(4)(5)" there shall be substituted "Section 16(8).".

The Attachment of Earnings Act 1971 (c. 32)

29. In Schedule 1 to the Attachment of Earnings Act 1971 (maintenance orders to which that Act applies), in paragraph 7, for the words "section 47 or 51 of the Child Care Act 1980" there shall be substituted "paragraph 23 of Schedule 2 to the Children Act 1989".

The Tribunals and Inquiries Act 1971 (c. 62)

30. In Schedule 1 to the Tribunals and Inquiries Act 1971 (tribunals under direct supervision of the Council on Tribunals) for paragraph 4 there shall be substituted —

"Registration of voluntary homes and children's homes under the Children Act 1989.

4. Registered Homes Tribunals constituted under Part III of the Registered Homes Act 1984."

The Local Government Act 1972 (c. 70)

31. — (1) In section 102(1) of the Local Government Act 1972 (appointment of committees) for the words "section 31 of the Child Care Act 1980" there shall be substituted "section 53 of the Children Act 1989".

(2) In Schedule 12A to that Act (access to information: exempt information), in Part III (interpretation), in paragraph 1(1)(b) for the words "section 20 of the Children and Young Persons Act 1969" there shall be substituted "section 31 of the Children Act 1989".

The Employment of Children Act 1973 (c. 24)

32. — (1) In section 2 of the Employment of Children Act 1973 (supervision by education authorities), in subsection (2)(a) for the words "guardian or a person who has actual custody of" there shall be substituted "any person responsible for".

(2) After that subsection there shall be inserted —

"(2A) For the purposes of subsection (2)(a) above a person is responsible for a child —

(a) in England and Wales, if he has parental responsibility for the child or care of him; and

(b) in Scotland, if he is his guardian or has actual custody of him.".

The Domicile and Matrimonial Proceedings Act 1973 (c. 45)

33. — (1) In Schedule 1 to the Domicile and Matrimonial Proceedings Act 1973 (proceedings in divorce etc. stayed by reference to proceedings in other jurisdiction), paragraph 11(1) shall be amended as follows —

(a) at the end of the definition of "lump sum" there shall be added "or an order made in equivalent circumstances under Schedule 1 to the Children Act 1989 and of a kind mentioned in paragraph 1(2)(c) of that Schedule";

(b) in the definition of "relevant order", at the end of paragraph (b), there shall be added "or an order made in equivalent circumstances under Schedule 1 to the Children Act 1989 and of a kind mentioned in paragraph 1(2)(a) or (b) of that Schedule";

(c) in paragraph (c) of that definition, after the word "children)" there shall be inserted "or a section 8 order under the Children Act 1989"; and

(d) in paragraph (d) of that definition for the words "the custody, care or control" there shall be substituted "care".

(2) In paragraph 11(3) of that Schedule—

(a) the word "four" shall be omitted; and

(b) for the words "the custody of a child and the education of a child" there shall be substituted "or any provision which could be made by a section 8 order under the Children Act 1989".

The Powers of Criminal Courts Act 1973

34. In schedule 3 to The Powers of Criminal Courts Act 1973 (the probation and after-care service and its functions), in paragraph 3(2A) after paragraph (b) there shall be inserted—

"and

(c) directions given under paragraph 2 or 3 of Schedule 3 to the Children Act 1989".

The Rehabilitation of Offenders Act 1974 (c. 53)

35.—(1) Section 7(2) of the Rehabilitation of Offenders Act 1974 (limitations on rehabilitation under the Act) shall be amended as follows.

(2) For paragraph (c) there shall be substituted—

"(c) in any proceedings relating to adoption, the marriage of any minor, the exercise of the inherent jurisdiction of the High court with respect to minors or the provision by any person of accommodation, care or schooling for minors;

(cc) in any proceedings brought under the Children Act 1989;"

(3) For paragraph (d) there shall be substituted—

"(d) in any proceedings relating to the variation or discharge of a supervision order under the Children and Young Persons Act 1969, or on appeal from any such proceedings".

The Domestic Proceedings and Magistrates' Courts Act 1978 (c. 22)

36. For section 8 of the Domestic Proceedings and Magistrates' Courts Act 1978 (orders for the custody of children) there shall be substituted—

"Restrictions on making of orders under this Act: welfare of children.

8. Where an application is made by a party to a marriage for an order under section 2, 6 or 7 of this Act, then, if there is a child of the family who is under the age of eighteen, the court shall not dismiss or make a final order on the application until it has decided whether to exercise any of its powers under the Children Act 1989 with respect to the child."

37. In section 19(3A)(b) (interim orders) for the words "subsections (2) and" there shall be substituted "subsection".

38. For section 20(12) of that Act (variation and revocation of orders for periodical payments) there shall be substituted—

"(12) An application under this section may be made—

(a) where it is for the variation or revocation of an order under section 2, 6, 7 or 19 of this Act for periodical payments, by either party to the marriage in question; and

(b) where it is for the variation of an order under section 2(1)(c), 6 or 7 of this Act for periodical payments to or in respect of a child, also by the child himself, if he has attained the age of sixteen."

39.—(1) For section 20A of that Act (revival of orders for periodical payments) there shall be substituted—

"Revival of orders for periodical payments.

20A.—(1) Where an order made by a magistrates' court under this Part of this Act for the making of periodical payments to or in respect of a child (other than an interim maintenance order) ceases to have effect—

(a) on the date on which the child attains the age of sixteen, or

(b) at any time after that date but before or on the date on which he attains the age of eighteen,

the child may apply to the court which made the order for an order for its revival.

(2) If on such an application it appears to the court that—

(a) the child is, will be or (if an order were made under this subsection) would be receiving instruction at an educational establishment or undergoing training for a trade, profession or vocation, whether or not while in gainful employment, or

(b) there are special circumstances which justify the making of an order under this subsection,

the court shall have power by order to revive the order from such date as the court may specify, not being earlier than the date of the making of the application.

(3) Any order revived under this section may be varied or revoked under section 20 in the same way as it could have been varied or revoked had it continued in being."

[*40. In section 23(1) of that Act (supplementary provisions with respect to the variation and revocation of orders) for the words "14(3), 20 or 21" there shall be substituted "20" and for the words "section 20 of this Act" there shall be substituted "that section".*]

41.—(1) In section 25 of that Act (effect on certain orders of parties living together), in subsection (1)(a) for the words "6 or 11(2)" there shall be substituted "or 6".

(2) In subsection (2) of that section—

(a) in paragraph (a) for the words "6 or 11(2)" there shall be substituted "or 6"; and

(b) after paragraph (a) there shall be inserted "or".

42. In section 29(5) of that Act (appeals) for the words "sections 14(3), 20 and 21" there shall be substituted "section 20".

43. In section 88(1) of that Act (interpretation)—

Note: The words *in italics* within square brackets were deleted by the Courts and Legal Services Act 1990.

(a) in the definition of "child", for the words from "an illegit-
imate" to the end there shall be substituted "a child
whose father and mother were not married to each other
at the time of his birth"; and

(b) in the definition of "child of the family", for the words
"being boarded-out with those parties" there shall be
substituted "placed with those parties as foster parents".

The Magistrates' Courts Act 1980 (c. 43)

44.—(1) In section 59(2) of the Magistrates' Courts Act 1980
(periodical payments through justices' clerk) for the words "the
Guardianship of Minors Acts 1971 and 1973" there shall be substituted "(or having effect as if made under) Schedule 1 to the
Children Act 1989".

(2) For section 62(5) of that Act (payments to children) there
shall be substituted—

"(5) In this section references to the person with whom a
child has his home—

(a) in the case of any child who is being looked after by
a local authority (within the meaning of section 22
of the Children Act 1989), are references to that
local authority; and

(b) in any other case, are references to the person who,
disregarding any absence of the child at a hospital
or boarding school and any other temporary
absence, has care of the child.".

The Supreme Court Act 1981 (c. 54)

45.—(1) In section 18 of the Supreme Court Act 1981 (restrictions on appeals to Court of Appeal)—

(a) in subsection (1)(h)(i), for the word "custody" there shall
be substituted "residence"; and

(b) in subsection (1)(h)(ii) for the words "access to", in both
places, there shall be substituted "contact with".

(2) In section 41 of that Act (wards of court), the following
subsection shall be inserted after subsection (2)—

"(2A) Subsection (2) does not apply with respect to a child
who is the subject of a care order (as defined by section 105
of the Children Act 1989)."

(3) In Schedule 1 to that Act (distribution of business in High
Court), for paragraph 3(b)(ii) there shall be substituted—

' "(ii) the exercise of the inherent jurisdiction of the High Court with respect to minors, the maintenance of minors and any proceedings under the Children Act 1989, except proceedings solely for the appointment of a guardian of a minor's estate;".

The Armed Forces Act 1981 (c. 55)

46. In section 14 of the Armed Forces Act 1981 (temporary removal to, and detention in, place of safety abroad or in the United Kingdom of service children in need of care and control), in subsection (9A) for the words "the Children and Young Persons Act 1933, the Children and Young Persons Act 1969" there shall be substituted "the Children Act 1989".

The Civil Jurisdiction and Judgments Act 1982 (c. 27)

47. In paragraph 5(a) of Schedule 5 to the Civil Jurisdiction and Judgments Act 1982 (maintenance and similar payments excluded from Schedule 4 to that Act) for the words "section 47 or 51 of the Child Care Act 1980" there shall be substituted "paragraph 23 of Schedule 2 to the Children Act 1989".

The Mental Health Act 1983 (c. 20)

48.—(1) For section 27 of the Mental Health Act 1983 (children and young persons in care of local authority) there shall be substituted the following section—

"Children and young persons in care.

27. Where—

(a) a patient who is a child or young person is in the care of a local authority by virtue of a care order within the meaning of the Children Act 1989; or

(b) the rights and powers of a parent of a patient who is a child or young person are vested in a local authority by virtue of section 16 of the Social Work (Scotland) Act 1968,

the authority shall be deemed to be the nearest relative of the patient in preference to any person except the patient's husband or wife (if any)."

(2) Section 28 of that Act (nearest relative of minor under guardianship, etc.) is amended as mentioned in sub-paragraphs (3) and (4).

(3) For subsection (1) there shall be substituted—

"(1) Where—

(a) a guardian has been appointed for a person who has not attained the age of eighteen years; or

(b) a residence order (as defined by section 8 of the Children Act 1989) is in force with respect to such a person,

the guardian (or guardians, where there is more than one) or the person named in the residence order shall, to the exclusion of any other person, be deemed to be his nearest relative."

(4) For subsection (3) there shall be substituted—

"(3) In this section 'guardian' does not include a guardian under this Part of this Act."

(5) In section 131(2) of that Act (informal admission of patients aged sixteen or over) for the words from "notwithstanding" to the end there shall be substituted "even though there are one or more persons who have parental responsibility for him (within the meaning of the Children Act 1989)".

The Registered Homes Act 1984 (c. 23)

49.—(1) In section 1(5) of the Registered Homes Act 1984 (requirement of registration) for paragraphs (d) and (e) there shall be substituted—

"(d) any community home, voluntary home or children's home within the meaning of the Children Act 1989."

(2) In section 39 of that Act (preliminary) for paragraphs (a) and (b) there shall be substituted—

"(a) the Children Act 1989."

The Mental Health (Scotland) Act 1984 (c. 36)

50. For section 54 of the Mental Health (Scotland) Act 1984 (children and young persons in care of local authority) there shall be substituted the following section—

"Children and
young persons in
care of local
authority.

54. Where—

  (a) the rights and powers of a parent of a patient who is a child or young person are vested in a local authority by virtue of section 16 of the Social Work (Scotland) Act 1968; or

  (b) a patient who is a child or young person is in the care of a local authority by virtue of a care order made under the Children Act 1989,

the authority shall be deemed to be the nearest relative of the patient in preference to any person except the patient's husband or wife (if any)."

The Matrimonial and Family Proceedings Act 1984 (c. 42)

51. In section 38(2)(b) of the Matrimonial and Family Proceedings Act 1984 (transfer of family proceedings from High court to county court) after the words "a ward of court" there shall be inserted "or any other proceedings which relate to the exercise of the inherent jurisdiction of the High court with respect to minors".

The Police and Criminal Evidence Act 1984 (c. 60)

52. In section 37(14) of the Police and Criminal Evidence Act 1984 (duties of custody officer before charge) after the words "Children and Young Persons Act 1969" there shall be inserted "or in Part IV of the Children Act 1989".

53.—(1) In section 38 of that Act (duties of custody officer after charge), in subsection (6) for the words from "make arrangements" to the end there shall be substituted "secure that the arrested juvenile is moved to local authority accommodation".

(2) After that subsection there shall be inserted—

"(6A) In this section 'local authority accommodation' means accommodation provided by or on behalf of a local authority (within the meaning of the Children Act 1989).

(6B) Where an arrested juvenile is moved to local authority accommodation under subsection (6) above, it shall be lawful for any person acting on behalf of the authority to detain him.".

(3) In subsection (8) of that section for the words "Children and Young Persons Act 1969" there shall be substituted "Children Act 1989".

54. In section 39(4) of that Act (responsibilities in relation to persons detained) for the words "transferred to the care of a local authority in pursuance of arrangements made" there shall be substituted "moved to local authority accommodation".

55. In Schedule 2 to that Act (preserved powers of arrest) in the entry relating to the Children and Young Persons Act 1969 for the words "Sections 28(2) and" there shall be substituted "Section".

The Surrogacy Arrangements Act 1985 (c. 49)

56. In section 1(2)(b) of the Surrogacy Arrangements Act 1985 (meaning of "surrogate mother", etc.) for the words "the parental rights being exercised" there shall be substituted "parental responsibility being met".

The Child Abduction and Custody Act 1985 (c. 60)

57.—(1) In section 9(a) and 20(2)(a) of the Child Abduction and Custody Act 1985 (orders with respect to which court's powers suspended), for the words "any other order under section 1(2) of the Children and Young Persons Act 1969" there shall be substituted "a supervision order under section 31 of the Children Act 1989".

(2) At the end of section 27 of that Act (interpretation), there shall be added—

"(4) In this Act a decision relating to rights of access in England and Wales means a decision as to the contact which a child may, or may not, have with any person."

(3) In Part I of Schedule 3 to that Act (orders in England and Wales which are custody orders for the purposes of the Act), for paragraph 1 there shall be substituted—

"1. The following are the orders referred to in section 27(1) of this Act—

(a) a care order under the Children Act 1989 (as defined by section 31(11) of that Act, read with section 105(1) and Schedule 14);

(b) a residence order (as defined by section 8 of the Act of 1989); and

(c) any order made by a court in England and Wales under any of the following enactments—

(i) section 9(1), 10(1)(a) of the Guardianship of Minors Act 1971;

(ii) section 42(1) or (2) or 43(1) of the Matrimonial Causes Act 1973;

(iii) section 2(2)(b), 4(b) or (5) of the Guardianship Act 1973 as applied by section 34(5) of the Children Act 1975;

(iv) section 8(2)(a), 10(1) or 19(1)(ii) of the Domestic Proceedings and Magistrates Courts Act 1978;

(v) section 26(1)(b) of the Adoption Act 1976."

The Disabled Persons (Services, Consultation and Representation) Act 1986 (c. 33)

58. In section 1(3) of the Disabled Persons (Services, Consultation and Representation) Act 1986 (circumstances in which regulations may provide for the appointment of authorised representatives of disabled persons)—

(a) in paragraph (a), for the words "parent or guardian of a disabled person under the age of sixteen" there shall be substituted—

"(i) the parent of a disabled person under the age of sixteen, or

(ii) any other person who is not a parent of his but who has parental responsibility for him"; and

(b) in paragraph (b), for the words "in the care of" there shall be substituted "looked after by".

59.—(1) Section 2 of that Act (circumstances in which authorised representative has right to visit etc. disabled person) shall be amended as follows.

(2) In subsection (3)(a) for the words from second "the" to "by" there shall be substituted "for the words 'if so requested by the disabled person' there shall be substituted 'if so requested by any person mentioned in section 1(3)(a)(i) or (ii)'."

(3) In subsection (5) after paragraph (b) there shall be inserted—

"(bb) in accommodation provided by or on behalf of a local authority under Part III of the Children Act 1989, or".

(4) After paragraph (c) of subsection (5) there shall be inserted—

"(cc) in accommodation provided by a voluntary organisation in accordance with arrangements made by a local authority under section 17 of the Children Act 1989, or".

60. In section 5(7)(b) of that Act (disabled persons leaving special education) for the word "guardian" there shall be substituted "other person who is not a parent of his but who has parental responsibility for him".

61.—(1) In section 16 of that Act (interpretation) in the definition of "disabled person", in paragraph (a) for the words from "means" to "applies" there shall be substituted "means—

> "(i) in the case of a person aged eighteen or over, a person to whom section 29 of the 1948 Act applies, and
>
> (ii) in the case of a person under the age of eighteen, a person who is disabled within the meaning of Part III of the Children Act 1989".

(2) After the definition of "parent" in that section there shall be inserted—

> ' "parental responsibility' has the same meaning as in the Children Act 1989."

(3) In the definition of "the welfare enactments" in that section, in paragraph (a) after the words "the 1977 Act" there shall be inserted "and Part III of the Children Act 1989".

(4) At the end of that section there shall be added—

> "(2) In this Act any reference to a child who is looked after by a local authority has the same meaning as in the Children Act 1989."

The Family Law Act 1986 (c. 55)

62.—(1) The Family Law Act 1986 shall be amended as follows.

(2) Subject to paragraphs 63 to 71, in Part I—

(a) for the words "custody order", in each place where they occur, there shall be substituted "Part I order";

(b) for the words "proceedings with respect to the custody of", in each place where they occur, there shall be substituted "Part I proceedings with respect to"; and

(c) for the words "matters relating to the custody of", in each place where they occur, there shall be substituted "Part I matters relating to".

(3) For section 42(7) (general interpretation of Part I) there shall be substituted—

"(7) In this Part—

(a) references to Part I proceedings in respect of a child are references to any proceedings for a Part I order or an order corresponding to a Part I order and include, in relation to proceedings outside the United Kingdom, references to proceedings before a tribunal or other authority having power under the law having effect there to determine Part I matters; and

(b) references to Part I matters are references to matters that might be determined by a Part I order or an order corresponding to a Part I order."

63.—(1) In section 1 (orders to which Part I of the Act of 1986 applies), in subsection (1)—

(a) for paragraph (a) there shall be substituted—

"(a) a section 8 order made by a court in England and Wales under the Children Act 1989, other than an order varying or discharging such an order"; and

(b) for paragraph (d) there shall be substituted the following paragraphs—

"(d) an order made by a court in England and Wales in the exercise of the inherent jurisdiction of the High Court with respect to children—

(i) so far as it gives care of a child to any person or provides for contact with, or the education of, a child; but

(ii) excluding an order varying or revoking such an order;

(e) an order made by the High Court in Northern Ireland in the exercise of its jurisdiction relating to wardship—

(i) so far as it gives care and control of a child to any person or provides for the education of or access to a child; but

(ii) excluding an order relating to a child of whom care or care and control is (immediately after the making of the order) vested in the Department of Health and Social Services or a Health and Social Services Board."

(2) In subsection (2) of that section, in paragraph (c) for "(d)" there shall be substituted "(e)".

(3) For subsections (3) to (5) of that section there shall be substituted—

"(3) In this Part, 'Part I order'—

(a) includes any order which would have been a custody order by virtue of this section in any form in which it was in force at any time before its amendment by the Children Act 1989; and
(b) (subject to sections 32 and 40 of this Act) excludes any order which would have been excluded from being a custody order by virtue of this section in any such form."

64. For section 2 there shall be substituted the following sections—

"Jurisdiction: general.

2.—(1) A court in England and Wales shall not have jurisdiction to make a section 1(1)(a) order with respect to a child in or in connection with matrimonial proceedings in England and Wales unless the condition in section 2A of this Act is satisfied.

(2) A court in England and Wales shall not have jurisdiction to make a section 1(1)(a) order in a non-matrimonial case (that is to say, where the condition in section 2A of this Act is not satisfied) unless the condition in section 3 of this Act is satisfied.

(3) A court in England and Wales shall not have jurisdiction to make a section 1(1)(d) order unless—

(a) the condition in section 3 of this Act is satisfied, or
(b) the child concerned is present in England and Wales on the relevant date and the court considers that the immediate exercise of its powers is necessary for his protection.

Jurisdiction in or in connection with matrimonial proceedings.

2A.—(1) The condition referred to in section 2(1) of this Act is that the matrimonial proceedings are proceedings in respect of the marriage of the parents of the child concerned and—

(a) the proceedings—
    (i) are proceedings for divorce or nullity of marriage, and
    (ii) are continuing;
(b) the proceedings—
    (i) are proceedings for judicial separation,
    (ii) are continuing,
and the jurisdiction of the court is not excluded by subsection (2) below; or
(c) the proceedings have been dismissed after the beginning of the trial but—
    (i) the section 1(1)(a) order is being made forthwith, or
    (ii) the application for the order was made on or before the dismissal.

(2) For the purposes of subsection (1)(b) above, the jurisdiction of the court is excluded if, after the grant of a decree of judicial separation, on the relevant date, proceedings for divorce or nullity in respect of the marriage are continuing in Scotland or Northern Ireland.

(3) Subsection (2) above shall not apply if the court in which the other proceedings there referred to are continuing has made—

(a) an order under section 13(6) or 21(5) of this Act (not being an order made by virtue of section 13(6)(a)(i)), or

(b) an order under section 14(2) or 22(2) of this Act which is recorded as being made for the purpose of enabling Part I proceedings to be taken in England and Wales with respect to the child concerned.

(4) Where a court—

(a) has jurisdiction to make a section 1(1)(a) order in or in connection with matrimonial proceedings, but

(b) considers that it would be more appropriate for Part I matters relating to the child to be determined outside England and Wales, the court may by order direct that, while the order under this subsection is in force, no section 1(1)(a) order shall be made by any court in or in connection with those proceedings."

65.—(1) In section 3 (habitual residence or presence of child concerned) in subsection (1) for "section 2" there shall be substituted "section 2(2)".

(2) In subsection (2) of that section for the words "proceedings for divorce, nullity or judicial separation" there shall be substituted "matrimonial proceedings".

66.—(1) In section 6 (duration and variation of Part I orders), for subsection (3) there shall be substituted the following subsections—

"(3) A court in England and Wales shall not have jurisdiction to vary a Part I order if, on the relevant date, matrimonial proceedings are continuing in Scotland or Northern Ireland in respect of the marriage of the parents of the child concerned.

(3A) Subsection (3) above shall not apply if—

(a) the Part I order was made in or in connection with proceedings for divorce or nullity in England and Wales in respect of the marriage of the parents of the child concerned; and
(b) those proceedings are continuing.

(3B) Subsection (3) above shall not apply if—

(a) the Part I order was made in or in connection with proceedings for judicial separation in England and Wales;
(b) those proceedings are continuing; and
(c) the decree of judicial separation has not yet been granted."

(2) In subsection (5) of that section for the words from "variation of" to "if the ward" there shall be substituted "variation of a section 1(1)(d) order if the child concerned".

(3) For subsections (6) and (7) of that section there shall be substituted the following subsections—

"(6) Subsection (7) below applies where a Part I order which is—

(a) a residence order (within the meaning of the children

Act 1989) in favour of a person with respect to a child,

(b) an order made in the exercise of the High Court's inherent jurisdiction with respect to children by virtue of which a person has care of a child, or

(c) an order—

(i) of a kind mentioned in section 1(3)(a) of this Act,

(ii) under which a person is entitled to the actual possession of a child,

ceases to have effect in relation to that person by virtue of subsection (1) above.

(7) Where this subsection applies, any family assistance order made under section 16 of the Children Act 1989 with respect to the child shall also cease to have effect.

(8) For the purposes of subsection (7) above the reference to a family assistance order under section 16 of the Children Act 1989 shall be deemed to include a reference to an order for the supervision of a child made under—

(a) section 7(4) of the Family Law Reform Act 1969,

(b) section 44 of the Matrimonial Causes Act 1973,

(c) section 2(2)(a) of the Guardianship Act 1973,

(d) section 34(5) or 36(3)(b) of the Children Act 1975, or

(e) section 9 of the Domestic Proceedings and Magistrates' Courts Act 1978;

but this subsection shall cease to have effect once all such orders for the supervision of children have ceased to have effect in accordance with Schedule 14 to the Children Act 1989."

67. For section 7 (interpretation of Chapter II) there shall be substituted—

"Interpretation of Chapter II.

7. In this Chapter—

(a) 'child' means a person who has not attained the age of eighteen;

(b) 'matrimonial proceedings' means proceedings for divorce, nullity of marriage or judicial separation;

(c) 'the relevant date' means, in relation to the making or variation of an order—

(i) where an application is made for an order to be made or varied, the date of the application (or first application, if two or more are determined together), and

(ii) where no such application is made, the date on which the court is considering whether to make or, as the case may be, vary the order; and

(d) 'section 1(1)(a) order' and 'section 1(1)(d) order' mean orders falling within section 1(1)(a) and (d) of this Act respectively.''

68. In each of the following sections—

(a) section 11(2)(a) (provisions supplementary to sections 9 and 10),
(b) section 13(5)(a) (jurisdiction ancillary to matrimonial proceedings),
(c) section 20(3)(a) (habitual residence or presence of child),
(d) section 21(4)(a) (jurisdiction in divorce proceedings, etc.), and
(e) section 23(4)(a) (duration and variation of custody orders),

for "4(5)" there shall be substituted "2A(4)".

69. In each of the following sections—

(a) section 19(2) (jurisdiction in cases other than divorce, etc.),
(b) section 20(6) (habitual residence or presence of child), and
(c) section 23(5) (duration and variation of custody orders),

for "section 1(1)(d)" there shall be substituted "section 1(1)(e)".

70. In section 34(3) (power to order recovery of child) for paragraph (a) there shall be substituted—

"(a) section 14 of the Children Act 1989".

71.—(1) In section 42 (general interpretation of Part I), in subsection (4)(a) for the words "has been boarded out with those parties" there shall be substituted "is placed with those parties as foster parents".

(2) In subsection (6) of that section, in paragraph (a) after the

word "person" there shall be inserted "to be allowed contact with or".

The Local Government Act 1988 (c. 9)

72. In Schedule 1 to the Local Government Act 1988 (competition) at the end of paragraph 2(4) (cleaning of buildings: buildings to which competition provisions do not apply) for paragraph (c) there shall be substituted—

> "(c) section 53 of the Children Act 1989."

Amendments of local Acts

73.—(1) Section 16 of the Greater London Council (General Powers) Act 1981 (exemption from provisions of Part IV of the Act of certain premises) shall be amended as follows.

(2) After paragraph (g) there shall be inserted—

> "(gg) used as a children's home as defined in section 63 of the Children Act 1989".

(3) In paragraph (h)—

   (a) for the words "section 56 of the Child Care Act 1980" there shall be substituted "section 60 of the Children Act 1989";

   (b) for the words "section 57" there shall be substituted "section 60"; and

   (c) for the words "section 32" there shall be substituted "section 53".

(4) In paragraph (i), for the words "section 8 of the Foster Children Act 1980" there shall be substituted "section 67 of the Children Act 1989".

74.—(1) Section 10(2) of the Greater London Council (General Powers) Act 1984 (exemption from provisions of Part IV of the Act of certain premises) shall be amended as follows.

(2) In paragraph (d)—

   (a) for the words "section 56 of the Child Care Act 1980" there shall be substituted "section 60 of the Children Act 1989";

   (b) for the words "section 57" there shall be substituted "section 60"; and

   (c) for the words "section 31" there shall be substituted "section 53".

(3) In paragraph (e), for the words "section 8 of the Foster Children Act 1980" there shall be substituted "section 67 of the Children Act 1989".

Annotation

Schedule 13: deals with consequential amendments that are technical in nature and update existing legislation to take account of changes in the Act, in order to ensure consistency between public general Acts of Parliament. *Paragraphs 8–10*, for example, deal with drafting and technical amendments in relation to education supervision orders and provisions in the Education Acts. *Paragraph 32*, dealing with the Employment of Children Act 1973 and *Paragraph 36*, dealing with the Domestic Proceedings and Magistrates' Courts Act 1978, mainly concern the effect of care and supervision orders and their interaction with other orders. Amendments in *Paragraph 46*, dealing with the Armed Forces Act 1981, *Paragraph 50* dealing with the Mental Health (Scotland) Act 1984 and others fall within the category of technical amendments. The following amendments in *Schedule 13* are of especial note.

Paragraph 1: amends the definition of "will" in section 1 of the Wills Act 1837. This is achieved by replacing reference to the disposition by will and testament or devise of the custody and tuition of any child with a reference to the appointment by will of a guardian of a child. It is clear that the former wording referred to the appointment of a guardian by will, and that it was desirable that the definition should refer to the concept of appointment of guardians, dealt with by section 5 of the Act, now that the concept of "custody" is wholly abolished.

Paragraph 2: amends section 1(1) of the Children and Young Persons Act 1933, which provides for a certain class of person to be guilty of an offence in certain circumstances. The class of person was formerly defined by references to persons having the "custody, charge or care of" the relevant child. As the concept of custody is abolished, this definition is replaced by a reference to persons having responsibility for the child concerned.

Paragraph 3: picks up four further references to "custody, charge or care" in the Children and Young Persons Act 1933 and amends them in the same way and for the same purpose as the amendment to section 1(1) explained in Paragraph 1.

Paragraph 4: updates section 10 of the Children and Young Persons Act 1933 by replacing the local education authority's duty to consider applying for an order under the Children and Young

Persons Act 1969 with a similar duty regarding applications for education supervision orders. The duty arises whenever a local education authority intends to prosecute a person who habitually wanders from place to place with a child of compulsory school age, thereby preventing the child from receiving education.

Paragraph 5: amends section 17 of the Children and Young Persons Act 1933 by providing a definition of persons having "responsibility for" a child for the purpose of those sections of Part 1 of the Act in which that expression occurs: see Paragraphs 2 and 3. This replaces the former definition of persons having custody, charge or care of children, which expression has been replaced in the body of the Act by reference to persons having responsibility for children.

Paragraph 6(1): adds proceedings for a care or supervision order to those circumstances in which (by virtue of section 34 of the Children and Young Persons Act 1933) a parent or guardian may be required to attend court. *Paragraph 6(2)(3)* also amends section 34 and requires that a supervisor appointed under the Act and a local authority which provides a child with accommodation under section 20 shall be informed of the child's arrest as soon as it is reasonably practicable to do so.

Paragraph 7(a): amends the definition of "guardian" for the purposes of the Children and Young Persons Act 1933 by replacing the reference to any person having for the time being the charge of or control over the child or young person concerned with a reference to any person having the actual care of such child or young person. The amendment is not intended to change the sense of the definition, but merely to update the terms used.

Paragraph 7(b): amends the definition of "legal guardian" for the purposes of the Children and Young Persons Act 1933 to include reference to guardians appointed in accordance with section 5 of the Act.

Paragraphs 8–10: deal with amendments to the Education Act 1944, to deal with applications for an education supervision order with respect to a child, among other things. Note that the supervisor under an education supervision order is required to advise, assist and befriend, and give directions to, the child concerned and his parents in such a way as will, in his opinion, secure that the child will be properly educated: see Schedule 3 Paragraph 12(1). In giving directions he must take into account the wishes and feelings of the child and his parents. "Parent" in this context has the wide meaning given in education legislation; it includes a person with parental responsibility for the child as well as anyone else who has care of him: see Schedule 3, Paragraph 21 and section 114(D) of the Education Act 1944, as inserted by Paragraph 10 of Schedule 13.

Paragraph 11: restricts the functions of a local authority under the National Assistance Act 1948 regarding the disabled, the aged or infirm to those who are aged eighteen or over. Part III of the Act provides comprehensively for the functions of a local authority towards those who are under that age and in need, as well as in some cases those who are not in need.

Paragraph 12: deals with amendments to the Reserve and Auxiliary Forces (Protection of Civil Interests) Act 1951, with regard to cases in which leave of the appropriate court is required before enforcing certain orders for the payment of money. It links also sections 21 to 33 of the Matrimonial Causes Act 1973 to Schedule 1 of the Children Act. Schedule 1 deals with financial provision for children.

Paragraph 13: amends the definition of "parent" for the purposes of the Mines and Quarries Act 1954. The former reference to a guardian or person having the legal custody of or control over a young person is replaced by reference to a person having parental responsibility under the Act. The new concept of parental responsibility subsumes all guardians under the Act and replaces the concept of custody.

Paragraph 14: deals with the Administration of Justice Act 1960 and relates to the publication of information relating to proceedings in private. Thus, rules which prevent the publication of details of children's cases which are heard in private in the High Court and county courts continue to have effect. The Children Act enables rules of court to be made to permit a magistrates' court to sit in private in proceedings in which powers under it may be exercised with respect to a child: see section 97(1).

Paragraph 15: amends the definition of "parent" for the purposes of the Factories Act 1961 in exactly the same way as the amendment to the same definition of "parent" for the purposes of the Mines and Quarries Act 1954: see Paragraph 13.

Paragraph 16: amends a definition contained in section 67(1A)(e) of the Criminal Justice Act 1967. Note the changes in the Act to the concept of care. Where a child is said to be in local authority "care" he is under a care order. "Care" no longer indicates a child who is accommodated by a local authority on a voluntary basis. In the Children Act children who are accommodated by or on behalf of a local authority are referred to as "looked after" by a local authority whether the accommodation is provided voluntarily or compulsorily: see section 20(3).

Paragraph 17: deals with changes to the Health Services and Public Health Act 1968. It links that Act with the Child Care Act 1980 and to the Children Act 1989.

Paragraph 27: makes an equivalent change to the Chronically Sick and Disabled Persons Act 1970 as is made by Paragraph 11 in respect of the National Assistance Act 1948.

Paragraph 28: relates to the Courts Act 1971 and deletes references to appeals to the Crown Court under the Children and Young Persons Act 1969, which are repealed by the Act.

Paragraph 45: amends section 18(1)(h) of the Supreme Court Act 1981 by replacing, in the list of interlocutory proceedings in respect of which leave is not needed for an appeal to be made, the references to "custody" and "access" with references to "residence" and "contact" as the latter two concepts will respectively replace the former ones under the Act.

Paragraph 45(2): amends Schedule 1 of the Supreme Court Act 1981, which provides for the distribution of business between the three divisions of the High Court, by partially redefining the work assigned to the Family Division in the light of the reorganisation of concepts and proceedings made by the Act. The former wording referred to the wardship, guardianship, custody or maintenance of minors including proceedings about access, except proceedings solely for the appointment of a guardian of a minor's estate.

Paragraph 48: amends section 131(2) of the Mental Health Act 1983 by substituting reference to the concept of parental responsibility created by the Act for the former reference. The purpose of section 131 is to ensure that minors who have attained the age of sixteen may voluntarily enter a hospital or mental nursing home for treatment. The effect of the former provision was that they might do so "notwithstanding any right of custody or control vested by law in his parent or guardian". The purpose of the amendment in Paragraph 48 is to preserve this effect while recasting it in terms of the concepts created by the Act, by providing that the fact that a person or persons have parental responsibility for the minor concerned is not to affect his ability to become a voluntary patient.

Paragraph 58: amends the regulation-making power in section 1 of the Disabled Persons (Services, Consultation and Representation) Act 1986 concerning the appointment of authorised representatives of disabled persons. Paragraph 28(a) replaces the power to provide for a parent or guardian to appoint the representative of a person aged under sixteen by an equivalent power in favour of a parent or another person who has parental responsibility for the child. This latter phrase will encompass both a guardian and a person who is not a parent but who has the benefit of a residence order in favour of the child. This provision which reflects the formula throughout the Act goes further than the former formulation in section 1 of the 1986 Act.

Paragraph 58(b): amends section 1(3)(c) of the 1986 Act which permits regulations to provide for a local authority to appoint the authorised representatives when the child is in their care. The reference to a child "in care" is replaced by a child who is "looked after" by a local authority, to ensure that children who are accommodated by local authorities on a voluntary basis receive the benefit of this provision.

Paragraph 59(2): makes an amendment to section 2(3) of the Disabled Persons (Services, Consultation and Representation) Act 1986 which follows from the amendment made by Paragraph 58(a).

Paragraph 59(3)(4): amends the list of premises in which the authorised representative may visit a disabled person and interview him in private to include accommodation provided under Part III of the Act.

Paragraph 60: replaces the word "guardian" by reference to a person who is not a parent but who has parental responsibility for the child for the reason given in relation to the equivalent amendment in Paragraph 58.

Paragraph 61(1) and (3): adds references to the Act for the purposes of the definition of "disabled person" and "welfare enactments". The former change follows from the amendment made in the National Assistance Act 1948: see Paragraph 11. Paragraph 61(2) and (4) defines the terms "parental responsibility" and "looked after by a local authority" to provide consistency with the Act.

SCHEDULE 14: TRANSITIONALS AND SAVINGS

Pending proceedings, etc.

1.—(1) Subject to sub-paragraph (4), nothing in any provision of this Act (other than the repeals mentioned in sub-paragraph (2)) shall affect any proceedings which are pending immediately before the commencement of that provision.

(2) The repeals are those of—

- (a) section 42(3) of the Matrimonial Causes Act 1973 (declaration by court that party to marriage unfit to have custody of children of family); and
- (b) section 38 of the Sexual Offences Act 1956 (power of court to divest person of authority over girl or boy in cases of incest).

(3) For the purposes of the following provisions of this Schedule, any reference to an order in force immediately before the commencement of a provision of this Act shall be construed as including a reference to an order made after that commencement in proceedings pending before that commencement.

(4) Sub-paragraph (3) is not to be read as making the order in question have effect from a date earlier than that on which it was made.

(5) an order under section 96(3) may make such provision with respect to the application of the order in relation to proceedings which are pending when the order comes into force as the Lord Chancellor considers appropriate.

2. Where, immediately before the day on which Part IV comes into force, there was in force an order under section 3(1) of the Children and Young Persons Act 1963 (order directing a local authority to bring a child or young person before a juvenile court under section 1 of the Children and Young Persons Act 1969), the order shall cease to have effect on that day.

CUSTODY ORDERS, ETC.

Cessation of declarations of unfitness, etc.

3. Where, immediately before the day on which Parts I and II come into force, there was in force—

- (a) a declaration under section 42(3) of the Matrimonial Causes Act 1973 (declaration by court that party to marriage unfit to have custody of children or family); or
- (b) an order under section 38(1) of the Sexual Offences Act 1956 divesting a person of authority over a girl or boy in a case of incest;

the declaration or, as the case may be, the order shall cease to have effect on that day.

The Family Law Reform Act 1987 (c. 42)

Conversion of orders under section 4

4. Where, immediately before the day on which Parts I and II come into force, there was in force an order under section 4(1) of the Family Law Reform Act 1987 (order giving father parental rights and duties in relation to a child), then, on and after that day, the order shall be deemed to be an order under section 4 of this Act giving the father parental responsibility for the child.

Orders to which paragraphs 6 to 11 apply

5.—(1) In paragraphs 6 to 11 "an existing order" means any order which—

    (a) is in force immediately before the commencement of Parts I and II;

    (b) was made under any enactment mentioned in sub-paragraph (2);

    (c) determines all or any of the following—

        (i) who is to have custody of a child;

        (ii) who is to have care and control of a child;

        (iii) who is to have access to a child;

        (iv) any matter with respect to a child's education or upbringing; and

    (d) is not an order of a kind mentioned in paragraph 15(1).

(2) The enactments are—

    (a) the Domestic Proceedings and Magistrates' Courts Act 1978;

    (b) the Children Act 1975;

    (c) the Matrimonial Causes Act 1973;

    (d) the Guardianship of Minors Acts 1971 and 1973;

    (e) the Matrimonial Causes Act 1965;

    (f) the Matrimonial Proceedings (Magistrates' Courts) Act 1960.

(3) For the purposes of this paragraph and paragraphs 6 to 11 "custody" includes legal custody and joint as well as sole custody but does not include access.

Parental responsibility of parents

6.—(1) Where—

    (a) a child's father and mother were married to each other at the time of his birth; and

(b) there is an existing order with respect to the child,

each parent shall have parental responsibility for the child in accordance with section 2 as modified by sub-paragraph (3).

(2) Where—

(a) a child's father and mother were not married to each other at the time of his birth; and

(b) there is an existing order with respect to the child,

section 2 shall apply as modified by sub-paragraphs (3) and (4).

(3) The modification is that for section 2(8) there shall be substituted—

"(8) The fact that a person has parental responsibility for a child does not entitle him to act in a way which would be incompatible with any existing order or any order made under this Act with respect to the child".

(4) The modifications are that—

(a) for the purposes of section 2(2), where the father has custody or care and control of the child by virtue of any existing order, the court shall be deemed to have made (at the commencement of that section) an order under section 4(1) giving him parental responsibility for the child; and

(b) where by virtue of paragraph (a) a court is deemed to have made an order under section 4(1) in favour of a father who has care and control of a child by virtue of an existing order, the court shall not bring the order under section 4(1) to an end at any time while he has care and control of the child by virtue of the order.

Persons who are not parents but who have custody or care and control

7.—(1) Where a person who is not the parent or guardian of a child has custody or care and control of him by virtue of an existing order, that person shall have parental responsibility for him so long as he continues to have that custody or care and control by virtue of the order.

(2) Where sub-paragraph (1) applies, Parts I and II shall have effect as modified by this paragraph.

(3) The modifications are that—

(a) for section 2(8) there shall be substituted—

"(8) The fact that a person has parental responsibility for a child does not entitle him to act in a way which would be incompatible with any existing order or with any order made under this Act with respect to the child";

(b) at the end of section 10(4) there shall be inserted—

"(c) any person who has custody or care and control of a child by virtue of any existing order"; and

(c) at the end of section 34(1)(c) there shall be inserted—

"(cc) where immediately before the care order was made there was an existing order by virtue of which a person had custody or care and control of the child, that person."

Persons who have care and control

8.—(1) Sub-paragraphs (2) to (6) apply where a person has care and control of a child by virtue of an existing order, but they shall cease to apply when that order ceases to have effect.

(2) Section 5 shall have effect as if—

(a) for any reference to a residence order in favour of a parent or guardian there were substituted a reference to any existing order by virtue of which the parent or guardian has care and control of the child; and

(b) for subsection (9) there were substituted—

"(9) Subsections (1) and (7) do not apply if the existing order referred to in paragraph (b) of those subsections was one by virtue of which a surviving parent of the child also had care and control of him."

(3) Section 10 shall have effect as if for subsection (5)(c)(i) there were substituted—

"(i) in any case where by virtue of an existing order any person or persons has or have care and control of the child, has the consent of that person or each of those persons".

(4) Section 20 shall have effect as if for subsection (9)(a) there were substituted "who has care and control of the child by virtue of an existing order."

(5) Section 23 shall have effect as if for subsection (4)(c) there were substituted—

"(c) where the child is in care and immediately before the

order was made there was an existing order by virtue of which a person had care and control of the child, that person."

(6) In Schedule 1, paragraphs 1 (1) and 14(1) shall have effect as if for the words "in whose favour a residence order is in force with respect to the child" there were substituted "who has been given care and control of the child by virtue of an existing order".

Persons who have access

9.—(1) Sub-paragraphs (2) to (4) apply where a person has access by virtue of an existing order.

(2) Section 10 shall have effect as if after subsection (5) there were inserted—

"(5A) Any person who has access to a child by virtue of an existing order is entitled to apply for a contact order."

(3) Section 16(2) shall have effect as if after paragraph (b) there were inserted—

"(bb) any person who has access to the child by virtue of an existing order."

(4) Sections 43(11), 44(13) and 46(10), shall have effect as if in each case after paragraph (d) there were inserted—

"(dd) any person who has been given access to him by virtue of an existing order."

Enforcement of certain existing orders

10.—(1) Sub-paragraph (2) applies in relation to any existing order which, but for the repeal by this Act of—

(a) section 13(1) of the Guardianship of Minors Act 1971;
(b) section 43(1) of the Children Act 1975; or
(c) section 33 of the Domestic Proceedings and Magistrates' Courts Act 1978,

(provisions concerning the enforcement of custody orders) might have been enforced as if it were an order requiring a person to give up a child to another person.

(2) Where this sub-paragraph applies, the existing order may, after the repeal of the enactments mentioned in sub-paragraph (1)(a) to (c), be enforced under section 14 as if—

(a) any reference to a residence order were a reference to the existing order; and

(b) any reference to a person in whose favour the residence order is in force were a reference to a person to whom actual custody of the child is given by an existing order which is in force.

(3) In sub-paragraph (2) "actual custody", in relation to a child, means the actual possession of his person.

Discharge of existing orders

11.—(1) The making of a residence order or a care order with respect to a child who is the subject of an existing order discharges the existing order.

(2) Where the court makes any section 8 order (other than a residence order) with respect to a child with respect to whom any existing order is in force, the existing order shall have effect subject to the section 8 order.

(3) The court may discharge an existing order which is in force with respect to a child—

(a) in any family proceedings relating to the child or in which any question arises with respect to the child's welfare; or
(b) on the application of—

(i) any parent or guardian of the child;
(ii) the child himself; or
(iii) any person named in the order.

(4) A child may not apply for the discharge of an existing order except with the leave of the court.

(5) The power in sub-paragraph (3) to discharge an existing order includes the power to discharge any part of the order.

(6) In considering whether to discharge an order under the power conferred by sub-paragraph (3) the court shall, if the discharge of the order is opposed by any party to the proceedings, have regard in particular to the matters mentioned in section 1(3).

GUARDIANS

Existing guardians to be guardians under this Act

12.—(1) Any appointment of a person as guardian of a child which—

(a) was made—

(i) under sections 3 to 5 of the Guardianship of Minors Act 1971;

(ii) under section 38(3) of the Sexual Offences Act 1956; or

(iii) under the High Court's inherent jurisdiction with respect to children; and

(b) has taken effect before the commencement of section 5,

shall (subject to sub-paragraph (2)) be deemed, on and after the commencement of section 5, to be an appointment made and having effect under that section.

(2) Where an appointment of a person as guardian of a child has effect under section 5 by virtue of sub-paragraph (1)(a)(ii), the appointment shall not have effect for a period which is longer than any period specified in the order.

Appointment of guardian not yet in effect

13. Any appointment of a person to be a guardian of a child—

(a) which was made as mentioned in paragraph 12(1)(a)(i); but

(b) which, immediately before the commencement of section 5, had not taken effect,

shall take effect in accordance with section 5 (as modified, where it applies, by paragraph 8(2)).

Persons deemed to be appointed as guardians under existing wills

14. For the purposes of the Wills Act 1837 and of this Act any disposition by will and testament or devise of the custody and tuition of any child, made before the commencement of section 5 and paragraph 1 of Schedule 13, shall be deemed to be an appointment by will of a guardian of the child.

CHILDREN IN CARE

Children in compulsory care

15.—(1) Sub-paragraph (2) applies where, immediately before the day on which Part IV comes into force, a person was—

(a) in care by virtue of—

(i) a care order under section 1 of the Children and Young Persons Act 1969;

(ii) a care order under section 15 of that Act, on discharging a supervision order made under section 1 of that Act; or

(iii) an order or authorisation under section 25 or 26 of that Act;

(b) deemed, by virtue of—

(i) paragraph 7(3) of Schedule 5A to the Army Act 1955;

(ii) paragraph 7(3) of Schedule 5A to the Air Force Act 1955; or

(iii) paragraph 7(3) of Schedule 4A to the Naval Discipline Act 1967,

to be the subject of a care order under the Children and Young Persons Act 1969;

(c) in care—

(i) under section 2 of the Child Care Act 1980; or

(ii) by virtue of paragraph 1 of Schedule 4 to that Act (which extends the meaning of a child in care under section 2 to include children in care under section 1 of the Children Act 1948),

and a child in respect of whom a resolution under section 3 of the Act of 1980 or section 2 of the Act of 1948 was in force;

(d) a child in respect of whom a resolution had been passed under section 65 of the Child Care Act 1980;

(e) in care by virtue of an order under—

(i) section 2(1)(e) of the Matrimonial Proceedings (Magistrates' Courts) Act 1960;

(ii) section 7(2) of the Family Law Reform Act 1969;

(iii) section 43 (1) of the Matrimonial Causes Act 1973; or

(iv) section 2(2)(b) of the Guardianship Act 1973;

(v) section 10 of the Domestic Proceedings and Magistrates' Courts Act 1978,

(orders having effect for certain purposes as if the child had been received into care under section 2 of the Child Care Act 1980);

(f) in care by virtue of an order made, on the revocation of a custodianship order, under section 36 of the Children Act 1975; or

(g) in care by virtue of an order made, on the refusal of an adoption order, under section 26 of the Adoption Act 1976 or any order having effect (by virtue of paragraph 1 of Schedule 2 to that Act) as if made under that section [; or].

[(h) in care by virtue of an order of the court made in the exercise of the High Court's inherent jurisdiction with respect to children.]

(2) Where this sub-paragraph applies, then, on and after the day on which Part IV commences—

(a) the order or resolution in question shall be deemed to be a care order;

(b) the authority in whose care the person was immediately before that commencement shall be deemed to be the authority designated in that deemed care order; and

(c) any reference to a child in the care of a local authority shall include a reference to a person who is the subject of such a deemed care order,

(and the provisions of this Act shall apply accordingly, subject to paragraph 16.

Modifications

16.—(1) Sub-paragraph (2) only applies where a person who is the subject of a care order by virtue of paragraph 15(2) is a person falling within sub-paragraph (1)(a) or (b) of that paragraph.

(2) Where the person would otherwise have remained in care until reaching the age of nineteen, by virtue of—

(a) section 20(3)(a) or 21(1) of the Children and Young Persons Act 1969; or

(b) paragraph 7(5)(c)(i) of—

    (i) Schedule 5A to the Army Act 1955;

    (ii) Schedule 5A to the Air Force Act 1955; or

    (iii) Schedule 4A to the Naval Discipline Act 1957,

this Act applies as if in section 91(12) for the word "eighteen" there were substituted "nineteen".

(3) Where a person who is the subject of a care order by virtue of paragraph 15(2) is a person falling within sub-paragraph (1)(b) of that paragraph, this Act applies as if section 101 were omitted.

(4) Sub-paragraph (5) only applies where a child who is the

Note: The words within square brackets were inserted by the Courts and Legal Services Act 1990.

subject of a care order by virtue of paragraph 15(2) is a person falling within sub-paragraph (1)(e) to [*(g)*] [h] of that paragraph.

(5) Where a court, on making the order, or at any time thereafter, gave directions [*under—*]

(a) [under] section 4(4)(a) of the Guardianship Act 1973; [*or*]

(b) section 43(5)(a) of the Matrimonial Causes Act 1973, [or]

[(c) in the exercise of the High Court's inherent jurisdiction with respect to children]

as to the exercise by the authority of any powers, those directions shall continue to have effect (regardless of any conflicting provision in this Act) until varied or discharged by a court under this sub-paragraph.

[*Cessation of wardship where ward in care*

16A. Where a child who is a ward of court is in care by virtue of—

(a) an order under section 7(2) of the Family Law Reform Act 1969; or

(b) an order made in the exercise of the High Court's inherent jurisdiction with respect to children,

he shall, on the day which Part IV commences, cease to be a ward of court.]

Children placed with parent etc. while in compulsory care

17.—(1) This paragraph applies where a child is deemed by paragraph 15 to be in the care of a local authority under an order or resolution which is deemed by that paragraph to be a care order.

(2) If, immediately before the day on which Part III comes into force, the child was allowed to be under the charge and control of—

(a) a parent or guardian under section 21(2) of the Child Care Act 1980; or

(b) a person who, before the child was in the authority's

Note: The words *in italics* within square brackets were deleted by the Courts and Legal Services Act 1990.
Note: The words within square brackets were inserted by the Courts and Legal Services Act 1990.

care, had care and control of the child by virtue of an order falling within paragraph 5,

on and after that day the provision made by and under section 23(5) shall apply as if the child had been placed with the person in question in accordance with that provision.

Orders for access to children in compulsory care

18.—(1) This paragraph applies to any access order—

(a) made under section 12C of the Child Care Act 1980 (access orders with respect to children in care of local authorities); and

(b) in force immediately before the commencement of Part IV.

(2) On and after the commencement of Part IV, the access order shall have effect as an order made under section 34 in favour of the person named in the order.

19.—(1) This paragraph applies where, immediately before the commencement of Part IV, an access order made under section 12C of the Act of 1980 was suspended by virtue of an order made under section 12E of that Act (suspension of access orders in emergencies).

(2) The suspending order shall continue to have effect as if this Act had not been passed.

(3) If—

(a) before the commencement of Part IV; and

(b) during the period for which the operation of the access order is suspended,

the local authority concerned made an application for its variation or discharge to an appropriate juvenile court, its operation shall be suspended until the date on which the application to vary or discharge it is determined or abandoned.

Children in voluntary care

20.—(1) This paragraph applies where, immediately before the day on which Part III comes into force—

(a) a child was in the care of a local authority—

(i) under section 2(1) of the Child Care Act 1980; or

(ii) by virtue of paragraph 1 of Schedule 4 to that

Act (which extends the meaning of references to children in care under section 2 to include references to children in care under section 1 of the Children Act 1948); and

(b) he was not a person in respect of whom a resolution under section 3 of the Act of 1980 or section 2 of the Act of 1948 was in force.

(2) Where this paragraph applies, the child shall, on and after the day mentioned in sub-paragraph (1), be treated for the purposes of this Act as a child who is provided with accommodation by the local authority under Part III, but he shall cease to be so treated once he ceases to be so accommodated in accordance with the provisions of Part III.

(3) Where—

(a) this paragraph applies; and
(b) the child, immediately before the day mentioned in sub-paragraph (1), was (by virtue of section 21(2) of the Act of 1980) under the charge and control of a person falling within paragraph 17(2)(a) or (b),

the child shall not be treated for the purposes of this Act as if he were being looked after by the authority concerned.

Boarded out children

21.—(1) Where, immediately before the day on which Part III comes into force, a child in the care of a local authority—

(a) was—

(i) boarded out with a person under section 21(1)(a) of the Child Care Act 1980; or
(ii) placed under the charge and control of a person, under section 21(2) of that Act; and

(b) the person with whom he was boarded out, or (as the case may be) placed, was not a person falling within paragraph 17(2)(a) or (b),

on and after that day, he shall be treated (subject to sub-paragraph (2)) as having been placed with a local authority foster parent and shall cease to be so treated when he ceases to be placed with that person in accordance with the provisions of this Act.

(2) Regulations made under section 23(2)(a) shall not apply in relation to a person who is a local authority foster parent by virtue of sub-paragraph (1) before the end of the period of twelve

months beginning with the day on which Part III comes into force and accordingly that person shall for that period be subject—

(a) in a case falling within sub-paragraph (1)(a)(i), to terms and regulations mentioned in section 21(1)(a) of the Act of 1980; and

(b) in a case falling within sub-paragraph (1)(a)(ii), to terms fixed under section 21(2) of that Act and regulations made under section 22A of that Act,

as if that Act had not been repealed by this Act.

Children in care to qualify for advice and assistance

22. Any reference in Part III to a person qualifying for advice and assistance shall be construed as including a reference to a person within the area of the local authority in question who is under twenty-one and who was, at any time after reaching the age of sixteen but while still a child—

(a) a person falling within—

(i) any of paragraphs (a) to [*(g)*] [(h)] of paragraph 15(1); or
(ii) paragraph 20(1); or

(b) the subject of a criminal care order (within the meaning of paragraph 34).

Emigration of children in care

23. Where—

(a) the Secretary of State has received a request in writing from a local authority that he give his consent under section 24 of the Child Care Act 1980 to the emigration of a child in their care; but

(b) immediately before the repeal of the Act of 1980 by this Act, he has not determined whether or not to give his consent,

section 24 of the Act of 1980 shall continue to apply (regardless of that repeal) until the Secretary of State has determined whether or not to give his consent to the request.

Note: The words *in italics* within square brackets were deleted by the Courts and Legal Services Act 1990.
Note: The words within square brackets were inserted by the Courts and Legal Services Act 1990.

T

Contributions for maintenance of children in care

24.—(1) Where, immediately before the day on which Part III of Schedule 2 comes into force, there was in force an order made (or having effect as if made) under any of the enactments mentioned in sub-paragraph (2), then, on and after that day—

    (a) the order shall have effect as if made under paragraph 23(2) of Schedule 2 against a person liable to contribute; and

    (b) Part III of Schedule 2 shall apply to the order, subject to the modifications in sub-paragraph (3).

(2) The enactments are—

    (a) section 11(4) of the Domestic Proceedings and Magistrates' Courts Act 1978;

    (b) section 26(2) of the Adoption Act 1976;

    (c) section 36(5) of the Children Act 1975;

    (d) section 2(3) of the Guardianship Act 1973;

    (e) section 2(1)(h) of the Matrimonial Proceedings (Magistrates' Courts) Act 1960,

(provisions empowering the court to make an order requiring a person to make periodical payments to a local authority in respect of a child in care).

(3) The modifications are that, in paragraph 23 of Schedule 2—

    (a) in sub-paragraph (4), paragraph (a) shall be omitted;

    (b) for sub-paragraph (6) there shall be substituted—

       "(6) Where—

          (a) a contribution order is in force;

          (b) the authority serve a contribution notice under paragraph 22; and

          (c) the contributor and the authority reach an agreement under paragraph 22(7) in respect of the contribution notice,

       the effect of the agreement shall be to discharge the order from the date on which it is agreed that the agreement shall take effect"; and

    (c) at the end of sub-paragraph (10) there shall be inserted—

       "and

          (c) where the order is against a person who is not a parent of the child, shall be made with due regard to—

(i) whether that person had assumed responsibility for the maintenance of the child, and, if so, the extent to which and basis on which he assumed that responsibility and the length of the period during which he met that responsibility;

(ii) whether he did so knowing that the child was not his child;

(iii) the liability of any other person to maintain the child."

SUPERVISION ORDERS

Orders under section 1(3)(b) or 21(2) of the 1969 Act

25.—(1) This paragraph applies to any supervision order—

(a) made—

(i) under section 1(3)(b) of the Children and Young Persons Act 1969; or

(ii) under section 21(2) of that Act on the discharge of a care order made under section 1(3)(c) of that Act; and

(b) in force immediately before the commencement of Part IV.

(2) On and after the commencement of Part IV, the order shall be deemed to be a supervision order made under section 31 and—

(a) any requirement of the order that the child reside with a named individual shall continue to have effect while the order remains in force, unless the court otherwise directs;

(b) any other requirement imposed by the court, or directions given by the supervisor, shall be deemed to have been imposed or given under the appropriate provisions of Schedule 3.

(3) Where, immediately before the commencement of Part IV, the order had been in force for a period of more than six months, it shall cease to have effect at the end of the period of six months beginning with the day on which Part IV comes into force unless—

(a) the court directs that it shall cease to have effect at the end of a different period (which shall not exceed three years);

(b) it ceases to have effect earlier in accordance with section 91; or

    (c) it would have ceased to have had effect earlier had this Act not been passed.

(4) Where sub-paragraph (3) applies, paragraph 6 of Schedule 3 shall not apply.

(5) Where, immediately before the commencement of Part IV, the order had been in force for less than six months it shall cease to have effect in accordance with section 91 and paragraph 6 of Schedule 3 unless—

    (a) the court directs that it shall cease to have effect at the end of a different period (which shall not exceed three years); or

    (b) it would have ceased to have had effect earlier had this Act not been passed.

Other supervision orders

26.—(1) This paragraph applies to any order for the supervision of a child which was in force immediately before the commencement of Part IV and was made under—

    (a) section 2(1)(f) of the Matrimonial Proceedings (Magistrates Courts) Act 1960;

    (b) section 7(4) of the Family Law Reform Act 1969;

    (c) section 44 of the Matrimonial Causes Act 1973;

    (d) section 2(2)(a) of the Guardianship Act 1973;

    (e) section 34(5) or 36(3)(b) of the Children Act 1975;

    (f) section 26(1)(a) of the Adoption Act 1976; or

    (g) section 9 of the Domestic Proceedings and Magistrates Courts Act 1978.

(2) The order shall not be deemed to be a supervision order made under any provision of this Act but shall nevertheless continue in force for a period of one year beginning with the day on which Part IV comes into force unless—

    (a) the court directs that it shall cease to have effect at the end of a lesser period; or

    (b) it would have ceased to have had effect earlier had this Act not been passed.

PLACE OF SAFETY ORDERS

27.—(1) This paragraph applies to—

    (a) any order or warrant authorising the removal of a child to a place of safety which—

      (i) was made, or issued, under any of the enactments mentioned in sub-paragraph (2); and

      (ii) was in force immediately before the commencement of Part IV; and

  (b) any interim order made under section 23(5) of the Children and Young Persons Act 1963 or section 28(6) of the Children and Young Persons Act 1969.

(2) The enactments are—

  (a) section 40 of the Children and Young Persons Act 1933 (warrant to search for or remove child);

  (b) section 28(1) of the Children and Young Persons Act 1969 (detention of child in place of safety);

  (c) section 34(1) of the Adoption Act 1976 (removal of protected children from unsuitable surroundings);

  (d) section 12(1) of the Foster Children Act 1980 (removal of foster children kept in unsuitable surroundings).

(3) The order or warrant shall continue to have effect as if this Act had not been passed.

(4) Any enactment repealed by this Act shall continue to have effect in relation to the order or warrant so far as is necessary for the purposes of securing that the effect of the order is what it would have been had this Act not been passed.

(5) Sub-paragraph (4) does not apply to the power to make an interim order or further interim order given by section 23(5) of the Children and Young Persons Act 1963 or section 28(6) of the Children and Young Persons Act 1969.

(6) Where, immediately before section 28 of the Children and Young Persons Act 1969 is repealed by this Act, a child is being detained under the powers granted by that section, he may continue to be detained in accordance with that section but subsection (6) shall not apply.

RECOVERY OF CHILDREN

28. The repeal by this Act of subsection (1) of section 16 of the Child Care Act 1980 (arrest of child absent from compulsory care) shall not affect the operation of that section in relation to any child arrested before the coming into force of the repeal.

29.—(1) This paragraph applies where—

  (a) a summons has been issued under section 15 or 16 of the

Child Care Act 1980 (recovery of children in voluntary or compulsory care); and

(b) the child concerned is not produced in accordance with the summons before the repeal of that section by this Act comes into force.

(2) The summons, any warrant issued in connection with it and section 15 or (as the case may be) section 16, shall continue to have effect as if this Act had not been passed.

30. The amendment by paragraph 27 of Schedule 12 of section 32 of the Children and Young Persons Act 1969 (detention of absentees) shall not affect the operation of that section in relation to—

(a) any child arrested; or
(b) any summons or warrant issued,

under that section before the coming into force of that paragraph.

VOLUNTARY ORGANISATIONS: PARENTAL RIGHTS RESOLUTIONS

31.—(1) This paragraph applies to a resolution—

(a) made under section 64 of the Child Care Act 1980 (transfer of parental rights and duties to voluntary organisations); and
(b) in force immediately before the commencement of Part IV.

(2) The resolution shall continue to have effect until the end of the period of six months beginning with the day on which Part IV comes into force unless it is brought to an end earlier in accordance with the provisions of the Act of 1980 preserved by this paragraph.

(3) While the resolution remains in force, any relevant provisions of, or made under, the Act of 1980 shall continue to have effect with respect to it.

(4) Sub-paragraph (3) does not apply to—

(a) section 62 of the Act of 1980 and any regulations made under that section (arrangements by voluntary organisations for emigration of children); or
(b) section 65 of the Act of 1980 (duty of local authority to assume parental rights and duties).

(5) Section 5(2) of the Act of 1980 (which is applied to resolutions under Part VI of that Act by section 64(7) of that Act)

shall have effect with respect to the resolution as if the reference in paragraph (c) to an appointment of a guardian under section 5 of the Guardianship of Minors Act 1971 were a reference to an appointment of a guardian under section 5 of this Act.

FOSTER CHILDREN

32.—(1) this paragraph applies where—

(a) immediately before the commencement of Part VIII, a child was a foster child within the meaning of the Foster Children Act 1980; and

(b) the circumstances of the case are such that, had Parts VIII and IX then been in force, he would have been treated for the purposes of this Act as a child who was being provided with accommodation in a children's home and not as a child who was being privately fostered.

(2) If the child continues to be cared for and provided with accommodation as before, section 63(1) and (10) shall not apply in relation to him if—

(a) an application for registration of the home in question is made under section 63 before the end of the period of three months beginning with the day on which Part VIII comes into force; and

(b) the application has not been refused or, if it has been refused—

(i) the period for an appeal against the decision has not expired; or

(ii) an appeal against the refusal has been made but has not been determined or abandoned.

(3) While section 63(1) and (10) does not apply, the child shall be treated as a privately fostered child for the purposes of Part IX.

NURSERIES AND CHILD MINDING

33.—(1) Sub-paragraph (2) applies where, immediately before the commencement of Part X, any premises are registered under section 1(1)(a) of the Nurseries and Child-Minders Regulation Act 1948 (registration of premises, other than premises wholly or mainly used as private dwellings, where children are received to be looked after).

(2) During the transitional period, the provisions of the Act of 1948 shall continue to have effect with respect to those premises to the exclusion of Part X.

(3) Nothing in sub-paragraph (2) shall prevent the local authority concerned from registering any person under section 71(1)(b) with respect to the premises.

(4) In this paragraph "the transitional period" means the period ending with—

    (a) the first anniversary of the commencement of Part X; or

    (b) if earlier, the date on which the local authority concerned registers any person under section 71(1)(b) with respect to the premises.

34.—(1) Sub-paragraph (2) applies where, immediately before the commencement of Part X—

    (a) a person is registered under section 1(1)(b) of the Act of 1948 (registration of persons who for reward receive into their homes children under the age of five to be looked after); and

    (b) all the children looked after by him as mentioned in section 1(1)(b) of that Act are under the age of five.

(2) During the transitional period, the provisions of the Act of 1948 shall continue to have effect with respect to that person to the exclusion of Part X.

(3) Nothing in sub-paragraph (2) shall prevent the local authority concerned from registering that person under section 71(1)(a).

(4) In this paragraph "the transitional period" means the period ending with—

    (a) the first anniversary of the commencement of Part X; or

    (b) if earlier, the date on which the local authority concerned registers that person under section 71(1)(a).

CHILDREN ACCOMMODATED IN CERTAIN ESTABLISHMENTS

35. In calculating, for the purposes of section 85(1)(a) or 86(1)(a), the period of time for which a child has been accommodated any part of that period which fell before the day on which that section came into force shall be disregarded.

CRIMINAL CARE ORDERS

36.—(1) This paragraph applies where, immediately before the commencement of section 90(2) there was in force an order ("a criminal care order") made—

(a) under section 7(7)(a) of the Children and Young Persons Act 1969 (alteration in treatment of young offenders etc.); or

(b) under section 15(1) of that Act, on discharging a supervision order made under section 7(7)(b) of that Act.

(2) The criminal care order shall continue to have effect until the end of the period of six months beginning with the day on which section 90(2) comes into force unless it is brought to an end earlier in accordance with—

(a) the provisions of the Act of 1969 preserved by sub-paragraph (3)(a); or

(b) this paragraph.

(3) While the criminal care order remains in force, any relevant provisions—

(a) of the Act of 1969; and

(b) of the Child Care Act 1980,

shall continue to have effect with respect to it.

(4) While the criminal care order remains in force, a court may, on the application of the appropriate person, make—

(a) a residence order;

(b) a care order or a supervision order under section 31;

(c) an education supervision order under section 36 (regardless of subsection (6) of that section); or

(d) an order falling within sub-paragraph (5),

and shall, on making any of those orders, discharge the criminal care order.

(5) The order mentioned in sub-paragraph (4)(d) is an order having effect as if it were a supervision order of a kind mentioned in section 12AA of the Act of 1969 (as inserted by paragraph 23 of Schedule 12), that is to say, a supervision order—

(a) imposing a requirement that the child shall live for a specified period in local authority accommodation; but

(b) in relation to which the conditions mentioned in subsection [*(4)*] [(6)] of section 12AA are not required to be satisfied.

(6) The maximum period which may be specified in an order made under sub-paragraph (4)(d) is six months and such an order may stipulate that the child shall not live with a named person.

(7) Where this paragraph applies, section 5 of the Rehabilitation of Offenders Act 1974 (rehabilitation periods for particular sentences) shall have effect regardless of the repeals in it made by this Act.

(8) In sub-paragraph (4) "appropriate person" means—

   (a) in the case of an application for a residence order, any person (other than a local authority) who has the leave of the court;
   (b) in the case of an application for an education supervision order, a local education authority; and
   (c) in any other case, the local authority to whose care the child was committed by the order.

MISCELLANEOUS

Consents under the Marriage Act 1949 (c. 76)

37.—(1) In the circumstances mentioned in sub-paragraph (2), section 3 of and Schedule 2 to the Marriage Act 1949 (consents to marry) shall continue to have effect regardless of the amendment of that Act by paragraph 5 of Schedule 12.

(2) The circumstances are that—

   (a) immediately before the day on which paragraph 5 of Schedule 12 comes into force, there is in force—

      (i) an existing order, as defined in paragraph 5(1); or
      (ii) an order of a kind mentioned in paragraph 16(1); and
   (b) section 3 of and Schedule 2 to the Act of 1949 would, but for this Act, have applied to the marriage of the child who is the subject of the order.

Note: The figure *in italics* within square brackets were deleted by the Courts and Legal Services Act 1990.
Note: The figure within square brackets were inserted by the Courts and Legal Services Act 1990.

The Children Act 1975 (c. 72)

38. The amendments of other enactments made by the following provisions of the Children Act 1975 shall continue to have effect regardless of the repeal of the Act of 1975 by this Act—

  (a) section 68(4), (5) and (7) (amendments of section 32 of the Children and Young Persons Act 1969); and
  (b) in Schedule 3—

> (i) paragraph 13 (amendments of Births and Deaths Registration Act 1953);
> (ii) paragraph 43 (amendment of Perpetuities and Accumulations Act 1964);
> (iii) paragraphs 46 and 47 (amendments of Health Services and Public Health Act 1968); and
> (iv) paragraph 77 (amendment of Parliamentary and Other Pensions Act 1972).

The Child Care Act 1980 (c. 5)

39. The amendment made to section 106(2)(a) of the Children and Young Persons Act 1963 by paragraph 26 of Schedule 5 to the Child Care Act 1980 shall continue to have effect regardless of the repeal of the Act of 1980 by this Act.

Legal aid

40. The Lord Chancellor may by order make such transitional and saving provisions as appear to him to be necessary or expedient, in consequence of any provision made by or under this Act, in connection with the operation of any provisions of the Legal Aid Act 1988 (including any provision of that Act which is amended or repealed by this Act).

Annotation

Schedule 14: makes detailed transitional provisions regarding orders made under the former law. Note that whilst the Children Act received the Royal Assent on 16 November 1989 and certain of its provisions became law immediately, nevertheless the bulk of its provisions are to come into force in October 1991, when the whole of the Act, with its profusion of regulations and rules of court, will be implemented.

Paragraph 1: provides that proceedings which are pending under the former law at the time the Act comes into force will continue unaffected by the new law. Paragraph 1 also deals with exceptions to this rule.

Paragraph 2: provides that an order in force on the day Part IV of the Act comes into force shall cease to have effect. Note that Part IV deals with care and supervision. The order referred to in Paragraph 2 is one dealing with a child or young person before a juvenile court.

Paragraph 3: deals with custody orders and the cessation of declarations of unfitness and provides for a declaration under section 42(3) of the Matrimonial Causes Act 1973 or an order under section 38(1) of the Sexual Offences Act 1956 to cease to have effect. Note that the Act replaces the order-making powers in the Matrimonial Causes Act 1973 and the Sexual Offences Act 1956.

Paragraph 4: provides that an order under the Family Law Reform Act 1987 which was in force at the commencement of the Children Act is deemed to be an order under section 4 of the new Act. Note that an order under section 4 of the Children Act *must* be made if a residence order is made in favour of a father: see section 12(1).

Paragraph 5: describes the orders to which paragraphs 6 to 11 apply.

Paragraph 6: deals with parental responsibility of parents. A person who otherwise would not have parental responsibility for the child but who had care and control or custody of a child under an existing order is given parental responsibility while that order lasts. Thus a father who does not have parental responsibilty for his child because he is not married to the child's mother, but who had care and control or custody under an existing order, is deemed to have a "parental responsibility order" in his favour: paragraph 6(4).

Paragraphs 7 and 8: deal with persons who are not parents but who have custody or care and control and those persons who have care and control. Thus, a person who may be a custodian under the Children Act 1975 is also treated in specific instances as if he had the benefit of a residence order. He may apply for a section 8 order without leave and if he had care and control of the child, rather than custody without care and control, certain other provisions apply.

Paragraph 9: deals with those persons who have access. Thus, a person with an access order under the former law is not given parental responsibility, but is treated for certain purposes in the Act as if he had a contact order.

Paragraph 10: deals with the enforcement of existing orders and provides a definition of "actual custody" in relation to a child. It provides for enforcement under section 14 which specifies that where a residence order is in force with respect to a child in favour of any person, an order under section 63(3) of the Magistrates' Courts Act 1980 may be enforced against a person in breach of the residence order. The only requirement in this respect is that such a person has had served upon him a copy of the residence order: see section 14.

Paragraph 11: deals with the discharge of existing orders. Existing orders regarding custody, legal custody, care and control and access may be discharged by a court, either on application or of its own motion in family proceedings: Paragraph 11(3). They are also brought to an end if the court makes a residence or care order under the Act: Paragraph 11(1).

Paragraph 12: provides for existing guardians to be appointed guardians under the Act. Thus, where a guardian's appointment took effect before implementation of the Act, he is treated as if he had been appointed under the Act: Paragraph 12(1).

Paragraph 13: deals with the appointment of guardians not yet in effect. Any appointment which has not taken effect by the commencement date of section 5 will only have effect in accordance with the Act, so that the rules which limit the circumstances in which appointments have effect apply.

Paragraph 14: deals with persons deemed to be appointed as guardians under existing wills. This is a transitional provision arising from the amendment to the Wills Act 1837 effected by Paragraph 1 of Schedule 13. The purpose of Paragraph 14 is to ensure that when the Act comes into force all existing appointments continue to have effect.

Paragraph 15: deals with children in compulsory care. Children under care orders under the former law, for example, under the Children and Young Persons Act 1969, are treated as if they had been made subject to a care order under section 31 of this Act. The same applies to children who were subject to a parental rights resolution.

Paragraph 16: deals with technical modifications to other Acts. Where a court has made directions to the local authority under powers which have been repealed these directions are preserved and may be varied or discharged.

Paragraph 17: deals with children placed with a parent while in compulsory care and relates to section 23(5). Note that section

23(5) provides that if a child who is in care is placed with a person falling within those categories defined in section 23(4)(a)(b)(c), the placement will be subject to regulations which derive from the Accommodation of Children (Charge and Control) Regulations 1988.

Paragraphs 18–19: deal with orders for access to children in compulsory care. Orders for access to a child in care made under the Child Care Act 1980 are treated as contact orders under section 34 of the Act. Section 34 enables a court to consider contact between a child in care and his parents or other persons.

Paragraph 20: deals with children in voluntary care. Where a child is in voluntary care at the time Part III of the Act comes into force, he is treated as provided with accommodation under section 20 of the Act. In line with the principles in Part III, if such a child had been placed with a parent, guardian or a person who had care and control of the child under a court order, he is not treated as provided with accommodation. Under the former law, it was not clear whether "voluntary care" continued in these circumstances.

Paragraph 21: deals with boarded out children. Note that placements under the former law of a child in compulsory care with a parent, guardian or a person who had the right to care and control of the child under a court order are in future treated as Accommodation of Children placements under the regulations which replace the Children (Charge and Control) Regulations 1988: see Paragraph 17. Other family placements are treated as if they had been made under the regulations which will replace the Boarding-Out (Foster Placement) Regulations 1988 under Paragraph 21.

Paragraph 22: provides for children in care to qualify for advice and assistance. Children who left care under the former law when they were sixteen or seventeen and are now under twenty one qualify for advice and assistance from the local authority in whose area they are. After care is subject to rules set out in section 24.

Paragraph 23: deals with emigration of children in care and provides that section 24 of the Child Care Act 1980 shall apply until the Secretary of State has determined whether or not to give his consent to the request for emigration. This is notwithstanding that the 1980 Act is repealed by the Children Act.

Paragraph 24: deals with contributions for maintenance of children in care. Orders under the former law requiring contributions to be made to a local authority for a child in care are treated as if they had been made under the Act.

Paragraph 25: deals with supervision orders. Supervision orders under the repealed provisions in the Children and Young Persons Act 1969 are treated as supervision orders under section 31: Paragraph 25(2). The new rule in the Act which restricts the duration of supervision orders to an initial period of one year is applied to old supervision orders, with modifications to allow the local authority time to apply for extension of an order which would have endured for more than one.year under the former law: Paragraph 25(3)(4)(5).

Paragraph 26: deals with other supervision orders. Supervision orders made under repealed provisions in divorce and other family proceedings are preserved for a maximum period of one year from the commencement of the Act.

Paragraph 27: deals with place of safety orders. Where a place of safety order was in force at the time of implementation of the Act, it continues to have effect as if the Act had not been passed. The only exception to this is that the power to apply for an interim order to continue to hold onto the child is repealed. Steps must be taken under the Act itself if authority is needed to hold onto the child once the place of safety order has run its course.

Paragraphs 28, 29 and 30: deal with the recovery of children. The implementation of the Act does not affect a summons or warrant issued to recover a child who is in care or under a place of safety order.

Paragraph 31: deals with voluntary organisations and parental rights resolutions. A further change in the Act is that a voluntary organisation will not be able to ask a local authority to pass a resolution vesting in them parental rights and duties with respect to a child whom they are looking after: see section 64 of the Child Care Act 1980. This power has been rarely used. Any existing resolutions will be brought to an end six months after the Act comes into force.

Paragraph 32: deals with foster children. Where a child was a foster child under the Foster Children Act 1980 at the time Part VIII of the Children Act comes into force and the circumstances are such that, unless exempted, registration as a children's home would be required, for three months after implementation the controls relating to private fostering will apply rather than those under Part VIII dealing with children's homes. Part VIII will bite three months after implementation, so that non-registration as a children's home is an offence, unless an application to so register has been made in that time and has not been refused or the arrangement has been exempted by the local authority from the controls of that Part.

Paragraphs 33 and 34: deal with nurseries and child minding. Persons and premises registered under the Nurseries and Child-Minders Regulation Act 1948 at the time of implementation of Part X continue to come within that Act for twelve months or until registration is effected under Part X, if sooner.

Paragraph 35: deals with children accommodated in certain establishments and relates to section 85(1)(a) or 86(1)(a). Note that a new duty is imposed on health and local education authorities which provide accommodation for a child for a consecutive period of more than three months. This three month period does not include time before the Act is implemented.

Paragraph 36: deals with criminal care orders. Existing criminal care orders will come to an end six months after the Act comes into force. Until that time the former law will continue to apply to them, for example, regarding the duration of the order and the right to apply for its discharge: see sections 15, 20 and 21 of the Children and Young Persons Act 1969. The six month period is intended to give local authorities the chance to apply for a care or supervision order under this Act if that would be appropriate.

Paragraph 37: deals with consents under the Marriage Act 1949. The Children Act substitutes in the Marriage Act 1949 a simpler and more coherent set of rules about those whose consent is required to the marriage of a child who is sixteen or seventeen: see Schedule 12, Paragraph 5, which amends the Marriage Act 1949. Where, however, a care order is in force, the consent of each person with parental responsibility for the child, including the local authority, is needed. Note that a care order brings an existing residence order to an end: see section 91(2). The purpose of Paragraph 37 is to ensure that where an old style custody order is in force, transitional provisions shall apply.

Paragraph 38: deals with the Children Act 1975 and provides for those provisions that shall continue to have effect notwithstanding the repeal of the 1975 Act. Note that Part II of the Children Act 1975 dealing with applications by qualified non-parents for custodianship and sections 85 to 87, which contained an explanation of certain general concepts such as parental rights and duties and legal custody, was the subject of study by the Law Commission in its "Family Law, Review of Child Law and Guardianship and Custody".

Paragraph 39: ensures that, notwithstanding the repeal of the Child Care Act 1980 by the Children Act, the amendment made to section 106(2)(a) of the Children and Young Persons Act 1963 remains. The Child Care Act 1980 is repealed in its entirety by the Children Act, which nevertheless replaces many of its provisions and makes certain exceptions such as the one covered by Paragraph 39.

Paragraph 40: ensures that the Lord Chancellor may make transitional and savings provisions in relation to the Legal Aid Act 1988: see also section 99. Note that children under sixteen are no longer assessed in terms of their parents' income but in their own right, a change introduced on 9 March 1990.

SCHEDULE 15: REPEALS

Chapter	Short title	Extent of repeal
1891 c. 3.	The Custody of Children Act 1891.	The whole Act.
1933 c. 12.	The Children and Young Persons Act 1933.	In section 14(2), the words from "may also" to "together, and". In section 34(8), "(a)" and the words from "and (b)" to the end. Section 40. In section 107(1), the definitions of "care order" and "interim order".
1944 c. 31.	The Education Act 1944.	In section 40(1), the words from "or to imprisonment" to the end. In section 114(1), the definition of parent.
1948 c. 53.	The Nurseries and Child-Minders Regulation Act 1948.	The whole Act.
1949 c. 76.	The Marriage Act 1949.	In section 3(1), the words "unless the child is subject to a custodianship order, when the consent of

Chapter	Short title	Extent of repeal
		the custodian and, where the the custodian is the husband or wife of a parent of the child of that parent shall be required". Section 78(1A). Schedule 2.
1956 c. 69.	The Sexual Offences Act 1956.	Section 38.
1959 c. 72.	The Mental Health Act 1959.	Section 9.
1963 c. 37.	The Children and Young Persons Act 1963.	Section 3. Section 23. In section 29(1), the words "under section 1 of the Children and Young Persons Act 1969 or". Section 53(3). In Schedule 3, paragraph 11.
1964 c. 42.	The Administration of Justcie Act 1964.	In section 38, the definition of "domestic court".
1968 c. 46.	The Health Services and Public Health Act 1968.	In section 64(3)(a), sub-paragraphs (vi), (vii), (ix) and (xv). In section 65(3)(b), paragraphs (vii), (viii) and (x).
1968 c. 49.	The Social Work (Scotland) Act 1968.	Section 1(4)(a). Section 5(2)(d). In section 86(3), the words "the Child Care Act 1980 or".

Chapter	Short title	Extent of repeal
		In Schedule 8, paragraph 20.
1969 c. 46.	The Family Law Reform Act 1969.	Section 7.
1969 c. 54.	The Children and Young Persons Act 1969.	Sections 1 to 3.
		In section 7, in subsection (7) the words "to subsection (7A) of this section and", paragraph (a) and the words from "and subsection (13) of section 2 of this Act" to the end; and subsection (7A).
		Section 7A.
		In section 8(3), the words from "and as if the reference to acquittal" to the end.
		In section 9(1), the words "proceedings under section 1 of this Act or".
		Section 11A.
		Section 14A.
		In section 15, in subsection (1) the words "and may on discharging the supervision order make a care order (other than an interim order) in respect of the supervised person"; in subsection (2) the words "and the supervision order was not made by virtue of section 1 of this Act or on the occasion of the discharge of a care

Chapter	Short title	Extent of repeal
		order"; in subsection (2A), the words "or made by a court on discharging a care order made under that subsection"; and in subsection (4), the words "or made by a court on discharging a care order made under that section".
		In section 16, in subsection (6)(a), the words "a care order or"; and in subsection (8) the words "or, in a case where a parent or guardian of his was a party to the proceedings on an application under the preceding section by virtue of an order under section 32A of this Act, the parent or guardian".
		In section 17, paragraphs (b) and (c).
		Sections 20 to 22.
		Section 27(4).
		Section 28.
		Sections 32A to 32C.
		In section 34(2) the words "under section 1 of this Act or", the words "2(3) or" and the words "and accordingly in the case of such a person the reference in section 1(1) of this Act to the said section 2(3) shall be construed as including a reference to this subsection".

Chapter	Short title	Extent of repeal
		In section 70, in subsection (1), the definitions of "care order" and "interim order"; and in subsection (2) the words "21(2), 22(4) or (6) or 28(5)" and the words "care order or warrant". In Schedule 5, paragraphs 12(1), 37, 47 and 48.
1970 c. 34.	The Marriage (Registrar General's Licence) Act 1970.	In section 3(b), the words from "as amended" to "1969".
1970 c. 42.	The Local Authority Social Services Act 1970.	In Schedule 1, in the entry relating to the Children and Young Persons Act 1969, the words "welfare, etc. of foster children"; the entries relating to the Matrimonial Causes Act 1973, section 44, the Domestic Proceedings and Magistrates' Courts Act 1978, section 9, the Child Care Act 1980 and the Foster Children Act 1980.
1971 c. 3.	The Guardianship of Minors Act 1971.	The whole Act.
1971 c. 23.	The Courts Act 1971.	In Schedule 8, paragraph 59(1).
1972 c. 18.	The Maintenance Orders (Reciprocal Enforcement) Act 1972.	Section 41.

Chapter	Short title	Extent of repeal
1972 c. 70.	The Local Government Act 1972.	In Schedule 23, paragraphs 4 and 9(3).
1972 c. 71.	The Criminal Justice Act . 1972.	Section 51(1).
1973 c. 18.	The Matrimonial Causes Act 1973.	Sections 42 to 44. In section 52(1), the definition of "custody".
1973 c. 29.	The Guardianship Act 1973.	The whole Act.
1973 c. 45.	The Domicile and Matrimonial Proceedings Act 1973.	In Schedule 1, in paragraph 11(1) the definitions of "custody" and "education" and in paragraph 11(3) the word "four".
1973 c. 62.	The Powers of Criminal Courts Act 1973.	In section 13(1), the words "and the purposes of section 1(2)(bb) of the Children and Young Persons Act 1969". In Schedule 3, in paragraph 3(2A), the word "and" immediately preceding paragraph (b).
1974 c. 53.	The Rehabilitation of Offenders Act 1974.	In section 1(4)(b) the words "or in care proceedings under section 1 of the Children and Young Persons Act 1969". In section 5, in subsection 5(e), the words "a care order or"; and in subsection (10) the words "care order or".

Chapter	Short title	Extent of repeal
1975 c. 72.	The Children Act 1975.	The whole Act.
1976 c. 36.	The Adoption Act 1976.	Section 11(5). Section 14(3). In section 15, in subsection (1), the words from "subject" to "cases)" and subsection (4). Section 26. In section 28(5), the words "or the organisation". Section 34. Section 36(1)(c). Section 37(1), (3) and (4). Section 55(4). In section 57, in subsection (2), the words from "and the court" to the end and subsections (4) to (10). In section 72(1), the definition of "place of safety", in the definition of "local authority" the words from "and" to the end and, in the definition of "specified order", the words "Northern Ireland or". In Schedule 3, paragraphs 8, 11, 19, 21, and 22.
1977 c. 45.	The Criminal Law Act 1977.	Section 58(3).
1977 c. 49.	The National Health Service Act 1977.	In section 21, in subsection (1)(a) the words "and young children".

Chapter	Short title	Extent of repeal
		In Schedule 8, in paragraph 1(1), the words from "and of children" to the end; in paragraph 2(2) the words from "or (b) to persons who" to "arrangements"; and in paragraph 3(1) "(a)" and the words from "or (b) a child" to "school age". In Schedule 15, paragraphs 10 and 25.
1978 c. 22.	The Domestic Proceedings and Magistrates' Courts Act 1978.	Sections 9 to 15. In section 19, in subsection (1) the words "following powers, that is to say" and sub-paragraph (ii), subsections (2) and (4), in subsection (7) the words "and one interim custody order" and in subsection (9) the words "or 21". In section 20, subsection (4) and in subsection (9) the words "subject to the provisions of section 11(8) of this Act". Section 21. In section 24, the words "or 21" in both places where they occur. In section 25, in subsection (1) paragraph (b) and the word "or" immediately preceding it and in subsection (2) paragraphs (c) and (d).

Chapter	Short title	Extent of repeal
		Section 29(4). Sections 33 and 34. Sections 36 to 53. Sections 64 to 72. Sections 73(1) and 74(1) and (3). In section 88(1), the definition of "actual custody". In Schedule 2, paragraphs 22, 23, 27, 29, 31, 36, 41 to 43, 46 to 50.
1978 c. 28.	The Adoption (Scotland) Act 1978.	In section 20(3)(c), the words "section 12(3)(b) of the Adoption Act 1976 or of". In section 45(5), the word "approved". Section 49(4). In section 65(1), in the definition of "local authority", the words from "and" to the end and, in the definition of "specified order", the words "Northern Ireland or".
1978 c. 30.	The Interpretation Act 1978.	In Schedule 1, the entry with respect to the construction of certain expressions relating to children.
1980 c. 5.	The Child Care Act 1980.	The whole Act.
1980 c. 6.	The Foster Children Act 1980.	The whole Act.
1980 c. 43.	The Magistrates' Courts Act 1980.	In section 65(1), paragraphs (e) and (g) and the paragraph (m)

Chapter	Short title	Extent of repeal
		inserted in section 65 by paragraph 82 of Schedule 2 to the Family Law Reform Act 1987.
		In section 81(8), in the definition of "guardian" the words "by deed or will" and in the definition of "sums adjudged to be paid by a conviction" the words from "as applied" to the end.
		In section 143(2), paragraph (i).
		In Schedule 7, paragraphs 78, 83, 91, 92, 110, 116, 117, 138, 157, 158, 165, 166 and 199 to 201.
1981 c. 60.	The Education Act 1981.	In Schedule 3, paragraph 9.
1982 c. 20.	The Children's Homes Act 1982.	The whole Act.
1982 c. 48.	The Criminal Justice Act 1982.	Sections 22 to 25. Section 27. In Schedule 14, paragraphs 45 and 46.
1983 c. 20.	The Mental Health Act 1983.	In section 26(5), paragraph (d) and the word "or" immediately preceding it. In section 28(1), the words "including an order under section 38 of the Sexual Offences Act 1956)".

Chapter	Short title	Extent of repeal
		In Schedule 4, paragraphs 12, 26(a), (b) and (c), 35, 44, 50 and 51.
1983 c. 41.	The Health and Social Services and Social Security Adjudications Act 1983.	In section 11, in subsection (2) the words "the Child Care Act 1980 and the Children's Homes Act 1982". In section 19, subsections (1) to (5). Schedule 1. In Schedule 2, paragraphs 3, 9 to 14, 20 to 24, 27, 28, 34, 37 and 46 to 62. In Schedule 4, paragraphs 38 to 48. In Schedule 9, paragraphs 5, 16 and 17.
1984 c. 23.	The Registered Homes Act 1984.	In Schedule 1, in paragraph 5, sub-paragraph (a) and paragraphs 6, 7 and 8.
1984 c. 28.	The County Courts Act 1984.	In Schedule 2, paragraph 56.
1984 c. 37.	The Child Abduction Act 1984.	In section 3, the word "and" immediately preceding paragraph (c). In the Schedule, in paragraph 1(2) the words "or voluntary organisation" and paragraph 3(1)(e).
1984 c. 42.	The Matrimonial and Family Proceedings Act 1984.	In Schedule 1, paragraphs 19 and 23.

Chapter	Short title	Extent of repeal
1984 c. 56.	The Foster Children (Scotland) Act 1984.	In section 1, the words "for a period of more than 6 days" and the words from "The period" to the end. In section 7(1), the word "or" at the end of paragraph (e). In Schedule 2, paragraphs 1 to 3 and 8.
1984 c. 60.	The Police and Criminal Evidence Act 1984.	In section 37(15), the words "and is not excluded from this Part of this Act by section 52 below", Section 39(5). Section 52. In section 118(1), in the definition of parent or guardian, paragraph (b) and the word "and" immediately preceding it. In Schedule 2, the entry relating to section 16 of the child Care Act 1980. In Schedule 6, paragraphs 19(a) and 22.
1985 c. 23.	The Prosecution of Offences Act 1985.	Section 27.
1985 c. 60.	The Child Abduction and Custody Act 1985.	Section 9(c). Section 20(2)(b) and (c). Section 25(3) and (5). In Schedule 3, paragraph 1(2).
1986 c. 28.	The Children and Young Persons (Amendment) Act 1986.	The whole Act.

Chapter	Short title	Extent of repeal
1986 c. 33.	The Disabled Persons (Services, Consultation and Representation) Act 1986.	In section 16, in the definition of "guardian", paragraph (a).
1986 c. 45.	The Insolvency Act 1986.	In section 281(5)(b), the words "in domestic proceedings".
1986 c. 50.	The Social Security Act 1986.	In Schedule 10, paragraph 51.
1986 c. 55.	The Family Law Act 1986.	In section 1(2), in paragraph (a) the words "(a) or" and paragraph (b). Section 3(4) to (6). Section 4. Section 35(1). In section 42(6), in paragraph (b) the words "section 42(6) of the Matrimonial Causes Act 1973 or", in paragraph (c) the words "section 42(7) of that Act or" and in paragraph (d) the words "section 19(6) of the Domestic Proceedings and Magistrates' Courts Act 1978 or". In Schedule 1, paragraphs 10, 11, 13, 16, 17, 20 and 23.
1987 c. 42.	The Family Law Reform Act 1987.	Section 3. Sections 4 to 7. Sections 9 to 16. In Schedule 2, paragraphs 11, 14, 51, 67, 68, 94 and 95. In Schedule 3, paragraphs 11 and 12.

Chapter	Short title	Extent of repeal
1988 c. 34.	The Legal Aid Act 1988.	Section 3(4)(c). Section 27. Section 28. In section 30, subsections (1) and (2). In Part I of Schedule 2, paragraph 2(a) and (e),

Annotation

Schedule 15: lists the enactments repealed by this Act. Note that the Act abolishes custody and access orders, together with their offshoots, unifies the many routes by which a child may be placed in the care of a local authority or under supervision and replaces the jurisdiction to make orders under fifteen statutes. Supervision orders may still be made in criminal proceedings under the Children and Young Persons Act 1969. The Act replaces order-making powers in the Custody of Children Act 1891, the Children and Young Persons Acts 1933–1969, the Nurseries and Child Minders Regulation Act 1948, the Sexual Offences Act 1956, the Family Law Reform Act 1969, the Guardianship Acts 1971–73, the Matrimonial Causes Act 1973, the Children Act 1975, the Domestic Proceeding and Magistrates' Courts Act 1978, the Child Care Act 1980, the Foster Children Act 1980, the Children's Homes Act 1982 and the Family Law Reform Act 1987. It also removes some order-making powers under the Adoption Act 1976.